Living in a Sacred Cosmos

Living in a Sacred Cosmos

Indonesia and the Future of Islam

BERNARD T. ADENEY-RISAKOTTA

For Mike with thanks.

Monograph 66/Yale Southeast Asia Studies

Library of Congress Control Number: *2018945016*
International Standard Book Number: paper 978-0-9850429-6-7
cloth 978-0-9850429-7-4

© 2018 by Yale University Southeast Asia Studies
New Haven, Connecticut 06520-8206

Distributor:
Yale University Southeast Asia Studies
P.O. Box 208206
New Haven, Connecticut 06520-8206
USA

Printed in U.S.A.

To Nona,

Farsijana R.C. Adeney-Risakotta, PhD

Without whose fierce faith, cheerful encouragement,
wise advice, practical support, and unwavering love
this book would never have been completed

Contents

List of Figures and Tables
    Figures   *ix*
    Tables   *ix*

Preface   *xiii*

Introduction   1

Part I. Islam and Modernity in Indonesia

  1   Whither Islam? Whose Islam? Which Muslims?   17

  2   Social Imaginaries in Indonesia and the West   37

  3   Cultures, Religions, and Modernities in Indonesia   57

Part II. Living in a Sacred Cosmos

  4   Enchantment and a Sacred Cosmos   81

  5   Islamic Modernism and Disenchantment   105

  6   Islam and Enchantment: Six Leaders   131

Part III. Traditional, Modern, and Religious Imaginations of Power

  7   Traditional Indonesian Imaginations of Power   157

  8   Modern Indonesian Imaginations of Power   179

  9   Muslim Imaginations of Power in Indonesia   201

Part IV. Nature, Women, and Conflict in a Sacred Cosmos

  10   Imaginations of Nature and Natural Disasters   229

  11   Imaginations of Women in Law and Practice   253

  12   Conflict, Intolerance, and Hope   277

Appendices

I Confidential Questionnaire on Indonesian
Social Imaginaries in English   303

II Confidential Questionnaire on Indonesian
Social Imaginaries in Indonesian   311

III Statistical Analysis of Questionnaire Responses
regarding the Supernatural, Dreams, Spirits, and
Accidents or Illness   319

IV Ethnic Variations in Muslim Views of Religion
and Power   337

V Indonesian Muslim Views of Nature and
Ethnic Variations   347

Notes   351

Glossary   379

References   383

Index   403

Figures and Tables

FIGURES

9.1   Islamic schools and branches of interpretation   203

9.2   How much should the Koran influence law?   208

9.3   The legality of religions in Indonesia   210

TABLES

0.1   Ethnicity of Questionnaire Respondents   9

3.1   Typology of Contrasting Social Imaginaries   75

5.1   Responses to Question II.D on the Unseen World   116

5.2   Muslim Responses to Question II.D (*Gaib*)
      by Ethnic Group   117

5.3   Responses by Religion to Question II.E on the
      Meaning of Dreams   118

5.4   Muslim Responses to Question II.E (Dreams)
      by Ethnic Group   119

5.5   Javanese and Moluccan Responses to Question II.F
      on Spirit Possession   121

5.6   Muslim Responses to Question II.F (Spirit Possession)
      by Ethnic Group   122

5.7   Responses to Question II.G on the Meaning of Sickness
      or Accidents by Religion   124

5.8   Javanese and Moluccan Responses to Question II.G
      on Illness and Accidents   125

5.9   Muslim Responses to Question II.G (Illness and
      Accidents) by Ethnic Group   126

6.1	Comparing Indonesian Muslim Leaders' Views of the Unseen World	152
7.1	Responses to Question IV.A on Imaginations of Power	164
7.2	Responses to Question IV.F on the Qualities of a Good Leader	172
7.3	Responses to Question III.C on the Characteristics of Good Government	175
7.4	Responses to Question II.C on the Characteristics of a Good Society	177
9.1	Responses to Questions III.E on the Basis of Law and II.B on Obedience to Law	206
9.2	Responses to Question IV.B on Government Regulation of Religions	212
9.3	Responses to Question III.D on Ideals for the Nation-State of Indonesia	214
9.4	Responses to Question III.B on Economic Ethics	223
10.1	Responses to Question III.G on Relation to Nature	233
10.2	Responses to Question IV.E on Meaning in Natural Disasters	248
11.1	Responses to Question IV.D on Ideal Relations between Women and Men	272

Appendices Figures

IV.1	Responses Questions III.E and II.B on Law	338
IV.2	Responses to Question IV.B on Government Regulation of Religion	339
IV.3	Responses to Question III.D on Ideals for the Nation-State of Indonesia	341
IV.4	Comparing Language	344

Figures and Tables, cont.

V.1   Javanese and Moluccan Responses to Question III.G
       on Relation to Nature   348

V.2   Muslim Responses to Question III.G, on Relation to
       Nature, by Ethnic Group   349

Preface

THIS BOOK IS THE OUTCOME of a long process. I was born in Shanghai, China, to an English father and an American mother and grew up in Asia, America, and Europe. But I have never lived anywhere that is as fascinating to me as Indonesia. In this book I try to understand why Indonesia is so interesting and whether it offers hope for the future of relations between Muslims and non-Muslims in the world at large.

After taking a degree from the University of Wisconsin–Madison in Asian studies, I first visited Java in 1972 at the age of twenty-three. I went back in 1973 and adopted my Javanese daughter, Rina, from Surabaya. I went on to study Asian religions and philosophy at University of London before completing a doctorate in international relations at the Graduate Theological Union and the University of California, Berkeley. In 1989 I had a sabbatical leave from teaching in Berkeley and was able to spend four months in Indonesia, three at a university and one spent island hopping in eastern Indonesia. In 1991 I resigned from my position in Berkeley to accept an invitation from a university in Salatiga, Central Java, to help start a graduate program on religion and society. What I anticipated as a few years' break from western academia turned into my life's work. In 1997 I married Farsijana Adeney-Risakotta, an Indonesian (Moluccan-Javanese) anthropologist, and we moved to Yogyakarta. In 1998 the thirty-two-year reign of President Soeharto came to a dramatic close and Indonesia began a process of major, democratic, structural reform.

For the past twenty-seven years I've had the honor of teaching in Indonesian universities and sharing with Indonesian colleagues and students an experience of almost unbelievably rapid social, political, economic, cultural, and religious change. At first I imagined this change as linear, shaped by the familiar paradigm of transition from rural, traditional cultures to urban, modern ones. It seemed to me that Indonesia was experiencing in just a few years changes that took centuries in Europe and the United States. Indeed, the simplistic paradigm of social change from traditional to modern societies is a lens that both reveals and conceals many useful insights. I quickly realized that much of what was happening in Indonesia was different from the changes that ushered in modernity in Europe and the United States. During my first years in Indonesia I employed western social theories to try to understand how social change in Indonesia resembled modernization in other countries. During my latter years I became more interested in how Indonesia is different. In this book I construct my own theories to explain that difference, especially in light of Indonesia as a Muslim, postcolonial society.

My analysis of Indonesia is shaped by western categories of thought that reflect the limitations and advantages of a western education in the social sciences and religion. My position as a foreigner in Indonesia includes both strengths and weaknesses. There are some aspects of Indonesia of which I will be eternally ignorant. An Indonesian child on the street feels (*rasa*) many things that I will never understand by virtue of her emersion since birth in Indonesian social, religious, linguistic, cultural, economic, and political structures. On the other hand, my location as a foreigner with multicultural experience and education gives me insights into Indonesian culture that are not commonly accessible to native-born Indonesians. In either case, whether especially ignorant or uniquely insightful, I am part of the community that is the object of my research.

This book uses theories to suggest answers to questions that are impossible to answer with certainty. My own theories have evolved over the past thirty years of my engagement with Indonesia and no doubt will continue to evolve. They are the result of a dialogue with many social theorists, historians, anthropologists, and Indonesianists whose names frequently appear in these pages. I have diverged from these scholars on important points, but my work would have been impossible without them. Inevitably the book was also shaped by the current crisis in relations between Islam and the West.

For many years I have been learning from my Indonesian colleagues and students. They are from many different ethnic groups and cultures, as well as from different religious communities and different parts of Indonesia. They have been my teachers and guides in my quest to understand Indonesia and the largest Muslim community in the world. I imagine that some of these colleagues, even now, will be amused at obvious mistakes or misunderstandings that crop up in my analysis. I hope they will also be surprised by new insights that result from having foreign eyes. Many of my best ideas come from them, while my errors are all my own.

My debts to those who have helped me refine my ideas are far too many to list. The Indonesian Consortium for Religious Studies (ICRS) in the Graduate School of Universitas Gadjah Mada (UGM) has been my primary academic home for the past twelve years. I'm thankful to the director, Siti Syamsiyatun and my friends and colleagues Jeanny Dhewayani, Dicky Sofjan, Leonard Epafras, Wening Udasmoro, and Fatimah Husein for their support on many different levels. I have cotaught courses with most of them and received critical feedback from them all, as well as from many students and other colleagues in classes, seminars, Wednesday Forums, workshops, conferences, focus group discussions, and joint research projects. My colleagues at the Center for Religious and Cross-Cultural Studies (CRCS), especially Zainal Abidin Bagir, Syamsul Ma'arif, and Irwan Abdullah, have challenged and sharpened my ideas.

The ICRS is a consortium of three universities: UGM, State Islamic University Sunan Kalijaga (UIN), and Duta Wacana Christian University (DWCU). I'm thankful for opportunities to teach at all three of these universities, as well as at Universitas Muhammadiyah Yogyakarta (UMY). Students and colleagues from all these universities have corrected my mistakes, challenged my theories, and forced me to sharpen my thinking.

I've been a faculty member in the graduate program of DWCU since 1997. For six years I was associate director of graduate studies at DWCU under the wise leadership of E. Gerrit Singgih. Gerrit was the person who first invited me to Yogyakarta, and he has helped shape my ideas for many years. He also helped found ICRS. My debts to him are too many to count. Colleagues at DWCU, such as J. B. Banawiratma, Yahya Wijaya, Paulus Widjaja and many others, also provided personal, intellectual, and institutional support. I am grateful to Singgih Santoso, the Dean of the Faculty of Business, who helped me analyze the statistics that are cited in this book. My work at ICRS has been dependent on four visionary rectors (presidents) at DWCU, including Henry Feriadi, Johan, Budiyanto and Aristarchus (like many Indonesians, the latter three have only one name), who supported the idea of a consortium of Muslim, Christian, and national universities and assigned me to work full time at ICRS.

It is impossible to pinpoint when the narrative developed in this book first began to evolve. Certainly it received a strong push when I enjoyed a sabbatical in 2002 as a fellow at the International Institute for Asian Studies (IIAS) at its branch at the University of Amsterdam, Netherlands. I'm grateful to the late Frans Huskens, who was instrumental in arranging my fellowship at IIAS. Unfortunately the book I started then on religion and power in Indonesia was never finished. Several articles came out of that year, but I could never satisfy myself that the book was "done." Some of the ideas, however, seeped into this book.

In 2013–14 I enjoyed a year's sabbatical in Boston at the Center on Culture, Religion, and World Affairs (CURA) at Boston University. I'm grateful to Robert Hefner for his invitation and gracious hosting at CURA. The Boston University and Harvard University libraries both provided wonderful help in locating abundant resources on Indonesia. I'm also thankful to Munir Jiwa, at the Center for Islamic Studies in the Graduate Theological Union, Berkeley, for two extended periods for research and writing there. My thanks also go to Michael Dove for the month of July 2016, which I spent in the Yale University library as a guest of the Council for Southeast Asian Studies, Yale. My thanks go to Anthony Reid, Robert Hefner, Nur Ichwan, Nelly van Doorn-Harder, the late John Raines, Michael Dove, and others who read parts of my work and offered critical feedback.

I am no different from many authors in reserving my deepest and most profound thanks for my family. I am thankful to Jen Marion Adeney, Rina and Glenn Woodfin, David, Isobel and Robbie Woodfin, and Peter Adeney, who continue to love and support me, even though my work requires that I live far from them. In ways that might surprise them, they make my work possible. Thanks, too, to my Indonesian family, Gen, Marlen, Youla, Dunant, Gaby, Ade, Vina, Syana, and Shalom and especially Oma, Iet, Tirza, and Hannah, whose love, prayers, and support give me strength and hope.

Certainly my greatest debt is to my wife, Farsijana R.C. Adeney-Risakotta. She doesn't write about a sacred cosmos, she lives in one. As an Indonesian anthropologist, she continually opens my eyes to things of which I am unaware. She has read and given me intelligent feedback on almost everything I have written. Her ideas, critical input, belief, and loving support undergird all my writing. This book is dedicated to her.

Bernard T. Adeney-Risakotta
Yogyakarta, Indonesia
31 March 2018

Introduction

IMAGINE A POSTCOLONIAL COUNTRY with the subtle, ritual politeness of China and Japan; the flamboyant, colorful myths of India; the modern political, economic, and social institutions of the West; and the highly religious, ethical monotheism of the Middle East. Is such a country possible? Indonesia is such a country and may suggest a new paradigm for the future of Islam. Indonesia is the largest and most dynamic Muslim country in the world.

This book explores how and why Indonesia is unique in the modern world. A major factor that makes Indonesia different from many other modern countries is Islam. Islam has been growing in influence in Indonesia since the fourteenth century but especially during the past fifty years (see Ricklefs 2012). The difference between the processes of modernization in Indonesia and Europe does not stem from the doctrinal teachings of Islam, which are in many respects similar to those of Christianity, but from many historical factors, including the association of modernity with the imperialist, colonialist, and capitalist powers that exploited Indonesia for centuries. Islam in Indonesia was and remains the most potent political force for mobilizing Indonesians against western domination.

Many Indonesians have an ambivalent attitude toward modernity, stemming from its association with European colonialism. These feelings are intensified by the perceived injustice of a worldwide capitalist economy dominated by wealthy nations. Further ambivalence is stimulated by western expressions of antipathy, in some cases verging on hatred, toward Islam. Many Indonesians abhor terrorism and actively oppose radicalism, but when western leaders issue wholesale accusations against Islam and ban or attack people from Islamic countries many Indonesians feel it as an attack on their fundamental religious identity.

1

Indonesians have enjoyed a rich civilization for thousands of years. But the modern capitalist world order, characterized by secular, scientific reason, is a western import. They have many reasons to distrust the current world order, including the hegemony of modern scientific reason. Most educated Indonesians appreciate the tremendous achievements of modern science, but they do not accept modern, secular, scientific rationality as the only, or even necessarily the most important, way of understanding reality. Both their religions and their ethnic traditions suggest alternative ways of imagining the world.

Indonesians also have an ambivalent attitude toward Arab, Middle Eastern hegemony in the interpretation and practice of Islam. Like western modernity, Arabism is also a foreign import. Indonesia is not a Middle Eastern state. Indonesian Muslims honor the Arabic origins of Islam but are ambivalent about attempts to impose Arabic culture on the practice of Islam in Indonesia. There is intense debate among Indonesian Muslims over whether and how the normative teachings of Islam can be rooted in Indonesian culture.

Many Indonesians switch effortlessly between modern, religious, and traditional concepts and practices. They treat modern, religious, and traditional languages as parallel, ideally complementary symbol systems, that are useful for different purposes in different contexts. Modernity, religion, and tradition are not three different things. In reality they are inseparable parts of one reality. They are concepts, ideal types, that enable one to observe the same reality through three different perspectives. For most of the world, modernity is religious and incorporates local traditions. Religion is modern and traditional. Religions are understood and practiced differently in different contexts because they are reconciled with modern ideas and local practices. Local traditions are constantly modified by interacting with both modern and religious ideas and practices. Living traditions are modern and religious.

Ideal types are useful for analysis, especially for delineating ways in which the social imaginaries of Indonesians are different from those of people in the West. Charles Taylor awakened my understanding of how western social imaginaries were constructed over a long period of time (Taylor 2003, 2007). Social imaginaries are not static, philosophical propositions, like worldviews. Nor are they subjective imaginations of reality constructed by individuals for their own private interests. Rather they are deep, intersubjective perceptions, stories, institutions, feelings, and practices that are constructed over centuries and shared by a large number of people who inhabit overlapping cultures. Taylor alerted me to constructed imaginations of political, social, economic, and cultural order that are widely shared in the West. Indirectly his account also reminded me that western social imaginaries are by no means universally assumed in Indonesia. One reason for this book is to better understand how the social imaginaries of the largest Muslim nation in the world differ from those of western countries.

One danger of constructing contrasting social imaginaries is to reify the ideal types. If we mistake ideal types for descriptions of reality, especially if they are constructed as binary opposites, they turn into stereotypes that conceal more than they reveal. "Invidious binary dualisms," such as traditional versus modern, secular versus religious, enchanted versus disenchanted, Indonesia versus the West, spiritual versus scientific, East versus West, and so on, not only oversimplify reality, but they actively mislead us into thinking that these polarizations are real. Like racial stereotypes, even if there is some truth in the oversimplifications, they do far more harm than good by encouraging people to make generalizations where none is warranted. This book tries to maintain a balance between using ideal types to analyze difference while constantly reminding the reader that differences and similarities between Indonesia and the West are far more subtle and complex than is suggested by ideal types.

In light of the work of Edward Said and Talal Asad, the use of social imaginaries as ideal types risks the charge of orientalism. Orientalists objectify their target of study (the orient) as exotic, "other," fascinating, and primitive. Orientalists are scientific subjects studying primitive objects. Their frames of reference are western, "universal" scientific categories, which may misconstrue or misunderstand their objects of research based on "universal" western definitions of such terms as *religion, tradition*, and *modernity*. For example, the term *disenchanted* is a western, Weberian expression that recalls a nostalgically missed age when people still believed in magic. One of my students suggested that even the venerable sociological terms *sacred* and *mundane* are western categories that are foreign to both Islam and Indonesian culture.

No one can analyze any culture or religion from a universal standpoint. We all view life through the lens of our own prejudices and opinions (cf. Gadamer 1975). Nevertheless, the approach in this book is descriptive, not normative. I am trying to describe Indonesian social realities as honestly and objectively as possible. My goal is not to judge what is right or wrong in Indonesia but to describe and understand the reality as best I can, with full consciousness of my own limited perspective.

By contrasting Indonesians "living in a sacred cosmos" with westerners "living in an impersonal universe," I risk polarizing the difference by using western categories of "sacred cosmos" and "impersonal universe," the former more "mystical East" in contrast to the more "rational West." If the ideal types of "sacred cosmos" and "impersonal universe" are taken as literal differences between Indonesia and the West, then the reader may be justified in suspecting that orientalism is embedded in this analysis.

At least three factors mitigate against this charge of orientalism. The first is that these are ideal types used for analysis of difference rather than literal descriptions of the difference. It is impossible to tell if most Indonesians live in a sacred cosmos or if most westerners live in an impersonal universe. Both of these terms are ideas, not empirical realities. I suspect that most human beings, no matter where they are from, experience some aspects of a sacred cosmos and some aspects of an impersonal universe. I don't really know how many Americans live with a consciousness of being surrounded by spiritual or supernatural powers. Certainly the popularity of charismatic Christianity, New Age or "eastern" practices, and eclectic spirituality in western countries suggests that many western people do not find an impersonal universe a very attractive place in which to live. In contrast, some Indonesians are deeply skeptical of mystical ideas and practices associated with a sacred cosmos. They much prefer to use reason and science to understand the mysteries of life. Ideal types may be useful for analysis but not for pigeonholing nations.

Second, this book tries to allow Indonesians to speak for themselves rather than just responding to "western" categories of social imaginaries. Orientalism assumes that the expert is the western scholar, while the object of study is the exotic eastern "other." Some western scholarly books on Indonesia only interact with other western scholars and show no serious interest in how Indonesian scholars define themselves.[1] The best defense against orientalism is to honor the people studied as subjects whose research, opinions, and perspectives are at least as important as those of the western, secularized social scientists who study them.

Third, orientalism falls into the Cartesian fallacy of separating subject from object, assuming a value-free, objective, scientific position on the part of researchers, in contrast to the emotionally invested, subjective, historically conditioned position of the objects of their research. In this book I position myself as a part of the phenomena that I am studying. There is no social-scientific researcher who is truly detached from the subject of his or her research. Every researcher is in some sense a part of what he or she is researching. In my case, this dynamic is intensified by my long involvement with and commitment to Indonesia. Studying Indonesia is like studying myself since I am part of this history.

My debt to Charles Taylor is evident throughout this book, especially for his account of how western culture moved away from "living in a sacred cosmos." Equally important is my debt to my mentor and friend, the late Robert N. Bellah. For several decades I exchanged ideas with Bob Bellah about two of his seminal concepts: the evolution of religion and the idea of "second naïveté." I was critical of both concepts. Bellah was careful to distance himself from normative ideas of evolution that locate later, more complex forms of religion as higher or better than earlier, simpler forms. He believed that human beings have evolved from simpler to more complex forms of cognition, which shape their understanding and practice of religion. But, he said, more complex forms, such as theoretic cognition, are not necessarily morally superior to simpler forms such as mimetic or mythic cognition. He showed how four axial civilizations developed theoretic thinking stimulated by an experience of transcendence. I find Bellah's types fruitful for analysis, even though I have serious questions about whether or not mimetic, mythic, ethical, and theoretic forms of cognition have ever been separated from each other or should be conceptualize as an evolutionary sequence. Bellah's analysis of China, India, the Middle East, and Greece as axial civilizations has been very useful for my theory since these four civilizations have had great influence on Indonesia. However, I wonder if theoretic cognition developed only in these four civilizations. Egypt and early Mesoamerican civilizations stand out as other candidates for axial civilization status.

Although I still have questions about Bellah's conception of "second naïveté," I have come to see it as a useful analytic concept concerning the ambivalence of belief in the presence of doubt or uncertainty. While some people live fully in "a sacred cosmos" (with a first naïveté), others choose to believe and practice their beliefs in spite of serious reservations at a rational level. This is common, not only in the secularized West but also in Indonesia. Still others (including Indonesians), practice a first naïveté with regard to modern scientific reason. They believe that reason and science are the only valid ways to understand reality.

As I was writing this book, three things bothered me. The first was my obvious Javanese bias. Living in Java for over twenty-five years cannot help but influence what one thinks of as "Indonesia"![2] I have traveled extensively in many parts of Indonesia, often accompanied by students and professors from those islands, but the overwhelming majority of my experience has been in Java. My travels and students made me aware of my Javanese bias but did not eliminate it. However, I did not want to give up my ambition to write about Indonesia as a unit of analysis.

A second concern was lack of statistical, empirical verification for my theories. My theories are supported by ample anecdotal evidence. I have many Indonesian stories that illustrate and support my ideas. But I was unaware of any empirical, statistical studies covering all of Indonesia that could substantiate my theories about Indonesian social imaginaries and experiences of living in a sacred cosmos.

A third weakness was my reliance on concepts and ideal types that are grounded in western social science and philosophy but perhaps are foreign to Indonesia. Concepts such as social imaginaries, sacred, cosmos, mundane, enchanted, science, tradition, religion, secular, modern, Indonesian, and western (as well as other ideal types) are not neutral. They may be foreign to both Islam and Indonesian culture. Used with subtlety these concepts can help us analyze a complex reality. But they always flirt with the dangers of essentialism, reification, and stereotyping. None of these ideal types exists in reality. They are better thought of as processes that are constantly changing and interpenetrating each other rather than as distinct "things." None can be separated from the others or exist apart from them.

In order to mitigate both my Java bias and my lack of statistical data, I received a grant from the Ford Foundation to research Indonesian social imaginaries, especially outside of Java. This grant enabled me to travel to many parts of Indonesia and distribute questionnaires among different religious and ethnic groups to test my hypotheses. The research utilized a questionnaire, refined over several months, to explore the primary symbol systems used by Indonesians to express their imagination of reality. The questionnaire included twenty-one questions, not including demographic data (see appendices I and II). Seven questions explored the respondents' imagination of the unseen, supernatural world (*gaib*). Seven explored their visions of a good society, and seven explored their imaginations of power, politics, and government. Each question asked respondents to choose one out of three possible answers that expressed their most cogent or powerful experience of reality or the ideal to which they aspired. In most cases, the three answers were not mutually exclusive. Many respondents agreed with all the answers. The three possible answers represented ideal types of traditional, religious, and modern or scientific social imaginaries. The goal was not to pigeonhole respondents into one of three categories but rather to see how traditional, religious, and modern symbol systems interact with each other on different topics.

I carried out most of the empirical research outside Java with assistance from Dr. Farsijana Adeney-Risakotta during 2015. With the help of many assistants in the locations chosen, we conducted extensive interviews and collected 2,492 questionnaires from most of the major ethnic groups and religious communities of Indonesia. The chapters that follow interpret the data gleaned from these questionnaires on how religion and ethnicity in various parts of Indonesia influence people's social imaginaries. The questionnaire explores people's experience of an enchanted cosmos, their imagination of power, and their vision of ideal relations between people and with nature.

All Indonesians use traditional, religious, *and* modern symbol systems to express the way they imagine the unseen world, political power, and a good society. According to our research, out of 46,769 answers in a questionnaire filled out by 2,492 people belonging to more than fifty ethnic groups, 24.3 percent of the answers were derived from symbol systems constructed as "traditional," 36.8 percent were "religious," and 39 percent were "modern." These percentages do not represent three different groups of Indonesians. Out of the 2,492 respondents, 2,491 (all but one) used all three symbol systems in their answers.

Our research was weighted toward young, educated people, who represent the future. Eighty-five percent of the respondents were under forty-six years old. Sixty-three percent were eighteen to twenty-nine years old, and 22 percent were thirty to forty-five years old. At least 96 percent were high school graduates, including approximately 82 percent who were students, university lecturers, teachers, or civil servants. This high percentage reflects the fact that most of the questionnaires were distributed in universities or higher education settings. Only 3.4 percent of respondents identified themselves as farmers or fishers. It is reasonable to assume that an older, less educated sampling would yield a higher percentage of traditional and religious answers.[3]

Our research did not presume to sample every ethnic group, province, religious community, age, or income bracket. Perhaps because of the preponderance of students and academics, 80 percent of respondents listed their income as less than US$225 per month. Of the respondents, 45.4 percent were men and 54.1 percent were women. The ethnic groups chosen for inclusion in the study were influenced by locations where I had former students or colleagues who could assist in the research. In order to simplify analysis of the statistics, we grouped several distinct ethnic groups into a single unit based on similarities in culture, religion, and geographic location. Ethnicity is already a constructed, contested grouping. Table 0.1 lays out the ethnic groups we constructed from the respondents' self-identification in order to simplify the task of comparative analysis.

In the interpretation of the data, this book only compares differences between ethnic groups (or groups of groups) from which there is a substantial sampling. The main comparisons are between Muslims, Protestants, Catholics, and Hindus. For ease of reading, I have kept the statistics to a minimum in the main body of the book, only showing a summary of our conclusions. The appendices show more statistical detail, as well as some of the reasoning behind our interpretations of the data. Readers should feel free to skip over statistical data that is not of interest to them. Those who want more detail should contact the author.

This book explores the ways in which the largest Islamic society in the world constructs a unique understanding of cosmic, social, and moral order. It is about the way an "enchanted" Islamic social imagination shapes different kinds of modernity unlike those constructed in the West. Many people believe that western modernity is more advanced than that found in the rest of the world. Thus, if they want progress, people should imitate modern western civilization. This book offers an alternative view. It shows how Indonesian Muslims, Christians, Hindus, and Buddhists integrate mimetic, mythic, ethical, and theoretic styles of cognition to structure their modern lives. Wilfred Cantwell Smith commented that if you only know

Table 0.1 *Ethnicity of Questionnaire Respondents*

Respondents		Frequency	Percentage	Valid Percent	
Valid	Jawa-Madura	463	18.6	18./	
	Sunda	108	4.3	4.3	
	Bali	217	8.7	8.7	
	NTT:[a] Flores, Manggarai, Lio, Ngada	164	6.6	6.6	38.2
	NTB[b]	3	.1	.1	38.4
	NTT: Sumba, Kupang, Timor, Rote, Alor, Sabu, Sawu	42	1.7	1.7	40.0
	Toraja, Rongkong, Luwu, Mamasa, Poso, Pamona, Rampi	113	4.5	4.5	44.6
	Makassar, Bugis, Mandar, Muna, Buton	193	7.7	7.8	52.3
	Papua, Biak, Suku-suku Papua	230	9.2	9.2	61.6
	Minahasa, Manado, North Sulawesi	79	3.2	3.2	64.7
	North Maluku, Halmahera, Ternate, Maluku, Ambon, Kei	207	8.3	8.3	73.1
	Dayak, Kalimantan, Banjar, South Kalimantan	78	3.1	3.1	76.2
	Tioghoa, Chinese	15	.6	.6	76.8
	Aceh, Gayo	196	7.9	7.9	84.7
	Batak, Nias	49	2.0	2.0	86.6
	Minang, Melayu, West Sumatra, Riau, Lampung, Komering, Tabuan, South Sumatra	313	12.6	12.6	99.2
	Indonesian multiethnic	14	.6	.6	99.8
	Non-Indonesian	4	.2	.2	99.9
	Lombok, Sasak	2	.1	.1	100.0
	Subtotal	2,490	99.9	100.0	
Missing		2	.1		
Total		2,492	100.0		

[a]NTT = Nusa Tenggara Timur, or East Nusa Tenggara. This is a chain of islands that forms a province in eastern Indonesia, the eastern part of the Lesser Sunda islands. I've divided NTT into two parts: ethnic groups on Flores, which are predominantly Catholic and ethnic groups on Sumba, West Timor, and nearby islands, which are predominantly Protestant.

[b]NTB = Nusa Tenggara Barat or West Nusa Tenggara. This province includes the western part of the Lesser Sunda islands, such as Lombok and Sumbawa, which are predominantly Muslim.

one religion you don't know any religion. If you learn about other religions, you will end up understanding your own religion much better. The same is true of western modernity. Learning about Muslim Indonesian forms of modernity will deepen the reader's understanding of western modernity. This book aims to illuminate both Indonesian and western forms of modernity.

Many Indonesians are affected by a polarized view of the world made up of essentialized categories such as East versus West, Islam versus the West, traditional versus modern, religious versus secular, Muslim versus Christian, and communal versus individualistic. This book deconstructs stereotypes and uncovers the complexity of Indonesia's modern, cultural, and religious identity. Many non-Muslims have one-dimensional, stereotyped views of Islam influenced by sensational media images and fear of the other. This book provides a complex, nuanced view of Islam that explores the interactions among religion, culture, and modernity. Islam in Indonesia does not represent global Islam. On the contrary, it is unique. Nevertheless, many aspects of an Islamic imagination of living in a sacred cosmos are not only true of Indonesia. They illuminate the social imaginaries of Muslim and other religious communities in many countries, including in the West.

This is a work of interpretive social science rather than normative evaluation. I'm trying to understand a very complex reality rather than arguing for a particular religious, moral, political, or theological perspective on Islam in the modern world. My biases in favor of tolerance, justice, and peace are obvious. But my priority is to describe the uniqueness of religious pluralism in the largest Muslim majority society in the world rather than to judge it. This book does not predict the future of Islam or Indonesia. However, it provides resources for building understanding between different religious and cultural communities. It suggests that Indonesian Islam provides a hopeful model for the future of Islam in a pluralistic world.

The central questions of the book are Why is modernity in Indonesia so different from modernity in the West, the Middle East, India, and China? Is it possible to live in a preaxial sacred cosmos while following an axial religion and living within postaxial modern institutional structures? And how might Islamicate culture in Indonesia contribute to a more just and peaceful world order in the years ahead? There is indeed a "clash of civilizations" in Indonesia, but it is not between Muslims and the West. Nor is it between Muslims and non-Muslims. Rather it is between different imaginations of reality that occur within different communities and, as often as not, also within a single human heart.

This book is divided into four parts with three chapters in each. Part I, "Islam and Modernity in Indonesia," lays out the main theories used to structure the book.

Chapter 1, "Whither Islam? Whose Islam? Which Muslims?," explores the central questions of the book regarding why Indonesian Islam is unique. The center of world Islamicate civilization is shifting to Asia. The chapter suggested that the well-documented rise of Islamic pietism, conservatism, and intolerance is not the only way to view Islam in Indonesia. The dominant metaphors that many scholars use to characterize Islamicate civilization in Indonesia are not wrong, but they obscure aspects that may be important for the future of human civilization.

Chapter 2, "Social Imaginaries in Indonesia and the West," explores how social imaginaries shape Indonesian experiences of modernity. While modern western social imaginaries (Taylor 2007) have increasing influence, they are in tension with traditional and religious social imaginaries about the unseen world (*gaib*), the political order, and the ideal society.

Chapter 3, "Cultures, Religions, and Modernities in Indonesia," outlines how Indonesia has been shaped by influences from China, India, the Middle East, and Europe. Indonesians integrate mimetic, mythic, ethical, and theoretic styles of cognition into their own imaginations of a sacred cosmos. Social imaginaries are sociolinguistic symbol systems, which interpenetrate and influence each other. Indonesians are fluent in three overlapping systems of meaning: the cultures of their ancestors, their religions, and the structures of modern society.

Part II, "Living in a Sacred Cosmos," explores Indonesian attitudes toward the unseen world of spirits and supernatural powers.

Chapter 4, "Enchantment and a Sacred Cosmos," explores the nature of a sacred cosmos through stories from different religious and ethnic communities in Indonesia. In a sacred cosmos individuals are embedded in communities that encompass ancestors and unseen powers. Communities are embedded in nature. The natural world has agency and includes powers that can communicate with the human community and affect its well-being. Nature is embedded in a single moral order, which includes both the community and nature. The moral order is embedded in God or some transcendent principle or power. Illustrated with stories, this chapter considers how to judge the "truth" of a sacred cosmos, especially with regard to the practices of magic.

Chapter 5, "Islamic Modernism and Disenchantment," asks whether or not Islamic modernism has stimulated a progressive disenchantment of the world for most Indonesians. This chapter examines how religion and magic were separated in the West and Indonesia. It summarizes empirical research on Indonesians' experience of an unseen world of spirits, communication through dreams, understanding of spirit possession, and affirmation of a moral meaning behind accidents and illness. It examines empirical evidence on whether or not the modernist movement to purify Islam has led to increasing disbelief in a world of unseen powers and spirits.

Chapter 6, "Islam and Enchantment: Six Leaders," presents the results of interviews with six prominent Indonesian Muslim leaders: two from Muhammadiyah (modernist), two from Nahdlatul Ulama (traditionalist) and two that are independent (nationalist). The interviews explore their conceptions of a sacred cosmos and their assessment of where the Muslim community in Indonesia is headed.

Part III, "Traditional, Modern, and Religious Imaginations of Power," explores imaginations and practices of power in various parts of Indonesia.

Chapter 7, "Traditional Indonesian Imaginations of Power," considers the influential theory that Javanese imagine power as an energy, or living "substance," that can be possessed regardless of its use. The chapter explores data from different religious and ethnic groups to see the extent to which Indonesians hold traditional views about substantive power, leadership, government, and society.

Chapter 8, "Modern Indonesian Imaginations of Power," explores the ways in which we can use modern and postmodern social theories to interpret Indonesian society. It asks how democratic institutions can bridge the huge differences between interest groups in Indonesia. How can Indonesians navigate rapid urbanization, a global capitalist economy, Islamic radicalism, the aspirations of the people, domination of the public sphere by money and violence, the hegemony of "truth regimes," and the use of symbolic violence by cultural elites?

Chapter 9, "Muslim Imaginations of Power in Indonesia," examines differences in the ways Indonesians imagine how religion should influence law, how the government should regulate religion, how religious imaginations shape society, and the power of religion in controlling the people. The chapter also explores how Indonesians imagine that religion empowers them through mimetic rituals, meaningful narratives, moral guidance, and theoretical reflection.

Part IV, "Nature, Women, and Conflict in a Sacred Cosmos," explores how living in a sacred cosmos that is traditional, religious, and modern shapes the ways Indonesians imagine nature, women, and religious conflict.

Chapter 10, "Imaginations of Nature and Natural Disasters," suggests that in Indonesia there is a complementary relationship, as well as tension, between different narratives about the meaning of nature and natural disasters. Indonesians use mimetic, mythic, ethical, and scientific approaches for conceiving their relation to nature and for dealing with natural disasters.

Chapter 11, "Imaginations of Women in Law and Practice," asks why Indonesian society is justly praised for empowering women but at the same time maintains highly patriarchal structures. The chapter explores tensions between traditional, Islamic, and modern national law, all of which are interpreted through local imaginations of women and ancient practices of patriarchy, gender balance, and equality in the public sphere.

Chapter 12, "Conflict, Intolerance, and Hope," explores Indonesian repertoires for addressing conflicts that arise from diversity. Indonesians are famous for their warmth, politeness, and gentleness, even with strangers. But there are also currents of violence and cruelty toward those constructed as cosmic enemies. The chapter discusses how Indonesians use mimetic rituals and competing narratives to both intensify and resolve conflict. It recaps the ways in which the book has answered the main questions about living in a sacred cosmos and the impact of Indonesia on the future of Islam in the modern world.

Part I
Islam and Modernity in Indonesia

PART I INTRODUCES questions about the nature of Islam and why Indonesia may make an important contribution for the future of human civilization. It explores why modernity in Indonesia is unique. Indonesians have different social imaginaries from the West, which integrate mimetic, mythic, moral and scientific ways of imagining reality. Indonesia is creating unique structures which integrate cultural traditions, religious practices and modern institutions.

1

Whither Islam? Whose Islam? Which Muslims?

Everything we see hides another thing. We always want to see what is hidden by what we see.

—René Magritte

Where is the Center of Modern Islamic Civilization?

THE CENTER OF ISLAMICATE CIVILIZATION in the world today is neither Saudi Arabia nor the Middle East. Rather it is Indonesia.[1] Indonesia is the most important country in the world about which most people know practically nothing.[2] Just as the center of Christianity is no longer in Europe or North America but has shifted to the Southern Hemisphere (Jenkins 2012), so the center of Islamicate civilization has shifted from the Middle East to Asia. Evidence for this change is supported by population statistics. Currently, 62 percent of Muslims live in Asia. Another 32 percent live in Africa. Relatively few of the world's Muslims live in the Middle East. Indonesia is by far the largest Muslim country on earth, with more Muslims living in Indonesia (215 million) than those who live in the entire Middle East.[3]

Population is not the whole story. Indonesia is also the most dynamic Muslim majority country, with incredible diversity between different streams of Islam, different ethnic groups, and different religious communities, which for the most part live side by side in harmony. Unlike many Muslim countries, Indonesia legally protects the right to hold different interpretations and practices of Islam. This creates space in which Indonesian Muslims can think about their faith without fear. I recall my shock when a visiting Muslim intellectual commented, during a discussion of Islam and hermeneutics in Yogyakarta, Indonesia, that if the opinion of one of my Muslim colleagues was expressed in his country he might receive a death fatwa. Muslim intellectuals from other countries often love Indonesia because they can freely express their honest questions about their faith without fear of prosecution.

If the center of Islamicate civilization has moved to Asia, it doesn't imply that Muslims in Asia are more peaceful and tolerant than Muslims in the Middle East. Many Middle Eastern Muslims are peaceful and tolerant, and many Asian Muslims are not. Pakistan is not exactly a model of peaceful tolerance. Indonesia is suffering a sustained attack by a minority of radicals who oppose openness to diverse ideas. Amply funded by Saudi Arabia, conservative and intolerant forms of Islam are growing in Indonesia. Harsh attacks by radicals have caused the mainstream majority to worry about the future.

Nevertheless, Indonesia has an ancient history of religious tolerance that is far more peaceful than the history of religions in Europe or the Middle East (see Reid 2014c). Through many centuries, Indonesia developed impressive social capital for dealing with religious diversity based on a social imagination of reality that is distinctively different from those of the West or the Middle East. Absolutist assertions that everyone must submit to a one and only truth feel foreign to most Indonesians. This respect for diversity is supported by rapid growth in economic prosperity, health, and education.

There is also a dark side to Indonesia. Indonesians have not always dealt with diversity in peaceful ways. The early exile of Hindus to the island of Bali, wars between different kingdoms, the brutal killings of 1965–66, the long authoritarian rule of President Soeharto, mass violence following his fall, and the growth of Islamic conservatism and radicalism have led many to question whether the admirable "tolerance of the Javanese" is only a peaceful facade over darker currents (Anderson 1965; see also Colombijn and Lindblad 2002). Minority groups such as the Shias, Ahmadis, Christians, Hindus, Buddhists, Confucianists, and followers of tribal religions sometimes experience oppression and violence. Racism against Chinese and Papuans is an ongoing source of injustice. Nevertheless, in spite of many serious and intractable problems, this book suggests that Indonesia is a source of hope for the future of relations between Muslims and non-Muslims.

The growing influence of Indonesia in the Muslim world has been ignored by many scholars.[4] Many Arab Muslims and orientalist scholars consider Indonesia to be a kind of backwater that practices an inferior form of Islam mixed with animistic beliefs. Both groups essentialize Islam, distinguishing "pure" (i.e., Arab) Islam from debased or folk Islam. From this perspective, Arabic language and culture are the normative measuring stick of authentic Islam. Many Muslims, including many Indonesians, agree. Koranic recitation in good Arabic is a measure of Muslim piety in Indonesia (Gade 2004). In one sense, Mecca and Medina in Saudi Arabia will always be the normative center of Islam because they are the location of the sacred narrative of the Prophet Muhammad and the Koran. This centrality is reinforced by the annual Haj. But Arabic language and culture are not necessarily the best measures of a successful Islamicate culture. Arab interpretations and practices of Islam may not be the standard by which all Muslim societies should be judged. According to many Indonesians, creating a community of justice, safety, and peace is closer to the teachings of the Koran than is the purity of Arabic culture.

Indonesia has experienced a dramatic renaissance in Islamicate civilization that has largely gone unnoticed outside the country. A dramatic flowering of Islamicate ideas, art, architecture, literature, political and economic structures, and civil society organizations is transforming the face of Indonesia. Most of the world remains ignorant of the thousands of books published every year in Indonesia, as they are in Indonesian, not English or Arabic. The Middle East is plagued by despotic regimes and is mired in seemingly endless conflicts and violence. Islam is increasingly seen by outsiders as a problem and a threat.[5] Islam evokes fear, not hope. This book suggests that there is hope that Islam may be a source of beauty, not only to Muslims but to the whole world. In Indonesia there are positive forms of Islamicate modernity that can contribute to world civilization.

Indonesia has the fourth-largest population in the world (after China, India, and the United States) and is the world's third-largest constitutional democracy. It enjoys stable democratic institutions, a growing economy, equal rights for women and non-Muslims, political freedom, and legal protection of human rights. As in all large countries, these legal ideals are far from perfectly enforced.[6] Nevertheless, changes over the past eighty years have been dramatic. In 1930 only 7.4 percent of the population could read (Ricklefs 2008:274). In 2016 there was more than 99 percent literacy among young people, including girls, and 93 percent literacy among the whole population.[7] Thousands of Indonesians are studying for postgraduate degrees in foreign countries. In 1955, the life expectancy of Indonesians was only thirty-seven years. Today it is about seventy-three years.[8] The children and grandchildren of parents who could not read or write and never experienced electricity or motor vehicles are now surfing the internet, flying to foreign countries, and forming study groups to discuss post-modern, postcolonial social theory. Indonesia is neither uniform nor static. It is changing at a dizzying speed. Like all large countries, it faces many intractable problems. No one knows what the future will bring. But whatever happens in Indonesia will affect the future of Islam in the modern world.

Many people are asking what the future of Islam will be, especially in relation to the West. Why are so many terrorist attacks associated with Islam? Why are millions of Muslim refugees flooding into western countries? How should we view the growing influence of Islam in the world? Twenty-three percent of the world's population are followers of Islam. Demographics suggest that this proportion will grow considerably larger in the coming years. In 2015 there were 1.8 billion Muslims, which was double the combined populations of Europe and the United States and equal to the combined populations of China and the United States. By 2060, according to the Pew Foundation, there will be almost 3 billion Muslims, including over 30 percent of the world population.[9] The future of the world is deeply connected to the future of Islam in the modern world.

Many people assume that Islam is identical to Arab culture. The "Arab Spring" of 2011 caused great excitement about the possibility of democracy taking root in Middle Eastern Muslim countries. But the degeneration of the Arab Spring into civil wars and the heating up of the rivalry between Saudi Arabia and Iran has led to general pessimism about the Middle East. Some even suggest that the Muslim world may be entering something like the Thirty Years' War, which decimated the population of Europe in 1618–48.[10]

This book explores the possibility that the future of Islam and Muslim relations with the non-Muslim world lies not in the Middle East but rather in the forgotten world of Indonesia. Indonesia is creating a unique kind of modernity, one that synthesizes mimetic, mythic, ethical, and theoretic imaginations of reality with modern institutions and values. The importance of Indonesia lies not in its similarity to the West (e.g., in its democratic institutions) but rather in its creation of a unique modernity forged out of thousands of years of interaction with the axial civilizations of China, India, the Middle East, and Europe (see Bellah 2011). Indonesia is a thoroughly religious, traditional, and modern society that is not following the expected paths of modernity or Islamic societies.

This book suggests that a key to understanding the importance of Indonesia lies in its distinctive social imaginaries (Taylor 2007). Social imaginaries include theories that shape our understanding of society. But they are not limited to ideas. They include common feelings, symbols, stories, and practices that determine what a society imagines is real. Social imaginaries make common practices possible. Indonesian social imaginaries are in dialectical tension between contrasting visions of reality. The outcome of this struggle is not clear, predetermined, or uniform. But many Indonesians hope that Islam Nusantara (Island Southeast Asian Islam) will contribute positive values to the whole world, not just the Muslim world. On the other hand, Muslim militants hope that Indonesia will become the world's most populous recruiting ground for *mujahidin* (warriors) in a "jihad" against the West.

Changing Perceptions of the West and the United States

In the year 2000, prior to the invasions of Afghanistan and Iraq, the United States had a surprisingly high approval rating of 75 percent among Indonesians, and it was even higher among young people (Holsti 2008).[11] During the struggle to overthrow the corrupt dictator President Soeharto in 1997–1998, many Indonesians looked on the United States as a symbol of democracy, freedom, clean government, and human rights. In early 1998 I was rather shocked to wake up one morning and find my whole neighborhood in Yogyakarta, Indonesia, festooned with American flags. They were symbols of freedom and democracy. The 9/11 attacks elicited a lot of sympathy for the American people, as well as grudging admiration for the bravery and sophistication of the attack on the symbols of American economic and military power (B. Adeney-Risakotta 2004).

However, many Indonesians viewed President Bush's invasions of Afghanistan and Iraq, his declaration of war against terrorism, and his rhetoric about a crusade as tantamount to a war against Islam.[12] US approval ratings crashed from 75 to around 15 percent in 2003, and there was a sharp rise in the popularity of radical Islamist groups.[13] It appeared that radicalism was on the rise, fueled by international geopolitical events such as the conflict between Israel and Palestine and the war in Iraq. The Indonesian economic crisis, which pushed a third of the country's new middle class back into poverty, also encouraged radicalism. Following the fall of Soeharto, from 1998 to 2002 ethnic and religious conflicts broke out in many parts of Indonesia, influenced by rapid decentralization, demilitarization, the economic crisis, and competition for political and economic resources.[14]

Since the 2004 elections, Indonesia has enjoyed political stability, democratic government and a steady improvement in the economy. After the election of Barak Hussein Obama, Indonesian approval of the USA crept back up to 63 percent (2009) and held at 62 percent in 2015.[15] Almost certainly the approval rating of the USA is now taking a dive, due to the election Donald Trump and his anti-Islamic rhetoric and policies. Trump's election was greeted with horror by most Indonesian Muslims. His indiscriminate, sweepingly negative rhetoric about Muslims encourages the perception that the West is at war with Islam. In contrast Trumps election was greeted with glee by radical Islamists, since his views are a mirror image of theirs. Both imagine themselves in an intractable war with evil opponents.

This book explores the character and direction of the Muslim community in Indonesia. From 2007–2017, it appeared that Islamic radicalism was declining. In the national elections, the great majority of Indonesian Muslims chose non-religious parties. Only one party is considered Islamist in ideology (PKS), but does it's best to appear as moderate as possible. For example, it does not openly advocate *Sharia* (the way of God) law and claims to fully respect democratic institutions and the protection of human rights. Yet even this "moderate" Islamist party only managed to garner 6.79 percent of the vote in the legislative elections of 2014, a decrease of over 16 percent in comparison with the previous election in 2009 and a steady decline over the previous 10 years.[16] On the other hand, many Indonesians are concerned about the recent growth of radicalism and intolerance (see chapter 12 in this volume).

Is Islam One or Diverse?

It is commonplace for foreigners to say that Islam in Indonesia is very different from Islam in the Middle East. From one perspective the statement is obvious and supported by abundant empirical evidence. It is equally true that the Muslim community in Saudi Arabia is quite different from that in Egypt. Both are very different from that in Iran, India, Turkey, Pakistan, or Yemen, each of which is strikingly different from the others. Even within Indonesia there are striking differences in how Muslims practice their faith. Nevertheless, the statement about different kinds of Islam is controversial. Most Muslims, wherever they are from, agree that Islam is one. There is only one Islam, the Islam revealed through the Prophet Muhammad and expressed in the Koran and Sunnah (stories about the sayings and actions of the Prophet).

Ever since the death of the Prophet, Muslims have differed in the way they interpret the Scriptures and apply them in their societies. Muslim conservatives oppose contextual interpretations and believe the words of God in the Koran should be exactly followed in all times and places. Therefore all Muslims should return to exact obedience to laws and practices revealed by the Prophet. The idea that there is only one Islam is used by the supporters of an Islamic caliphate, as is asserted by the Islamic State of Iraq and Syria (ISIS) to claim that the caliphate is the one true representative of Islam. Everyone, Muslim or non-Muslim, must submit to the caliphate. According to this view, only a caliphate can restore the unity of Islam. Anyone who opposes it is *kafir* (pagan) and at war with Islam.

Most Muslims in the world do not agree that ISIS is the one true representative of Islam. Most Muslims see ISIS as a heretical caricature of true Islam. According to a Pew Foundation study, less than .03 percent of Indonesian Muslims were Wahabi/Salafi followers in 2005 (Arab-based fundamentalist streams of Islam) and most Wahabi/Salafi followers did not agree with the teachings and practices of ISIS.[17] Thousands of Europeans with secular backgrounds have gone to join ISIS, even while millions of Muslims in ISIS-controlled territories have fled to Europe. In contrast, only a few hundred Indonesians have set out to fight for ISIS. Nevertheless, the government and major Muslim organizations are concerned enough to set up task forces to combat the growth of radicalism in Indonesia.

There is a hot debate in Indonesia over whether it is proper to speak of Indonesian Islam (Islam Nusantara, the "Islam of the Archipelago") or if the better language is "Islam in Indonesia." This may seem like splitting hairs to outsiders, but great matters are at stake in the debate. Those who promote the term Islam Nusantara insist that there are unique forms of Islam in Indonesia that are not only valid but actually superior to Islam as it is practiced in the Middle East. Members of Nahdlatul Ulama (NU), an organization that claims forty to fifty million members,[18] insist that Islam Nusantara is a unique, authentic, contextualized expression of Islam that differs from Islam in the Middle East. According to NU, Islam Nusantara is a national treasure that must be protected from globalized attempts to define a single form of valid Islam determined by Saudi Arabia. More conservative groups reject the term Islam Nusantara on the grounds that there is only one Islam, the one taught by the Prophet. They may acknowledge that there are legitimate differences in interpretation and practice, but they reject spiritual or ritual practices that are not directly authorized by the Koran and Sunnah.

An example of this debate occurred when a Javanese Muslim performed a Koranic recitation in the National Palace before President Joko Widodo (Jokowi) in May 2015. Controversy erupted when the Koranic scholar recited the Koran accompanied by traditional Javanese gamelan music. To conservative Muslims, this was scandalous as it represented an "innovation" (*bid'ah*) not authorized by the Koran. But for those who advocate Islam Nusantara it was a perfectly valid expression of Javanese Islam.

The Growth of Conservative Islam in Indonesia

The dramatic growth of orthodox Islamic piety in Indonesia is apparent. Several fine studies have convincingly documented an accelerating process of "Islamisation" in Java (e.g., Hefner 2000; Beatty 2009; Ricklefs 2012, Bruinessen 2013). Java is not alone. Islamisation has had a profound impact on all parts of Indonesia. Indeed it is part of a global phenomenon. Indonesia not only has the largest Muslim population in the world, but it is also a country in which Islam is becoming more and more dominant in all areas of life. M. C. Ricklefs's masterful three-volume history of religion in Java proposes three stages in the development of Islam there. From the fifteenth century to about 1830, the Muslims of Java achieved a "mystic synthesis" in which most Javanese saw no contradiction between Islam and their pre-Islamic beliefs (Ricklefs 2006). From about 1830 to 1965, Muslims became increasingly polarized between the *abangan* (peasant, syncretist Muslims) and the *santri* (observant, conservative Muslims) (Ricklefs 2007). According to Ricklefs, since 1965 the institutions that supported the *abangan* have collapsed and the *abangan* way of life is rapidly disappearing, replaced by the Islamisation of all of life (2012).[19]

To many non-Muslim observers, this is an alarming development, captured dramatically in the title of Andrew Beatty's *A Shadow Falls: In the Heart of Java* (2009). In colonial times, some Europeans feared the Islamic side of Indonesia and mythologized the tolerant, Hindu-Buddhist heritage of ancient Java and Bali (see Anderson 1965). Nancy Florida has shown that western scholarship on ancient Javanese literature was distorted because researchers ignored abundant Islamic Javanese texts in favor of Hindu-Buddhist or mystical texts (1995). What they *saw*, the heritage of a rich Hindu-Buddhist civilization, clouded their vision of the deep impact of Islam on this civilization. Following the Reforms of 1998ff, some observers were torn between admiration for the process of democratization and alarm over the dramatic growth of Islamic piety. On the one hand, they denounced the authoritarian government of President Soeharto but were tacitly grateful for his suppression of militant Islam. On the other, they praised the growth of democracy while lamenting the rapid growth pietistic Islam.

Categories and Classifications

What we see is often determined by predetermined categories we hold in our minds. No single person has influenced the ways in which religion is viewed in Indonesia as much as Clifford Geertz. Geertz is well known for his division of Javanese Islam into syncretistic Muslim Abangan (peasants), orthodox Muslim Santri (pious, conservative traders) and mystic Muslim Priyai (aristocrats) (1960). Geertz suggested that the Abangan and Priyai, who included the great majority of Javanese Muslims in the 1950s, were only Muslims on the surface. Underneath their superficial Muslim forms lay a Javanese civilization shaped by centuries of Hindu and Buddhist influence. This typology continues to exercise enormous influence on ideas about Islam in Java. The categories do not describe the sociopolitical, cultural, economic, and religious realities of today, but they are still shaping assumptions, especially among those who regret the apparent collapse of *abangan* and *priyai* forms of Islam. The current situation in Indonesia is interpreted as a process of loss: the loss of a unique and rich cultural heritage that was shaped by Hinduism and Buddhism.

There are at least three ways to respond to Geertz. First, some scholars argue that he was simply wrong. His analytic categories were overly ambitious as he tried to create one overarching system of comparison that combines religion, class, economics, politics, and culture. As a result he ignored the complex ways in which these categories overlap. It is possible for the same person to be a *priyai* by class and political role, a *santri* by religious practice and economic activity, and an *abangan* in terms of animist beliefs and cultural lifestyle. Many Javanese combine aspects of all three types. The same person may be a *santri* on Fridays and during Ramadan, an *abangan* on Saturday night or when enjoying Javanese art forms, and a *priyai* in following certain mystical disciplines. Besides oversimplifying Javanese religious life, Geertz was insufficiently aware of the rich diversity within Islam. Influences that he attributed to pre-Islamic Hinduism and Buddhism can just as easily be traced to sufism or other streams within Islam (Woodward 1989).

Such criticisms include many valid observations but miss the power and usefulness of Geertz's typology. Ideal types are not descriptions but rather analytic categories for examining complex realities. Geertz never claimed that everyone in Java fit neatly into one of his three streams (*aliran*). Rather he provided tools with which to analyze these three broad currents in what is essentially a single river, which includes thousands of smaller subcurrents. Even if Javanese Muslim practices can be traced to Islamic sources from China, India, Persia, and the Middle East, it does not necessarily mean that these sources were untouched by ideas that were consonant with Hinduism and Buddhism. The concept of "circulatory history" suggests that different civilizations have been influencing each other for millennia (Duara 2015). It is futile to argue over the original source of influential ideas and practices. The power of Geertz's typology continues to be felt, even in the writings of his severest critics. They still use his categories even as they deny their relevance.

A second response to Geertz is to suggest that his three categories were accurate descriptions of divisions within Javanese society at the time when he was conducting his research in the 1950s in the village of Pare. Following Ricklefs, we may view Geertz's categories as helpful analytic categories up to the present, even though the *abangan* and *priyai* variants have declined in influence. One of the many virtues of Ricklefs's nuanced history is that he puts to rest the notion of an essential, unchanging Javanese civilization. Java was not always polarized between *santri* and *abangan*. In fact the term *abangan* did not even exist until the late nineteenth century. Most Javanese Muslims combined Islamic piety with a mystical acceptance of local beliefs and practices. Later, in the 1950s, the *abangan* stream was so strong that Geertz suggested it would be difficult for a Javanese to become a true Muslim because Javanese civilization was so much at odds with Islamic civilization (1960:160). But in the twenty-first century, according to Ricklefs, the *abangan* way of life has been so completely undermined that "There is now no significant opposition to the deeper Islamisation of Javanese society" (2012:446). The *abangan* and *priyai* have been swallowed up by the *santri*.

This is certainly one way to interpret this history, but it tends to reify the types, treating *abangan* and *santri* as if they are mutually exclusive social groups. Ricklefs's three-volume history is so rich in empirical detail that the reader is continually reminded of the complexity of the dialectical overlap between the *abangan* and *santri*. Still, the narrative of polarization and conflict and the increasing defeat of one "type" by the other are in danger of being reified as fact rather than recognized as a theory about the meaning of this history. Long before the term *abangan* came into common use, there were polarized conflicts between more and less strict interpretations of Islam, such as the Padri Wars in West Sumatra (1803–37).[20] Even after the apparent eclipse of *abangan* institutions, *santri* institutions are still deeply influenced by *abangan* practices and beliefs.

A third response to Geertz's three types is to emphasize that they are heuristic tools that bring some things into focus while obscuring others. Even in the 1950s there was no such thing in reality as a pure *abangan*, *priyai*, or *santri*. They were ideal types, not real people. Geertz's typology was not the only way to categorize religious currents among the Javanese in the 1950s. An astute observer could have identified five types, ten, or only two. President Sukarno employed three types: nationalists, religionists (Islamists), and communists (*nasakom*). Others used categories such as modernists, traditionalists, and Islamists, or scripturalist versus substantialist Islam (e.g., Effendy 1998). Human beings and groupings are always more complex than any type. Geertz's three types were extraordinarily useful constructs that helped us to see things to which we would otherwise have been blind. The types are still valuable, as shown in Ricklefs's narrative, as categories to help us understand cultural change, even though they no longer describe major divisions in Indonesian society. A bigger problem is that the types distract us from seeing other things that may be more important. Other categories open up different kinds of insights.

Geertz's characterization of *abangan* Muslims as fundamentally Buddhist/ Hindus for whom Islam was no more than a superficial veneer, has been widely discredited in light of more recent developments (e.g., Woodward 1989; Florida 1995). Geertz was certainly mistaken about the superficiality of Islam in Java. But in our haste to correct the master, we may forget his more basic insight, later elaborated by Denys Lombard, that Indonesians are made up of many layers of ancient civilizations (see Lombard 1996a, b, and c). Indonesians are part of a global, historical circulation of rituals, stories, laws, and theories from many different interacting sources. Indonesian Islam is shaped by an ongoing centuries-old process of the circulation of mimetic, mythic, ethical, and theoretic imaginations of reality. Indonesian Islam is a product of its own prehistoric ethnic cultures, as well as Confucianism, Taoism, Hinduism, Buddhism, Islam and Christianity. When discussing human evolution, Robert N. Bellah often said, "Nothing is ever lost." That which came before is still a part of us. In Indonesia influences from China, India, the Middle East, and Europe are deeply rooted in the imaginations of most Indonesians to this day.

The resurgence of public Islamic piety in Indonesia is undeniable. For some western observers, there is something close to panic at the thought that what they love about Indonesia may be passing away. I am not competent to judge whether the kind of Islamisation that is happening in Indonesia is a positive or negative trend. How we name things carries normative weight. Instead of naming this phenomenon "Islamisation" or the "resurgence of Islam," we might call it the "renaissance of Islam" in Indonesia to call attention to the flowering of Islamic art, architecture, intellectual discourse, literature, philosophy, social science, theology, music, and so on. While there has been a decrease in some *abangan* and *priyai* practices, this does not mean that Indonesian Islam has become more narrow and uniform. In fact the Muslim community in Indonesia is more diverse today than it has ever been. Education and the global circulation of ideas (including radical ideas) have led to far greater diversity in the understanding and practice of Islam in Indonesia than ever before.

The long-term effects of a renaissance of Islam in Indonesia, or in any other part of the world, are still unknown. Zhou Enlai was reputedly asked what he thought about the French Revolution. He thought for a long time, while his listeners grew impatient. Finally, to their confusion, he replied, "It's too soon to tell."[21] I don't think he was making a joke. The ultimate outcomes of western civilization, for which the French Revolution was a pivotal event, are still unfolding. From a postcolonial, ecological, or pacifist perspective, the French Revolution might be viewed as a disaster. This book examines the current realities of Indonesia through a different lens than that of Islamisation or the dialectic between *santri* and *abangan*, modernist and traditionalist, scripturalist and substantialist, or radical and moderate. Instead, the book examines how Indonesian social imaginaries about a sacred cosmos shape a different kind of modernity in Indonesia than there is in the West.

René Magritte, a Belgian surrealist artist, wrote, "Everything we see hides another thing. We always want to see what is hidden by what we see." The dramatic growth of conservative Islamic piety is an important reality we can see. But it also hides some things. Dramatic religious, political, economic, and cultural changes may hide from view the continuities in Indonesian society that are the product of centuries. The so-called *abangan* and *santri* may be more alike than we thought. Even Indonesian Muslims, Christians, and Hindus may be more alike than some would imagine. This book focuses on how social imaginaries in Indonesia shape an "enchanted" perspective on reality that transcends different streams of religion in Indonesia. By shifting the categories to social imaginaries rather than different categories of Muslims, new questions emerge. Different questions result in different insights regarding the interaction among religion, imagination, and modernity in Indonesia.

Mimetic, Mythic, and Theoretic Styles of Cognition

Robert N. Bellah's monumental book on religion in human evolution is premised on Merlin Donald's theory of cognitive evolution from mimetic to mythic to theoretic (Bellah 2011). According to Bellah, the great axial civilizations of China, India, Israel, and Greece gave birth to new powers of scientific, universalizing, analytic, critical, abstract, and theoretic thought. Theoretic cognition gave birth to the modern world. It also changed the role of religion in the world.

A theory of axial civilizations was first proposed by Karl Jaspers at the end of World War II. Jaspers had an ethical agenda and opposed the common western assumption that the modern world is a western invention rooted in Greek thought and Christian theology. He disagreed with Georg Wilhelm Hegel's thesis that the axis of history was the life of Jesus Christ. According to Hegel (and Max Weber), modernity is a Christian, western invention. On the contrary, Jaspers suggested that modernity came from multiple sources.

Bellah took up Jasper's theory that human evolution was working in similar ways in different places, most notably between 800 and 200 BCE, to make possible the modern world. There were similar cognitive breakthroughs during the axial age when China (Confucius, Lao Tze), India (Vedas, Upanishads, Buddha), the Middle East (Isaiah, Jeremiah, Amos), and Greece (Socrates, Plato, Aristotle) all gave birth to theoretic culture.[22] If there are multiple axial civilizations, that may help explain why there are multiple modernities. The development of theoretic cognition gave rise to different philosophies, practices, and religions in China, India, the Middle East and Greece. There is more than one path to modernity.

José Casanova suggests that "preaxial" religions were premised on a single, unified cosmos of meaning with two parts: the sacred and the profane (Casanova 2012:200). Preaxial, mimetic religions are focused on rituals, which imitate (mimic) or reproduce the sacred order (see Durkheim [1912] 1915). Since these rituals are located in sacred time and space, they enable practitioners to reconnect the sacred and the profane and find their proper place within one cosmos. Bellah suggests that mimetic rituals owe their origins to the human capacity for play. Only when humans are "offline," that is, not absorbed in work to ensure their survival, do they have time for play. A fundamental form of play is imitation (mimicry).

This book explores how preaxial, mimetic consciousness founded on experience of a unified cosmos is a part of Indonesian practices of Islam, as well as of other religions. The call to prayer (*sholat*) five times a day is a mimetic ritual that intends to reproduce a proper order between humankind and God, between the creature and the Creator, between the microcosmos and the macrocosmos. They re-create order through sacred space in the midst of the disorder of everyday (profane) life.

According to Merlin Donald's theory of cognitive evolution, mimetic cognition, which was focused on ritual, led to mythic cognition, focused on narrative. Mythic cognition also began in the preaxial age and shaped consciousness of reality through narratives, which explored depths of meaning that were not available through mimetic rituals. Myth did not eliminate mimetic consciousness (sacred rituals), but carried it forward into the axial age.

Stories are still the primary means of making sense of reality in Indonesia. Whether it is ancient Indian stories (from the *Ramayana* and *Mahabharata*) used in all-night shadow puppet plays (*wayang kulit*), nationalist narratives of Majapahit glory, sacred stories of the trials of the Prophet, tragic tales in modern Indonesian film, New Order myths of progress and development, or postmodern novels about changing sexual identities in an urban jungle, Indonesians make sense of their lives by means of stories. Some of my students dream of the day when Islam will rise again and take its place on the world stage as the most noble of religions. Their imagination is shaped by a narrative about God's final revelation through the Prophet Muhammad and the past glories of Islamic civilization.

The axial age breakthrough was the discovery of the transcendent realm and the ability of human beings to distance themselves from mundane existence. The axial age broke the unity of a single cosmos and posited a transcendent realm of the gods or God, which was greater than the everyday world. No longer did the primary duality between the sacred and the profane exist within a single cosmos. Rather, reality was divided in two: the mundane realm of everyday life and the transcendent realm of God, Heaven, Nirvana, or the gods. Consciousness of transcendence enabled people to think critically about the mundane world.

Islam is an axial religion par excellence. In Islam the transcendence of God is unrivaled, and God is far above the foolishness of puny human beings. Some of my Indonesian Muslim friends have permanent black bruises on their foreheads. This is because five times a day they bang their heads on ceramic tile, acknowledging the greatness of God and their own unworthiness. For the most part, the ones I know are gentle, humble people who would no more take up a gun to kill an infidel than they would kill their own mothers.

Dividing the transcendent from the mundane did not eliminate mythical cognition but rather gave it a whole new realm above the earth about which to tell stories. Nevertheless, mythical cognition gradually gave birth to theoretic, abstract, universalizing thought. The idea of transcendence gave rise to self-critical distancing and reflection about mundane life in the light of universal, transcendent truths. Not only stories but also principles, laws, formulas, theories, and models added a huge new repertoire of meaning systems to explain what had been previously thought of as a mystery. In this book I distinguish between two streams of theoretic thought: the ethical and the empiric. The ethical appealed to transcendent revelation and reason to distinguish what is good, just, and right from what is evil, unjust, and wrong. The empiric drew on reason and empirical evidence to create theories that explain causation within the universe.

According to Donald, theoretic cognition led to the postaxial, secular age of the modern world. In the postaxial age of theoretic cognition, the primary dichotomy is no longer between sacred and profane (preaxial) and transcendent and mundane (axial) but rather between the religious and the secular (postaxial) (Casanova 2012:199). At least in the West, science, verifiable knowledge, public discourse, the marketplace, and government all exist in the sphere of the secular, whereas religious beliefs and ethical practices are in the sphere of individual, private beliefs and practices. Mimetic rituals, sacred stories, and ethical commitments are subjective, personal, and private. In contrast, rational scientific thought is public.

Although Bellah believed that the theoretic civilizations of modernity are far more complex than the mimetic and mythic civilizations of the past, he did not believe that this made them better morally. Complexity is not a normative category. Complex theoretic systems make possible far greater assimilation and sharing of knowledge. But they are not morally better. In fact Bellah feared that theoretic modern civilizations are leading to human extinction. The most alarming evidence of this is the ecological crisis.

Bellah argued that "nothing is ever lost." His theory of human evolution suggests that what we are now contains everything that went before. He stressed that theoretic cognition does not supersede or replace mythic and mimetic culture. In fact the polarization of theoretic thinking and ethics has led to a profound crisis in modern life that threatens our existence. In the modern, western world, theoretic cognition has become so dominant over mythic and mimetic ways of thinking that we have lost hold of the meaning of our lives. Meaning is grounded in narratives, stories, myths, rituals and art, which cannot be reduced to theoretic propositions or limited to private life.

Indonesia is different from the West, not primarily because it is still dominated by preaxial, mimetic cosmic rituals and axial myths. Western cultures are also saturated with rituals and myths. Many people in the West still inhabit a sacred cosmos. Even the most technologically advanced societies cannot live without mimetic rituals and mythical narratives.[23] Indonesia is different because of the way it fuses preaxial cosmic traditions and rituals, religious experiences of transcendence and morality, and modern ideas, institutions, and structures. This book suggests that Indonesia is simultaneously preaxial, axial, and postaxial.

Bellah, following Donald, constructs the categories of mimetic, mythic, and theoretic as evolutionary growth in the process of cognition from the simple to the more complex. Mimetic and mythic cognition are categorized as preaxial, while theoretic cognition is axial and postaxial or modern. I prefer to think of mimetic, mythic, ethical, and theoretic as ideal types that are useful for analyzing different ways of imagining/knowing the world. They are not distinct periods in history. It may be useful to imagine an "axial age" (800–200 BCE) where theoretic thought was born through discovery of the transcendent. But these dates only mark the four civilizations that left written records we can decipher. The first large temple structure (Gobekli Tepe in Turkey) was built more than ten thousand years ago, more than seven thousand years before the axial age. I suspect that the erection of huge monolithic stones in circles implied some form of theoretic thought, as well as mimetic and mythic cognition.[24] Theoretic cognition probably came much earlier than the axial age and in many more civilizations, which for various reasons did not leave records that we can read.

Mimetic, mythic, ethical, and theoretic cognition can never be completely divorced from each other. For example, mimetic rituals imply the need for a theory and story to justify and explain their meaning. They are also connected to an ethical evaluation that is linked to the imagination of a moral order.

Unlike many people in the West who imagine that planet Earth is a speck in the universe, without meaning, most Indonesians imagine that they live in a sacred cosmos. Mimetic rituals, sacred stories, and moral judgments are not separated from theoretic "secular" thought. They are part of the same reality. In the West, religion and ethics are (ideally) separated from the public sphere. Not so in Indonesia.

Indonesian Innovation: Modernity without the Secular

Most Indonesian Muslims are deeply suspicious of the secular. They associate secularism with atheism, the decline of religion, and banishment of religion to the private sphere. They are quick to point out that Indonesia is neither an Islamic nor a secular state. The first principle on which the Republic of Indonesia was founded is the Great Unity of Deity (*Ketuhanan yang Maha Esa*). There is only One God over all Indonesians, no matter what their religion. The unity of God is the basis for affirming the unity of humanity and the unity of many different ethnic groups and religions in one nation. The state officially recognizes six religions: Islam, Protestantism, Catholicism, Hinduism, Buddhism, and Confucianism. All Indonesians are encouraged to adopt one of these religions. All "world religions" are considered good. Indonesia is a multireligious, monotheistic nation-state that rejects both the classic choices between a monoreligious and secular state.[25]

In Indonesia, religions are not meant to be relegated to the private sphere, as if they have no relevance to politics, economics, social relations, or law. Most Indonesian Muslims believe that religion is the basis not only for private morality but for public morality as well. Even in the hard sciences, many Muslims have an a priori conviction that true religion will never come into conflict with the findings of science. Religion should be part of all serious thinking about anything and everything. Public national universities are not described as secular but rather as multireligious or religiously neutral.

A leading Indonesian Muslim intellectual, Dr. Nurcholis Madjid, became famous in 1970, when he published an article defending "secularism" as an important principle in politics. His article caused such a storm of criticism that he later disavowed his use of the term *secularism*, although he did not withdraw his basic argument. Madjid did not use an argument drawn from human rights, political theory, or the autonomy of science to back up his defense of the secular. Rather he used a theological argument. He suggested that Muslim political parties that claim to represent Islam are actually idolatrous because they equate their limited political interests with the will of God. This violates the foundational doctrine of Islam, Tauhid. According to Tauhid, nothing should be equated with or joined to God. God is alone, above all human interests or understanding. Those who equate their human interests with God's will are idolatrous (elevating something human to the level of God).

Madjid argued that Muslim political parties implicitly claim a divine warrant for their parochial interests. This deceives people into confusing the will of God with a human agenda for gaining power. According to Madjid, this violates Tauhid by joining a human organization to God (1978). Madjid's famous slogan "Islam Yes, Islamic Politics No" is still debated in Indonesia today.[26] Madjid retracted his use of the term *secularism* not only to dampen political criticism but also because he did not mean to imply that religion should be separated from politics, as in the western model (the separation of church and state), but only that no political party should claim a divine warrant for a human agenda. Like most Indonesians, Madjid opposed Indonesia becoming an "Islamic state." Also like most Indonesians, Madjid believed Islamic values and practices should inform every area of Indonesian life.

Few scholars still defend the theory that secularization is an inevitable partner of increasing rationality and modernity (see Berger 1999). Most of the world, including the United States, is more religious now than it was one hundred years ago. Indeed there is some evidence that religion is one of the most powerful agents of rationalization and modernization. Less obvious is the question of whether or not increasing rationalization and moderniza-tion, while not leading to a decline in religion, does lead to the progressive "disenchantment" (Weber) of the world. In an enchanted world, human beings are surrounded by unseen powers. Does rapid social, political, economic, and technological change, along with higher education, weaken belief in magic and a unified moral cosmos? In most western countries, many people consign magic to fantasy and superstition. Is that also happen-ing in Indonesia? This book explores to what extent most Indonesians still live in a sacred cosmos and experience an unseen world of spirits and powers (see Adeney-Risakotta 2014a, 2017).

Chapter 2 explores the theory of social imaginaries and how they have shaped different kinds of modernity. Indonesian social imaginaries incorporate "western" social imaginaries but are also in dialectical tension with them. In order to highlight this tension, the next chapter elaborates on Charles Taylor's interpretation of western social imaginaries and contrasts them with alternative Indonesian ways of imagining the world.

2

Social Imaginaries in Indonesia and the West

Our solid American citizen awakens in a bed built on a pattern which originated in the Near East. ... He throws back his covers made of cotton (domesticated in India), linen (domesticated in the Near East) or silk (discovered in China). ... He puts on his slippers (adapted from moccasins invented by Indians). ... He takes off his pajamas (a garment invented in India) and washes with soap (invented by the ancient Gauls). ... His shoes are made from skins tanned by a process invented in ancient Egypt. ... He ties a strip of brightly colored cloth around his neck, which is a survival from ... 17th-century Croatians. ... He glances through his window (made of glass invented in Egypt). If it is raining, he puts on overshoes (made of rubber discovered by the Central American Indians) and takes an umbrella (invented in southeastern Asia). On his head, he puts a hat made of felt (a material invented in the Asiatic steppes) ... he stops to buy a paper, paying for it with coins (an ancient Lydian invention). ... His plate is made from a type of pottery invented in China. His knife is of steel (an alloy first made in southern India). His fork is *a medieval Italian invention*, and his spoon is a derivative of a Roman original. He begins his breakfast with an orange (originally from the eastern Mediterranean), a cantaloupe (from Persia), or perhaps a piece of African watermelon. With this, he has coffee (from an Abyssinian plant) with cream and sugar. (Both the domestication of cows and the idea of milking them originated in the Near East, while sugar was first made in India.) ... He goes on to waffles (cakes made by a Scandinavian technique from wheat domesticated first in Asia Minor). Over these he pours maple syrup (invented by Indians) ... he may have an egg (... first domesticated in Indo-China) or thin strips of bacon (... domesticated in Eastern Asia ...). When our friend has finished eating, he settles back to smoke (an American Indian habit). Tobacco was domesticated in Brazil. ... He reads the news of the day (printed in characters invented by ancient Semites on material invented in China by a process invented in Germany). ... He thanks a Hebrew deity in an Indo-European language that he is "100% American."

—Ralph Linton

SINCE I MOVED TO INDONESIA in 1991, many Indonesians have asked me, "Why do you love Indonesia?" Since I never knew how to answer, I used to just make a joke and say "I love the funny hats that people wear!" The flippant answer hinted at something more profound. The exuberance of Indonesian culture gives permission for people to wear many different kinds of head coverings that derive from many cultures. Different ethnic groups from thousands of different islands each have their own unique traditional dress. Some people improvise with bits of cloth or styles borrowed from many cultures. The relatively recent popularity of the Muslim head covering (*jilbab* or *hijab*) has not subdued the exuberance of Indonesian culture. A great proliferation of styles, colors, accessories, and fabrics are worn by Indonesian women. The popularity of Muslim head coverings put some hair salons out of business. In response, new "*jilbab* salons" have opened where women can have ever more elaborate styles of cloth and jewelry designed for their personal *jilbab*s.

A most dramatic display of sartorial eclecticism occurs during parades around the ancient palace (*kraton*) of Yogyakarta on special holy days such as Maulud or Grebeg. The traditional guards and retainers of the sultan dress in sumptuous costumes that borrow from Old Javanese, Portuguese, French, English, Dutch, Arab, Chinese, Indian, and other fashions that were in style in various centuries. The result is uniquely Indonesian. Nowhere else in the world can you see such an eclectic mix of styles unless it is in other parts of Indonesia. Certainly the *adat* (traditional) clothing of the Moluccan islands is at least as spectacular as that found in Java or Bali. Nevertheless, as much as I love Javanese batiks, Sumba *ikat*, (hand woven cloth) and the unique fabrics handwoven on many different islands, the importance of Indonesia is not derived from its people's clothing.

Indonesia is a treasure of human civilization because it has constructed a unique world that blends influences from all four of the great axial civilizations that shaped the modern world. The same might be said of all modern societies. The process of globalization has been going on for centuries. No country in the world has escaped the influences of China, India, the Middle East, and Greece. These civilizations are not insulated or monolithic. They have also deeply influenced each other. Although many countries are dominated by one or two of these broad civilizations, Indonesia has adapted all four into a unique social construction of reality. The social construction of reality in Indonesia has led to social imaginaries that differ remarkably from those of the West.

Social Imaginaries and Modernity

Clifford Geertz argues that culture does not exist primarily as ideas *in* the human mind that are then expressed in "acts" or applications. Rather, culture exists *between* human beings. Culture is not something a person *has* but is constitutive of what it means to be human, for "there is no such thing as a human nature independent of culture" (1973:49). There is no space in human experience that is not cultural space. In other words, there is nothing that human beings think, perceive, experience, feel, or do that is not affected by their culture. Culture is a network of symbol systems, constructed over time by a society with influences from many sources, which constitutes its members' identity as a people.

Culture is never monolithic. It is always complex and diverse. It has major and minor currents. Often different currents of culture work at cross-purposes and are logically contradictory. Living culture is always in the process of change. There is no essential Indonesian, Muslim, Javanese, Moluccan, or Minang culture. All are constantly interacting with many overlapping symbol systems as well as material reality. All living cultures, like all living people, are in the process of change. Change involves continuity and discontinuity. Nothing changes without carrying over some of what was left behind. Practices that have persisted for hundreds of years are not obliterated, even if they are no longer practiced. Nothing is ever lost. They only find new shapes and symbols with which to express themselves. For example, perhaps Indonesian Muslim women create such colorful, intricate head coverings, unlike anything you might see in the Middle East, because their imagination of what is good and beautiful is not just the product of Arab Islam but also incorporates colorful elements from India, an aesthetic sense of decorum from China, and recent fashion trends from Japanese pop culture.

Practices, which are socially constructed, reveal the moral world in which a group lives better than propositions do. Propositions are abstractions derived from a preexisting social reality. Practices are constructed publicly and socially out of a shared imagination of what is real. What people do in their relationships with each other tells you more about their values than what they say. Shared practices are only possible because of shared social imaginaries. Cross-cultural research on values has been plagued by the substantial empirical gap between what people say are their values and what they actually do (Deutscher 1973; Hofstede 1980:18; Adeney 1995:48). Social imaginaries are better inscribed in practices than they are in words. The dichotomy is artificial, as there is a dialectic involved: practices and the words that make sense of them mutually influence each other. The study of practices reveals how social imaginaries are lived out by a community (de Certeau 1984).

Michel de Certeau sees everyday practices as clues to how people, especially the marginalized, spontaneously use their creativity to express their values in the cracks and empty places of the prevailing social structure. Enduring political, economic, social, and religious structures are created and sustained by the powerful as "strategies" for the maintenance of "reality" according to their own definition. Such social structures are real and dominate most peoples' lives most of the time. But they lack the power to eliminate all values that do not conform to the structure. Individuals and small groups have dissident values that are expressed in "tactics" (de Certeau 1984) or "hidden transcripts" (Scott 2012).

The dominant "strategies," that structure most peoples' lives in Indonesia are the global economy and an equally globalized Islam. The state in Indonesia serves as an agent of capitalism and Islam, promoting both economic growth and orthodox religion. The practices of Indonesian traditional *adat* cultures are constructed as compatible with both economic growth and orthodox religion. In rural contexts where *adat* law is still strong, the traditions of the ancestors may even qualify as dominant strategies of control. Nevertheless the practices of traditional *adat* frequently express values that are not supported by the dominant structures of either global religion or global capitalism.

This became vivid to me one day as I was reading a high school, government-issued textbook on Islam used by the niece of a Javanese mystic with whom I was staying. The text listed beliefs and practices that were certain to result in condemnation to eternal hellfire. Among them were practices integral to the everyday mystical habits of my Muslim host family. It didn't seem to bother this family at all that, according to the teaching in the schools, they were all going to hell!

How do Indonesians imagine the world? It is a foolish question. Of course it depends on the Indonesian. How do Americans or Chinese or people from India imagine their place in the human community? The answer is that it depends on the person. In an increasingly complex, diverse, and globalized world, different people imagine social reality differ-ently. The same answer applies if we address religious communities. How do Muslims imagine a good society? It depends on which Muslim you ask. Is there single Buddhist view of politics or a dominant Christian under-standing of economics? Do all atheist humanists hold the same image of a good society? Obviously not. There is such a great diversity of views that it is dangerous to make generalizations. Oversimplifications lead to stereo-types and prejudice. Globalization leads both to homogenization ("the McDonaldization of the world") and diversification, in which ever smaller groups of people react to homogenizing global culture by asserting their own unique identities and linking up with like-minded people through the internet (Miller 2014).

Two Javanese Muslims living on the same street in Yogyakarta, Indo-nesia, may have fundamentally different perspectives on what is a good society. Iqbal may think far more like Robert, an Irish Catholic living in Boston, than he does like Ahmed, who lives next door, even though they are both Muslims. Susanti, an Indonesian Chinese Catholic social activist, may have more in common with Fatimah, an Iranian intellectual, than she does with Angelica, her own sister, who is fascinated with Lady Gaga and dreams of competing on *Indonesian Idol*. Sharing the same address, citizen-ship, religion, ethnicity, or blood is no guarantee of a uniform imagination about what is a good society.

That is part of the problem with the theory of a "clash of civilizations." It encourages assumptions that there are monolithic civilizations, which are in eternal conflict. The opposite assertion, that different civilizations are in essential harmony, is equally suspect. As Martha Nussbaum demonstrated with regard to India, there are as many clashes within civilizations as there are between them (2007).

The cultural traditions, religious communities, and structures of moder-nity in Indonesia all compete with and influence each other. The social imaginaries of Indonesia are in an ongoing process of change that includes great diversity but also striking elements of commonality. Most Indonesians believe in a cosmos that is "enchanted," with many supernatural powers. For most Indonesians, their religion is not something they chose but rather a primordial part of their identity that shapes their perceptions of cosmic, social, and moral order. At the same time, modern institutions, technology, practices, and ideas structure the lives of most Indonesians.

Modernity is not singular but plural. Modernity in Yogyakarta is remarkably different from modernity in Berlin, Singapore, Lima, Tokyo, Nairobi, or San Francisco. Different modernities are shaped by different social imaginaries, which are often grounded in religious faith (Taylor 2003). Social imaginaries are different from both social theory and theological conviction. They cannot be expressed as a rigidly defined set of ideas. Rather they include the imagination of a moral order that is grounded in a story about the meaning of human society in relation to a normative conception of reality. Charles Taylor explains, "The social imaginary is not a set of ideas; rather it is what enables, through making sense of, the practices of a society" (2). For example, certain attitudes toward religious diversity make sense because of a particular imagination of what makes a good society. Routine practices create their own social imaginary. It is futile to ask which came first, the social imaginary or a particular tactic for dealing with diversity. A practice is impossible without a prior imagination of what it might mean. On the other hand, the social imagination is constantly modified by changes in practices. Thus social imaginaries are never static or fixed. They are always in process, changing through "the intervention of previously unidentified variables" (Liddle 1996:145).

Considering the widely different practices of people from even the same religion, it is apparent that there is no single social imaginary associated with each religion. Not all Muslims imagine the same moral order. The same is true of Christians, Hindus, Buddhists, or any other religious (or nonreligious) group. Sometimes people from different religions share the same social imaginary about the moral order that should govern society, even though the religious convictions that legitimate their social imaginary may be different. Inter-religious dialogue between people who share the same social imaginaries is relatively easy. Their religious convictions may be different, but they share a similar imagination of what is real and good.

On the other hand, people from the same religious community may imagine a moral order different from those of other members of the same faith. That is one reason why conflicts between people who profess the same religion are often more acute than conflicts between people of different religions. Within our graduate program in inter-religious studies in Yogyakarta, the most heated debates are usually between people of the same religion. For example, Calvinist Christians who can listen with empathy to Muslims may find it hard to show the same respect to Pentecostal

Christians. Similarly, conservative Muslims who get along fine with Christians often find it difficult to accept the views of progressive Muslims who have a different social imaginary. Even when people share the same religious beliefs, they may imagine their political and social reality very differently. They not only interpret the political reality of the world differently, but they also disagree about how we should live together in the world and what an ideal society should look like.[1]

Sometimes common practices give birth to the same social imagination among people with very different religious backgrounds. Living and working with people of other faiths ("the dialogue of everyday life") may unify their social imaginations. In 2006 we had a very destructive earthquake in Yogyakarta, as a result of which about fifty-seven hundred people died and three hundred thousand lost their homes. For about a month our house served as a field kitchen. Dr. Farsijana Adeney-Risakotta, who is an Indonesian Christian, worked round the clock with Muslim colleagues in the Indonesian Women's Coalition (KPI), distributing food and basic supplies to people who were in desperate need. One evening toward the end of this period Farsijana commented that she felt she was much more like her Indonesian Muslim colleagues than she was like the American Christian women she had met. Common practices had created an "imagined community" that was not bounded by a single religious faith. There was no melding of religious differences, but in a time of crisis everyone shared the same imagination of what needed to be done.

Social imaginaries include two aspects, hermeneutical and normative, which are intertwined. The hermeneutical, or interpretive, aspect includes a vision of the moral order which governs human relations. For example: "There are no free lunches" or "What goes around comes around." This aspect is more than just a worldview that can be described by means of propositions. It includes feelings, emotions, stories about the past, and visions of the future. For example, when Confucius talked about the ancients and the ideal order that existed under Yao, Shun, and Yu the Great, he was invoking a social imaginary of the golden age that should guide the present practices of a virtuous king (Waley 1938:18).

The hermeneutical aspect of a social imaginary is not primarily a description of the way things work in the "real world" of the present. The present may be decadent and heading for disaster, as Confucius recognized during the chaotic Warring States period in China. However, neither is it just a utopian vision of an indefinite future. A powerful social imaginary is based on the conviction that a real moral order guides the way humans are meant to live in societies. This imagined community (Anderson [1983] 1991) includes a conception of how power should function (politics) and what a just ordering of the economy should be. Often present evils are assumed to have resulted from a failure to live in conformity with the moral order. Therefore a social imaginary is also normative, or prescriptive: it tells us how to live.[2] It condemns certain practices and justifies others on the basis of an overarching vision of social reality. Often it includes implicit repertoires of practices for dealing with problems in the society.

Charles Taylor argues that western modernity is characterized by a social imaginary that has spread from particular influential theories, which are only understood by an intellectual elite, to become fundamental imaginations of social life that have become practically universal in the West. A social imaginary appears self-evident to those who hold it. It is hard to conceive of any other way to imagine the world. That may be one reason why people who hold different social imaginaries have such a hard time understanding each other. The things that seem obvious to one party seem irrational to the other (see MacIntyre 1981). Each is embedded in its own intersubjective narrative about the world,[3] which encompasses a long history of traditions, practices, and beliefs that gives rise to opposing conceptions of what is rational and just (MacIntyre 1988).

This might imply that people from different traditions cannot speak with each other because they inhabit different social imaginaries. But the social structures and practices that support a social imaginary are seldom monolithic. Most modern people are affected by multiple plausibility structures for competing social imaginaries. They are shaped by different social imaginaries, which they make use of in different contexts for different purposes. Peter Berger writes, "The modern individual exists in a plurality of worlds, migrating back and forth between competing and often contradictory plausibility structures, each of which is weakened by the simple fact of its involuntary coexistence with other plausibility structures" (1969:55).

Plausibility structures are institutionalized. They legitimize a particular way of imagining the world. Examples include the government of Indonesia, Yale University, NU, the Pope, the Muslim organization Muhammadiyah, Amnesty International, the Majelis Ulama Islam, the United Nations (UN) Universal Declaration of Human Rights, a local chess club, a popular style of music, a corporation selling jeans or Muslim head coverings, and so on. We all inhabit multiple plausibility structures, which pull our imaginations of the moral order in different directions.

Many people in the West believe in a spiritual world, but unlike Indonesians they believe with a "second naïveté," accompanied by many empirical questions and doubts (Bellah [1970] 1991).[4] Many Indonesians experience an unseen world with a first naïveté. It is not something they believe in but rather something they directly experience. For many religious believers in the West, faith is more like a practice and a decision than it is a direct experience. One reason for this is that most public institutions of knowledge are secular. Faith is excluded from public institutions. Peter Berger outlines the power of "plausibility structures" in supporting our imagination of reality. He writes, "[I]t is only as the individual remains within this structure that the conception of the world in question will remain plausible to him. The strength of this plausibility, ranging from unquestioned certitude through firm probability to mere opinion, will be directly dependent upon the strength of the supporting structure" (1969, 45).

Most educated westerners are rooted in a secular age in which their "historical consciousness" (Gadamer 1979) constantly reminds them that their experiences of reality are socially and historically constructed, including their perception, or lack thereof, of an invisible world. Reality is socially constructed (Berger and Luckmann 1989). Some western social scientists readily agree that an Indonesian experience of an unseen, supernatural world is a social construction. But they operate as if their own secular perspective is an unmediated social scientific view of reality. In fact, all reality is socially constructed, including their own. There is no privileged perception of the "facts" of reality.

Charles Taylor's narrative of the growth of modernity shows how a secular age was constructed in the West step by step over several hundred years (2007). According to him, our secular age is not the simple result of growing rationality and progressive disproof of irrational superstition. A scientific, materialist understanding of the world is not just what is left after we have subtracted all the irrational grounds for religious belief. Rather, the secular age of the modern western world was constructed as an alternative moral order based on a different understanding of the self and the social world (Taylor 1989). A modern social order "disembedded" individuals from society, society from nature, and nature from an overarching moral order. Max Weber showed that modern capitalism did not just rise out of the collapse of an older tradition of morality but was influenced by the construction of an alternative conception of moral order ([1930] 1961). Similarly, according to Taylor, our secular age is based on the imagination of a moral ordering of society that excludes religion from politics, economics, science, and the world of verifiable human knowledge.

Taylor suggests that there are three meanings to "a secular age." One is that religion has been substantially removed from public life. Second, many people no longer believe in or practice religions as they have been traditionally understood. Third, belief in God has become an option, a choice that individuals can make. It is this third aspect of secularity that Taylor suggests is the most significant.

Religion has become a choice rather than a primordial identity. Non-association with a religion is something that almost everyone in the West can imagine. Large numbers of people in the West find it difficult to believe in God or a spiritual world. Even for those who do practice a religion, it is not an automatic, unproblematic choice. In some sense they choose to believe in spite of doubts. Others choose not to practice a religion in spite of occasional religious feelings. Just like agnostics or atheists, most religious believers in western countries imagine a disenchanted world in which nature proceeds by fixed laws and magic is simply an escapist fantasy. Even devout religious practitioners in the West inhabit a disenchanted world. For many, religion is a private source of meaning, but it is not a public source of knowledge.

The disenchanted world of the West includes a particular theory of the mind that Taylor calls "a buffered self." A buffered self is a mind that is protected and separated from the outside world. With a buffered self, we assume that what happens inside our minds, is the product of our psychological processes rather than the voice of spirits or powers from outside. Freud's revolutionary idea of the unconscious mind enables us to assume that the strange images and the stuff of dreams, which may disturb our consciousness, all come from within our subconscious. Our senses take in stimulus from the world outside that may be processed into dreams or fantasies, but only psychotic people think that the voices in their heads come from powers outside themselves.

Taylor's narrative of the growth of modern, social imaginaries is not an empirical description of how everyone perceives reality in the West. His modern social imaginaries are ideal types of dominant trends in secularized western societies. The phenomenal growth of Evangelical and Charismatic Christianity, New Age "Eastern" religions, Sufi Islam, and other spiritual movements suggests that many people still inhabit (or try to inhabit) an enchanted universe, even in the West. Tanya Marie Luhrmann's study of Charismatic Evangelical churches in the United States, Ghana, and India suggests that Charismatic Christians in the United States have to work harder to overcome their "buffered self" than their counterparts in Africa and Asia do. They experience the voices of God and spirits in their minds, but, unlike the Ghanaians and Indians, they have to practice and learn to overcome their doubts (see Luhrmann 2012).[5]

Modern social imaginaries are metaphors that most people in the West use to make sense of society, government, the economy, public space, and many other aspects of modern life. Social imaginaries are the lenses through which everything else makes sense. Taylor's conceptualization of modern social imaginaries illuminates the western societies where I have lived. However, his ideal types are not nearly so self-evident when applied to Indonesia. That does not mean they are irrelevant. The western social imaginaries also influence Indonesian consciousness. But they are one out of a repertoire of symbol systems used to make sense of the world. Indonesians have four axial civilizations living within them.

Conceptualizing Modern Western Social Imaginaries

Modern western social imaginaries cannot be reduced to a list of concepts any more than a painting can be adequately described in terms of the ideas it suggests. Nevertheless, there are at least fifteen interlocking ideas embedded in modern western social imaginaries.[6]

1. Modern western societies imagine themselves as having been formed by individuals. Individuals are the basic unit of society.

2. These individuals have certain basic and equal human rights.

3. Together they form a society based on an implicit social contract.

4. The social contract guarantees the human rights of each individual.

5. Society exists for the sake of the people. Society should serve everyone.[7]

6. The purpose of government is to protect the rights of individuals so they can seek their own well-being by cooperating with each other in safety.[8]

7. A good society guarantees maximum individual freedom for all its members. Freedom of the individual is the most fundamental of liberal values.

8. With their freedom, rights, and security guaranteed, individuals are responsible for achieving their own prosperity.

9. Thus the dominant institution within the modern, western social imaginary is the economy, not the government.[9]

10. The moral order of society is based on the sovereignty of the people expressed in democratic institutions.

11. Political legitimacy is based on the consent of the governed, who are imagined as individuals.[10]

12. All the individuals within an ideal society should have equal freedom, equal rights, and equal opportunities.

13. This includes the idea of a rule of law, which does not discriminate on the basis of race, wealth, class, gender, religion, ideology, culture, or sexual preference.[11]

14. Law should be the result of a consensus founded on free and rational deliberation or debate, based on a constitution that protects everyone's human rights.

15. Society is always in the process of change through progress, development, evolution, or devolution.[12]

Social Imaginaries in Indonesia

Social imaginaries are symbolic representations that make use of dominant metaphors. They are ideal-type assumptions that most people take for granted. The fifteen metaphors listed above as modern western social imaginaries are also present in the imaginations of Indonesians. However, they are not always the dominant metaphors through which Indonesians imagine reality. Western imaginations about society are deeply secular, while most Indonesians are equally influenced by metaphors drawn from their religions and traditional cultures.

Most people are not limited to a single symbolic vocabulary. They can switch from one set of symbols to another and even combine metaphors that are logically inconsistent if it suits the context and purpose of their discourse. Different symbol systems are appropriate when you are playing different "language games" (Wittgenstein 1953). Just as someone playing football cannot apply the rules of basketball to the game, so the language we use in a business negotiation might not be appropriate in a mosque. According to my research, virtually all Indonesians combine modern, religious, and traditional social imaginaries. They don't choose one over the others. The following "Indonesian" ideal-type social imaginaries are deliberately constructed in contrast to the western concepts. They should not be construed as representing the way all Indonesians think.[13]

1. The basic unit of society is the family, not the individual. Families, clans, villages, tribes, ethnic groups, and provinces are all more significant than individuals.

2. Some people have more rights than others. Rights are always modified by duties to those who are older or above you in a hierarchy. Just as children have no right to betray their parents, so inferiors have no right to betray their superiors. All human rights are subordinate to God. Islam means submission.

3. Society is not based on a social contract between individuals but rather is a family bound together by God in a shared history that goes back thousands of years. Both "social contract" and "family" are metaphors, not literal descriptions of society. The economic metaphor of a social contract feels cold and unattractive to many Indonesians. In classes I teach at UMY, most of my undergraduate students prefer the metaphor of Indonesia as a family over the metaphor of society based on a social contract.

4. Society is not primarily a community of equal individuals. Everyone in Indonesia is addressed using familial titles that indicate their relative age or social status. Even siblings who are very close in age refer to each other with titles that indicate whether they are older or younger. Not only language but also social practices reflect a consciousness of this social

hierarchy. My two nieces from Manado are sisters and close friends, but they never address each other as equals. They seldom even use each other's names. Instead they address each other as Older Sister (Kak) or Younger Sister (Dik). Usually (though not always) the younger defers to the older.[14]

5. The primary purpose of society is not to serve individual self-interests. The goal of a good society is harmony (*rukun*), peace (*damai*), and balance between groups that are different (see Magnis-Suseno 1984; Keeler 1987).

6. The government should be like a parents who are responsible for the virtue of their "children." Protecting the rights of individuals may be important, but it is subject to the needs of society as a whole and the law of God. Rights are seldom equal, as often the government protects the rights of the majority (e.g., Sunni Muslims) over the rights of disapproved minorities (e.g., Ahmadis). Government is like a parent who should set a good example and teach the people to be good. In Indonesia this often comes under the rubric of government-sponsored "character education," as well as required religious education and courses on Pancasila (five basic principles which are the official national ideology and foundation of the constitution) from kindergarten to university.

7. Protection of maximum freedom for all individuals is not the responsibility of government. The government should suppress activities and ideas that violate societal moral norms. The law against pornography and "pornoaksi" (pornographic behavior) is an example of a situation in which the government, with the backing of the largest Muslim organizations (NU and Muhammadiyah), legislated Muslim norms of dress and morality in spite of widespread opposition from non-Muslim groups.[15] Some Indonesians feel the government is insufficiently vigilant in protecting religion and public morality. Therefore they form militias to attack places of vice or groups that they consider threats to Islamic values, such as bars, nightclubs, gambling dens, and brothels. The police are often reluctant to interfere because they, too, are Muslims and don't want to be perceived as protecting vice.

8. The government, like a parent, is responsible for the prosperity and well-being of its "family." The government should not just protect the freedom of the marketplace so people can work to further their own interests. Rather the state should own the most crucial means of production, protect the people from sharp rises in prices, provide subsidized or free services and goods to the poor, and create conditions that lead to prosperity.

9. In principle, most Indonesians imagine the government, not the marketplace, as the dominant institution in society.

10. The moral order of society is not based on the sovereignty of the people but rather on the will of God. The Indonesian Constitution enshrines the idea of the sovereignty of the people expressed through representative democratic institutions. However, in our research about 60 percent of Indonesians imagined legitimate political authority to be either the representative of God (30 percent) or a parent (30 percent). Just 39 percent imagined political legitimacy as coming from and responsible to the people. Those who believe political authority comes from God or is like a parent may also believe in the sovereignty of the people and democratic institutions. They mix their metaphors. During the days before the fall of President Soeharto, I was surprised to see Latin graffiti sprayed on a wall in Yogyakarta. It read, *Vox Populi, Vox Dei*, the Voice of the People is the Voice of God. In a secular setting this phrase could be interpreted as meaning that the voice of the people has replaced the voice of God. But in the context of Indonesia in 1998, it almost certainly meant that God speaks through the voice of the people. God's will is expressed by the people: President Soeharto should step down.

11. Regarding the consent of the governed, many Indonesians imagine their nation as a primordial unit that has existed for thousands of years. The modern nation-state of Indonesia was established in 1945 and internationally acknowledged in 1949, but the nation of Indonesia is imagined as being much older. Both presidents Sukarno (the revolutionary hero and first president of Indonesia 1945–1965), and Soeharto 1966–1998, emphasized the ancient nature of Indonesia, symbolized by the great precolonial empires of Sri Vijaya, Majapahit, and Mataram, which ruled most of the archipelago (see Anderson [1983] 1991). Indonesia is imagined as a family tied together by blood and tears, culture and history, not a contract between individuals who chose to band together to further their own self-interests in 1945.

An illustration of this social imaginary, was revealed in a comment by former president Megawati Sukarnoputri concerning the secession of East Timor. Ibu Mega (Mother Mega) lamented that the secession wounded her deeply because part of her family was refusing to be united with her. This helps explain the surprising lack of sympathy on the part of most Indonesians, including human rights activists, both for the secession of East Timor and for the demands for independence made by West Papua. The intense emphasis on the slogan, Negara Kesatuan Republik Indonesia (NKRI—the Unity and Indivisibility of Indonesia) is based on this imagination of Indonesia as a primordial reality, established by God, rather than the recent result of political expediency. This does not mean that the "consent of the governed" has no place in the social imagination of Indonesians. But it is applied almost exclusively to Indonesia's right of independence from western colonialism and neocolonialism, not the right of certain peoples to secede from the country.[16]

12. Freedom and equality are fundamental elements in a western social imaginary. These ideas are hotly contested in Indonesia. According to our research, about 50 percent of those surveyed believed the state should protect the religious rights of everyone, without regard to their religion. However the other 50 percent did not consider human rights to have highest priority with regard to religious difference. Thirty-five percent felt that the first duty of the state is to maintain harmony and find a solution to conflicts that can be accepted by all. Another 15 percent felt that the state should support the six officially recognized religions and suppress heretical groups.

13. Most Indonesians imagine Indonesia to be a tolerant, religiously diverse society in which all citizens should enjoy equal protection under the law, no matter what their religion, race, gender, or ideology. In principle, all religions and ideologies enjoy equal standing before the law as long as they do not violate Pancasila or the Constitution. The first principle of Pancasila states that Indonesia is based on the Great Unity of Deity, which is taken to imply monotheism. Historically this has justified discrimination against atheists (especially communists) and the nonrecognition of indigenous tribal religions.

Particularly contentious is the law against "blasphemy," which has been used to justify discrimination against minority groups that claim to belong to one of the recognized religions but differ on important points from the orthodoxy asserted by the majority. The most prominent example is discrimination against the Ahmadiyah sect, which claims to be part of Islam. Its members have the legal right to exist but are forbidden to spread their teachings (see Lindsay and Pausacker 2016). In addition, based on the Blasphemy Law, some Sunni Muslims have advocated (without success) that Shia Islam should be banned in Indonesia as it is in Malaysia and some other Sunni-majority countries. In April 2010, the Constitutional Court upheld the Blasphemy Law, which has been used to oppress minority groups.

The court gave the following justification: "The state—consistent with the mandate of the Constitution—also has a responsibility to upgrade piety and noble character. The religious domain is a consequence of the acceptance of Pancasila ideology. In the Pancasila state there may be no activities that cause estrangement from religious standards and religiosity."[17]

One reason that the Constitutional Court review did not strike down the Blasphemy Law is that it was supported by mainstream Muslim organizations such as NU and Muhammadiyah, which claim 70 million members between them. The social imaginary of many Indonesians includes the assumption that government should protect "religion" from deviant interpretations and public morality from expressions that offend the sensibilities of the dominant Muslim majority. The conviction of the former governor of Jakarta on charges of defaming religion is an ominous example of the use of the law for political purposes.

14. In contrast to the West, most Indonesians believe that religion is the indispensable foundation of law. According to our research, 68 percent of Indonesians surveyed believe that law should be based on religion.[18] That does not imply that they do not approve of rational discussion, democratic deliberation, or a search for consensus. Open deliberation (*musyawarah*) and consensus (*mufakat*) are enshrined in Pancasila and the Constitution. They are an ancient part of the traditions (*adat*) of most ethnic groups in Indonesia. But religious teaching is an integral part of the process. Legal discourse is not secular but rather deeply religious. Law is neither secular nor neutral. In practice the teachings of the Koran are subject to different interpretations. As a result, there is an ongoing, open-ended discourse about which laws are consistent with the Koran (El Fadl 2001). In Islam there is no "Pope" who can bring the discussion to a close.[19] This also results in legal pluralism as different interpretations are enshrined in law (*hukum*) in different times and places (Adeney-Risakotta 2016b; see also chapter 11 in this volume). Perhaps for that reason, most Indonesian Muslims believe that public law should be based on the broad ethical principles of Sharia rather than on detailed Muslim laws (*fiqh*) from a different context (see chapter 9 in this volume).

15. A social imaginary of progress (*kemajuan*), development (*pembangunan*), and evolution was a central part of the Indonesian social imaginary promoted by Soeharto. Indeed, it still provides hope for many Indonesians. They imagine their country as becoming better, richer, stronger, and more

honored in the world. They imagine progress, not only economically but also politically and socially.

Nevertheless there is an older imaginary, common in Indonesia, that sees history not as an ascent from lower to higher but rather as a cycle of changes that keep turning back on themselves. In this vision, we are not progressing but rather repeating ourselves. Repeating ourselves does not necessarily imply that we are about to enter a golden age. Rather we may be stuck in an era of madness (*edan*). Indonesian literature and film are dominated by tragic themes in which all striving, hope, and conflict finally result in death and despair. This is in stark contrast to western popular culture, which specializes in happy endings. These days many Indonesians prefer to watch Hollywood blockbuster movies. Social imaginaries are changing. According to our research, about 50 percent of Indonesians now view history through the metaphors of development and progress, while 34 percent use traditional, cyclical metaphors of fate. Another 15 percent prefer religious metaphors of predestination and God's will.

Conclusion

There is no essential, unchanging core of Indonesian (or Javanese, Batak, Acehnese, Dyak, Bugis, etc.) culture. The social imaginaries and cultures of Indonesia are in a constant process of change and adaptation. Nevertheless, Indonesia has been shaped by thousands of years of a social process in which tolerance for religious and cultural diversity was essential for survival. This has built up a reservoir of social capital that bodes well for the continuing construction of a modern, religious, and enchanted social order in which diversity is not only tolerated but actively celebrated.

Merlin Donald suggests that human intelligence is not primarily in the mind of one person but rather is distributed throughout whole societies (2012:49). Each person knows very little compared to the knowledge, skills, institutions, and processes spread throughout a culture. Dialogic civilization makes it possible to learn not only from the single individuals with whom we talk but also from the civilization of which we are only a small part. Computers make accessible knowledge that is spread throughout vast networks. The idea of circulatory history reminds us that these networks do not stop at national or civilizational borders but rather circulate around the world. The genius of Indonesia may not lie in a particular group that we consider most enlightened or congruent with our own personal values. The genius of Indonesian civilization is distributed throughout the society, perhaps including some aspects that are alien to western scholars.

This book explores how Indonesian social imaginaries are rooted in people's experience of living in a sacred cosmos in which individuals are rooted in society, society is rooted in nature, nature is rooted in a moral order, and the moral order is rooted in God. Many Muslims all over the world experience reality as sacred and meaningful. In contrast, for some people in the West there is no sacred cosmos, no primordial human community, no human grounding in nature, no cosmic moral order, and no God.[20]

Indonesians can help us to see things of which we are ignorant. Indonesian social imaginaries are not only valuable to them. They have things to teach the world. What is the identity of Indonesia as a multireligious, multicultural society in relation to the rest of Islam and the world? What are the commonalities among Indonesian Muslims, Christians, Hindus, Buddhists, Confucianists, and followers of the many different indigenous religions (*agama suku*)? What are the differences between Indonesian Muslims from different ethnic groups? How did Indonesia come to be one of the most beautiful, tragic, amazing, and complex civilizations on earth? Can Indonesia contribute to the peace, justice, and well-being of the coming world? This is much too big an agenda for one book. But just because we cannot answer these questions, it doesn't mean we shouldn't try.

The following chapter provides a brief narrative overview of the historical processes that shaped Indonesian social imaginaries. It suggests that the theory of axial civilizations provides a tool for analyzing how mimetic, mythic, ethical, and theoretic ways of knowing formed Indonesian social imaginaries through centuries of interaction with China, India, Arabia, and Europe.

3

Cultures, Religions, and Modernities in Indonesia

> Long before the Portuguese and Spanish inaugurated Europe's Age of Exploration, even before the Vikings ventured across the North Atlantic, on the other side of the globe another seafaring race had already spread over two oceans. The geographical spread of these Austronesian-speaking peoples far surpassed that of the world's next largest cultural linguistic grouping, Indo-Europeans.
>
> —Ann Kumar

THE BRILLIANT INDONESIANIST Daniel Lev, not long before his death in 2006, commented to Farsijana and I that the difference between him and us was that we had hope for the future of Indonesia. He was deeply discouraged about the state of the country, especially the weakness of Indonesian law and human rights. There are plenty of good reasons not to have hope. It is not difficult to construct a very pessimistic picture of the future of Indonesia. Hope is not the same as prediction and should not be confused with optimism. This book does not claim to predict the future and is not based on confidence in the ability of Indonesia to overcome its myriad problems and become the savior of the world. Far from it. But this book is premised on the conviction that Indonesia has constructed a unique and precious culture, which is part of the worldwide social capital of Islam and human civilization. The theories constructed in this chapter have the merit of both explaining a complex reality and providing tools with which we can work toward a future that has hope. The beauty and tragedy of Indonesia are a legitimate source of hope.

A Historical Construction of Modern Indonesia

Indonesian culture is composed of diverse island cultures that have interacted with each other for millennia, fought with each other, traded with each other, settled in each other's spaces, intermarried, and sometimes oppressed each other. That would be enough to make an interesting country. More than that, Indonesia has been a meeting place for the great civilizations of the world.

More than 1.5 million years ago, *Homo erectus* (Java Man) came to Java. More than 700,000 years ago, *Homo floresiensis* (Hobbit People) came to these lands, drawn by the warm climate, fertile soil, and abundant food.[1] More than 45,000 years ago, modern human Austronesians (*Homo sapiens*) settled these islands, migrating from Africa.[2] These early humans were oceangoing travelers, coming not only from southern China, Taiwan, and the Philippines but from Africa, India, China, and Japan. According to Ann Kumar, Indonesian ancestors mastered oceangoing navigation before China, the Middle East, or Europe did (Kumar 2012; see also Kumar 2009). There is strong evidence of prehistoric travel between Java and Madagascar, off the coast of Africa. Traditional theories suggest that Japanese culture was transformed through contact with Korea and China around 300 BCE. However, Kumar argues, on the basis of growing genetic, linguistic, and cultural evidence, that Japan was actually transformed even earlier through contact with travelers from Java (2009). Indonesians were not only recipients of cultural influences from China, Japan, and India, but they also traveled to these places in their own right.

Indonesia interacted with China, India, the Middle East, and Europe over many centuries. Since prehistoric times, competing religious beliefs and imaginations of reality have spread throughout the Indonesian archipelago. Gradually Mahayana Buddhism and Hinduism, especially the worship of Shiva (Shaivism) gained sway over most of the archipelago. For centuries at different times, the great empires of Srilendra and Sri Vijaya (Buddhist) and Majapahit and Mataram (Hindu and Muslim) asserted their dominance over almost all of present-day Indonesia and beyond, into other parts of Southeast Asia. Indonesians integrated local religious practices with new influences from China and India (Ricklefs 2008; Reid 2015a). Sumatra and Java occupied a key position in the maritime trade routes between China and India. One reason why Indonesia has retained so much diversity is that it resisted absorption into either of these powerful civilizations and retained its own indigenous traditions. Drawing on the work of James C. Scott, Anthony Reid suggests that many ethnic and cultural groups in the archipelago remained essentially stateless. They assimilated what was useful, or necessary for survival, from the regional powers and foreign traders who encroached on their territories. But no single empire subjugated or enforced a uniformity of culture and religion on them (Reid 2015b; see also Scott 2009).

For hundreds of years, Muslim and Christian traders also came to Indonesia from China, India, Persia, and the Middle East. In the late thirteenth and fourteenth centuries the first Islamic sultanates were established in North Sumatra, spreading their influence down to the northern coast of Java and later up to the northern Moluccas. According to early Javanese literature and legends, Islam was spread throughout Java by nine Muslim apostles or saints (*wali songo*), some of whom were Chinese. They used peaceful means, including ancient Indian literature (primarily the *Ramayana* and *Mahabharata*) and leather shadow puppets (*wayang kulit*). In the fourteenth century Islam spread rapidly in Java. By the sixteenth it had overthrown the social order based on Hinduism and Buddhism (Shaivism and Mahayana).[3]

Christianity was brought to Southeast Asia first by Nestorian traders from Persia, who probably established churches in Sumatra in the seventh century. However, as elsewhere in Asia, Nestorian Christianity disappeared with few remaining traces (Aritonang and Steenbrink 2008). Later traders from Portugal, Spain, the Netherlands, and England competed with Arab traders for the spice trade. In the early sixteenth century, Fr. Francis Xavier, S.J., arrived, and Catholic Christianity gained a foothold in eastern Indonesia. A century later, in 1605, the Netherlands established the first Protestant church in the Moluccan Islands. During the twentieth century, Christianity spread rapidly in other parts of Indonesia, and it remains a significant minority religion (10 percent of the population) in a largely Islamic society (87 percent).

Far from being just passive recipients of influence from these great axial civilizations, Indonesians selectively received and shaped the influences from multiple cultures to gradually form their own unique identity and story. The diversity of Indonesian culture is thus not just a diversity of groups with different cultural characteristics. It is the diversity of different "layers" of culture that mutually enriched each other. These layers are virtually impossible to distinguish from each other because ideas and practices from China, India, the Middle East, and Europe interacted and mutually influenced each other over many centuries (Lombard 1996a, 1996b, 1996c).

Historical influences among these cultures go both ways. They are circulatory, mutually enriching each other. According to Geertz, Indonesia's "proper genius has ... always lain in her ability to work out practicable adjustments among her constituent cultures and to absorb the great host of external influences impinging on her while still, somehow, maintaining a distinct and over-all unique character" (1983:154).

Four Axial Civilizations in Indonesia: Chinese, Indian, Middle Eastern, and Greco-Roman

Most of the world's great civilizations are dominated by the social imaginaries of just one of the four great axial civilizations. Indonesia has absorbed all four while still, in the words of Geertz, "maintaining a distinct, overall, unique character" (1983:154). The civilizations of China, India, the Middle East, and the West each include mimetic, mythic, ethical, and theoretic styles of cognition, all of which have contributed to Indonesian culture.

The axial breakthrough, in the eighth through the second centuries BCE, came with development of the transcendent cognitive ability to step back and objectify mundane reality based on the assumption of a transcendent realm that is both the source and judge of the life we experience in this world. Thus, according to Bellah, the achievement of the Hebrew prophets in the Middle East was similar to that of Confucius and Lao Tse in China, the Vedas and Upanishads in India, and Plato and Aristotle in Greece. They were all characterized by theoretic cognition.

Building on Merlin Donald's theory of cognitive evolution from mimetic to mythic to theoretic, Bellah saw Abrahamic, prophetic religion's preoccupation with ethical monotheism as one of the first rationalizing forms of theoretic thought.[4] Bellah's ideas were influenced by Max Weber's theory of an evolution from magic to priestly religion and from priestly religion to prophetic ethical monotheism. Weber saw ethical monotheism, or prophetic religion, as a rationalization of religion, superseding magic and priestly religion. Counter to Bellah, I think it is useful to separate ethical from theoretic cognition. Weber's assumption that theoretic cognition is more rational than mimetic and mythic cognition is problematic. Mimetic, mythic, ethical, and theoretic cognition are all forms of rationality. Just as mimetic rituals follow a different logic from mythical storytelling or theoretical analysis, so ethical cognition follows a different logic from the other three. All four axial civilizations experienced cognitive evolution that encompassed mimetic, mythic, ethical, and theoretic forms of cognition. The four categories are tools of analysis, not distinct periods or sharply differentiated forms of thought or action.

Mimetic rituals are infused with mythical stories, ethical convictions, and theoretical ideas. Similarly, myths may be mimetic, creating a world through stories that imitate the microcosmos of human lives in order to embody an ethical narrative and give flesh to a theory. Ethical thinking is also infused with mimetic rituals, such as participation in the death of Christ during the Mass, or stoning the devil in the city of Mina during the Haj. Stories are not only means for passing on moral understanding to the next generation; they are the primary way we think about what is right and wrong. Theoretic cognition is also compounded of mimesis, myth, and ethics. Theories imagine, abstract, and imitate what is believed to be true based on a certain narrative. The narrative behind a theory includes values. A personal standpoint—the values and goals behind a theory—is what makes knowledge possible (Polanyi 1958; Kuhn 2012).

China

Indonesia is deeply influenced by Chinese culture. There is irony in the history of Indonesian oppression of Chinese Indonesians, who are sometimes referred to as "descendants" of China (*keturunan*) rather than indigenous Indonesians (*pribumi*), even though they have lived for hundreds or even thousands of years in Indonesia. Chinese Indonesians officially make up only 1.2 percent of the population, but they have influence far greater than their minority status might indicate. After thousands of years of intermarriage between Chinese and other ethnic groups, a much higher percentage of Indonesians are part Chinese. Former president Abdurrahman Wahid (Gus Dur) caused a stir when he publicly announced in 2008 that he was "genuinely part Chinese." He said that some of his ancestors were pure Chinese, although he also had Arab and Indian blood.[5] Most Indonesians have Chinese blood. Intermarriage is not the only reason. Since early Indonesians migrated from southern China, most Indonesians probably have Chinese ancestors.

As the "Middle Kingdom" (*Zhongguo*), China considered itself to be the center of the earth, and it viewed those outside its borders as barbarians.[6] There is early evidence of contact between Indonesia and China. In the third century BCE, Chinese courtiers put cloves in their mouths to ensure that their breath would be sweet when addressing the emperor. The fabled spice islands of the Moluccas, in eastern Indonesia, were the only place in the world where cloves grew.[7] In the seventh century CE, Yijing, a Chinese Buddhist monk, visited Sri Vijaya in Sumatra several times, where he studied Sanskrit and the Malay language. There is evidence that in the fourteenth century Chinese traders in the Moluccan Islands, were buying spices in Ternate and Tidore (Reid 2000). In the fifteenth century, Admiral Zheng He carried out seven massive voyages to Southeast Asia, India, and Africa. He visited Java and Sumatra on six of them. But after Zheng He's death the ocean voyages ceased, and every reference to them was deleted from Chinese books.

In the Forbidden City of Beijing, I was surprised to see a classic Javanese batik pattern (Mega Mendung) reproduced in stone carvings from the Ming dynasty (fifteenth century). Subsequently I saw the same design reproduced in other Chinese objects. There is no way to know if the design originally came from Java and was adopted by the Chinese or if traders brought a Chinese design to Java. Either or both could be true. Influences are circulatory, like chickens and eggs. No one knows which came first.

Confucianism is now recognized as an official religion in Indonesia (unlike in China where it is considered a cultural philosophy), but the influence of Confucian and Taoist social imaginaries goes far beyond the relatively small number of Confucianists. The preeminence of family as a social metaphor for all of society may have come from China, as did the emphasis on revering ancestors. Confucian ancestral values, meritocracy, and mimetic rituals to ensure cosmic balance are deeply embedded in Indonesian culture. Taoist and Mahayana Buddhist values from China are also part of the ways in which many Indonesians imagine reality. The Taoist belief that magical power can be obtained by conforming to the Tao and seeking harmony with nature is part of Indonesian imaginations of the natural order.

Confucianism and Taoism both posit a close connection between the microcosmos and macrocosmos, which is also common in Indonesia. Many Indonesian villages located on different islands and populated by various ethnic groups carry out mimetic rituals to ensure a proper relation between the microcosmos and macrocosmos, especially at the time of harvest and village cleansing. In some Muslim villages, traditional food offerings to the spirits are replaced with Islamic prayers and recitations from the Koran. The forms of the ritual vary, but the mimetic content is similar. The villagers perform local "micro" rituals that imitate the "macro" effects they hope to achieve, such as fertile soil, the goodwill of the ancestors, and the blessing of God on their efforts. Ideas about a relationship between the microcosmos and the macrocosmos are found in the earliest Indonesian literature, as well as in ancient Greece, China, the Middle East, and India (see Lach 1965).

From China, Indonesia absorbed highly ritualized, hierarchical social relations based on the analogy of the family. The highly complex, hierarchical Indonesian bureaucracy, with its emphasis on loyalty to the Bapak (Father), may have been influenced by thousands of years of contact with Chinese bureaucracies. Ritual speech and extremely formal, polite, and hierarchical social relations, especially in Java, are part of the mimetic character of Indonesian social practices, which are similar to those of China. Refined speech, suppression of emotion, and practices to ensure harmony (*rukun*), may be more pronounced in Java, but they are part of the Asian character of all of Indonesia. Mimetic rituals of family loyalty, submission to elders, and reverence for the ancestors are ancient Chinese values that are virtually universal across Indonesia. Most Indonesians today continue to be shaped by the mimetic, mythic, ethical, and theoretical culture of ancient China.

India

India has also indelibly marked the civilizations of Indonesia. Starting at least two thousand years ago, Indians spread their languages, religions, and cultures to many parts of Asia, including Indonesia (Aoyama 2007). More than thirteen hundred years ago, Dharmakirti, a Sri Vijayan Buddhist scholar from Sumatra moved to India and taught in the famous Nalanda University. His theories became normative in Tibet and are still taught today. A thousand years ago there were Javanese scholars studying in southern India.

Beginning in the sixteenth century, Arab, Portuguese, Chinese, Spanish, Dutch, French, and English traders all struggled for control of the trade with India. With such a long history and so many different contending cultures, India enjoys boundless diversity (see Nussbaum 2007). Radical Hindu nationalists argue that there is an essential, primordial, unchanging Indian culture that should be purified of all the polluting elements that have come from outside. They consider Indo-Aryan culture as not only native to India but even the source of most world civilizations. But this is an illusion. India, too, is the product of thousands of years of interaction with other cultures.

Early traders called Indonesia the East Indies because the Hindu and Buddhist cultures of ancient Indonesia were perceived to be an extension of India. Java's is one of the few Southeast Asian civilizations to have an ancient written literature. In Old Javanese, up to 90 percent of the words are derived from Sanskrit. The modern Indonesian language (Bahasa Indonesia) also borrows many words from Sanskrit (Aoyama 2007). The impact of India on Indonesia may be connected to what Ronit Ricci has calls "literary networks" (2011a). Ricci observes that Javanese Sri Lankan Muslims, whose ancestors came to Sri Lanka in the seventeenth century, still retain an imagination of Java, which is kept alive through stories. An example is an 1897 manuscript found only in Sri Lanka, the *Hikayat Tuan Gusti*, about the fifteenth-century apostle of Islam, Sunan Giri (Ricci 2011b).[8] Imaginations of the past were transformed into stories that addressed the current concerns of the Javanese Muslim community in Sri Lanka.

Trade networks across the Indian Ocean between Java and India have existed for millennia. Transportation between Java, Sri Lanka, and India was easier five hundred years ago than it was between northern and southern India. Traders don't only trade in goods. They also trade in stories and exchange documents. The seventh-century Chinese Buddhist monk Yijing stopped in Sri Vijaya in southern Sumatra on his way to collect Buddhist manuscripts in India. He continued on to India but returned to Sumatra because there was such an abundance of Indian Buddhist manuscripts there. There he studied Sanskrit and recorded that there were a thousand monks in the city studying Buddhist texts. After returning to China he came back to Sumatra with additional supplies of paper and ink to translate some of the abundant Indian Buddhist texts into Chinese. Literary networks may help explain the domination of Indian myths and stories in Indonesian classical and modern art. Eighth-century Borobodur, the largest ancient Buddhist temple in the world, includes stone carvings of hundreds of stories from India.

Even today it is amazing how much Indonesian art, literature, music, dance, film, television, political discourse, and economic practice is dominated by the myths and stories of India. Stories from the *Ramayana* and *Mahabharata* epics repeat themselves with almost monotonous regularity, not only in traditional art forms such as *wayang kulit* but even in postmodern, progressive works of art. For example, the internationally acclaimed film *Opera Jawa*, directed by Garin Nugroho, presents a surrealistic, nostalgic yet thoroughly modern reinterpretation of the *Ramayana* myth in the context of modern Java.[9]

Popular culture in Indonesia is also infused with Indian imaginations of reality. It may seem somewhat mystifying that conservative Indonesian Muslims are addicted to Bollywood movies or fanatically follow television series about Hindu gods and goddesses. Even the Indonesian music and dance styles of *dandut* and *keroncong* are influenced by Indian imaginations of reality. Indonesian *keroncong* music uses western-style instruments, such as the ukulele, guitar, violin, and double bass, and is derivative of Portuguese fado music. It is thought to have evolved from the music played by Portuguese slaves in Indonesia in the sixteenth century, adapted by Indonesian young toughs. In spite of its use of European instruments, Javanese *keroncong* uses a five-tone scale, is influenced by gamelan, and imitates the sounds of an Indian sitar.[10] Since modern fado developed in the nineteenth century, it is possible that it was influenced by earlier Portuguese contact with India and Indonesia. Influences circulate.

I used to play my violin with a neighborhood Javanese *keroncong* group. I'm generally good at improvisation and prefer to play by ear, so the lack of written music was no problem. I can generally reproduce a western melody on my violin after hearing it once or twice. But I could never get my ears around the imaginative musical universe of my *keroncong* group. The other players in the group always seemed to know where the music was going. They moved together with the music, bringing it to each new stage of the musical narrative. But even after years of playing with them I could never feel (*rasa*), the meaning of the music. I liked the music we made, but I couldn't feel it in my bones. My friends in the group were good-naturedly tolerant of my fumbling incompetence, but unlike them I never knew whether the next note was going to go up or down!

Like an elusive *keroncong* melody, the impact of China and India on Indonesia is more hidden today than is the impact of Islam and western modernity. Islamic symbols and western political, economic, and social institutions are prominent throughout Indonesian society. But China and India exist in the cracks. They are not separate streams of particular groups of Indonesians.[11] Rather, China and India are part of the Indonesian soul. They are part of an Indonesian social imagination. China and India are integrated into Indonesian Islamicate practices of modernity. Indonesia was never assimilated into Indian or Chinese civilization. Yet China and India are part of Indonesia. They are part of what makes Indonesia an Asian, rather than a Middle Eastern or western, country.

The Middle East

While Indonesia is Asian, it is not like either China or India, in part because it has been transformed by Islamic civilization. Islam dominates the public sphere in Indonesia. An Islamic renaissance has changed the face of Indonesia over the past thirty years. But Islamicate culture has been developing in Indonesia for over a thousand years. The understanding and practice of Islam by different Indonesian Muslim communities have continually evolved to adapt to changing local, regional, and global contexts. Global religion is changing local practices, in part propelled by modernization and increasing individualism.

Southeast Asian countries have been deeply religious for millennia. The recent increase in public piety in Southeast Asian countries reflects the increasing "individuation" of religious practices. Skills that used to be monopolized by religious professionals are now practiced by millions of ordinary believers. In Indonesia, Islam is no longer primarily the concern of a religious elite. Global communications media, increasing prosperity, education, and democratization have led to more and more people practicing their faith publicly and seeking their own personal religious experience. This does not mean they are "more religious" than before. Rather, the forms of religious practice and belief are changing from predominantly communal practices led by a religious elite to personal religion that is the responsibility of all the members of the community.

Middle Eastern (Judeo-Christian-Islamic) civilization in Indonesia includes a strong emphasis on ethical imaginations of reality.[12] While Judaism has few followers in Indonesia, Jewish monotheistic, prophetic concern with the ethical has been assimilated into Christianity and Islam. As the dominant religious community in Indonesia, the Muslim *umat* (community) is overwhelmingly oriented toward a moral imagination of reality. Most Indonesians, including both Muslims and Christians, think in categories of right or wrong (*benar atau salah*), good or bad (*bagus atau jelek*), permitted or forbidden (*halal atau haram*), sinful or not sinful (*dosa atau bukan dosa*), and good or evil (*baik atau jahat*).

An amusing example of this binary orientation occurred during Ramadan when I was fasting along with a Javanese Muslim mystic family. After the call to prayer at sundown, a young man named Ari and I celebrated the end of the daylight fasting hours by lighting up clove cigarettes.[13] Ari had misspent part of his youth as a young hoodlum (*preman*) but had repented, returned to a rigorous, mystical form of Islam, and was anxious to live right. I casually joked that we probably shouldn't be smoking, as it was not good for our health. Ari was concerned by my comment and asked, "But it's not a sin, is it?" For Ari, healthy or not healthy were not that important. More important was whether or not it was sin (*dosa*), forbidden (*haram*), or wrong (*salah*).

In Indonesia the concern with morality is not confined the private sphere. Public law is meant to incorporate morality and guide the society toward goodness. Muslims view Sharia (the way of God) as absolute truth, which must be obeyed. However, there are great differences in Muslim interpretations of how "the way of God" should be applied in society. For example, some Muslims view the essence of Sharia as justice, peace, human rights, and responsibilities, which can be formulated differently in different places and times. Others understand Sharia as an ancient law code that grew up in the centuries after the prophet, detailing proper dress for women and specific punishments for various crimes.

Interactions among traditional, religious, and state concerns about morality are exemplified in Pancasila, the five founding principles of the nation. Pancasila is from Sanskrit and literally means five principles. These principles form the beginning of the Constitution and the official ideology of the Republic of Indonesia.[14] All five bear the mark of the ethical Islamicate civilization that transformed Indonesia. They are moral principles infused with traditional, religious, and modern conceptions of morality. The five principles include the following.

1. The Great Unity of Deity (*Ketuhanan Yang Maha Esa*). This principle is fundamental to Semitic ethical monotheism and the Muslim concern for *Tauhid* (Arabic دي‌حوت) or absolute monotheism. The principle does not include *Allah*, the standard word for God used by both Muslims and Christians, but rather *Ketuhanan*, which literally means "Lordship" but carries the meaning "deity." This negotiated language accommodates traditional commitments to preserve harmony between different religious communities.[15] It accommodates modern concerns with religious freedom in a pluralistic nation-state.

2. One just and civilized humanity (*Kemanusiaan yang adil dan beradab*). The unity of human kind is based on the religious conviction that God created all people. Since there is only one God, who created all people equal, it follows that there is only one humanity. This reaffirms traditional Indonesian commitments to tolerance of difference and the modern idea of one just and civilized humanity, which includes all ethnic and religious groups.

3. The unity of Indonesia (*Persatuan Indonesia*). Indonesians understand the unity of the nation as founded via God's providence in creating one nation out of many different ethnic and religious groups. It is based on the Indonesian motto "They are different, but the same" (*Bhinneka Tunggal Ika*), taken from a traditional mystic poem. National unity is connected to independence and freedom from foreign domination.

4. Democratic society, guided by the wisdom of consultation and consensus between the people's representatives (*Kerakyatan yang dipimpin oleh hikmat bebijaksanaan, dalam permusyawaratan perwakilan*). "Consultation" (*musyawarah*) and "consensus" (*mufakat*) are Arabic words that have been used for centuries to describe how traditional Indonesian villages make decisions communally. The principle of dialogue and consensus are explicitly linked to modern ideas of representative government and democracy.

5. Social justice for all the people of Indonesia (*Keadilan sosial bagi seluruh rakyat Indonesia*). The principle of social justice for all is rooted in all three Semitic religions, but it also conforms to traditional law and the modern nationalist passion for freedom and justice.

In addition to the powerful influence of Chinese and Indian rituals, narratives, and ethics, most Indonesians are shaped by Muslim rituals, stories, and ethics. Moral categories of cognition, especially those of Islam, are diffused throughout society and reinforced with Abrahamic rituals and stories. Most Muslims believe that Indonesian law should be based on the ethical values and principles of religion. At a time when some western societies are abandoning religiously based social ethics, at least in the public sphere, Indonesia is embracing Judeo-Christian-Islamic morality with great intensity.[16]

Europe and North America

The fourth axial civilization that is deeply imbedded in Indonesia is the Greco-Roman civilization of the West. Spanish, Portuguese, Dutch, English, French, and North American civilizations have had an impact on Indonesia for centuries. Most Indonesians phrase the story of Dutch influence in negative terms, as 350 years of colonial exploitation. The Dutch grew rich by exploiting the natural resources and cheap labor of Indonesians. The Dutch "golden age" of the seventeenth century was a period when most of Europe was mired in economic depression, natural disasters, and political chaos (Toulmin 1990). But the Netherlands grew incredibly wealthy in part because it defeated its Arab, Spanish, Portuguese, and British competitors and established a monopoly over the spice trade.

The Netherlands did not formally colonize Indonesia until after the Dutch East India Company (VOC) went bankrupt in 1799 and the Netherlands established direct rule over most of Indonesia. However the VOC first appointed a governor in Ambon in 1605 and gradually used divide-and-rule tactics to gain political and economic control over larger and larger areas of what it called the Dutch East Indies. At the beginning of the nineteenth century the East Indies came under the control of the French Republic and then was governed by Sir Thomas Stanford Raffles of England from 1811 to 1815, before reverting again to Dutch control. After narrowly winning the Java War of 1825–30 the Dutch gradually gained control over all of present Indonesia (Carey 2008). According to Dutch government policy, Indonesia was defined as a *wingewest*, a region for making profit. In 1901 the Netherlands acquired a conscience and instituted the "Ethical Policy," which stated that Indonesia should be governed for the benefit of the people and not just for profit. The policy was underfunded and often opposed by powerful members of the Dutch colonial administration. It was abandoned by the time of the Great Depression in 1929 (Ricklefs 2008).

Whether motivated by self-interest or altruism, the Netherlands' legacy has profoundly shaped modern Indonesian life. The Netherlands established modern, rationally structured institutions of administration, law, education, science, health care, and government. These ideas and institutions were not created by the Dutch alone but emerged in various forms throughout the world as colonial powers influenced each other and had their ideas changed and modified by resistance and local practices in Africa, America, China, Europe, India, and Asia. The Dutch introduced educated Indonesians to many of the fruits of Greco-Roman, European civilization, including its rituals, myths, ethics, and theories. Ideas about nationalism, sovereignty of the people, the rule of law, social justice, and revolution helped fuel the Indonesian struggle for independence.

Today the dominant political, economic, and social institutions that structure the lives of Indonesians are primarily derived from the legacy of Greco-Roman culture.[17] The concept of the modern nation-state, based on the sovereignty of the people, rule of law, human rights, equality, and constitutional democracy, shapes political relations in Indonesia. Whether they like it or not, Indonesians compete in a capitalist, global marketplace. Even farmers on remote islands are aware of the current exchange rate between the rupiah and the US dollar because it affects the market price of their products.

As a non-Muslim, I recall once feeling regret that so much of the public sphere is dominated by Islam in Indonesia. I wondered why TV programming has to be interrupted at least twice a day by the call to prayer (*azan*). The call to prayer occurs five times a day, but most stations stop their programs in the morning and evening to broadcast it, usually accompanied by pious images of people at prayer and beautiful scenes from around Indonesia.[18] Then I realized that the call to prayer is actually a relatively mild domination of public space compared to that of the commercial interests of modern capitalism. Advertisements interrupt television programming not five times a day but more than five hundred times, with thirty to fifty advertisements per hour! If you travel down a major road in any Indonesian city, almost everywhere you look there is a commercial message. The upsurge in public piety is dwarfed by the flood of capitalist propaganda.

Not only the economy, but personal habits and social relations are dominated by western-derived, globalizing social institutions. The primary institutions of socialization are not the mosque or the longhouse but rather modern education, mass media, and the internet. From nursery school to university, children are socialized to adapt to modern life. Everything from daily tooth brushing to romantic gender relations is shaped by western institutions of health and concepts of the self. In Indonesia some conservative Islamist groups instigated a campaign to prevent young people from celebrating Valentine's Day on the grounds that it is not Islamic. It appears that this will be a futile effort to counter western notions of romantic relations as long as there are internet cafés on every other corner offering virtually free (pirated) downloads of Hollywood movies.

Globalization is an ancient phenomena in Indonesia. As a crossroads of trade and a rich source of natural resources, cheap labor, and a rapidly growing market, Indonesia has become the target of competition among many different civilizations. Each has left its mark on Indonesia, but probably none has had a greater impact than the modern West. Modern, scientific, theoretical thought shapes not only how Indonesians see the natural world but also the institutions and structures that organize their lives. Even increasing religious piety, not to mention radicalism, may be an indirect fruit of the overwhelming influence of the western world. While western theoretic ideas and institutions are transforming social, political, economic, religious, and cultural life, many Indonesians are looking for something that is not western, that is lasting and secure, to shape their identity. Capitalism is widely perceived as a system based on greed that is destroying the environment and causing radical inequality between the rich and the poor. Yet it is inescapable. Indonesians struggle to hold on to the sacred cosmos of their ancestors, to be faithful to their religions, and at the same time to live within a modern world dominated by the West.

Tradition, Religion, and Modernity

The social imaginaries of Indonesians are determined by a dialectical interaction among the social imaginaries of their ancestors, their religions, and their modern scientific consciousness. Most Indonesians are fluent in three different symbol systems and can switch from one to another according to which is most useful. They use different language in a neighborhood meeting, a mosque, or an office. Tradition, religion, and modernity are ideal types that are useful for analysis. They are not descriptions of mutually exclusive symbol systems, let alone different groups of people. Indonesian "traditions" are infused with both religious and modern ideas. Similarly Indonesian religious practices are shaped by cultural traditions and modern ideas. Indonesian modernities are thoroughly religious and infused with traditional practices. People negotiate among systems of symbols to create a uniquely Indonesian and religious modernity. While some Indonesians tend to use one of these three cultural-linguistic streams as their dominant "language," everyone uses all three streams when it is useful to them.

If we consider the differences in social imagination generated by the symbol systems of cultural tradition, religion, and modernity, we might be tempted to divide Indonesian society into three types, each of which is primarily shaped by one of the three contrasting symbol systems. But this would obscure more than it enlightens. We might learn something by analyzing those who are primarily oriented toward their ethnic traditions, those whose primary orientation is to their religion, and those whose primary reference point is modernity. However, that is a very rough analytic tool that hides the extent to which cultural traditions, religion, and modernity infuse each other and shape all Indonesians. The three categories are overlapping and mutually interpenetrating. Indonesian people and societies are traditional, religious, and modern, not one or the other. Even the most traditional or religious person is shaped in a million unconscious ways by the modern world. Similarly, even the most modern urbanite is still shaped by his or her culture and religious background.

Particular religions should not be identified with one of these three categories. For example, local tribal religions are not necessarily more "traditional" than Islam or Christianity. They are traditional in a different way. Similarly, Islam is not necessarily more "religious" than tribal religions, Hinduism, or Christianity. Rather, it is religiously different. Christianity may be more influenced by western traditions, but it is not more modern. Islam, tribal religions, and Buddhism are shaped by different imaginations of modernity. Just as all religions employ mimetic, mythic, ethical, and theoretic symbol systems, so all religions are traditional, religious, and modern.

Tribal religions might be imagined as "traditional" or "preaxial" because they inhabit a unified sacred cosmos. But in Indonesia highly educated, postmodern intellectuals perform ancient tribal rituals to reassert their ethnic roots. Islam may be imagined as more "religious" or "axial" because it separates God from the world and seeks to suffuse all areas of life with religious meaning. But most Muslims still live in a sacred cosmos suffused with power, even while they work in multinational corporations that operate through secular institutions. Christianity may be imagined as "modern" or "postaxial" insofar as some Christians construe religion as a private matter that should not interfere with the public realms of modern science, politics, and economics. But Indonesian Christians do not generally segregate their faith from either secular reason or traditional rituals. Most inhabit a sacred cosmos.

The imagination of these religions as polarized into categories of traditional, religious, and modern may underlie the theory of the clash of civilizations. It also lends itself to an evolutionary imagination of progress from primitive superstition to dogmatic religion to liberal-minded personal religion. Such an approach distorts empirical reality and leads to stereotypes rather than understanding.

An evolutionary perspective stimulates condescension toward what are considered the "lower types." Even worse, an ideology such as the clash of civilizations theory has the potential power of a self-fulfilling prophecy. The more people believe in and act on an imagination of the world as embroiled in a primordial, eternal clash between civilizations the more their behavior will mimic conflict and hatred.[19] The "war on terror" and travel bans targeting certain Muslim countries promote the imagination of a clash of civilizations and stimulate the growth of "radical" Islam, which sees itself as inherently opposed to western modernity. Ironically, the most powerful tool for spreading radical ideas is the internet.

Indonesians imagine a complex world where different social imaginaries are useful in different contexts. The shift between different imaginations of reality is seldom a conscious, rational decision. Sometimes it is dictated by social context or a person's habitus. For example, the rituals of certain holy days shape an imagination that honors and venerates the ancestors. Religious liturgies draw participants into prayer and worship of God. But when people enter a school or office, they step into a different kind of imagined world. They don't worship their boss, no matter how much he would like it! If there is a clash of civilizations, it is often a clash within our own selves as we struggle to integrate incommensurate symbol systems.[20]

Each of the three sets of ideas, practices, symbols, feelings, and institutions renders a world. We are all shaped by the community into which we were born and internalize, as part of our fundamental imagination of reality, the ways in which the society around us imagines the world (internalization). Our intersubjective, internalized imaginations are modified by our experiences and personalities and occasionally even by conscious thought. What we experience as reality we project into the world (externalization) and then participate in creating the plausibility structures that transform our imaginations into objective reality (objectification) (Berger and Luckmann 1989).

Berger and Luckmann's well-known theory of the social construction of reality includes the social construction of religion. Different communities construct their practices and institutions differently, according to their interpretation of the revelation. There is diversity of practices even in one religion, one nation, and one century, let alone in various religions, in the whole world, throughout history. Such diversity alerts us to the limits of our knowledge. All religions struggle to understand how their authoritative teachings fit into the social imaginaries of their age and culture. We are shaped by our milieu, but we are also capable of shaping it. The "imagined community" of most Indonesians includes stories, dreams, practices, and hopes from many different sources. (see Anderson [1983] 1991). Social imaginaries are symbolic "languages" that depend on different plausibility structures. One person interacts with many different kinds of institutions and settings in which different plausibility structures make different social imaginaries useful. In our questionnaire, respondents were asked to choose one of three answers, whichever felt the strongest or most appropriate for them.[21] Most people did not necessarily disagree with the other two answers. All three symbol systems made sense to them. The questionnaire induced tension because for many people it was hard to choose. Most people agreed with all three answers but followed the directions and chose the one that "felt" most compelling. Therefore the questionnaire did not test whether the respondent was traditional, religious, or modern, but rather which symbol systems were more or less powerful for them in different situations.

Conclusions

This chapter argues that modern Indonesia has been shaped by four great axial civilizations, each of which is an "axis" of the modern world. Indonesia has not been annexed to any of these civilizations. It is neither Indian nor Chinese nor Middle Eastern nor western. Indonesia is Indonesia, a unique civilization that is continually appropriating cultural riches and transforming them, all the while resisting assimilation to its powerful neighbors.

Table 3.1 *Typology of Contrasting Social Imaginaries*

	Tradition of the Ancestors	Religion (Islam and Christian)	Modern Democratic Ideals
Basis of society	Society is a micro-cosmos modeled after eternal macrocosmic reality of hierarchical relations and power. Primordial Unity	Society is based on the will and purpose of God and governed by God's law. There is only one God.	Society is based on the will of the people and is governed for their benefit. All people are equal.
Role of government	Like a good parent, government should lead by inner power and ex-ample to achieve balance, stability and peace. Good government follows the way of the ancestors.	As ordained by God and as God's representative, government should lead people to hold true beliefs and live moral lives, by rewarding the good and punishing those who go astray.	Government should protect the right of all citizens to have maxi-mum freedom to follow their own beliefs andseek prosperity through economic exchange.
Dominant metaphors of political society	Family Harmony Loyalty Hierarchy	*Umah* (community) Obedience to God Moral order Equality under God	Social contract Individual freedom Justice Equality
Basis of law	*Adat* (tradition) Rule of the ancestors Harmony with spirits and nature Ethnic groups have a right to follow their traditional beliefs.	Sharia (God's will) Holy Scriptures Each religion should fol-low divine law according to the teaching of its Scriptures.	Reason and agreement. Law should be secular, impartial, neutral, and treat all citizens as equal without regard to reli-gion, race, sex, culture, or ideology.
Attitude toward history	Cyclical, repeats itself Tragic Mysterious Acceptance of fate	Linear, hope in God Judgment Day Heaven and hell Submission to the will of God	Progress, hope in science and development Open, undetermined Possible apocalypse

Some years ago a student of mine took me to attend the dedication of a church in a remote village in Ambon, Moluccas. We traveled in a car with the governor of the province and the head of the Moluccan Protestant Church (GPM). After several hours of driving, we arrived at the village where a huge, cathedrallike church towered over a village of simple huts. The villagers had spent decades of toil and sacrifice to build this magnificent temple to God, even while the people had to live very simply. We received a VIP welcome. We walked down a path bordered on both sides with young women dancing in traditional Moluccan dress. I heard the strangest music, which animated the dancers. The music was familiar but different from anything I had ever heard. There was an orchestra playing western-style instruments. There were trumpets, trombones, flutes, violins, guitars, drums, and gongs. I couldn't stop smiling when I realized that most of the instruments were made of bamboo. The local materials transformed the sound of the instruments so that what they played sounded nothing like western music.

When I examined the traditional costumes of the women and men, I felt like I had entered a time warp, like I was in the Twilight Zone. There were neck ruffles that recalled the court attire of fifteenth-century Portugal, frills and puffy sleeves from sixteenth-century Spain, red pantaloons that might have been worn in a seventeenth-century French court, early Dutch peasant dresses, Polynesian touches such as bare feet, English waistcoats with gold buttons, batik fabrics from Java, handwoven clothing from eastern Indonesia, and Indian silks. Naturally some were dressed in western attire, including black suits with white shirts and ties and black Dutch dresses and veils, as well as jeans and t-shirts sporting misspelt American slogans topped off with baseball caps. Some wore uniquely Mollucan dress, including headgear festooned with bird of paradise feathers, but all of it was Mollucan. The people had drawn from diverse centuries and civilizations to create completely unique costumes that exist nowhere in the world outside of Indonesia.

After numerous ritualized speeches of welcome, we entered the church, which looked very European from the outside. But inside the western architecture the pulpit was shaped like a gigantic pink seashell. Then I saw the pipe organ: the pipes were made of bamboo! The worship and dedication service had all the liturgical forms of a nineteenth-century Dutch Reformed church, but I suspected that even these traditional forms had a different meaning to the worshipers than they did to Calvinists in the Netherlands.

After the worship, they had laid out a feast. The food was similarly eclectic, with elements from all over the world, as well as from different parts of Indonesia. There was one table dedicated to Moluccan dishes. Other tables served Javanese, western, Chinese, Indian, and eastern Indonesian dishes.

This eclectic mixing of cultures is not unique to Ambon. It can be seen at countless Javanese wedding receptions. Prior to the reception, the couple perform many elaborate rituals to ensure the blessing of their ancestors, families and community, their fertility and the blessing of Allah. At the reception, the wedding couple stands on a diadem in front of elaborate Javanese thrones, dressed in a wide variety of traditional Javanese clothing, often styled like the dress of a Javanese Prince and Princes. They are flanked by their parents on either side, also dressed in traditional Javanese dress. You enter the hall and pass through a receiving line of sumptuously dressed retainers and join the long line to pay your homage and offer congratulations to the couple and their parents. Meanwhile a Muslim *ustad* (guru) recites prayers and blessings from the Koran in musical Arabic. The typical feast that follows offers food derived from many different countries and parts of Indonesia. Often there is a rock band, playing popular Western music with a sexy singer belting out romantic lyrics. Usually there is a professionally produced video, showing the happy couple riding bikes together and visiting romantic locations, wearing casual Western dress, with Muslim accessories.

The eclectic material culture expressed in these two stories (from the Moluccas and Java) only hints at the rich architecture of Indonesian minds and hearts. The religious communities of Indonesia are different from those in Saudi Arabia, the Netherlands, India, and China. They are different because they resisted assimilation and retained the rich cultural diversity of their own land. This diversity includes layers of meaning derived from millennia of interactions with the great civilizations of humankind. Whether or not Indonesia will continue to value this richness is an open question and part of the subject of this book. The following chapter uses stories to illustrate the ways in which many Indonesians experience reality as a sacred cosmos.

Part II
Living in a Sacred Cosmos

PART II EXPLORES Indonesian attitudes toward the unseen world of spirits and supernatural powers. To what extent do the traditions of the ancestors still shape the experience of everyday life in Indonesia? How can we assess the truth of competing narratives of magic, Islam, and modernity in the stories of Indonesians? How do Muslim leaders from different streams of Islam interpret a sacred cosmos? What is the impact of modernist Islam on the disenchantment of everyday life?

4

Enchantment and a Sacred Cosmos

"The ecological thought" … is a vast, sprawling mesh of interconnection without a definite center or edge. It is radical intimacy, coexistence with other beings, sentient and otherwise.

—Timothy Morton

The Nature of a Sacred Cosmos

AN ENCHANTED COSMOS is one in which we are surrounded by powers. There are magic and miracles, spirits, *jins*, and supernatural powers. God is an ever-present agent who acts in the world. In a sacred cosmos there is a single moral order that governs both natural and supernatural phenomena. Individuals are embedded in communities, which are in turn embedded in nature. Nature and human societies are part of a moral order that governs all existence and is ruled by God.

Most modern, educated people in western countries (including religious believers), understand that they are located on the planet Earth in a solar system in the Milky Way galaxy in the universe. The universe is a material, natural reality, the object of scientific research (physics, astronomy). It is almost unimaginably large, billions of years old, and totally impersonal. Within the immense scale of the universe's time and space, human beings are tiny specks without significance. If there is meaning in life, it is not to be found in nature (the "objective" world of science) but in the subjective worlds of art, religion, emotion, and relationships. In contrast, those who inhabit an enchanted cosmos understand themselves as part of a web of meaning that is governed by transcendent powers.

Unlike an impersonal universe, a cosmos includes both material and immaterial or supernatural phenomena. A cosmos includes a moral order, a social order, and a physical order. The moral, social, and physical orders are aspects of the same reality, which is grounded in God. The macrocosmos (*jagad gede*) of the outer world, including the physical universe and the invisible powers, and the microcosmos (*jagad cilik*) of intimate, hidden, and secret meanings are reflections of each other. The meaning of the whole of history may be contained in the meaning of this one fleeting moment or one tiny space. In a cosmos, facts and their meaning, knowledge and ethics, reality and fate, are undivided.

Charles Taylor describes the "great disembedding" of modern secular societies as follows.

> This society had no place for the ambivalent complementarities of the older enchanted world: between worldly life and monastic renunciation, between proper order and its periodic suspension in Carnival, between the acknowledged power of spirits and forces and their relegation by divine power. The new order was coherent, uncompromising, all of a piece. Disenchantment brought a new uniformity of purpose and principle. The progressive imposition of this order meant the end of the unstable postaxial equilibrium. The compromise between the individuated religion of devotion, obedience, or rationally understood virtue, on the one hand, and the collective, often cosmos-related rituals of whole societies, on the other, was broken, and in favor of the former. Disenchantment, reform, and personal religion went together. (2004:49–50)[1]

Many modernizing Southeast Asian societies have not experienced disenchantment or "disembedding" in anything like the same way as in the West. What Taylor called the "ambivalent complementarities of the older enchanted world" are still an everyday lived reality in Indonesia. For example, life is a rhythm between prayer and mundane pursuits, ascetic practices and joyful celebration. During the month of Ramadan the day is spent in fasting while the night is spent in feasting. While there is no societywide cultural equivalent of Carnival, there are many opportunities in which the Javanese passion for order, politeness, gentleness, and harmony are suspended in favor of culturally tolerated expressions of chaos.

Examples include locally specific rituals that involve young Javanese men running around nearly naked for midnight ritual bathing, spirit possession, *jatilan* dances, the *ogah-ogah* parades of Bali, the horse battles of

Sumba, and the bull races of Madura. Negative examples include extremely aggressive driving, violence toward "deviant" groups in expressing religious emotions, mass village violence against petty criminals, and anarchic behavior following football games. Most Indonesians acknowledge the power of local spirits, ghosts, and spiritual beings. Many perform various rituals to keep them happy while acknowledging that there is only one God who deserves our worship. There is still an uneasy balance between communal, cosmos-sustaining rituals and individuated, ethically oriented religion.

The same tension holds true for the relation between the latest findings of modern science and belief in an unseen world. Many well-educated Indonesians believe in both. The distinguished philosopher and astronomer Karlina Supelli commented to me in a private conversation that her attempts to understand how God interacts with quantum physics only address the intersection of theology with the latest findings of natural science. The unseen world of a sacred cosmos cannot be verified or falsified by science. Science is not the only means of understanding what is real. This chapter tells stories about the ways in which Indonesians experience a sacred cosmos. It closes with reflections on how we may think of the "truth" of these accounts.

There are four characteristics of living in a sacred cosmos (Taylor 2007). First, individuals are embedded in communities. In a sacred cosmos, the community is not limited to the living or the human. The community includes ancestors and unseen powers. Second, communities are embedded in nature. Human society and the natural world are part of each other, not just in the biological sense but also in a personal and social sense. The natural world has agency and includes powers that can communicate with the human community and affect its well-being. Third, nature is embedded in a moral order. Just as nature is not impersonal, so it is not ruled by amoral, neutral physical laws alone. It is part of a single moral order that includes both the human community and nature. Fourth, the moral order is embedded in God. God, who is understood differently in different religious and ethnic communities, is sovereign over the entire sacred cosmos.

A wise philosopher from India once commented at the beginning of a conference, "I have so little time that I'm just going to tell stories." This chapter uses narratives to illustrate how these four characteristics are experienced by many Indonesians.[2]

Individuals Are Embedded in Communities of
the Seen and Unseen World

In a sacred cosmos the primary reality is community, not the individual. A person knows who they are because they are part of a primordial community. The community is not a voluntary association. It assumes solidarity based on blood, faith, ritual, language, and nation (see Tönnies [1887] 2001). This community includes the living, the ancestors, and unseen powers (Chambert-Loir and Reid 2002; Ricklefs 1998)

While we were conducting research in a mountain town in Flores, a young man told us the story of how the spirit of his grandmother helped him fight injustice. The man was born and raised on land that had been passed down through many generations of his ancestors. He inherited the land, built a house on it, and farmed it. A wealthy outsider came and produced documents claiming that the land belonged to him. The case went to court, but he had no official deeds to the land or money to hire lawyers or bribe the judge. Nevertheless he knew this was the land of his ancestors and his by right. Since he would not vacate the land, his enemy hired a gang of thugs to drive him away. One night they burned down his house and threatened his life. The young man prayed to God and performed rituals to honor his ancestors. He built a simple house of bamboo and settled in with a friend to see what would happen. One day thirty thugs came to drive him off the land. He and his friend were terrified. All they could do was pray. Gradually a very strong feeling came over him. If his ancestors wanted him to have the land, they would have to defend him. Otherwise he and his friend would just stay in their hut and die. He cried out to his ancestors for help. Suddenly a sound like a rushing wind filled the hut. The spirit of his grandmother came and possessed his body. Although he was a small man with no experience of fighting, he rushed at the thirty approaching gangsters. He felt huge and powerful, invincible. Perhaps the gangsters saw something other than one small man because they cried out in fear and fled from the land. Since then no one has dared to bother him. He rebuilt his house and farms his lands with confidence that it is protected by his ancestors.

This story illustrates a sharp contrast between those who live in an impersonal universe and those who live in a sacred cosmos. In an impersonal universe, there are no ancestral spirits or miracles. There are impersonal institutions of law that may or may not deliver justice. Often the strong or the wealthy trample the rights of the weak. There is not much we can do about it apart from working to improve the rule of law and defending the rights of the powerless. But in a sacred cosmos we are surrounded by powers. The powers may be good, neutral, or malevolent, but they are real. Rituals are needed to maintain good relations with the unseen world and keep the cosmos in balance. Communities include the ancestors. Violation of the traditional laws (*adat*) of the ancestors can bring real physical retribution, including sickness, alienation, and death. Even when there is no justice in this life, there will be justice after we join the ancestors on the other side of the grave.

In May 1998, President Soeharto was forced from office. About a year later Abdurrahman Wahid (Gus Dur) became president of Indonesia.[3] Before he became president, I talked with him about his beliefs in a sacred and embedded cosmos. Gus Dur had just accepted an invitation to visit Israel and join the Board of Directors of the Peres Center for Peace. Politically this was a dangerous thing to do, since Israel is unpopular in Indonesia. His enemies gleefully attacked him in the press as a "friend of Israel." Gus Dur had many moral and rational explanations about why it was right for him to join the Peres Peace Center, but he also had a supernatural explanation. He said that if it was wrong to go to Israel and join the peace center his guru would tell him not to go. I asked him who this Guru was. He replied that his teacher was Kyai Hasyim Asy'ari. Hasyim Asy'ari was his grandfather, the great Islamic ulama who founded NU. Hasyim Asy'ari died in 1947. I asked Gus Dur how his guru communicated with him since he was dead. Gus Dur replied that he frequently had dreams in which his teacher told him what he should do. He was convinced that if going to Israel was wrong his guru would tell him. Gus Dur was embedded in a community that transcended the limits of death and waking consciousness.[4]

Many Indonesians from different ethnic and religious communities experience communication from powers outside their minds through dreams. When someone dies, a common topic of conversation is who has had a dream that foretold the death. In fact it is considered unusual if a death comes unexpectedly, with no warning in a dream. Sometimes even religious conversion takes place through the agency of dreams. For example, Ibu Ngatimah, who worked for me when I first came to Indonesia, was a devout Catholic who attended Mass early every morning. She told me that she had converted from Islam to Catholicism some years ago. I asked her why, and she replied that Jesus came to her in a dream and told her that she should follow him.[5]

Abrahamic religions often attempt to "purify" their converts from "syncretism" with local beliefs. However, the social imaginaries that underlie local beliefs are not easy to eradicate. Social imaginaries are always hybrid human constructions, which borrow symbols from many different sources, as illustrated by the following story.

The Tobaku people in the highland mountains of Central Sulawesi converted to Christianity in the early twentieth century as a result of the efforts of Salvation Army missionaries from the United States.[6] They consider themselves fervent Evangelical Christians (Kristen fanatik). But on one occasion, after a wedding feast in the mountains, the elders of the church were dismayed when most of the people at the feast became violently sick to their stomachs. Visiting American missionaries assumed that there must have been food poisoning due to something served at the feast. The elders had a different explanation. After prayer and seeking God's direction, they declared the sickness had been caused by their ancestors because the bride had failed to ask permission from her parents when she left her village.

When the tearful bride was asked why she didn't ask permission, she explained that she thought it was unnecessary because both her parents had already passed away. To the dismay of the visiting Americans, this was not considered an adequate excuse. The elders believe they are "surrounded by a great cloud of witnesses." The community includes both the living and the dead. Reverence for the ancestors may be even more important than honoring living parents since ancestral spirits are known to cause problems in families that ignore them.

Communities Are Part of Nature, Both Seen and Unseen

In a sacred cosmos, nature is part of the human community. Humans are part of nature biologically, socially, economically, religiously, and culturally. Nature and the human community are part of a unified meaning system. Human meanings are seen in natural events. Natural processes, such as fertility of the soil, amount of rain, natural disasters, death and life, global warming, and so on, are all signs for those who have eyes to see. Certain places are sacred, usually because they are inhabited by unseen beings or powers. Graves, sacred places, and natural wonders such as mountains, large rocks, and trees are all revered. Many become the sites of pilgrimages of Indonesians from all religions. Nature has agency; it interacts with the human community in both positive and negative ways.

Most Javanese in Yogyakarta believe that harmony in society and with nature can be assured by maintaining a balance between the male power of the volcano to the north, Grandfather Merapi (Mbah Merapi), and the female power of the ocean to the south, the Queen of the South (Kanjeng Ratu Kidul). Many believe these powerful beings are real, although they offer differing theological explanations to account for their existence. Some Javanese mystics believe that the Queen of the South is the offspring of a goddess who was cursed because she married a human and then was charged with ruling the supernatural beings who inhabit the coast and ocean. Many Muslims believe that she is a *jin* and the queen of the *jins* who inhabit the wild oceans of the south coast of Java. *Jins* are mentioned in the Koran. They are spiritual beings created by God from fire and may be good, evil, or neutral. Every year the sultan carries out rituals to honor the female power of the Queen of the South and the male power of Grandfather Merapi.

Some years ago my wife and I bought an old Javanese teak house from her Javanese Muslim uncle. The house was built by my wife's great-grandfather in 1822, in Prambanan, near the famous eighth-century Hindu temple complex. With the family's permission, we moved the house to land on the cliffs overlooking the south coast of Java close to Langse Cave.[7] A devastating earthquake hit Yogyakarta in 2006. Fifty-seven hundred people died and around three hundred thousand homes were destroyed, including the entire neighborhood in Prambanan where our house had stood. Our Javanese Muslim family believe the ancestors "whispered in our ear" that we should move the family heirloom, so that it would be saved.

The epicenter of the earthquake was just off the south coast of Java, so it made sense to assume that the Queen of the South was involved in creating the earthquake. Perhaps the proper cosmic rituals to honor the queen had been lacking. Or she was angered by increasing pollution of the rivers, commercialization of the beaches, and general degradation of the environment. Since we had reassembled our house on the cliffs just a few kilometers from the epicenter of the earthquake, on the day of the quake we assumed it had been destroyed. To our amazement, it was undamaged. This confirmed the conviction of our Javanese neighbors that the house is full of power.

When we were conducting research in Bali, our niece took us to a lovely beach called Tegalwangi (Fragrant Place). My wife Farsijana started filming as she hiked down the path and onto the beach. Suddenly a huge wave swept her off her feet and flung her against the rocks. Her face crashed into the jagged rocks and she felt great pain. She felt like her whole face has been smashed in. After recovering her feet she was surprised to learn that she was fine. She just had a few mild scratches. To her surprise, after she was "kissed" (*dicium*) by the rock, suddenly she smelled (*mencium*) a wonderful fragrance. None of the rest of us smelled the beautiful scent of Tegalwangi.

A few days later we were leading a seminar at the Institute Hindu Dharma Negeri (IHDN) in Denpasar and Farsijana shared the story of her experience. A Balinese Hindu professor offered his interpretation of what happened. He explained that our bodies contain all the elements that occur in nature, including the elements in rocks and fragrances. He suggested that the elements in the rocks in Tegalwangi were *cocok* (compatible with) the elements of rock in Farsijana's body. They established a vibration between her body and the rocks such that the rocks attracted her to them. The rocks kissed her face (*mencium*) such that she could smell (*mencium*) the hidden fragrance of Tegalwangi.

The Balinese professor used several different styles of thinking in his explanation. There was mimesis between the microcosmos of Farsijana's body and the macrocosmos of the physical world of rocks, ocean, and beach. Mimetic cognition is also revealed in the wordplay in the double meaning of *cium*, which can mean either "kissed" or "smell." He thought in narrative about the myth of a hidden beach that would only reveal its fragrance to the right person, a person who was kissed by the rocks. The professor also used vocabulary drawn from scientific modernity. Chemical elements in the body and nature created a molecular vibration that caused attraction between two objects. He shifted among mimetic, mythic, and scientific symbol systems to make sense of our interaction with nature.

Nature Is Part of a Moral Order

Many Indonesians make no sharp distinction between the outer and inner worlds that make up reality and are sometimes related to each other as macrocosmos (Javanese *jagad gede*) to microcosmos (*jagad cilik*). The outer world (*lahir*), includes the physical, material, social, legal, economic, political, cultural, and religious. It can be analyzed with rational, empirical methods. But it is also linked to the inner world (*batin*), which includes spirits, character, forces, conscience, authority, powers, obedience, *jins*, virtue, and miracles. This inner world cannot be understood using reason alone, but it is not opposed to rationality, as in the western dichotomy between rationality and irrationality or objectivity and subjectivity. Most Indonesians highly value rationality, science, and modern education. But they think their usefulness, however impressive, is limited. They can't teach us how to be *ikhlas* (committed to giving of yourself in service to others), *pasrah* (submitted to the will of God), *tanpa pamrih* (without self-interest), *mengalah* (allowing yourself to be defeated knowing that you are stronger than the other), *gotong royong* (working together for the good of all), or *rukun* (living in harmony with others) (See Magnis-Suseno 1984).

The inner and outer are not the same as western categories of material and spiritual. All things, both material and spiritual, have an inner and outer dimension. For example, a material, outward action, such as soliciting bribes (*lahir*), may cause inner corruption (*batin*), which in turn can make you physically sick (*lahir*). Or maybe your inner corruption (*batin*), caused by despair and poverty (*lahir*), leads you to accept bribes, which causes you to become rich, powerful, and honored by your community. But the inner rot goes deeper. Or perhaps your inner rot and outer prosperity are the result of you having sacrificed someone you love to a malignant spirit (*tuyul*), who has given you great success in business in exchange for your soul. In that case, there will come a time of reckoning in this world or the next.

If everything has inner and outer aspects that are related to each other, then it makes no sense to dichotomize reality into a material, rational, objective, empirical world that is separate from a spiritual, irrational, subjective, imaginative world. The inner world is not less real, less objective, less rational, or less material than the outer world. We just don't understand the inner world as well unless we are highly trained in inner world disciplines (*kebatinan*).

Even if we are trained in inwardness (*kebatinan*), the word *understand* is misleading. What we need is *rasa*, which encompasses in one concept feeling, understanding, intuition, sensing, and taste. *Rasa* encompasses both the inner and outer worlds in one faculty of perception. In economic practices, this explains why sometimes an Indonesian businessperson will sell a product for a loss, not because of a rational calculation of profit but because he or she feels *cocok* with the buyer. *Cocok* means "comfortable with," "compatible with," or "in sync." You are appropriate for each other, you fit, and there is a common feeling that transcends profit or loss. The outer reality of a sale is matched with an inner reality of common feeling such that the transaction is *pulung*. It is fated, not in the bad sense of being forced by an outer power but in the positive sense of two halves finding their matching inner reality to make a whole. Even if this sale results in a loss, it might change your luck and bring you further, more profitable sales.

One of Indonesia's most creative, brilliant figures was the Javanese Jesuit architect Father Mangunwijaya. Father Mangun was a brilliant architect, novelist, historian, and social activist. He moved into a squatter village on the garbage-strewn banks of a river named Kali Code in Yogyakarta. He lived there for many years, working for the rights of the poor and resisting government attempts to evict them in order to build a Holiday Inn. He helped empower the people to transform their slum into a beautiful, simple, garden village with painted murals, libraries, winding paths, art performances, flowers, schools, running water, and sanitation. Although he won many international awards for his architectural works, which made use of local materials, modern ecological ideas, and Indonesian cultural forms, he won his greatest honor for his work among the poor. In 1992 Father Mangun won the Aga Khan Award, which is often referred to as the Muslim equivalent of the Nobel Prize, for his transformation of a slum.

In 1997 I was invited to a celebration of Father Mangun's birthday with a few friends in the home of my colleague Dr. Th. Sumarthana. The group included some of the leading intellectual and religious leaders in Indonesia, including Abdurrahman Wahid (Gus Dur). The small gathering was in Yogyakarta, near the base of Mount Merapi, one of the most active volcanoes in the world. It had just erupted, killing some people and forcing the evacuation of several villages. As we ate dinner, the topic of conversation moved to the meaning of the volcanic eruption. The consensus of the group was that it meant the fall of President Soeharto was imminent. The group also suggested that Gus Dur was a reincarnation of Semar, the Javanese high god who was incarnated in the form of a comical, crude, and lowly servant. He was destined to take a major role in the coming cataclysmic events. At the time, Soeharto had just been "elected" to another five-year term and controlled a powerful military. I didn't think Soeharto would step down anytime soon unless he died. But within a year, in fact, Soeharto was forced out of office and the following year Gus Dur became president of Indonesia.

For that small group, nature was part of a moral order. Somewhat like in a Shakespearean play, the workings of nature were perceived as signs of a disturbance in the sociopolitical moral order. A volcanic eruption was a sign of the end of a political regime for those who "had eyes to see." The natural power of Mount Merapi and the political power of the ruler were both part of the same moral order. Both were embedded in a moral order governed by God. In this discourse, Javanese power is not amoral, as suggested in Benedict R. Anderson's brilliant analysis (1990) but rather rooted in an overarching moral order of reality with God at the summit. The eruption of Mount Merapi did not cause the fall of Soeharto but rather was a sign of change. Both were part of the same structure of meaning.

These multireligious Indonesian leaders were certainly postaxial, perhaps even postmodern. They had no problem with abstract theoretical thinking. Some held PhDs from leading western universities. But their world was still enchanted. They lived in a unified moral cosmos where social, scientific, spiritual, and moral processes were embedded in each other within a single reality. The microcosmos reflects the macrocosmos and vice versa.

A Moral Order Grounded in God

In a sacred cosmos the moral order has a transcendent reference. The moral order is grounded in God, the Tao, Nirvana, or some other meaningful power. During the dangerous days leading up to the fall of Soeharto in 1998, rumors were flying thick and fast. Some Muslim activists expressed fear and confusion over rumors of a conspiracy led by international capitalists and the American Central Intelligence Agency (CIA) to keep Soeharto in power. Father Mangun told them to calm down. He said our job was to work for justice, democracy, human rights, and peace within our own local communities. We could not control the bigger forces, but we could change the way we lived. Our job was to be faithful and leave the final outcome to God.

Father Mangun was embedded in a local, multireligious community and rooted in a natural landscape that was part of an overall conception of the Good. The fact that he was Catholic did not matter to the many Muslims who revered him. They shared the same understanding of a morally ordered cosmos that transcended the chaos of human failings because it was subservient to the will of God. Father Mangun passed away in 1999, but he lived just long enough to see the prophecy made at his birthday party come true.

A social imaginary that sees all reality as having an outer and inner dimension (*lahir* and *batin*) grounded in God is not necessarily comfortable. There may be serious tensions between what the outer world seems to demand and what feels right (*rasa cocok*) from within. A famous Javanese poet of the nineteenth century, Ronggowarsito, illustrated the tensions in the link between the inner and outer worlds (Florida 1995; Ricklefs 2007). He predicted that in the cycles of history there comes an era of *edan*, which literally means "madness" or "chaos." The moral order has broken down, and the times are "out of joint." During this period, those who are evil flourish in an outward sense (*lahir*), while those who are virtuous in their outward actions (also *lahir*) go hungry. His poignant question regards how to live with yourself and act in such a time. He concludes that even though it appears that those who are careless and follow the path of madness are happy, God wills that those who remember who they are and are careful will be happier in the end. If you act on your inner knowledge of virtue by following virtuous outward practices, then in an outward sense you may be destroyed. If you don't succumb to the madness of the outer world, then you will not share in the spoils. On the other hand, if you give in to the madness, then you are in danger of destroying your inner life (*batin*). Ronggowarsito's poem follows in my free translation.

> Witness the era of madness:
> It is so difficult to act.
> Can't stand to follow the madness,
> But if you don't act crazy
> You don't share the spoils.

Hunger is waiting at the door.
Nevertheless, according to God's will,
No matter how happy are the morally careless,
Those who remember and stay on guard
Will be happier in the end.[8]

Ronggowarsito's poem expresses a feeling (*rasa*) that the events of the outer world (*lahir*, the macrocosmos), including the physical world of nature, are linked to the political economy of the social order, which is in some sense the *batin* of the natural world. Many Indonesians are attracted by the ideas, practices, and narratives engendered by western social imaginaries, but they do not feel the radical secularity of the social and natural worlds that is part of the air most people breathe in the western world, especially in the world of secular universities. Some Indonesians' alienation from "the West" is caused by the radically secular assumptions about the basis of society. They feel that the basis of the human community is the will of God, not primarily the will of the people.

A Javanese Muslim Shaman: Living in Three Worlds

Some years ago I lived with a Javanese Muslim shaman and his family in a village on the slopes of Mount Merbabu in Central Java.[9] He and his family were rooted in Javanese mysticism, deeply Islamic and also modern. Embah (Grandfather) Selamat's mission in life was to serve God and people regardless of whether they were rich or poor and regardless of their race, religion, or position. His clients included simple villagers and some of the most powerful leaders in the country.[10] He had many disciples who came to him for instruction in *kebatinan* ("inwardness" or Javanese mysticism). Magic was heavily involved, and communion with spirits and *jins* was common.[11] On certain conjunctions of the Javanese and Arabic calendar, Embah went into a trance state where he claimed to see into the past and future and the souls of people. He slept very little, meditated a lot, fasted two days a week, and had a constant stream of clients who came to him at all hours of the day and night. He was a traditional healer, a combater of black magic, and a purveyor of spells, talismans, and supernatural solutions to every problem in the book. He frequently bathed in the middle of night at sacred springs and prayed at the graves of his ancestors.

Embah was well known as a man of power and obviously enjoyed his success. Yet he believed his power was dependent on his lack of self-interest (*tanpa pamrih*). If he became self-seeking and ambitious, his success would dry up. Embah derived his power from ascetic practices (*bertapa*) and meditation (*samedi*), especially as performed in places of power such as the tombs of the nine great prophets of Java (*Walisongo*). Suffering was his path to power and egolessness the key to his success. From a thin and hungry wandering juggler sleeping in mosques, casting out demons, healing the sick, learning from monkeys, and predicting winning numbers for gamblers, Embah evolved into a jovial, successful shaman. Though prosperous, he continued to practice asceticism (*bertapa*) to retain his power.

Embah was also a sincere Muslim who carried out the five pillars of Islam with great enthusiasm. He prayed (*sholat*) five or more times a day and often proclaimed the Shahada in Arabic: "There is no God but God, and Muhammad is his Messenger."[12] He fasted during Ramadan and also every Monday and Thursday during the rest of the year. Embah was generous to those around him, not only giving the required tithe (*zakat*) but also sharing his wealth with the whole village. He never asked for money from those he helped. While I lived with him he sponsored *pengajians* (readings from the Koran) and invited famous Kyais to come and preach to all the villagers. At such events he, his wife, and neighbors cooked for the whole village, as well as for disciples and *santri* who came from surrounding villages.[13] He went on the Haj to Mecca, sacrificed a goat during Idul Adha, and was in charge of building a large mosque in his village.[14]

Embah Selamat was also a modern man. He drove his own car, used a cell phone, kept up with national and international news, and rode in airplanes. Although he never charged for his services, his wealthy clients showered him with gifts, opening up opportunities for international travel and the purchase of modern technology. Embah was a counselor as well as a healer. He listened to people's problems and offered sage advice. Although he had dropped out of grade school, he knew a little about modern psychology and used terms like *emotional stress*, *psychosis*, and *mental illness*.

Embah also worked for the Coca-Cola Company and had his own office at a nearby factory. Coca-Cola took him around to its plants, where he meditated in a special room, usually in the middle of the night. He often left for his office at the Coca-Cola plant at 11:00 PM. He drove his own car to the factory, forty minutes away. Embah performed rituals to protect the factory from black magic, to bring peace and harmony to the workers, and to give virtue to the water used in Coke. He ensured the prosperity of the business by means of prayer and meditation. The company even flew him to other countries to perform similar services. His position was something like Vice President for Spiritual Affairs. Embah, and his employers, combined mysticism, Islam, magic, and modern capitalism.

A Shaman's Integration of Magic and Ethical Religion

Influenced by Weber and Anderson, I thought Embah Selamat's practice of magic was divorced from ethical considerations. He wasn't concerned with the moral practices of his clients but said he would serve anyone who asked for help. Some of his most powerful clients were of seriously questionable character. However, I came to see that his practice of magic encompassed a view of nature that was embedded in a moral order.

Embah often switched between three different cultural-linguistic symbol systems. Sometimes when he talked about clients who were highly agitated he would say that they were possessed by an evil spirit or *jin*. He would give them specially blessed water, a *jimat* (usually a little bag containing an Arabic verse from the Koran), or secret mantras to drive out the spirit. He might tell them to bathe seven times in the middle of the night on a certain conjunction of the Javanese and modern calendars at seven different springs. Since his calling and profession were as a healer, the language of Javanese mysticism (*kebatinan*) was his primary language.

Sometimes when talking about clients with remarkably similar symptoms to someone possessed by a *jin*, Embah used Muslim ethical discourse and said they were burdened by sin and failure to follow God's commands. He would encourage them to pray, perform *sholat*,(the five, daily required acts of Muslim ritual worship) and ask for God's mercy and forgiveness. He would encourage them to be *pasrah* (submissive to the will of God) and *ikhlas* (willing to serve and accept whatever was the result). Embah sometimes suggested that they should fast and pray or attend koranic reading groups. In good Islamic fashion, he stressed that everything good comes from God and only God can help a person overcome his or her problems.

On other occasions, Embah Selamat used modern psychological language. He would say that agitated clients were experiencing great emotional stress due to natural causes, such as unemployment, failure to pass an exam, or marital infidelity. He would advise them to calm down, think through their problems, and find their own solutions. Embah Selamat was a good listener and often served as a free counselor.

Embah understood magic as derived from nature, which included both an outer aspect (*lahir*) and an unseen, inner reality (*batin*). When talking to me about a *jimat*, he would say that it had power to cure an illness and then explain to me that it symbolized the power of God, who could use it to cure a person if that person really believed. The word *symbol* is a very abstract, modern term suggesting that something operates on multiple levels. Embah saw the *jimat* as a real object of power that could bring about a supernatural result. But as a good Muslim he acknowledged that all power came from God and the success or failure of the cure was in God's hands. His use of the word *symbol*, combined with his basic understanding of psychology, provided a link among the physical object of the *jimat*, the mysterious power of a transcendent God, and the psychosocial needs of his clients. Embah used the different languages of magic, ethical religion, and modern psychology for different audiences and different purposes.

Embah Selamat's practices helped "render a world," which throws the light of contrast on western conceptions of reality. The social imagination revealed in Embah's practices helps us see the moral cosmos in which he lived. Embah inhabited multiple cultural-linguistic systems without any sense of contradiction. His practices made sense of his world and provided the resources for a virtuous life. His practices created meaning. Multiple webs of meaning can make sense of the same experience.

The Meaning of Asceticism in Javanese Mysticism

Three related metaphors clarify why Embah practiced asceticism to obtain power: compensation, balance, and sacrifice. Anderson suggests that in Javanese tradition "ascesis follows the law of compensation that is funda-mental to the Javanese sense of the balance of the cosmos."[15] Spiritual powers are not free; you have to pay for them. You pay with your own suffering. Ascetic practices are a kind of bargaining. You offer God your physical pain and weakness in exchange for something you want. It may be spiritual power or something as simple as the recovery of a sick child. The powers of the spiritual world want to know how serious you are and what you are willing to give up. It is not only the degree of suffering offered. The purity of heart of the petitioner makes a difference. Ascetic practices are a means through which petitioners offer all of themselves to God in exchange for whatever God chooses to give. The mystical ideal of compensation is justice.

There is a balance in the cosmos of good and evil, suffering and happiness, power and weakness. To stave off evil, prevent suffering, or increase power, a mystic maintains the balance by voluntarily accepting evil, suffering, and weakness. Extra weakness in one sphere makes possible extra power in another. There is a light and dark side to everything. If we want the light side, we must be willing to accept the dark as well. Embah often spoke of the suffering and abuse he experienced as a child. Those dark experiences balanced his extraordinary success later.

Sacrifice is another exchange metaphor in which something good is sacrificed in exchange for preventing evil or achieving something better. One Sundanese mystic explained sacrifice as a means of feeding spiritual powers. They need blood. From time to time there are inexplicable disasters in which many people die. The mystic suggested that blood must be shed to appease the powers that inhabit the earth.

Sacrifice is also a form of scapegoating in which the guilt of the many is deflected onto the sacrificial victim. A more sinister form of the sacrifice metaphor is the idea that certain supernatural powers must be paid for with a life. An evil spirit may require the souls of petitioners, or someone close to them, if they are unable to pay in a different way. Some Javanese believed that when Ibu Tien, the wife of President Soeharto died it was because the president had sacrificed her to retain his hold on power.

Language and Religion as Sociolinguistic Systems

The Sapir-Whorf hypothesis suggests that language forms the reality we experience. George Lindbeck views religion as a sociolinguistic symbol system (1984), which cannot be definitively verified or falsified except in terms of its own assumptions and internal coherence. Whether or not a *pusaka* (object of power) actually has a *jin* living in it, is a channel for the power of God, or is a symbol that induces "long-lasting moods and motivations" (Geertz 1973) is a matter of different sociolinguistic systems. If we assume that a western, scientific, empiricist worldview is not "the objective truth" but rather one powerful means of describing experience, then it follows that this language is limited and those within it cannot perceive or experience certain things that are obvious to someone else. The eyes of faith see things that are simply not there for the skeptic. Timothy Morton suggests that every being has limited perception. For example, a human being cannot perceive what a fly perceives and vice versa (2010).

If the worldview of *kebatinan* (inwardness) is not "the truth" but rather only one means of describing experience, then it also follows that the language of supernatural power will not perceive aspects of causation that seem obvious to a "scientific" observer. Embah, like most Indonesians, stands at a meeting point between sociolinguistic systems. In describing different people with similar symptoms as possessed, sinful, or crazy, he shifts between different symbol systems without any sense of incongruity. He happily mixes the categories. All three languages are part of his unified moral cosmos. All three explain reality but with different categories. The categories might not make sense to someone who lives in a different moral order (see Foucault 1997).

Bruce Olson recounts living with members of an isolated tribe in Columbia. He lived with them for several years without leaving their mountain villages. At one point there was serious dysentery spreading through the villages. Olson suspected it was caused by contaminated water. He left his village and traveled for many days to a city where he bought a microscope and disinfectant with which to treat the water. When he got back, he put a drop of water under the microscope and observed the microbes wriggling around like little worms. Then he called the local shaman and asked her to look through the microscope. He said, "Auntie, by looking through this glass, what do you see in the water? Can you see all the little evil spirits that are living in the water?" She observed the tiny creatures with amazement and replied, "Yes, little brother, there are so many evil spirits and they are so lively!" Olson asked if she thought those evil spirits were making people sick. She thought it was likely. He suggested that she try applying a drop of medicine to the water to see what happened. The shaman applied a drop of disinfectant and watched all the wriggling spirits shrivel and die. From then on she went from village to village, praying over the water, chanting her spells, and applying disinfectant to the drinking water. The little evil spirits were driven from the water, and many lives were saved (Olson [1973] 2006).

When Olson showed microbes to a shaman and demonstrated how a powerful medicine could kill "the little spirits that cause disease," he was mixing two sociolinguistic systems, two worldviews. Both languages may be "true" in a sense. The words *evil spirits* and *microbes* are from alternate languages that each contain elements of truth not revealed in the other. In this particular case, the language of science provides a more powerful explanation of the origins of the disease and cure than the language of evil spirits does. That is not necessarily the case for all differences between scientific language and the languages of myth and ritual. A scientific discourse on the psychological benefits of altruism may convey far more superficial meanings than the biblical story of the Good Samaritan. Social imaginaries that include evil spirits may have rich meanings that are lost to a secular imagination. Social imaginaries informed by mimetic, mythic, ethical, and theoretic cognition have richer resources for constructing meaning in life than social imaginaries restricted to materialist assumptions alone do.

Interpretations of Truth in the Powers of a Shaman

There are six ways to interpret the truth of this narrative about a shaman. First, shamans like Embah Selamat may be charlatans. Like the fabled sellers of snake oil, charlatans are out to deceive the gullible. Even if they don't ask for payment, their real goal is to make money. Indonesia has a plethora of print and online tabloids dedicated to mysticism, magic, and all things supernatural. A striking feature of these publications is their advertisements for the services of paranormal shamans. Some of these shamans, like televangelists, have their own TV shows, which are usually aired late at night. The disreputable connotation of the word *dukun* (shaman) is evidence that many Indonesians view shamans as con men. Many Indonesians distinguish between the deceivers and authentic shamans. Even if a shaman's spells and cures do not work, it does not necessarily mean that he or she is a crook. The shaman simply might not be *cocok* (appropriate or fitting) for you. Many Indonesians shop around, looking for a shaman who is *cocok* for them.

Second, some see a shaman like Embah as occupying a liminal space between traditional modes of thinking and scientific rationality. From this perspective, beliefs in magic and spiritual beings are irrational superstitions that are destined to pass away as human beings become more educated. Embah might not be a deceiver but just premodern. A venerable metaphor in social science is that of traditional ways of life giving way to rational, modern, scientific consciousness. For many classical writers, this was not a metaphor but a fact that they strove to understand and explain.[16] More recent social science is rightly suspicious of simplified assumptions that modern consciousness is necessarily more rational than traditional understandings of the world (see Placher 1989:chap. 4).

Third, some believe that a shaman is in touch with a real world of spirits and powers that modern western people are unable to perceive. Materialist cultures are plagued with a particular kind of blindness. They only see the material world that is subject to empirical verification. A shaman has the power to see much more. Modern people have forgotten what was once apparent to most people, especially those trained in mysticism. From this perspective, shamans have real spiritual powers that give them superior perceptions of reality. The popularity of New Age spirituality and Charismatic Christianity in the West is an indication that this view is not confined to Asia or the nonwestern world.

Geertz wrote that if you ask Balinese villagers who have just come out of trance during a Barong dance whether they believe the Barong is real they would look at you like you were crazy (1973:118). They don't believe with a "second naïveté" (Bellah [1970] 1991) because it is useful, culturally meaningful, beautiful, or a form of resistance. They know without doubt that the Barong spirit is real.

Fourth, many Indonesians think that the spirit world is real but religious believers should have nothing to do with it. Their only prayers should be to God. Only God is worthy of reverence. The powers of the shaman come from either evil spirits or other powers that religious believers should avoid. Religious or traditional leaders can cast out evil spirits or heal people of spiritual possession, but ordinary believers should have nothing to do with mystical powers. This explains why a significant percentage of people who indicated on our questionnaire that they "don't believe" in *gaib* (the unseen world) nevertheless believe that spirit possession is real.

Once I attended a Javanese *jatilan* trance dance where the dancers ate glass, acted like animals, and appeared to be in a deep trance. I asked my pious Muslim neighbor, who is a modernist Muslim leader, what he thought of it. He said the dancers were truly possessed by *jins* (*makluk halus*), but they were crude beings who were lower than humans. In his view the dance was *sia-sia* (useless) and debased both the dancers and their audience. I asked if he thought such spirit possession dances should be banned. He said no, but as people became better educated and closer to God they would abandon such useless cultural rituals.

A fifth perspective views the rituals and practices of a shaman as a cultural-linguistic system that symbolically expresses (symbols of) and re-creates (symbols for) the reality experienced by authentic subjects (see Geertz 1973). Anna Tsing's study of Dyak women shamans in the Meratus mountains of South Kalimantan interprets their language and practices as expressions of the oppression experienced by doubly marginalized people in "out of the way places" (1993). As Dyak followers of the Kaharingan tribal religion, the shamans are marginalized by the dominant religious, ethnic, and economic classes of Indonesia (e.g., Muslim, Javanese, or Banjar). As women shamans they are further marginalized in their own tribe, in which shamans are typically male.[17] Tsing shows how the women creatively adapt different vocabularies from the groups that oppress them (e.g., government officials, Islamic teachers, or male shamans) in order to survive and create a space in which to exist. Even though Dyak Kaharingan shamans were traditionally women, patriarchal structures of official religion have separated the role of "priest" (*basir*) from that of "spirit medium" (*pendita*). Currently all the priests (*basir*) are male.

Michael Taussig, weaves together shamanic rituals and colonial, postcolonial, and Catholic practices of power and oppression in Colombia. (1991). Shamanic "wild men" use their altered states of consciousness to create different kinds of power in resistance to the hegemonic powers of the colonial and postcolonial political and religious order. Taussig describes his own project as

> the politics of epistemic murk and the fiction of the real, in the creation of Indians, in the role of the myth and magic in colonial violence as much as in its healing, and in the way that healing can mobilize terror in order to subvert it … through the tripping up of power in its own disorderliness. That is why my subject is not the truth of being but the *social being* of truth, not

whether facts are real but what the politics of their interpretation and representation are. (XIII).

Taussig points to the sociopolitical reality of practices regardless of their "truth." Sometimes, if there is a question that cannot be answered, it makes sense to ask a different question. Neither Tsing nor Taussig addresses the question of whether or not the metaphysical realities assumed in the shaman's practices really exist. They assume that the practices are real and that they render a bitter social reality. They are a means of both oppression and resistance. They are "weapons of the weak" wielded against their oppressors (Scott 1985). Their social reality is powerful enough without our speculating about the efficacy of trance, drugs, or magic in the material world. With Michel Foucault, they assume that knowledge creates power and power knowledge. By practicing "unauthorized" systems of knowledge and power, the shamans create "hidden transcripts" or "tactics" that are not subject to the hegemonic control of the power elite (Scott 2012; see also de Certeau 1984).

This perspective breaks through the epistemological dilemma of how to verify or falsify that which is inherently unverifiable and unfalsifiable. It affirms the symbolic power of alternative discourses without bringing a positivist judgment on their account of what is real. Shamanic practices play a powerful mimetic role in resisting and subverting oppressive power structures. Their stories are myths that reveal a deeper truth.

The discourses of Taussig and Tsing would hardly be comprehensible to the subjects of their research. A postmodern, postcolonial perspective is tolerant and nonjudgmental, but it is a view from the outside (*etic*), which implies that social scientists are not a part of the phenomena under consideration. They can choose not to judge because the practices of a sacred cosmos are not integral to their own social imaginaries. The same neutrality might not be possible for someone who is fully a part of the community.

Sixth, there is a perspective from within (*emic*). Most Indonesians live in a sacred cosmos not because of its political or social power in resisting the hegemony of the powerful. Rather they really believe that they are in the hands of God and surrounded by spirits and powers who inhabit sacred space in the real world. The tenets of a sacred cosmos are consistent with teachings of their religions. They may not believe in all aspects of a sacred cosmos, but they don't doubt its basic existence. Their social imaginaries are hybrid, combining scientific, religious, and traditional imaginaries.

Every social scientist has a standpoint. There is no neutral ground unaffected by the perspective of the analyst. I am part of what I am studying. I am part of the 98 percent of Indonesians who live to some degree within a sacred cosmos. The term *participant observer* assumes that the social scientist is a secular observer who uses participation as a strategy to get closer to the objects of observation. I am a participant observer, but my primary identity is as a participant in Indonesian social history. "Observer" implies the ability to stand back and observe as honestly and critically as possible. Theoretical analysis demands distance, which facilitates the ability to understand without bias. I try to do that without forgetting that my perspective is shaped by identification with Indonesia as my home. Participation is not just a strategy to enrich observation; observation is my strategy for understanding the community of which I am a part.

Like most Indonesians, my perspective is hybrid. I believe less about a sacred cosmos than many colleagues and more than others. Perception is influenced by participation in legitimation structures. It is easier to experience a sacred cosmos in Indonesia because you are surrounded by people and legitimation structures that reinforce its reality. Nevertheless, I find it difficult to believe anything with a "first naïveté." "Historical consciousness" stimulates awareness that everything I feel, think, and experience is the product of a historical process (Gadamer 1979).

Conclusions

Not all Indonesians live in a sacred cosmos, just as not all westerners live in an impersonal universe. In Indonesia modernization is accompanied by increasing religious piety but also rationalization and "disenchantment." In Flores we had an interesting conversation with three highly educated priests. One deeply believed in the power of the unseen world. He gladly performed rituals to maintain cosmic balance. The second priest half believed. He believed but had doubts. He lived in a sacred cosmos but believed with a "second naïveté," having doubts but choosing to practice his traditions because they made sense of his life. The third stated frankly that he did not believe in spirits or supernatural beings. He felt that such beliefs were incompatible with modern education. He still performed mimetic cosmic rituals, for example, to prevent a bad dream from coming true, because the people in his parish would be upset if he did not.

The three priests are convenient ideal types for all Indonesians: those who fully live within a sacred cosmos (first naïveté), those who half believe and continue the practices (second naïveté), and those who don't believe in unseen powers other than God. They may or may not interpret mimetic rituals in rationalist terms as socially useful. I suspect that increasing numbers of Indonesians are aligned with the second priest.

The following chapter explores the link between religious "modernization" (or rationalization) and disenchantment. Based on empirical research in various parts of Indonesia, it interprets the evidence on whether or not "disenchantment" is really happening and if it is related to the conservative, "modernist" turn in Indonesia.

5

Islamic Modernism and Disenchantment

The fate of our times is characterized by rationalization and intellectualization and, above all, by the disenchantment of the world.
— Max Weber

Is There a Link between Islamic Modernism and Disenchantment?

THE BIRTH OF SECULAR MODERNITY in the West included rejection of a dialectical relation between the rational demands of ethical religion and the ritualistic management of unseen powers. Reformed Christianity tried to unify ethical religion with a scientific conception of the natural world based on belief in prophetic revelation and rationally ordered creation. In Indonesia, Islamic modernism also seeks to cleanse religion of magic and rituals that show reverence toward powers other than God. Islam is also a highly ethical religion with a strong emphasis on law and morality. This chapter asks What is the impact of Islamic modernism on experience of a sacred cosmos in Indonesia?

Increasing education, modernization, and science did not bring secularization to Indonesia. Indonesia is both modern and deeply religious. However, it is less clear whether or not it is becoming more "disenchanted." Increasing religious piety is compatible with modern scientific rationality (see Berger 1999). In fact modernist religion is often a vehicle for promoting scientific rationality at the expense of the experience of living in a sacred cosmos. Modern education and institutional structures of theoretical knowledge may be undermining belief in the unseen powers of a sacred cosmos. Ironically, as in seventeenth-century Europe and America, the strongest forces for disenchantment in Indonesia may be religious.

While the European Reformation and Enlightenment were homegrown reform movements that appeared to promise utopia through science and true religion, both western science and Islamic modernist reform in Southeast Asia are foreign imports. In a postcolonial age there is widespread skepticism about foreign imports, especially from the West but also from the Middle East.[1] Some Indonesians may appear to accept both Islamic modernism and western science without allowing either to change their experience of the unseen world. Even though there has been a huge increase in emphasis on personal, individuated devotion and obedience to the orthodox demands of religion, collective rituals to maintain cosmic and communal order are still common.

My initial hypothesis was that modernist Islam (e.g., Muhammadiyah) is a powerful force for disenchantment, somewhat similar to the Reformation in Europe. According to this hypothesis, disenchantment means loss of the vital experience of living in a sacred cosmos. This process may be stimulated by modern science and education, but it is legitimized by a modernist, Islamic attack on magic and all interactions with the unseen world (apart from God). Just as Weber argued that not only material factors influenced the rise of modern capitalism but rather the construction of a whole new Protestant ethos, so I wondered if Indonesia was experiencing disenchantment as a result of a new, modernist Islamic ethos that separates "magic and beliefs" from "religion." This hypothesis was strengthened by the fact that the Indonesian government has not acknowledged indigenous tribal religions (*agama suku*) as "religions" but rather categorized them as cultural beliefs (*kepercayaan*). They are widely perceived as primitive practices (animism, magic) that are destined to pass away as they are replaced by true "world religions." Recently the Constitutional Court ruled that indigenous religions (*agama suku*) should have the right to list their group in the religion column of their national identity card (KTP). This was a major victory for the rights of indigenous peoples, but it is too early to tell how it will affect how the government treats "local beliefs."

It is impossible to prove whether the hypothesis of modernist Islam bringing disenchantment is true because it is based on ideal types. There are no such things as pure modernist or traditionalist Muslims. Likewise there is no such thing as purely "living in a sacred cosmos" or purely "living in a disenchanted universe." Animism, tribal religions, and magic are also ideal types that include a huge variety of beliefs and practices, including modern practices and influences from world religions. These ideal types simplify a million different variations on how human communities construct their imagination of reality. Nevertheless, it is possible to make a strong rational argument based on ideal types. My goal is not proof but rather a convincing interpretation of Islam and disenchantment that is grounded in both theory and empirical evidence. The evidence presented in this chapter suggests that most Indonesians still live in a sacred cosmos and that modernist Islam has not had as much impact on beliefs in an unseen world as I initially suspected. This conclusion is strengthened by the interviews presented in the following chapter.

The first part of this chapter explores how the concepts of religion and magic were constructed in the West and particularly influenced by the thought of Max Weber. We also examine how the distinction between religion and magic has been integrated with Islamic and Indonesian understandings of modernity. The second part of the chapter summarizes the statistical results of our empirical research on beliefs and practices related to a sacred cosmos in Indonesia. The broad question of the chapter is whether Islamic modernism has stimulated a progressive disenchantment with the world for most Indonesians. We explore this question with reference to people's experience of an unseen world of spirits, communication through dreams, understanding of spirit possession, and affirmation of a moral meaning behind accidents and illness.

Modern Constructions of a Dichotomy between Religion and Magic

The idea of disenchantment, like the idea that magic is separate from religion, is modern. Max Weber was the first to use the word *disenchantment* in a famous lecture titled "Science as a Vocation" in 1917 at Munich University (Weber 1946; see also Veer 2014:118). Weber believed that modernity is defined by rational analysis of all reality and the progressive disenchantment of the world (*entzauberung*). He wrote, "Not anymore, like the savages, for whom there were such (uncontrollable) powers does one have to resort to magical means to control the spirits or to supplicate them. But technical means and calculation can do this. Above all, this implies intellectualization as such." Peter van der Veer suggests that Weber was above all a theorist of "disenchantment" (rather than secularization). One of Weber's most original contributions was to suggest that religion itself, through the rationalizing process of the Protestant Reformation, could be a powerful force for disenchantment. Protestantism attacked "superstition" and the community-defining sacramental rituals of Catholicism, thereby opening the door to rationalization and individualized ethical religion.

Weber developed a popular evolutionary theory of religion that was proposed by the influential nineteenth-century pioneers of anthropology and comparative religion Edward Tyler and his disciple James Frazer. According to this theory, animism and magic are the original "primitive" forms of religion. Magic is just primitive science through which human beings attempt to explain and control powers that are beyond their understanding. With developing technology and the growth of cities, individualistic magic evolves into priestly religion, which includes professional leaders who mediate with the gods on behalf of the society. Further rationalization takes place as belief in many gods and powers gives way to belief in one great God over all (monotheism). Monotheism justifies the centralization of power. But increasing rationalization leads to the rise of prophetic religion, in which prophets stand up to corrupted power in the name of a higher ethical code revealed by God. Thus is born a rationalized, ethical religion. Tyler, Frazer, Weber, and many generations of social scientists since believed that it was only a matter of time before ethical religion itself would be replaced by scientific rationality (secularization).

The universal category of "religion," as an umbrella under which animism, Confucianism, Taoism, Hinduism, Buddhism, Jainism, Judaism, Christianity, Islam, Baha'i, and so on could all be gathered as particular instances of the same thing (i.e., "world religion"), is itself a modern idea born of Platonic and Enlightenment ideas of universal truth. "Religion," as a category, rose out of a theory of religious evolution and the comparative study of religions as an academic discipline (Veer 2014). It also took place within a context of western, post-Christian, secular intellectuals who no longer believed in God but nonetheless derived their understanding of religion from Christianity (Asad 1993).

Modernist Muslim Constructions of Religion

In Indonesia the idea of religion as a universal category found fertile ground in both Islam and the national ideology. Islamic teaching suggests that the oneness of God was revealed in imperfect ways through many different prophets, culminating in the final and most perfect revelation through the Prophet Muhammad. This enables Muslims to define all religions as good, at least if they are monotheistic. All monotheistic religions that existed prior to the Prophet Muhammad are from God. The national ideology of Pancasila makes the goodness of all monotheistic religions the first principle on which is founded the nation-state of Indonesia. A very broad and liberal definition of *monotheism* allows the nation to include Buddhists, Hindus, and Confucianists, as well as Christians, within this framework, thus enabling national unity that includes the overwhelming majority of Indonesians.

Modern ideas of an evolutionary division between magic (defined as superstition or false science) and ethical religion (defined as rational and modern) was an Enlightenment project to find universal truth at the height of the western imperial age of colonialism. A theory of the evolution of religion was part of a theory of the evolution of human civilization. Western Europe believed itself to be the apex of civilization, as proved by its subjugation of most of the world through colonial imperialism. Similarly, Christianity was considered the apex of religion, cleansed of superstition. Christianity proved to be an important moral justification for western imperialism, even though the relationship between the two was often strained.

The irony of the complex connections between Christianity and imperialism is exemplified by the Opium Wars between Britain and China. When China was defeated, the British forced China to open its doors to opium, trade, and Christian missionaries. The missionaries then became moral crusaders opposing opium and the worst aspects of colonial exploitation. They were also powerful advocates for modern education and science, including the ending of "primitive superstitions" (Veer 2014). Their civilizing mission provided justification for colonial domination even while opposing some of its worst excesses.

A dichotomy between magic and religion was not an original part of Islam. The unseen cosmos of supernatural powers, including *jins*, ghosts, and spirits, is assumed in the Koran and Sunnah, just as it is in the scriptures of Christianity, Hinduism, and Buddhism. It is a vital part of the religion practiced by many Muslims and other religious communities in Indonesia today. The division of magic and religion fit well with Indonesian strategies for nation building and modernization. World religions were distinguished from "tribal religions," which were demoted to the status of primitive, or "prereligious," cultural beliefs.

Indonesian Islam also experienced a "Reformation," which included some of the same currents as the Protestant Reformation in Europe. The movement in Indonesia is called "modernist Islam." As with the Protestant Reformation, modernist Islam seeks to cleanse Islam of superstition and accretions of traditions that are not warranted in the original revelation (*sola scriptura*). Modernist Islam believes that new (modern) interpretations of Scripture (*ijtihad*) are valid as long as they are rational and do not violate its original intent. But *bid'ah* (innovations not warranted by Scripture) and *syirik* (anything that tends toward polytheism or the worship of powers other than God) are forbidden. Like the Puritan reformers in Europe, Muslim reformers forbade interaction with the unseen world, not because they believed it was unreal or an irrational myth but because they believed that only God should be worshiped.

Just as the Protestant Reformation was fed by rapidly changing social, economic, and political factors in Europe, so Islamic modernism is fed by the same familiar narratives of nationalism, progress, and scientific modernization. According to this narrative, disenchantment is not an exclusively European phenomenon but a universal movement of increasing rationality. It is a necessary part of becoming "modern." Evolutionary narratives of religion can be assimilated into Islam, especially those that marginalize practices associated with "uncivilized," animistic, or magical practices that lack koranic validation. Those who still worship ancestors, appease spirits, guard cosmic balance through rituals, and practice magic are not defined as following another religion but rather as not yet religious (*belum beragama*). They are *kafir* (pagans).

This explains an event that initially puzzled me. During the Soeharto era, even though Christian missionary work was severely curtailed in Muslim Java, the government gave Christian missionaries permission to operate in the highlands of Sulawesi. The "animist" peoples in the mountains were considered not yet religious. From the perspective of Muslim officials, conversion to Christianity would be better than not having any religion. Christians brought modernity, development, and monotheism to "primitive" people. Later they could make even more progress toward civilization by converting to Islam.

Much has been written about the "civilizing mission" of western colonialism. Britain, Portugal, France, and Spain justified worldwide imperialism on the basis of spreading civilization, including Christianity, to uncivilized peoples. By end of the nineteenth century, the Netherlands had become more cynical about its role in the Dutch East Indies, which was defined not as a missionary field but as a "field for profit taking." With the exception of the Moluccan Islands (Spice Islands), the Dutch did not allow mission work with "natives." They recognized Islam as a potentially powerful unifying force of opposition and did not want missionaries to upset the delicate balances of power that enabled them to divide and conquer.

The most serious challenges to Dutch domination of Indonesia came from "holy wars" fought under the banner of Islam. These included the Padri Wars in Minangkabau (1821–38), under the leadership of Imam Bonjol and Haji Miskin; the Java War (1825–30), led by Prince Diponegoro in Yogyakarta; the Banten Tjilegon Uprisings (1888), led by Haji Wasit and Tubagus Haji Ismail; and the bloodiest of all, the Holy Wars of Aceh (1873–1904), which left tens of thousands dead.

In part because of the horrendous news of massacres of whole villages by the colonial army in Aceh and reports of extreme poverty in Java, the Netherlands acquired a conscience and declared an "Ethical Policy" in 1901. This policy opened Indonesia to missionaries and led to the establishment of schools and hospitals in many parts of the country. The Ethical Policy was originally intended to improve the material conditions of the people by returning some of the wealth that had been taken out of Indonesia since 1867. However, the policy was underfunded and sometimes opposed by Dutch colonial officials. It was marred by paternalism and cultural chauvinism. It had limited success and was largely abandoned by the end of the 1920s when the Great Depression hit. Nevertheless, it helped stimulate a modernist Muslim reaction, in part because of the effectiveness of Protestant and Catholic missionaries in founding modern schools.

In 1912 Haji Ahmad Dahlan founded Muhammadiyah in Yogyakarta. Leaders of Muhammadiyah believe that the Ethical Policy was actually a secret systematic attack on Islam in Indonesia constructed by the sophisticated

Dutch missionary and orientalist Christiaan Snouck Hurgronje.[2] The attack had two faces. The first was a wave of cultural westernization and Christianization directed toward the elite through modern education. The second the encouragement of syncretistic, Hindu-influenced Islam among the masses of poor people. This included encouraging superstitious, animist practices and rituals that are not authorized in Islam (*bid'ah*). Muhammadiyah was founded to counteract both threats by simultaneously purifying Islam of superstition and heretical practices and providing modern, rational education in an orthodox Islamic context. Purification of Islam required a rational, modern interpretation of the Koran and Sunnah.[3] Islamic modernism, as represented by Muhammadiyah, was a counter "civilizing mission" meant to prevent Christianization and guide people away from the primitive magical practices of Islam toward true, universal, ethical Islam. As such it unconsciously absorbed the western dichotomy between magic and religion.

When I came to Indonesia, one of my first surprises was to discover that my assumed categories about the meaning of *traditional* and *modern* did not apply. Nahdlatul Ulama was referred to as traditionalist Islam, while Muhammadiyah was called modernist Islam. In the West, the term *traditional Christians* would describe fundamentalist or conservative Christians who believe in the infallibility of the Bible. Conversely, the modernist movement in Christianity was powered by liberals who were open to new interpretations of the faith. In Indonesia the categories are not exactly reversed, but they go by a completely different logic.

Traditionalist Islam (NU) includes many who are very open to new interpretations and practices. They are traditionalist in that they value the traditional, unique practices of Islam in Indonesia and reject calls for a return to a "pure" (Arab) form of Islam. They are not scriptural literalists but are open to and tolerant of a great variety of beliefs and practices that conservative Muslims consider *bid'ah* (without scriptural warrant) or *syirik* (polytheistic). Nahdlatul Ulama was founded in 1926 to explicitly counteract Muhammadiyah and oppose the domination of Wahabi Arab Islam. It denied that Muhammadiyah represented Indonesian Islam and pledged to uphold freedom of Islamic belief and to preserve the traditional Islamic practices of Indonesia. Today many young NU intellectuals are attracted to postmodern thought and deconstructionism. Nahdlatul Ulama claims that it has forty to fifty million members and owns around seven thousand boarding schools and forty-four universities. In addition it is heavily represented in state-funded universities and institutes of Islamic studies, as well as Muhammadiyah-owned institutions.[4]

In contrast, many of those affiliated with modernist Muhammadiyah are far more conservative in both doctrine and practice. They are generally scripturalists who want to follow the letter of the law as revealed in the Koran and Sunnah and interpreted by modern reason. They are open to modern principles of interpretation as long as the goal is to discover the original meaning of the text. Their emphasis is not on blindly following the Koran and Sunnah but rather on using reason and science to reinterpret Scripture in ways that are both faithful to the text and appropriate for the modern day. Because of their emphasis on reason and science, their strongest emphasis is on modern education. Currently Muhammadiyah has about thirty million members and operates more than 10,000 schools and 172 universities and colleges throughout Indonesia.

Muhammadiyah and NU are massive, vital, civil society organizations, both of which oppose radicalism and the use of violence in the name of religion. Together they resist attempts to turn Indonesia into an Islamic state. They also reject secularism. Instead they think Indonesia should be a monotheistic state that respects religious freedom and human rights. Some scholars think both NU and Muhammadiyah are losing influence because they have been unable to convert their massive numbers into electoral victories. An alternate interpretation is that they are victims of their own success. Each is so massive and influential that it includes tremendous diversity. Unlike in the past when people voted more along the lines of primordial ethnic and religious affiliation, blindly following the instructions of their leaders, now Indonesians are much more independent, ignoring parties and primordial identities to follow their individual consciences.

Empirical Research on a Sacred Cosmos in Indonesia

This book suggests that most Indonesians live in a sacred cosmos. However, I wondered to what extent the vigorous movement of Muslim modernism is undermining or even eliminating the experience of living in a sacred cosmos. Is disenchantment a general phenomenon for all religious and ethnic groups in Indonesia? Do most Indonesians prefer scientific reason to supernatural or religious language to describe their experience of reality? For those who prefer modern, scientific symbol systems, does that imply that they no longer believe in an unseen world of supernatural powers? Is Islamic modernism the major factor influencing disenchantment in Indonesia? Are Muslims more disenchanted than non-Muslims? How does ethnicity affect disenchantment? Which is stronger, the correlation between religion and disenchantment or the correlation between ethnicity and disenchantment?

In part to find answers to these questions, we constructed a questionnaire with twenty-one questions, not including demographic data (see appendices I and II). Seven of the questions are directly related to living in a sacred cosmos and disenchantment. In this chapter I summarize the responses to four of these questions, including experience of a world of supernatural spirits and powers, communications through dreams, interpreting the meaning of spirit possession, and finding moral meaning in "natural" events such as accidents and illnesses. In each of the questions, respondents were asked to choose their preferred response between answers that used modern scientific language, religious language, or the language of traditional Indonesian beliefs. For most questions, the answers are not mutually exclusive. They are intended to discover which of the symbol systems is closest to each respondent's imagination.

Our questionnaire was completed by 2,492 participants. These included Muslims, Protestants, Catholics, Hindus, and Buddhists from around fifty different ethnic groups. [5]

In the following sections we summarize the statistical results for four of the questions. A more detailed analysis of the statistical data is discussed in appendix III. Interpretation of the answers to the questions on these topics is not simple. They were not intended to indicate the absolute beliefs or experiences of the respondents but rather whether they explained the respondents' experience with modern rationalistic language, religious language, or language that corresponds to more traditional, indigenous experiences of the unseen world. In many cases the respondents felt that all three languages expressed their feelings, but they chose the language that felt most appropriate to their imagination of what is real or true. What follows are the questions.

The Unseen World and Scientific Reason

Question II.D on experience of the unseen world

Which of the following best expresses your experience?

1. I often experience the presence of spiritual powers around me, such as spirits of ancestors, *jins*, ghosts, and other spirits, etc.

2. Sometimes I experience miracles, angels or God's supernatural protection.

3. I never experience supernatural, mystical events. I think it is better to use science and rationality to understand the mysteries of life.

The responses to this question suggest that most Indonesians believe that the unseen world exists but many fewer experience direct communication with unseen powers. About 36 percent replied that they had never had a supernatural experience with the unseen world (*gaib*) and did not believe in it. Fifty-two percent had had supernatural experiences but framed them in religious terms as encounters with God or angels. Only 12 percent said that they had frequent awareness of or communication with the unseen world. Thus 64 percent reported that they had experienced communication with unseen spiritual powers while 36 percent were skeptics. However, of these, 80 percent showed in their answers to other questions that they believed the spiritual, unseen world exists but thought they should have nothing to do with it.

The perception that the unseen world of mysterious powers (*gaib*) is real but religious believers should not "believe" in it or participate in utilizing its powers was revealed by an interesting anomaly in our research. Out of 2,492 respondents, more than a third said they had never experienced the unseen world of mysterious powers, that they did not believe in it, and that we should use reason and science to understand the mysteries of life. However, of the 36 percent who chose this "modern" rationalist answer concerning the unseen world, more than 55 percent believed that spirit possession is real and spirits should be controlled by either traditional leaders (37 percent) or religious leaders (18 percent). On the basis of just these two questions, it appears that only 16 percent of the 2,492 respondents did not believe that the world of spirits is real. Thus 84 percent of Indonesians believe in some form of communication with the unseen world. Even of the

16 percent who said they did not believe in spirits, most believed that God spoke to them through dreams, sickness, or natural disasters.

Taking into consideration their answers to other questions, apparently only 5 to 6 percent or less of Indonesians do not believe that an unseen world exists (36 percent minus 80 percent of 36 percent = 6 percent). This is consistent with the judgment of the Islamic leaders interviewed in chapter 6. Even those who doubted the existence of an unseen world apart from God said that they were a small minority. They said the vast majority of Muslims believe in unseen spirits.

Most Indonesians (52 percent) interpret their experience of the supernatural through the language of religion and God. Thirty-six percent chose the scientific language of reason. This means that 88 percent preferred either religious or scientific language. It is hard to determine from these data whether or not Islamic modernism is the major factor influencing the preference for these two symbol systems. Both Muslims and non-Muslims equally preferred these two languages. In fact non-Muslims had a significantly higher preference (56 percent) for religious language than Muslims did (46 percent). That might mean Islamic modernism has a minimal effect. But it could also mean that Islamic modernism has influenced the preferred language of 88 percent of Muslims while other kinds of religious

Table 5.1 *Responses to Question II.D on the Unseen World*

	Java Muslims	Java Non-Muslims	Molucca Muslims	Molucca Non-Muslims	Indonesia Muslims	Indonesia Non-Muslims
Traditional language: often, spirits	8%	11%	19%	14%	12%	12%
Scientific language: never, use reason	42%	44%	45%	44%	42%	32%
Religious language: sometimes, God	50%	44%	36%	42%	46%	56%
Religious or scientific language	92%	88%	81%	86%	88%	88%
Totals	100%	100%	100%	100%	100%	100%

modernism have influenced 88 percent of non-Muslims. Of course there are other variables as well. The fact that the great majority of our respondents were well educated is certainly a factor. Another factor is ethnicity. The statistics show that ethnicity has a significant influence on the symbol systems people prefer.

Dreams and the Unconscious

During our research we heard many stories about supernatural communication through dreams. The stories came from people from all ethnic and religious groups. Former President Abdurrahman Wahid (Gus Dur) famously made many decisions based on dreams. Many people believe that dreams often warn of an impending death or accident. Nevertheless, the results of our empirical research do not support the conclusion that many Indonesians rely on dreams for reliable information about the mundane

Table 5.2 *Muslim Responses to Question II.D (Gaib) by Ethnic Group*

Ethnic Groups	Traditional Frequent *Gaib* Experience	Modern Never Don't Believe	Religious Occasional God's Presence	Modern/ Religious
Java/Madura	8%	42%	50%	92%
Sunda	10%	51%	39%	90%
Makassar/Bugis	8%	38%	54%	92%
Minang/West Sumatra	14%	44%	42%	86%
Aceh	20%	38%	42%	80%
All Indonesian Muslims	12%	42%	46%	88%
All Indonesian Non-Muslims	12%	32%	56%	88%
All Indonesians	12%	36%	52%	88%

world. The statistics from across Indonesia are summarized in this section. More analysis can be found in appendix III.

How do you think we should interpret dreams?

1. Dreams are usually the product of our own, psychological processes. However, sometimes God or unseen powers speak to me in dreams.

2. Dreams are all in our head. They are simply psychological expressions of our unconscious mind.

3. God and/or other spiritual powers often speak to me in dreams. Dreams are an important source of communication and knowledge about the real world.

In spite of anecdotal evidence, most Indonesians do not frequently receive communication through dreams. In our interviews we discovered that Indonesians like to tell stories about one or more times when they had a remarkable dream that came true. However a majority (60 percent) believe that dreams are just a psychological process within our own minds. Less than half of non-Muslims (48 percent) have had dream experiences that they believe are communications from outside their minds.

Table 5.3 *Responses by Religion to Question II.E on the Meaning of Dreams*

Religions	Traditional Frequent Experience	Modern Never, Purely Psychological	Religious Occasional God Speaks	Modern/ Religious	Traditional/ Religious	Total
Muslims	8% 105	60% 766	32% 402	92% 1,168	40% 507	100% 1,273
Protestants	9% 66	45% 332	46% 335	91% 667	55% 401	100% 773
Catholics	23% 44	53% 102	24% 47	77% 149	57% 91	100% 193
Hindus	17% 44	55% 138	28% 70	83% 208	45% 114	100% 252
Buddhists	—	—	100% 2	100% 2	100% 2	100% 2
All Non-Muslims	13% 154	48% 572	39% 454	87% 1,026	52% 608	100% 1,180

In my interview with Syafi'i Ma'arif (see chapter 6), his first response was to say that he absolutely did not believe in dreams. But after reflection he revised his answer to acknowledge that there may be exceptional people who receive communication through dreams, citing the example of Jacob in the Scriptures. This example shows that even those who say that dreams are purely a psychological process might not rule out the possibility that some people receive communications that way.

The prevalence of modern psychological answers suggests that modern Freudian ideas about the unconscious mind are widespread in Indonesia, at least among those who are well educated. Since more people from all ethnic groups and religions preferred psychological answers over religious answers, this may be interpreted to mean that modern ideas have a stronger influence than Islamic modernism.

Religious differences are significant. More non-Muslims experience supernatural messages through dreams (52 percent) than Muslims do (40 percent). There are certain standard stories of symbolic correlations between dreams and reality that transcend religious and ethnic boundaries. For example, some Muslims and Christians believe that if you dream that you

Table 5.4 *Muslim Responses to Question II.E (Dreams) by Ethnic Group*

Ethnic Groups	Traditional	Modern	Religious	Modern/ Religious	Traditional/ Religious
Java/Madura	7%	58%	35%	93%	42%
Sunda	8%	60%	32%	92%	40%
Makassar/Bugis	5%	62%	33%	95%	38%
Minang/West Sumatra	7%	67%	26%	93%	33%
Aceh	18%	56%	26%	82%	44%
All Indonesian Muslims	9%	60%	31%	91%	40%
All Indonesian Non-Muslims	14%	48%	38%	86%	52%
All Indonesians	11%	54%	35%	89%	46%

break a tooth it means someone close to you will die. Some ethnic groups have religious rituals that people can perform to prevent a bad dream from coming true.

Ethnic differences don't seem to be much of a factor, at least among Muslims. The statistics from different Muslim ethnic groups are remarkably similar. The one exception is Aceh, where 20 percent of people said they frequently receive messages through dreams. But even in Aceh, 38 percent gave a modern, psychological interpretation. Cultural differences may be a significant factor, especially when combined with religion. While Javanese and Moluccans are virtually identical in their experience of meaning in dreams, non-Muslims outside Java have a higher percentage of belief in dreams than Muslims do for the whole country.

An interesting anomaly in our research is that of the 11 percent who relied on dreams for frequent communication about the outside world a significant number did not believe in spirit possession as it was framed in the question If all the students in a high school class lost normal consciousness and did not know who they were, how should such an event be interpreted and faced? For the relatively small group who often experienced communication through dreams, 71 percent expressed belief in spirit possession while 29 percent thought it was a psychological phenomenon. This 29 percent is interesting because it seems to indicate that frequent experience of communication through dreams does not necessarily correlate with belief in spirit possession. In follow-up interviews we discovered that some respondents who thought that the above situation was probably the result of mass hysteria nevertheless thought that individual spirit possession was very real.

Spirit Possession and Psychology

If all the students in a high school class lost normal consciousness and did not know who they were, how should such an event be interpreted and faced?

1. This is possession by an evil spirit, which should be exorcised by a religious leader.
2. This is mass hysteria and a doctor of psychology should be called.
3. This is spiritual possession, which can be controlled by a shaman or paranormal.

The religious answer (no. 1, evil spirit possession) and the traditional answer (no. 3, spirit possession) equally indicate belief in spirit possession. The difference is in whether or not the spirit is labeled evil and whether a paranormal/shaman or a religious leader should handle it.

An expert informant from Flores said that the framing of this question revealed a Java bias. He is a *tokoh* (expert) in Manggarai *adat* (traditions from the Manggarai area of Flores) and a retired principal of a public high school. According to him, mass possession of school children is a Java phenomenon that he believes is purely psychological. Therefore he chose the modern psychological answer to this question. He does not doubt that possession by spirits is real, but he believes it is an individual phenomenon. He then told me the dramatic story of an incident in which one of the students in his school was possessed by a spirit. The boy not only did not know himself and spoke in a different voice, but he also had superhuman strength and could lift things that even a very strong man would be unable to budge. This made the situation quite dangerous for my respondent. If he dealt with it wrongly, he could be killed. He brought the boy into his office with him alone. He prayed for him and politely asked the spirit to leave. Fortunately, in this situation he was successful and the boy was restored to his normal mind.

In some parts of Indonesia, shamans routinely go into trance and claim to be possessed by a spirit, often by one of their ancestors. In the Dyak Kaharingan religion, shamans are distinguished from religious leaders. Shamans are traditionally women who bring messages to the people from

Table 5.5 *Javanese and Moluccan Responses to Question II.F on Spirit Possession*

	Javanese Muslims	Javanese Non-Muslims	Moluccan Muslims	Moluccan Non-Muslims	Indonesian Muslims	Indonesian Non-Muslims
Traditional spirit possession	38%	18%	33%	53%	42%	42%
Psychological explanation	40%	69%	33%	34%	34%	40%
Religious evil spirit	22%	13%	34%	13%	24%	18%
Religious or traditional	60%	31%	67%	66%	66%	60%

the ancestors. Religious leaders may also experience trance/possession, but their main role is to lead the community in the performance of rituals that maintain a proper relation with unseen powers.

The "Java bias" in the questionnaire, which asks about mass possession rather than possession of an individual shaman, means that some respondents who chose the modern psychological answer also believe in spirit possession by individuals. Nevertheless, even with this limitation, the statistics show that belief in spirit possession is high in Indonesia.

Sixty-five percent of Indonesians from all ethnic and religious groups believe that spirits really do possess people. Of these believers, traditional language which does not label the spirits as evil, is twice as popular (43 percent) as religious language about evil spirits (22 percent). In many parts of Indonesia, there is a balance or competition for power between religious and traditional (*adat*) leaders. Our research suggests that when it comes to spirit possession, most people prefer to call on the *adat* leader or shaman, rather than the religious leader. Not having watched too many Western

Table 5.6 *Muslim Responses to Question II.F (Spirit Possession) by Ethnic Group*

Ethnic Groups	Traditional Spirit Possession	Modern Psychological	Religious Evil Spirit	Traditional/ Religious
Java/Madura	38%	40%	22%	60%
Sunda	36%	40%	24%	60%
Makassar/Bugis	49%	33%	18%	67%
Minang/West Sumatra	51%	28%	21%	72%
Aceh	41%	32%	27%	68%
All Indonesian Muslims	43%	34%	23%	66%
All Indonesian Non-Muslims	42%	38%	20%	62%
All Indonesians	43%	35%	22%	65%

horror films about possession (!), they do not see spirit possession as necessarily a bad thing. As in the story related earlier about the young Flores man possessed by his grandmother, possession may be by the spirits of ancestors who just want to communicate with the living community.[6]

There is remarkable similarity in the ratios of belief and disbelief from all different religious and ethnic groups, indicating that belief in spirit possession is not much affected by religion or ethnicity. However people from the island of Java (Javanese and Sundanese) are slightly more skeptical (40 percent) than the norm (35 percent). Meanwhile people from Minang/West Sumatra have the highest percentage of belief (72 percent) compared to the norm (65 percent).

Meaning of Sickness or Accidents and Natural Causation

If you experienced a serious accident or unusual illness, what might it mean?

1. Accidents and sickness don't have any particular meaning. They happen by accident and just mean you are unlucky.

2. It may mean that you are under attack by an evil spirit or spiritual power.

3. Perhaps the suffering is God's way of speaking to and reminding you.

Our research suggests that the great majority of Indonesians still believe that "natural events" have personal or social meaning. A very high percentage of people from all religious and ethnic groups believe there is meaning in serious accidents or illness (86 percent). A very low percentage (5 percent) attributed suffering caused by serious accidents or illness to spiritual attacks (with the partial exception of Aceh, with 11 percent). Only 14 percent of Indonesians felt that sickness or accidents were purely the result of natural causes and had no meaning.

The low percentages choosing the traditional and modern responses should not be overinterpreted. As I have shown, the large majority who see illness or accidents as ways in which God speaks to us (81 percent) do not necessarily reject the idea that illness or accidents also have natural causes or that they may sometimes be caused by spiritual attack. Many believe that even if an accident was caused by black magic or an illness was caused by bacteria God allowed it and can speak to them through it.

Most Indonesians from all religions have a strong belief in God's sovereign will. The proper response to misfortune is to be *pasrah* (submitted to God's will). Even if the cause of an accident is a motorcycle without brakes, the first response of Muslims, Christians, and Hindus is to ask what God is saying to one in this situation. In fact that was Machasin's first response to that situation, which he related in our interview (see chapter 6). Even though he was one of the few who did not believe there is meaning in sickness or accidents, it cost him an effort not to see his own accident as a message from God. Similarly, even if they know their sickness is caused by a mosquito, Indonesians will still ask what God is saying to them if they come down with dengue fever. If they are Hindus, the question might be Why is it my karma to experience this suffering? What is God, or the unseen powers that surround us, saying to me?

When I first came to Indonesia, a young student at my university died while participating in training exercises in the campus military program.[7] I heard rumors of serious physical abuse inflicted on the cadets in the program, who were forced to go through a very harsh regime to prove themselves. The military refused to allow an autopsy of the body. I knew

Table 5.7 *Responses to Question II.G on the Meaning of Sickness or Accidents by Religion*

Religions	Traditional Spiritual Attack	Modern Chance	Religious God Speaks	Modern/ Religious	Totals
Muslims	5%	10%	85%	95%	100% 1,256
Protestants	3%	16%	81%	97%	100% 725
Catholics	6%	24%	70%	94%	100% 190
Hindus	7%	21%	72%	93%	100% 248
Buddhists	—	50% 1	50% 1	100% 2	100% 2
All Non-Muslims	4%	18%	78%	96%	100% 1,180

the family and went to the funeral. What shocked me was that the deeply grieving family were *pasrah* (resigned to God's will) and trying to let go of their beloved son. They did not want to push for an investigation let alone sue the university. They believed that the accident was God's will. They did not imagine the feelings expressed in the famous Dylan Thomas poem, "Do not go gently into that good night / Rage, rage against the dying of the light" (Thomas 1952). Of course in the climate of Soeharto's militaristic New Order, protesting would have been dangerous and probably futile.[8] But this family demonstrated what the statistics from this question on our questionnaire suggest: most Indonesians believe that God is involved in all that happens, and we need to accept God's will and let go.

A similar attitude was displayed by Syafi'i Ma'arif when he told us about the deaths of two out of three of his children at an early age (see note 1). He said this test was extremely severe (*ujian sangat berat*) but he had never in his life been angry with God. He believed that everything that happens to him is God's will. He thought it was very funny when I confessed to him that I had often been angry with God.

Former president Susilo Bambang Yudhoyono (SBY) is another leader who would have chosen the religious answer even if he also believed in attacks by spiritual beings. When he was campaigning for president, he claimed that he and his family were being spiritually attacked via black magic.[9]

Table 5.8 *Javanese and Moluccan Responses to Question II.G on Illness and Accidents*

	Javanese Muslims	Javanese Non-Muslims	Moluccan Muslims	Moluccan Non-Muslims	Indonesian Muslims	Indonesian Non-Muslims	All Indonesians
Traditional spiritual attack	3%	0%	16%	4%	5%	4%	5%
Modern just chance	8%	26%	11%	11%	11%	19%	14%
Religious God speaks to me	89%	74%	73%	85%	84%	77%	81%
Religious or modern	97%	100%	84%	96%	95%	96%	95%

Table 5.9 *Muslim Responses to Question II.G (Illness and Accidents)*
by Ethnic Groups

Ethnic Groups	Traditional Spiritual Attack	Modern Chance	Religious God Speaks	Religious/ Modern	Religious/ Traditional
Java/Madura	3%	8%	89%	97%	92%
Sunda	1%	11%	88%	99%	89%
Makassar/ Bugis	3%	7%	90%	97%	93%
Minang/West Sumatra	4%	7%	89%	96%	93%
Aceh	11%	21%	68%	89%	79%
All Indonesian Muslims	5%	11%	84%	95%	89%
All Indonesian Non-Muslims	4%	19%	77%	96%	81%
All Indonesians	5%	14%	81%	95%	86%

Some who chose the religious answer also believed that some accidents or illnesses occur by chance. Many Indonesians believe that nothing happens by chance. God speaks to them in all that happens. However, some also believe that natural disasters result from natural processes or human destruction of the environment.[10] The choices between the three answers are not mutually exclusive.

Conclusions: Religion and Disenchantment in Indonesia

If disenchantment means imagining that we live in a closed, natural universe fully governed by natural causation, then this chapter has demonstrated that the great majority of Indonesians are not "disenchanted." Indonesians from all religious communities and ethnic groups live in a sacred cosmos. They believe there is "a ghost in the machine." Most believe that God and other unseen beings are always around them. Almost half experience messages through dreams, and even those who think dreams are just a psychological process believe that God and other beings communicate with us in a variety of other ways. Most Indonesians believe that spirit possession is real and prefer the traditional language, which does not assume that only evil spirits possess humans. Ancestors sometimes communicate through mediums. The great majority believe that God speaks to us through suffering.

The impression that most Indonesians live in a sacred cosmos is supported by the finding that only 1.3 percent of the 2,492 respondents to our questionnaire chose exclusively rationalist or materialist responses to all seven questions pertaining to the unseen world. In all, 98.7 percent chose a religious or traditional response to at least one of the seven questions, indicating that they find meaning in experiences that transcend the limits of rational or materialist explanations.

Charles Taylor suggests that modern, secular people have a "buffered self," one in which most modern western people assume that all that happens in their minds derives from their own psychological processes. There is no communication from beings or powers outside our minds that can break into our thoughts. Freud taught us that we all have extensive subconscious minds, which break into our consciousness through dreams and/ or occasionally through visions, psychotic episodes, or mystical experiences. There are no real external powers that intrude into our internal psychological processes.

The buffered self is by no means universally experienced, even in the West, as attested by the popularity of various kinds of charismatic and mystical movements in both Christianity and other religions that promise direct communication with the Divine (see Luhrmann 2012). The fact that a majority of Indonesian, young, educated people (54 percent) do not experience dreams as a source of knowledge about material reality may indicate that the buffered self is an increasing reality in Indonesia. However, the fact that most Indonesians (84 percent) have experienced spiritual powers and/ or believe that there are spirits capable of "possession" (*kesurupan*) should caution us about generalizing about a buffered self, which is impervious to communication from outside the mind.[11]

Most Indonesians prefer religious language about God's presence and activity in their lives over mystical language about spirits and unseen beings. They believe in spirits, but religion is their default language for explaining the meaning of unseen powers, receiving mysterious communications, or giving meaning to illness and accidents. They still prefer traditional language to explain their understanding of spirit possession. The overall preference for religious language may be the result of Islamic modernism, but if so, there are equally strong elements of religious modernism in the non-Muslim religions. Muslims are not more disenchanted than non-Muslims but rather the reverse.

Unfortunately we do not have baseline statistics to compare the language preferred by Indonesians today with the language they would have chosen one hundred years ago. If we did, I suspect that one hundred years ago, when Muhammadiyah was founded, a much higher percentage of Indonesians (especially Muslims) would have chosen traditional over religious or modern language. This might indicate that Islamic modernism has had a profound impact on the social imaginaries of Indonesians. If so, I imagine that modern education is a stronger influence than changing religious beliefs. Muhammadiyah and the Indonesian government have built a vast network of modern schools and universities. One hundred years ago most Indonesians could not read or write.

Not only literacy but also the internet and global media have opened up tremendous access to all kinds of modern knowledge. Access to scientific knowledge about the universe is increasing at an exponential rate. Nevertheless, as Zainal mentioned in his interview (see note 9), this has not led most Indonesians to doubt that they live in a sacred cosmos. Rather they are finding more and more creative ways to express their belief that life has meaning. Indonesians are becoming increasingly religiously pious and well educated. According to Machasin, the more pious people become the more they believe in *gaib* and all kinds of mysterious powers.

Indonesia is not just Java, even though more than half the population lives on this one island. Our research shows that there are significant differences on these four questions that are influenced by local ethnic beliefs. Sometimes local cultural beliefs are stronger than differences in religion. Islamic and non-Islamic modernism is stronger in Java (including Sunda) than on the outer islands. Nevertheless, in spite of many local variations, the overall picture is clear. Most Indonesians from all religious and ethnic groups live in a sacred cosmos. The following chapter adds nuance to this conclusion by showing a variety of ways in which different Muslim intellectual leaders interpret their experience of a sacred cosmos.

6

Islam and Enchantment: Six Leaders

The true threat to the world today comes from the mad ambitions of states and capitalists bent on destroying non-modern cultures. It is the so-called developed countries that plunder the planet's resources without showing the least concern for consequences they are incapable of foreseeing.
—René Girard

THIS CHAPTER IS BASED on interviews with Muslim intellectuals, including four men and two women. The six leaders include two representatives from Muhammadiyah, two from NU, and two who are unaffiliated. The interviews reveal to what extent these leaders live in a sacred cosmos and how they construct the relation between Islam and a sacred cosmos. The interviews also explore where they think Indonesia is heading.

The interviews reveal the complexity with which Indonesian Muslims view and inhabit a sacred cosmos. These leaders do not represent all Indonesian Muslims. They are prominent leaders with doctorates and extensive international experience. They are critical of narrow, intolerant, dogmatic interpretations of religion. They don't represent a growing minority of Muslim conservatives who believe there is only one true way to be a good Muslim. They do represent a great diversity of Indonesian ways of negotiating complex interactions among Islam, beliefs about the unseen world, and scientific knowledge. Each of them is different from all the others.

The interviews help break down simplistic stereotypes about different kinds of Muslims in Indonesia such as modernist, traditionalist, and postmodern. These Muslim leaders don't fit into fixed categories. They are all in process, with hybrid identities that have changed over time, and are still adjusting to rapid social change. All of them can be considered devout Muslims, although their interpretations of what it means to practice their religion in the modern world are quite varied.

Interview with Ahmad Syafi'i Ma'arif

Prof. Dr. Ahmad Syafi'i Ma'arif is one of the leading Muslim public intellectuals in Indonesia and is often quoted in national and international media. Syafi'i was the thirteenth head (Ketua Umum Pimpinan Pusat) of Muhammadiyah from 2000 to 2005. He is the founding director of the Maarif Institute and the author of many articles and books. Syafi'i was born in 1935 in a village in West Sumatra. His mother died when he was still an infant, and he was raised by his uncle and aunt. Due to economic hardship and revolution, he faced many obstacles in getting an education. But he persisted and eventually received his first doctorate at the Institute for Teaching and Education (Institut Keguruan Ilmu Pendidikan—IKIP) in Yogyakarta before going on to earn a further master's degree at Ohio University and a PhD at the University of Chicago, where he studied with Fazlur Rahman. My first impression of Syafi'i when we met in 1997 was of his warmth, friendliness, and intense curiosity. He seemed very down to earth and free of arrogance. When we met in his home for this interview, twenty years later, he showed the same openness, humility, and honesty.

Syafi'i has a deep faith in God. He believes that God has been with him at every step and that it is only by the grace of God and national independence that he was able first to come to Java from a simple village in West Sumatra and then to travel the world and meet many interesting people. Syafi'i bows to the ground and worships God (*sholat*) five times every day. If he ever misses a prayer time, he feels something is lost in his life. But he quickly adds that not all of his prayer times are *khusyuk*, (engrossed in the presence of God). He says he is a normal human being, so sometimes his prayers are superficial. But his life is fully committed to God and Indonesia. He has written that commitment to Islam, Indonesia, and humanity are all part of the same breath for him (Ma'arif 2015). That is part of what enables him to take controversial positions without fear.

Syafi'i and his wife have had three children, but two of them died of illness at the ages of twenty months and five years. These losses were extremely heavy tests (*ujian sangat berat*) to his character. But he says he has never been angry with God, not even when in deep grief. He was and is *pasrah*, submitted to the will of God.

Syafi'i's first response to a question about *gaib* (powers of the unseen world) was to say that he tends not to believe in unseen beings or powers other than God. He only believes in God. But then he quickly revised his answer to say that he believes that Satan, demons, evil spirits, and so on exist. He frequently asks God for protection from evil, whether it is human evil or spiritual evil. However, Syafi'i has never experienced the presence or power of spirits or unseen beings. He has no experience of spirit possession, but he believes it exists. In fact he acknowledges that there is possession by evil spirits as well as possession by *jins* or spirits who use a medium to communicate. But he doesn't want anything to do with them. He doesn't trust in *gaib*. He doesn't want to use that kind of power or even pay attention to it. According to his understanding of Islam, our prayers and attention should only be given to God. In Islam, he says, we are required by the Koran to believe in *gaib* but we are forbidden to pay too much attention to it.

When I asked him about dreams, Syafi'i vigorously denied that they could be anything other than a psychological process. He said he absolutely does not believe in dreams. But then, on reflection, he qualified his answer by saying that perhaps there were some special people, like Jacob in the Scriptures, who received communication through dreams. Regarding illness or accidents, Syafi'i believes they are a way that God speaks to us. They are not just chance but rather a test of our faith. On the other hand, he feels that natural disasters do not necessarily have any theological meaning. They are simply the result of natural causes, sometimes brought on by human actions that degrade the environment.

As might be expected by a leader of Muhammadiyah, Syafi'i affirmed that *bid'ah* (spiritual practices not authorized by the Koran and Sunnah) and *syirik* (worshiping anything other than God) are a danger to the Muslim community. But according to him, a far greater threat is the danger of Arabism. The Islamic community in Indonesia is divided and broken (*perpecahan*) because of the conflicts between Arab elites in the Middle East. He declared that Arabic Islam has been destroyed (*hancur*). Arabic Islam was torn apart by conflicts between Arab elites, which broke out not long after the death of the Prophet. These ancient conflicts have been exported to the entire Muslim world, including Indonesia. Arab Muslims blame all their problems on outside powers such as the United States or Israel. But they fail to honestly face their own failures. Conflicts related to narrow and absolutist interpretations of religion and the struggle for power are far from the true teachings of Islam. The greatest danger facing the Muslim community in Indonesia is not *bid'ah* or *syirik* but Arabism. Syafi'i affirmed that Islam in Indonesia is different from Islam in the Middle East. He has hope for future contributions of Indonesian Islam to world civilization. But he said the key is education. Indonesia is the largest Muslim country in the world, but he regrets that the quality of Muslims in Indonesia is still low.

Interview with Siti Syamsiyatun

Dr. Siti Syamsiyatun (Atun) is the director of ICRS, an interreligious, interdisciplinary, international doctoral program and research center in interreligious studies based at UGM. It is cosponsored by UGM, UIN, and DWCU. Atun received her master's degree from McGill University in Montreal and her PhD from Monash University in Melbourne. Her main research subject is Islam and gender. Atun was one of the first Indonesian women to receive a PhD in Islamic studies, and she has won numerous international honors, including a Fulbright fellowship. Atun is from an influential Muhammadiyah family and has written extensively on Islam and women in the context of the Aisyiyah, a Muhammadiyah women's organization founded in 1917. In addition to her leadership in inter-religious studies, she is a permanent faculty member of the Dakwah and Communication Faculty of UIN. She lives in the strongly Muhammadiyah town of Kota Gede near Yogyakarta.

Atun does not frequently experience the presence of the unseen world, but she doesn't have any doubts about its reality. She has many stories about *gaib* and believes God helps and protects her in her daily life. For example, to qualify to study overseas she had to take a language exam at a time when her English was not very strong. The night before the exam she prayed and randomly studied materials on refugee issues. The topic of the readings on the exam was refugees. She doesn't know why God helped her but speculates it was because of her parents' godliness and their prayers for her.

One time when she was suffering from allergies, she had difficulty breathing and sleeping because of a severe cough. She dreamed that a woman dressed in white came to her in her bed. The woman greeted her in Arabic, *Assalamualaikum!* She laid her hand on Atun's chest. Immediately her breathing eased, and when she woke her cough was gone. While Atun affirms that dreams are usually just the way our unconscious mind processes our experiences, she believes that God or other powers, sometimes communicate through dreams.

In her old family home, she believes there are unseen beings who sometimes take things or move them around. One time she left a bracelet on her dresser. When she got up in the morning it wasn't there. They searched the house, but it had disappeared. The next night she dreamed it was in an old broken dresser in the garden that she hadn't touched for years. She went to the dresser in the garden, and sure enough, the bracelet was there. Because small things often disappear, she and her family sometimes speak to the unseen beings, saying, "If our things are borrowed please don't keep them too long." Atun does not consider this a real prayer, let alone worship, but rather just a request. It is similar to her common practice of uttering an Arab prayer to ask permission when she enters a graveyard or an empty house.

Atun confessed that she half believes and half doesn't believe traditional Javanese interpretations of dreams. For example if you dream that you are swimming in clear, clean water it means something good will happen. If you dream of swimming in dirty water, it means you will get sick. If you dream of defecating, it means someone will die. Atun said that often such dreams seem to come true, but she still has her doubts.

Atun believes that spirit possession is real. Sometimes, she said, it is just a symptom of psychological problems, especially when there is mass possession of young students. They are very susceptible to suggestion, and when they have a lot of stress panic can spread among them and cause them to lose normal consciousness. Real possession can be either negative, from an evil spirit, or positive, as when an ancestor, *jin*, or good spirit uses someone as a medium to communicate to the community. Atun's most vivid experience of possession happened in New Delhi. She was in a small group of Indonesian academics with the Indonesian ambassador to India. Suddenly the ambassador went into a trance. His voice changed into the voice of a very old man. He spoke very angrily with a dean who was present because he had stopped performing the five daily prayers and attending Friday worship (*sholat*). Then he turned to warn another friend that he was being tempted by a woman and should remain true to his wife. When he came out of the trance he said he had been possessed by the spirit of his grandfather. Atun was really shaken by the experience.

Regarding sickness or accidents, Atun believes that everything in life happens for a purpose. Nothing is just by chance. In all that happens, God is speaking to us. She relates this to the doctrine of Sunnatullah natural law. God established laws to govern everything in nature, human beings, and spiritual beings. Sunnatullah includes not only the physical laws of nature but also the moral law of what is good and evil and how we should respond. If she is sick or has an accident, Atun asks what God is trying to tell her. This does not mean that everything that happens is good. Atun believes that if she gets sick or has an accident it could be because she is being attacked by an evil spirit or *jin*. But even in that case God has allowed it and can use the experience to speak to her.

Sunnatullah also applies to natural disasters. God can use them to speak to us. However, Atun preferred traditional rather than religious language as her primary explanation for natural disasters. Natural disasters are a sign that nature and humanity are out of balance. As a result of human evil, our ancestors and the unseen powers of the sacred cosmos become angry. The result is a natural disaster. Of course she knows that the causes are complex and include natural causes, human agency, the agency of spiritual beings, and the will of God.

Atun views power as primarily a relationship between human beings, which anyone can attain by rational means such as a position within a political structure, superior knowledge, wealth, or control of technology. However, she also affirms the traditional Javanese belief that power can be obtained by mystical means such as fasting, asceticism, or connection to a spiritual being. It can also be obtained through possession of an heirloom (*pusaka*) that contains mysterious power. When she was little, many people believed in *ingu-ingu*, taking care of an invisible being (*makluk halus*) in order to obtain wealth. Generally, Atun thinks that seeking power by mystical means is unwise. Usually the power obtained by such means is only physical or material power and may be evil. It's better to stay away from it.

Atun said that most Muhammadiyah members have views similar to hers. In fact she said that the overwhelming majority believe in *gaib* (the unseen world). Belief in *gaib* is required for all Muslims because it is frequently mentioned in the Koran. Perhaps a difference from NU is that Muhammadiyah members believe that Muslims should stay away from the invisible powers of *gaib*. They should only worship God, face their problems using rational means, and not seek power from the unseen world. Muslims should not depend on shamans or magic. Nevertheless, according to Atun, most Muhammadiyah members are much more relaxed than in the past regarding charges of heresy based on participation in cultural traditions that are not authorized by the Koran (*bid'ah*) or revering beings other than God (*syirik*). She said that many people still pray in graveyards to obtain a blessing or become rich. While Atun does not approve of such practices, she doesn't think they are necessarily *syirik*. When people go on pilgrimages to a graveyard or other sacred place, they might be praying only to God but hoping that the power of the place, or the beings that inhabit it, will make their prayers to God more effective. According to Atun, increasing piety among Muslims is actually increasing belief in *gaib* and mystical practices rather than the opposite.

I asked Atun about a conflict in Kota Gede (the city where she lives) between Muhammadiyah and the Kraton (the sultan's palace), which manages an ancient mosque (Mesjid Gede) and a sacred spring. The German anthropologist Judith Schlehe described a cultural festival that includes a parade (*kirab budaya*) to the ancient mosque and sacred spring in Kota Gede (2016). According to her, complex negotiations took place between the sultan's palace and Muhammadiyah, which allowed the parade but downplayed the mystical aspects of the cleansing of the sacred spring. The festival was construed as a purely cultural event for the purpose of drawing tourists. Publicly, the leaders of both parties denied that there was any religious or spiritual meaning to the festival. Privately, traditional leaders from the palace admitted that the ritual cleansing of the sacred spring was the summit and purpose of the festival. But both parties downplayed the ritual cleansing in public. The ritual cleansing, designed to please the local *jins*, was performed surreptitiously, when the attention of the spectators was directed elsewhere. Schlehe suggests that the commodification of culture as a tourist spectacle allowed traditional practitioners to carry out their rituals (surreptitiously) in a context dominated by the more puritanical Muhammadiyah.[1]

Atun added an interesting perspective to this account. According to her, the conflict between the Kraton and Muhammadiyah has a long history. A major point of tension arose when Muhammadiyah built a separate mosque (Mesjid Perak), rather than attending the ancient Mesjid Gede. A major bone of contention was that the Kraton leaders of Mesjid Gede did not urge everyone to attend Friday prayers at the mosque. They said it was sufficient that the *kaum* (the group of Muslim leaders) prayed at the mosque on behalf of the people.

According to Atun, there is no problem with the ritual cleansing of the sacred spring. In fact it is done every Friday. She said that everyone in Kote Gede believes there are *jins* living in the spring. Muhammadiyah members only differ with some in thinking that Muslims should not glorify (*memuliakan*) the *jins* or overly honor them. One should only pray to God. Nevertheless, the sacred spring in Atun's town is a popular destination for pilgrims. She said that many powerful and famous people *tirakat* there, usually at midnight. *Tirakat* means to order your inner self through fasting, meditation, prayer, reading the Koran, bathing in a sacred place, or performing other ascetic disciplines.

Atun's viewpoint does not contradict Schlehe's account, but it adds the perspective that the difference between the Kraton and Muhammadiyah is not that one side believes in supernatural beings while the other does not but rather that they differ in how they think we should respond to them, especially in a public ceremony. One side thinks we should honor them, while the other side thinks we should leave them alone.

Interview with Muhammad Machasin

Prof. Dr. H. Muhammad Machasin was the general director for Islamic organizations (Ditjen Bimas Islam) in the Department of Religion of Indonesia. From 2010 to 2015 he was on the Central Governing Board of NU (Rais Syuriyah PBNU—Pengurus Besar Nahdlatul Ulama—The Great Leaders of NU). Prior to that, Machasin held a variety of high positions, including director of Islamic higher education in the Department of Religion and head of NU for the province of Yogyakarta. He is also a professor of the history of Islamic cultures at the State Islamic University Sunan Kalijaga.[2] Machasin was born in 1956 in Purworejo, Central Java. He studied Arabic language and literature at IAIN Sunan Kalijaga and then went on to study Islamic philosophy, history, and mysticism (*tasawuf*) at the same school, where he received his doctorate. Machasin is a humble and gentle man, a Muslim scholar who worships five times a day and is obedient in following the requirements of his faith. He has been outspoken in advocating tolerance and dialogue both between different religions and between different streams of the same religion.

As might be assumed of a prominent Muslim leader of NU, Machasin affirmed his belief in the unseen world (*gaib*). Belief in *gaib* is required for Muslims, according to Machasin, because the Koran (Holy Scriptures) is from the unseen world and was revealed by God through the Prophet Muhammad. The Koran tells us that all true Muslims should believe in *gaib*. However, Machasin has doubts concerning many of the common beliefs about *gaib* held by most members of NU. He suggested that many rituals practiced by traditional Javanese Muslims have cultural value, even though he doubts the literal, metaphysical reality of the beings or realities invoked by the practices. Machasin suggested that traditional NU practices are analogous to the Christmas celebrations of European Christians. They might still light candles even though they do not believe in the original meaning of them.

When he was a young man, until about the age of thirty, Machasin believed in the literal existence of spirits, *jins*, and unseen beings or powers. Once he went to a graveyard in the middle of the night to seek a blessing so that he might pass his exams. Now he doesn't believe in such beings or powers. When I asked him about spirit possession, he admitted that there is a lot that he doesn't understand. In front of his house there is a large old banyan tree. When children play near the tree, they frequently are "possessed." He does not presume to understand it. It is a mystery. He does not believe that they are literally possessed by a spirit or unseen being. He just doesn't understand it.

Machasin admitted that part of him still believes in the powers of *gaib*. For example, when he was nominated for the position of rector (president) of his university, he was walking on the street and was hit by a young man who was driving a motorcycle with no brakes. It made him wonder if God was warning him not to accept the nomination. But he rejected that feeling (*rasa*) and chose to follow his reason (*nalar*) rather than following an irrational feeling. In the end he was not elected rector, but he felt it was still wiser to follow his mind rather than his feelings. Machasin said there are very few members of NU like him, persons who don't believe in spirits, *jins*, and unseen powers. The overwhelming majority live their lives with a consciousness that they are surrounded by unseen powers.

Sometimes Machasin also believes in them because he feels their presence. But he tries hard not to believe. I asked him why, and he gave three reasons. First, his modern education disposes him to believe in rational causes. Second, in his experience of life, belief in unseen powers is futile; belief in *gaib* doesn't help anyone solve their problems. Just because you don't understand something does not mean it was caused by a super-natural being. Several times during our interview, Machasin repeated that there is a lot he does not understand. Third, he tries not to believe because using your reason to study the Koran and modern science is far more productive. *Gaib* is mysterious and unclear, whereas Islam and study of the Scriptures bring clarity about how to live. Modern theories of interpretation help him to understand how the words of the Koran can be both the words of God and the words of the Prophet. Modern science helps him understand natural causation.

Machasin is rather pessimistic about the growth of reason and science in Indonesia. He feels that the growth of piety and intolerance are not the result of an increase in understanding but rather the opposite. Many Muslims don't want to think or use their minds. They would rather see the world as black and white. The more pious people become the more they believe in magic and *gaib*. Nevertheless, he acknowledges that there is tremendous diversity among Indonesian Muslims. Many Muslims in NU are very tolerant and open to modern education. But it is the intolerant extremists who shout the loudest.

On most markers of a sacred cosmos in our questionnaire, Machasin would be considered a rational secularist. He doesn't believe in unseen beings or powers, messages through dreams, meaning in natural events or sickness, spirit possession, or supernatural means of gaining power. He believes we should use reason and modern science to solve our problems. His lack of belief is a choice based on education and experience, not religious dogma. He is not concerned that belief in *gaib* might be unortho-dox (*bid'ah* or *syirik*). As a leader of NU, he would defend the right of Javanese Muslims to continue with their sacred beliefs and rituals. He him-self would not hesitate to participate in *selamatans* (sacred meals) or village cleansings (*bersih desa*), which appeal for a good harvest. But he interprets them as rich cultural and social symbols that can be freed from their original metaphysical meanings.

Machasin was raised in a strong NU context where a sacred cosmos was the assumed reality. By admitting that a part of him occasionally still feels the presence of unseen powers, he occupies a liminal space between his cultural roots and his modern scientific assumptions. This is a reversal of

Bellah's "second naïveté." Machasin is a devout Muslim who believes in modern science and rationality in spite of his occasional feelings of being surrounded by an unseen world of power and meaning. In contrast, Bellah's western idea of second naïveté is of someone who assumes that we live in an impersonal universe of scientific cause and effect but chooses to believe and practice religion because it gives meaning to life. Machasin chooses to believe in science because it makes more sense of his life.

In a published interview Machasin suggested that three things characterize the practice of Islam in Indonesia.[3] First, the practice of Islam in Indonesia is very good. It is better than anywhere else in the world. In terms of tolerance, worship, and consistency between beliefs and practices, Indonesia excels compared to other Muslim countries. Second, the practice of Islam in Indonesia is always in a social context and affected by the maturity level of the people. Religious groups that use violence against those who are different from them are immature and childish. Even though they are a small minority, they seem to be growing, and that is worrying. Third, many Indonesians have an inferiority complex. They think that anyone from the Middle East knows more than them about Islam. Anyone who is Arab is looked on as an ulama, even if he or she is ignorant of religion. Similarly, they have an inferiority complex vis-à-vis the West with regard to science. Machasin believes that Indonesians need to grow up and gain self-confidence. They are not necessarily behind in religion or knowledge from the Middle East or the West.

Interview with Muhammad Iqbal Ahnaf

Dr. M. Iqbal Ahnaf is a permanent faculty member in the CRCS at UGM. The CRCS is an interdisciplinary master's program in religious studies. Iqbal directs the CRCS program in public education. He studied at the State Islamic University Sunan Kalijaga and went on for a PhD at Victoria University in Wellington, New Zealand. His research was on radical movements in Islam. He is the author of *The Image of the Other as Enemy: Radical Discourse in Indonesia* (2006) and has taught peace studies at Eastern Mennonite University in the United States. Iqbal is a local leader of NU, with which he has been associated all his life. He is from East Java where his father is a modest NU *kyai* (head of an Islamic school) and has a mosque in his home. His father is a very pious Muslim and, like many *kyai*, also a healer and paranormal.

Since his father is a *kyai*, Iqbal grew up in a context in which interaction with the unseen world is common. He said that his father has a guardian spirit (*qodem*).[4] Various family members have seen or heard the guardian or other spiritual beings. Some are bothered or frightened by them. Members of the family often hear knocking or other noises for which there is no rational explanation.

Iqbal said that when he was in his early twenties he was half awake on his bed and a *makluk halus gaib* (supernatural being from the unseen world) came to him. He was paralyzed with fear and could not move. His father came to him, and the being disappeared. He believes the being was his father's guardian. Iqbal doesn't often feel the presence of *gaib*, although he believes it is always there.

Iqbal thinks that most dreams are just the fruit of our unconscious mind. However, there have been a few times, such as in the story above, when he believed that God or another being came to him in a dream. Like most Indonesians, Iqbal has no doubt that spirit possession is real. He believes that evil spirits, *jins*, and ancestral spirits are all capable of entering people. They may be good or evil. On the other hand, he acknowledges that psychology also plays a role in possession. Some possessions may just be symbolic expressions of psychological problems. Psychological problems make a person more vulnerable to possession. But not all possession is a problem. Sometimes it is a positive experience of connection with the unseen world. Shamans like his father may be possessed by good spirits who open their eyes to see the past and future.

According to Iqbal, if he became ill or had an accident his primary response would be to look for what God is trying to tell him through the suffering. He believes there is meaning in all that he experiences. However, he also assumes that a sickness or accident can be caused by an attack by an evil spirit or other creature of *gaib*. Iqbal suggests that we are an integral part of nature and we should revere the earth of our ancestors. We need to guard the balance between human needs and our environment. Natural disasters are caused by a lack of balance or harmony between human beings and nature. Human greed and exploitation not only upset the balance, but they also make our ancestors angry.

Iqbal suggested that power is best thought of rationally as a relationship between people. Everyone has power, which is the fruit of knowledge (à la Foucault). Education, an institutional position, technology, media, and wealth are all means of increasing the power of one person over another. However, that doesn't mean that power cannot also be obtained through spiritual practices like meditation, fasting, and prayer in sacred places. Power also inhabits certain objects and places. When Iqbal got married and moved into a new house, his father planted a sacred stone in the house. Iqbal believes the stone protects him and his family from evil, especially the supernatural powers of *gaib*.

According to Iqbal, the great majority of members of NU are extremely mystical and fully believe in *gaib*. They perform many rituals to maintain a good relationship with the unseen world. In fact he sees himself as more rational than most NU members because of his extensive travel and western higher education. He has no concerns about charges of *bid'ah* or *syirik* against members of NU. He believes the Islam practiced by NU is far superior to the narrow, intolerant views promoted by Arab elites from the Middle East. It is also closer to the true teachings of religion. One reason he is an NU activist is because he wants to combat intolerance and narrow interpretations of Islam.

Interview with Wening Udasmoro

Dr. Wening Udasmoro is the dean of the Faculty of Cultural Sciences (FIB) at UGM. She studied French language and literature at UGM for her undergraduate and master's degrees. She went on to earn a second masters and a PhD from the Faculty of Economics and Social Sciences at the University of Geneva, Switzerland. Prior to being elected dean, she was head of the French Department. Her main research interests are French literature, sexuality, and gender studies. She is influenced by French social theory, especially the thought of Pierre Bourdieu.

Wening is the daughter of the founder of a large school of traditional Indonesian martial arts (*pencak silat*) in Magelang, Central Java. Following the death of her father, she became the head of the school (Ketua Perguruan Pencak Silat Kembang Setaman). Her father performed many acts of strength for which there is no scientific explanation. Some of her students also have powers and can perform feats that are difficult to explain.

Wening herself has no direct experience with *gaib* (the supernatural world) and tends not to believe in spirits, spiritual beings, *jins*, or magic. She said she used to believe in many traditional Javanese legends such as omens in dreams or signs in ordinary experience. For example, if you dream of a lizard falling on you (or if a lizard actually does fall on you), it means that someone close to you will get sick. If you dream of losing a tooth, it means that someone close to you will die.[5] Gradually she gave up such beliefs because they did not match her experience of reality. She feels that if you believe such stories you will go looking for evidence that they are true. People reconstruct their experiences to fit their beliefs. Wening said that when she was young her father told her that she could not perform magical feats of *pencak silat* because she was too rational.

Although she does not rationally believe in the unseen beings of *gaib*, Wening is still scared of them and does not like to go near graveyards at night or other sacred places (*tempat keramat*). She feels very frightened in such places. She laughed deprecatingly at herself, but without shame, as she told me of her fears. She feels (*rasa*) the power of *gaib* and tries to stay away from places that frighten her. Nevertheless, she chooses not to believe in *gaib*. As a teacher of martial arts, she urges her students to give priority to the disciplined practice of techniques rather than praying in graveyards or trying to obtain magic. I asked when she began to lose her belief in *gaib*. She said it was when she became an adult who was not afraid to express herself and make her own decisions.

Wening has seen much apparent evidence of the powers of *gaib*, but she always looks for a rational explanation. Some of her students go into trance and believe they are possessed by a spirit. She can't explain their behavior but believes it is purely psychological. It generally happens to students who are not emotionally stable and are under great stress. Wening suggests that some stories of *gaib* are social constructions designed to protect personal interests. They are part of a habitus that supports a person's status within a power structure (Bourdieu 1977). She gave an example of competing Javanese shamans who all claimed to have a personal ghost (*hantu*) at their service.

Wening is a Muslim, but she does not wear a *jilbab* (head scarf, *hijab*). She prays (*sholat*) but is not strict in following all the rules of Islam. She feels that true Islam is shown in your actions, behavior, and character, not in your strictness in following certain rituals. True religion is not for your own personal benefit. It should not be focused on gaining your own salvation. Rather it is to live consistently for the sake of others, especially those who are weak. True religion is for the community, not for personal gain. She remarked wryly that some would say she is not a Muslim because she does not believe in *gaib*. However, according to her, those who use violence to enforce a particular narrow interpretation of their religion are not Muslims. They are just using religion to try to find a personal identity.

Wening believes that the majority of Indonesians in Indonesia are like her in that they have a more flexible understanding of Islam. In fact she speculated that 55 percent of Muslims in Yogyakarta are not strict in following Islamic rituals. However, she acknowledged that most of them believe in *gaib* and the surrounding powers of an unseen world. Within the context of the university and among highly educated Muslim intellectuals, she insisted that there are many like her who do not believe in *gaib*.

While Wening tends toward rational explanations for everything, she thinks that human beings have many hidden powers that are not understood by science. Supernatural feats of strength, such as the ability of some her students to break very strong reinforced concrete blocks with their bare hands through inner power, is an example. Perhaps we will understand such power in the future, but for the present it is mysterious. While Wening herself does not believe in *gaib* or practice the rituals of Javanese mysticism, she respects those who do and will defend their right to follow their own beliefs. She has no patience for intolerance and does not believe that *bid'ah* (innovation) or *syirik* (trusting in powers other than God) are a serious problem in Indonesia. Followers of Javanese mysticism are not *musyirik* (heretical). Religious fanaticism and intolerance are much more dangerous to true Islam than Javanese mysticism.

Wening shows many of the signs of "disenchantment." She believes in God, and there is a part of her that fears spirits and ghosts. She respects Javanese mysticism and rituals that link us to the unseen world. However, she chooses to live her life on the basis of a modern, rational, tolerant, ethical, and scientific imagination of reality. On the one hand, she believes that modern education undermines belief in magic and *gaib*, as well as narrow intolerant expressions of religion. On the other hand, she believes that history is not linear but cyclical. Nationalist, *abangan* Muslims like her are constrained by the current hegemony of pietistic, conservative Islam. According to Wening, pietistic Muslims associated with Muhammadiyah, NU, and the radical groups are not the majority. They are actually a minority. Nationalist, *abangan* Muslims like her are the majority and in time will reassert themselves. Currently they are silent because they are lazy (*malas*). They don't want to risk speaking out against the current dominance of pietistic religion. But history will turn, and the true power of the Indonesian Muslim majority will be revealed.

Interview with Zainal Abidin Bagir

Dr. Zainal Abidin Bagir is the executive director of CRCS at UGM. He specializes in the philosophy of religion, religion and science, and religion and ecology. He is the author of *Science and Religion in the Post-colonial World: Interfaith Perspectives* (2005). Zainal was born in Surakarta, Indonesia. He received a bachelor's degree in mathematics from the Bandung Institute of Technology. His master's degree in Islamic philosophy was earned at the International Institute of Islamic Thought and Civilization in Malaysia. He was selected for a Fulbright scholarship and earned his PhD in the history and philosophy of science at Indiana University. He is not affiliated with either NU or Muhammadiyah but was a Muslim activist and writer for a leading Islamic journal before becoming the head of CRCS.

Zainal suggested that many Muslims in Indonesia are beyond "disenchantment" and are now experiencing "reenchantment." Whereas formerly they had a great concern about being "rational" and accepting both the findings of natural science and the orthodox teachings of their religion, now many are rediscovering the richness of their traditions, including the more mystical practices of their ancestors. Previously he and other modern Muslim intellectuals were much more rigid in their interpretation and rejection of *bid'ah* (innovation) and *syirik* (polytheism). Now they have a better appreciation of cultural traditions. Zainal said that in Indonesia there is abundant support for the reality of a sacred cosmos because there are so many artistic, mystical, and traditional groups practicing rituals that connect them to the unseen world (*gaib*).

Zainal affirmed that he often experiences *gaib*, but he experiences it more as energy and power than as personal beings like spirits and *jins*. He gave an example of looking at a beautiful tree and feeling strong positive energy, which empowers him. In contrast, when he looks at a pile of garbage that people have thrown around, he feels negative energy, which weakens him. He doesn't exactly believe in spirits or *jins* as personal beings because he has never directly experienced them. However, he is open to the possibility that they exist and tends to believe credible witnesses who have seen them. But he is skeptical about all types of spirit possession and thinks it is related to psychological problems or processes. I asked Zainal what he thought of trance dances, like Jatilan, which actively seek spirit possession. He said he thought it is a psychological means of emptying the dancers' minds and opening them to all kinds of suggestions. He said he has watched such performances and never felt any unusual power.

In the questions I asked him related to a sacred cosmos, Zainal tended to answer with either traditional or modern symbol systems. He didn't choose religious language as a response to any of the questions. However, he said his Islamic faith is very important to him. He prays/worships (*sholat*) five times a day and feels that if he skips a prayer time there is something missing from his life. However, he tends to think of God in terms of energy and power rather than as a personal being. Regular worship ideally connects him to the ground of being and the power that infuses nature and the cosmos. He acknowledged that this connection with the unseen world of power and energy does not happen every time he performs the *sholat*. Sometimes he is in a hurry and just goes through the motions. Zainal is deeply committed to Islam, not just for his own personal experience but because he is part of a worldwide community, which has shaped his identity.

Since Zainal often senses the unseen world of *gaib*, he does not have a "buffered mind." This is confirmed by his experience of communication through dreams. Zainal felt that most of his dreams were just his subconscious mind processing experience, but he has experienced dreams that came true. He did not interpret them as a message from a personal God or spirit. Rather he felt that the power that infuses the cosmos was communicating with him. Zainal knew people who frequently received messages through dreams and tended to believe them.

Regarding finding meaning in sickness or an accident, Zainal was ambivalent. On the one hand, he felt that sickness or illness is due to natural causes and should not be attributed to evil spirits or other personal beings. On the other hand, he acknowledged that we humans seek meaning in suffering and it is possible that the energy of the cosmos may communicate with us or even attack us through illness or an accident. However, his own experience of *gaib* tended to be positive rather than negative. Perhaps God or nature might speak to him through an illness, not as a negative warning but rather to help him find meaning and life.

Interpretation, Analysis, and Comparison of the Interviews

The six interviews provide a fascinating picture of a range of Indonesian Muslim attitudes and experiences of living in a sacred cosmos. Syafi'i Ma'arif's views contrast with those of Siti Syamsiyatun, though both of them are prominent members of Muhammadiyah. As might be expected in an organization with more than twenty-nine million members, there is considerable variation. Syafi'i is from the more progressive wing of Muhammadiyah, and as the top leader from 2000 to 2005, he took it in a tolerant, humanist direction. His successor, Prof. Dr. Din Syamsuddin, while also opposed to radical, intolerant versions of Islam, was more conservative in upholding a narrower interpretation of "true" Islam with less tolerance for those who diverged from it. I suspect that their views of the unseen world are quite similar. The difference between them is probably in how tolerant each is toward those who hold different viewpoints.

In the interview, Syafi'i expressed considerable ambivalence. It appeared that his gut instincts were to not believe in *gaib* or a supernatural, invisible world. On the other hand, he is a sincere and pious Muslim who recognizes that the existence of an unseen, supernatural world is clearly affirmed in the Koran. It is also linked to God's agency in the world. Since Syafi'i believes that God is active in his life and the world, he believes that the unseen world is real. Consistent with Muhammadiyah's commitment to purify Islam of superstitious practices and use modern science to properly interpret the world and the Scriptures, Syafi'i is committed to keeping a healthy distance from *gaib* and relating only to God. In practice he is a rationalist, with little interest in anything supernatural apart from God. He "believes" in *gaib* as a doctrine, but he wants nothing to do with any part of it except God. God is part of *gaib* (the unseen world) and the center of his life. But for the rest of seen and unseen reality, he prefers to understand it through the eyes of reason. Unlike more intolerant members of Muhammadiyah,

Syafi'i showed little interest in prosecuting Indonesian Muslims who continue to perform cosmic rituals to maintain harmony with the lesser powers of the unseen world. For Syafi'i the real threat to Islam is Arab extremism and intolerance, not syncretism with traditional beliefs and practices. Cultural practices of dubious orthodoxy should be combatted by modern education and religious teaching, not repression or violence.

In contrast, Siti Syamsiyatun has no existential doubts about the reality of *gaib*. She is a leader among Muhammadiyah women and shares with Syafi'i the conviction that Muslims should not use magic or seek power through relations with beings from the unseen world. Like him, she is inclined to be tolerant toward those who continue to perform cosmic rituals to maintain harmony between the seen and unseen worlds. But unlike him, she lives in both worlds. The unseen world of supernatural beings is not just a doctrine to her but rather an existential reality. She is careful not to worship or glorify any power other than God, but she is very aware that she is surrounded by the unseen world. In contrast, Syafi'i believes that *gaib* is real because it is part of orthodox Islamic teaching. But he has no direct experience of *gaib* except for the presence of God. Syafi'i experiences a sacred cosmos centered on God. Atun lives in a sacred cosmos that is centered on God but also includes the seen and unseen worlds as part of her community.

The contrast between Atun (of Muhammadiyah) and Machasin (of NU) is very striking. Atun believes in the unseen world of spiritual powers, and Machasin doesn't. They break the stereotypes. As might be expected of a prominent leader of NU, Machasin is tolerant of Javanese traditions and practices that assume there is a sacred cosmos inhabited by spiritual beings. But unlike the majority of NU members, he does not believe they are real. Rather, he uses science, reason, and a rational interpretation of Scriptures to interpret experience. Atun has no doubts about the reality of unseen spiritual beings, but, consistent with Muhammadiyah, she doesn't think they should be glorified or worshiped.

Unlike Syafi'i, who believes in the existence of the unseen world for doctrinal reasons but thinks we should keep our distance from it, Machasin uses modern hermeneutics to interpret the unseen world as a symbolic reality that should be respected for its cultural value. The only part of *gaib* in which he really believes is God and the Koran, which he believes came from the unseen world. Machasin shows a high tolerance for ambiguity, which allows him to acknowledge that he sometimes feels the presence of unseen powers and that there are many mysteries he doesn't understand. However, he chooses to follow reason rather than his feelings.

In terms of existential experience, Machasin (of NU) appears to be much closer to Syafi'i (Muhammadiyah) than Iqbal (NU). Both Syafi'i and Machasin are skeptical of the usefulness of imagining an unseen world apart from God. In contrast, Atun (Muhammadiyah) appears to be much closer to Iqbal (NU) in that both expressed a strong conviction that the world of spirits and supernatural powers is a metaphysical reality. Both Syafi'i and Machasin acknowledged that their scientific imagination of reality is rare among the great majority of members of both Muhammadiyah and NU. While neither Syafi'i nor Atun saw bid'ah or syirik as major threats to Indonesian Islam, they were true to the principles of Muhammadiyah in agreeing that we should keep our distance from gaib. In contrast, consistent with the teachings of NU, Machasin and Iqbal saw no problem in upholding traditional Javanese rituals that are intended to appease or delight the spirits.

Even more complexity is added if we include the views of Wening and Zainal. Wening used the term nationalist to characterize herself. The Javanese martial arts tradition is steeped in mysticism (kejawen). Therefore I expected Wening to strongly affirm the reality of the unseen world since she is the head of a martial arts school. In contrast, discourse about religion and science is often dominated by attempts to rationalize religion so as to integrate it with science. Therefore I expected Zainal to be skeptical of the unseen world of supernatural powers since he is one of Indonesia's leading experts on religion and science.

To my surprise, Wening appeared quite secular in outlook while Zainal strongly stated his belief in unseen supernatural powers. Wening viewed both Muhammadiyah and NU as overly conservative and expressed her conviction that true Islam is meant to serve humanity rather than worrying too much about the supernatural. Meanwhile, Zainal said that he often has direct experiences of the unseen world. Ironically, Wening acknowledged that while she doesn't believe in spiritual beings she is afraid of them and steers clear of graveyards and mystical places of power. Like Machasin, she acknowledged that there is much she doesn't understand, but she believes that science will ultimately explain these mysteries. Also like Machasin, Wening feels the presence of unseen powers, but she chooses to follow her rational mind rather than her feelings. Perhaps Wening was influenced by her French literary studies in a secular European context, whereas Zainal was influenced by studying science and religion in the more religious context of the American Midwest.

While Wening acknowledged that she is not terribly strict in following the requirements of Islam, Zainal strongly affirmed his orthodox practices. Nevertheless, Zainal showed ambivalence in affirming traditional under-standings of a sacred cosmos. On the one hand, he said his experience of God is not so much of a personal God as of a power that permeates reality. So, too, with spiritual beings. He does not believe in spirits and *jins* but rather in the infusion of all reality with powers beyond our comprehension. Unlike Wening, Zainal did not appear afraid of these powers but rather experienced them as positive forces. Zainal believes that spirit possession is a purely psychological process, but he acknowledges that certain people he respects claim to have had direct experience of spirits. He did not rule out their existence, even though he has not experienced them directly.

Zainal said that he was raised by a father who was extremely pious and strictly orthodox, believing in *gaib*, but careful to have nothing to do with any powers other than God. He contrasted this with his own teenage son, who has far more scientific knowledge about the physical world than prior generations but is much more open to nonrational explanations. According to Zainal, science is uncovering many things that demystify the world. But science cannot give meaning to our lives. Reenchantment is a process, after disenchantment, through which we create meanings that transcend the materialist explanations of science. Thus, "Science takes things apart and asks how they work, religion puts them back together and asks what they mean" (Sacks 2011:284).

These six interviews do not reveal a strong correlation between Muham-madiyah and disenchantment. All of these expert witnesses agreed that the great majority of members of both Muhammadiyah and NU believe in the metaphysical reality of *gaib*. None thought that increasing piety and conser-vatism were accompanied by decreasing belief in an unseen world, but rather the opposite. The more pious people become the more they believe in the unseen world. In terms of the beliefs and experiences of these six Muslim leaders, there was no correlation between Muhammadiyah and disenchantment and NU and enchantment. I did not choose these six for their views. I expected the Muhammadiyah leaders to be more disenchanted and the NU leaders to have a stronger belief in *gaib*. In fact both Muhammadiyah leaders expressed strong belief in *gaib* while one of the NU leaders was a skeptic. Muhammadiyah leaders did follow their type by suggesting that we should stay away from building relations with *gaib*, whereas NU leaders were tolerant of *gaib* rituals.

Four of the six Muslim leaders expressed the strong belief that spiritual beings or powers apart from God exist and can affect us. The other two (Machasin and Wening) do not believe in such beings or powers. Five of the six experienced feelings of the presence of unseen powers. Ironically the one who categorically denied ever experiencing the presence of unseen beings or powers (Syafi'i) expressed belief in their existence. One out of two from both Muhammadiyah and NU had no doubts about the metaphysical reality of *gaib* (Atun and Iqbal). Both had vivid experiences of the supernatural. In contrast, the other two representatives of Muhammadiyah and

Table 6.1 *Comparing Indonesian Muslim Leaders' Views of the Unseen World*

Indonesian Muslim Leaders	Belief in the Reality of Gaib	Personal Experience of Gaib	Participation in Gaib Rituals	Toleration of Gaib Rituals	Confidence in Scientific Reasoning	Lives in a Sacred Cosmos
Syafii Maarif (Muhammadiyah)	Moderate	Weak	No	Moderate	Strong	Yes
Siti Syamsiyatun (Muhammadiyah)	Strong	Strong	No	Moderate	Moderate	Yes
M. Machasin (NU)	No	Moderate	Yes	Strong	Strong	Yes
M. Iqbal Ahnaf (NU)	Strong	Strong	Yes	Strong	Moderate	Yes
Wening Udasmoro (Independent)	No	Moderate	Yes	Strong	Strong	Yes
Zainal Abidin Bagi (Independent)	Strong	Strong	Yes	Strong	Strong	Yes
Common Stereotypes of Islamic Groups						
Muhammadiyah	Yes	Moderate	No	No	Strong	Moderate
NU	Yes	Strong	Yes	Yes	Weak	Strong
Nationalist/Mystic	Yes	Strong	Yes	Yes	Moderate	Strong
Radical Islamist	Yes	Strong	No	No	Weak	Strong

NU (Syafi'i and Machasin), appeared to be functional rationalists, choosing to trust science and Scripture to explain the meaning of experience.

There was no gender correlation regarding enchantment and disenchantment in this group. Many Indonesians think that women are more sensitive to the unseen world and are, for example, more susceptible to trance and spirit possession. In some communities, most mediums are women. However, in this group one woman was a strong rationalist and the other (from Muhammadiyah) had many experiences of the unseen world. The men were similarly split but hard to characterize: three of the four had experienced *gaib*, but one of the three did not believe in it. The one male who said he had never experienced the unseen world, apart from God, believed that spirits and *jins* exist.

All six of the leaders interviewed still inhabit a sacred cosmos. However, the symbolic languages they use to express their social imaginaries are quite varied. They all believe in God or a transcendent power and practice their beliefs through more or less orthodox religious rituals. All believe in an unseen, supernatural reality, although they differ in their existential experience, beliefs, and practices regarding the way we should relate to it. Table 6.1 compares the views of the six Muslim leaders.

The next part of the book includes three chapters that explore one aspect of a sacred cosmos, the nature of power. Chapter 7 considers traditional, or "Javanese," views of power and the ways in which they interact with religious and modern conceptions in the social imaginaries of Indonesians.

Part III
Traditional, Modern, and Religious
Imaginations of Power

PART III EXPLORES imaginations and practices of power in various parts of Indonesia. First, it examines theories of a radical difference between Javanese and western imaginations of power and the extent to which Indonesians from various different religious and ethnic groups still hold traditional imaginations of power as substantive "energy." Second, it explores modern and postmodern ideas of power that are used by Indonesian intellectuals to understand rapid social change. Third, it explores the power of Islam in people's everyday lives.

7

Traditional Indonesian Imaginations of Power

Power is that intangible, mysterious and divine energy, which animates the universe. It is manifested in every aspect of the natural world, in stones, trees, clouds and fire, but is expressed quintessentially in the central mystery of life, the process of generation and regeneration.

—Benedict R. Anderson

THIS CHAPTER EXPLORES cultural perceptions and practices of power in Indonesia under four clusters of ideas. The first is the influential ideal-type theory of Javanese and western concepts of power. The chapter explores the usefulness of this theory as a tool for understanding traditional Indonesian imaginations of power. We also examine the empirical results of a question regarding power on our questionnaire to see how widespread mystical, substantive imaginations of power in Indonesia are.

The second section examines Indonesian traditional, religious, and modern ideas of an ideal leader. This section also has a theoretical and empirical component, including interpretation of the preferred choices of our respondents from around Indonesia regarding their imagination of the characteristics of an ideal leader.

The third section explores Indonesian imaginations of an ideal government. As with all the questions on our questionnaire, respondents were asked to choose among languages that we classified as traditional, modern, or religious. The answers reveal which symbol system is most cogent according to the respondent.

The fourth section focuses on the ideal characteristics Indonesians hope will be embodied in their society. What kind of power would they like to see diffused throughout society? Power is not only exercised by elites; it is also revealed in the ability of a society to achieve its ideals.

Living in a sacred cosmos is not only about belief in magic. It also encompasses a moral and religious imagination of power. This chapter shows how traditional, religious, and modern imaginations of power are interconnected in relation to imaginations of the sources of power and the ideals of leadership, government, and society.

Magical and Substantive Imaginations of Power

In a celebrated article, Benedict R. Anderson created an ideal-type analysis of ancient Javanese concepts of power that are fundamentally different from western concepts. He believed that ancient Javanese practices are still influential in the political behavior of Indonesians. Anderson's theory explains Javanese power in terms of four basic differences from western concepts of power.

1. *Power* in the West is an abstract word that describes a relationship of domination or influence between people, whereas in Java *kekuasaan* (power) is something concrete and substantial. A Javanese can own power independent of his relationship with other people. Certain objects are powerful because of the living energy or being that inhabits them. Ownership of such objects confers power on the owner. Power "is not a theoretical postulate but an existential reality. Power is that intangible, mysterious, and divine energy which animates the universe" (Anderson 1990:22).

2. In the West, sources of power are extremely diverse. Power can derive from technology, wealth, social status, knowledge, organization, charisma, formal office, and many other sources. In contrast, Javanese power is homogeneous and derives from only one source. According to Anderson, Javanese believe that power is located in all of nature but ultimately derives from God alone. Power emanates from God and is ultimately a single, unified reality.

3. Anderson suggests that westerners believe power is continually created anew and is without any inherent limits. Therefore there is no limit to the accumulation of power. For example, with the creation of the nuclear bomb, destructive power is now much greater than it ever was before. Good organization can increase everyone's power. In contrast, Javanese believe that the sum total of power in the universe is fixed and unchanging. Power does not increase or decrease except with regard to its division

between people (or places). This means that if power increases in one place it must decrease in some other place. Power is a zero-sum game. "For political theory, this has the important corollary that concentration of power in one place or in one person requires a proportional diminution elsewhere" (Anderson 1990:23).

4. According to Anderson, western concepts of power include a moral dimension such that power is subject to ethical judgments. Power is morally ambiguous. Power can be used for good or evil. It can be legitimate or illegitimate, right or wrong, and true or false. In contrast, Javanese power has no relation to morality. Javanese power is a kind of energy that exists throughout the cosmos. Power is like the strength of the wind or the eruption of a volcano, which cannot be evaluated in moral terms. We may or may not like the effects of power, but, like the eruption of a volcano, they are not subject to ethical judgments. "Power is neither legitimate nor illegitimate. Power is" (Anderson 1990:24).

Every theory is built on a framework of assumptions. Anderson's theory is based on concepts of power and social evolution derived from Max Weber. Following Weber, Anderson thought Javanese culture was evolving from traditional to modern. Anderson wrote about Javanese power in part to dispute Weber's conception of power as having three types: traditional, charismatic, and legal/rational. According to Anderson, there are only two types. Charismatic power is a part of traditional power. "One could then argue that when Weber contrasted charismatic with traditional or rational-legal domination, he was the victim of a sort of optical illusion. In reality, there were only two general forms of domination, one linked to substantive and the other to instrumental/relational concepts of power. ... [A]ll traditional authority was charismatic, and all charismatic authority traditional" (Anderson 1990:79).[1]

Ideal-type analysis creates a polarity, or dichotomy, for the purpose of contrast and clarification, not empirical description. No one thinks in just a "western" or "Javanese" way about power. Anderson's work magnifies two contrasting extremes about what power is. It is a heuristic model to help us think, not an empirical description.[2] Anderson's typology illuminates many things, including significant aspects of President Sukarno's and President Soeharto's styles of leadership. Sukarno was the first President of Indonesia, holding power from 1945–1965. The essential difference between the two types is between a substantive model of power as an "energy" that can be possessed independent of its use and an abstract model in which power is a relational process between two or more people. Anderson's Weberian assumptions about social evolution from traditional to modern societies are problematic, but his ideal types are productive for discussion.[3]

Indonesian political behavior is far more complex than either of these types would indicate. The anthropologist Koentjaraningrat pointed out that Anderson exaggerated the mystic and supernatural elements in ancient Javanese literature.[4] According to him, even in ancient times Javanese people could distinguish fact from fiction in a good story. Many Indonesians believe in the substantive, supernatural aspects of power without denying the more mundane, abstract, relational, and rational realities of power politics. Thus the first pair of contrasting types (abstract relational power vs. concrete substantive power) is misleading. Most Javanese see no conflict between these two types. They are not evolving from one conception to the other but rather creating a complex new synthesis.

Most Indonesians agree that all power derives from God and is ultimately one. But not many think that all power is homogeneous. Even Javanese mystics don't think all kinds of power are alike. A Javanese shaman (*dukun*) explained to me why I must go to different graveyards to amass different kinds of power. He said that each of the ancient Muslim apostles (*Wali Sanga*) was powerful in a different way. One had the mystical power to do supernatural things (*sakti*). Another was extremely rich but had no supernatural powers. A third lived simply and had no powers but had great moral presence and authority (*berwibawa*). The shaman explained that if I wanted to get rich it was no good meditating and praying at the graveyard of a sage who had great wisdom but no wealth. Similarly, if I sought supernatural power I shouldn't meditate at the grave of a wise or wealthy sage. Each of the nine traditional saints of Java had a different kind of power, and each could provide help only in his area of power.

Anderson's third set of polarities suggests that Javanese power is limited whereas western power is unlimited. Many people of all cultures view power as a zero-sum game (I win means you lose). But that does not mean they really think power is limited. A Javanese mystic may hesitate to reveal his deepest esoteric secrets to his disciples until he is on his deathbed because he fears losing power. But every day the mystic teaches his students and gives them various kinds of power without losing his own. Sometimes power politics is a zero-sum game, but Indonesians are aware of all kinds of ways to increase different kinds of power.

The fourth type contrasts western ethical conceptions of power with amoral Javanese power as simply a natural force. In my experience, Indonesians all see a relationship between power and morality. They are very moralistic in their discussions of power and politics. In contrast, there is a strong stream of "value-free political realism" in western political science flowing from Machiavelli through Hobbes and Rousseau and up to Hans Morganthau, Henry Kissinger, and Kenneth Waltz (see Adeney 1988).[5] Many western political philosophers supported a value-free approach to politics based on presumptions of self-interest as a law governing all human behavior. Of course Anderson is correct in his assessment that the question of legitimacy, justice, and the morality of power is also a major stream in the history of western political discourse.

However, the same can be said about Indonesia. Ancient Javanese literature connected power and morality. Religious leaders who were not connected to the court functioned as moral critics, or prophets, who were admired because of their courage in criticizing those in power (Anderson 1990). In Javanese morality, the possession and retention of power is contingent on being without self-interest (*tanpa pamrih*) (Magnis-Suseno 1984). Anyone who rules according to selfish ambition will lose his or her power. Sincere shamans (*dukun*) in Indonesia all offer their services without asking for payment because they believe that if they ask for money they will lose their power. Indonesian stories from the *Ramayana* and *Mahabharata* are all tales about power and morality. For most Indonesians, morality is not based on abstract, Kantian ethical principles. Rather, it includes a confusing mix of traditions (*adat*), religion, mysticism, and pragmatism (Magnis-Suseno 1984).

According to Koentjaraningrat, moral authority (*kewibawaan*) was a basic requirement in ancient Javanese conceptions of power (1984:135). Authority (*wibawa*) implies moral presence and virtue. Those who are shamed (*dipermalukan*) by having their sins exposed to public view lose their authority and their ability to lead or rule. Indonesians like to think of their culture as a culture of shame (*budaya malu*), and they frequently lament the lack of shame in corrupt political leaders.[6]

Anderson's conception of Javanese power is much simpler than that of western power: Javanese power is one, homogeneous, limited, amoral energy. In contrast, western conceptions of power are complex: power is extremely varied, unlimited, relational, and ethical. Such a contrast deserves to be questioned and may reflect evolutionary assumptions that Indonesia is evolving from simple, traditional, hierarchical practices to complex, progressive (*lebih maju*), democratic practices.

Anderson's evolutionary assumptions about the transition from traditional to modern types of power is also widely held by Indonesians. According to some, substantive conceptions of power are superstitious, feudal, and authoritarian. They are gradually being replaced with rational democratic ideas that are more appropriate for the modern world. This may be true, but it is only one way to interpret the transitions that are going on in Indonesia. Indonesians are experiencing very rapid social, political, and economic change. But to characterize that change as progress from traditional communities to modern society obscures as much as it enlightens. Cultural traditions and religious commitments are changing through interactions with modern ideas and education. They are not necessarily being left behind. Change is not progressing from primitive to modern. Rather, traditional practices and religious commitments are being transformed through interactions with modernity. Modernity is also being transformed through its integration with cultural traditions and religious beliefs. This book argues that Indonesia is constructing new, unique forms of modernity that incorporate many aspects of its traditional religious culture.

How widespread are traditional substantive views of power in Indonesia? To find the answer, we formulated a question about power in our questionnaire on Indonesian social imaginaries as follows.

Questionnaire Question IV.A on the nature and sources of power

> *Which of the following statements is the best description of power?*
>
>   1. Power can be obtained by fasting, ascetic practices, or from a magical object such as a *keris* (sacred Javanese dagger).
>
>   2. Power describes the relations between people. Anyone can exercise power over another person through use of superior knowledge or technology or by holding a higher position in the structure.
>
>   3. Only the will of God determines who is given power.

The first, "traditional" response assumes a substantive view of power as something that an individual can own, similar to Anderson's theory of Javanese conceptions. The second, "modern" response corresponds to the "Western" conception of power in Anderson's theory. Power is a relationship subject to negotiation. The third, "religious" response understands power as completely in the hands of God. The religious response could fit into either the "western" or "Javanese" concepts of power, but it is closer to the Javanese conception since it includes a supernatural element.

The results of our research show that the great majority of Indonesians chose the "modern" language as their preferred imagination of power. Overall, of the 2,433 participants who answered this question, 66 percent chose the modern response, 31 percent chose the religious response, and just 3 percent preferred the traditional language. The traditional imagination of power was preferred by just 3 percent of Muslims, 2 percent of Protestants, 1 percent of Catholics, 1 percent of Hindus, and none of the Buddhists. Muslims preferred the modern response (72 percent), compared to 49 percent of Protestants, 72 percent of Catholics, 83 percent of Hindus, and all the Buddhists.

If we compare ethnic groups, it appears that not many Javanese had read Anderson's book because only 1 percent chose the "Javanese" concept of power! There was not much difference between Javanese Muslims and non-Muslims except that 86 percent of Javanese Catholics favored modern language (compared to 69 percent of Javanese Muslims). Among Moluccans, 3 percent chose the traditional answer. Most Moluccan Muslims preferred modern language (55 percent) over religious language (40 percent), whereas Moluccan Christians preferred religious language (60 percent) over modern language (38 percent). Acehnese seemed to have the most traditional views as 13 percent of them chose the traditional answer. Most Acehnese preferred modern language (63 percent) over religious language (24 percent).

Most religious groups strongly preferred the modern, relational imagination of power over the religious imagination of God as the one who determines who has power. The one exception was the Protestants. They were divided 49 to 49 percent between modern and religious language. Hardly anyone seemed to favor the traditional language.

Several things stand out in these figures. Muslims have a very high preference for the modern relational understanding of power. Just 25 percent of them chose the theocentric answer, that God is the one who determines who is powerful. This is actually less than the Protestants and Catholics. Twice as many Protestants than Muslims said that power is in the hands of God. Mainline Protestants in Indonesia mostly belong to Reformed Calvinist churches, so their high level of religious responses may be related to a strong doctrine of predestination and divine sovereignty.

The very high percentage of Hindus (83 percent) who preferred to think of power as an abstract structural relationship is also striking. The majority of Hindu respondents were from Bali, "the home of the gods," where religious practices are dominated by interactions with spiritual beings. Therefore it might be expected that more of them would have preferred the magical, substantial conception of power. However, that was not the case. Of course a strong preference for the modern relational language does not mean they do not believe in the substantive conception of power as well.

Another figure that stands out is the relatively high percentage of Acehnese (13 percent) who preferred the traditional conception. Since the

Table 7.1 *Responses to Question IV.A on Imaginations of Power*

Groups	Traditional Power as Substance	Modern Power as Relational	Religious Power Comes from God
Muslims	3%	72%	25%
Protestants	2%	49%	49%
Catholics	1%	72%	27%
Hindus	1%	83%	16%
Buddhist	0%	100%	0%
Non-Muslims	2%	59%	39%
Javanese Muslims	1%	70%	29%
Javanese Protestants	0	67%	33%
Javanese Catholics	0	86%	14%
All Javanese	1%	70%	29%
Moluccan Muslims	5%	55%	40%
Moluccan Protestants	2%	38%	60%
All Moluccans	3%	46%	51%
All Acehnese (Muslims)	13%	63%	24%
All Indonesians	3%	66%	31%

percentage of Acehnese who chose theocentric religious language (24 percent) is similar to that of all Muslims (25 percent), it means that they chose modern language 10 percent less than all Muslims.

The difference between Javanese and Moluccan Protestants is striking. Two-thirds of the Javanese Protestants preferred modern language, and the other third chose religious language. Moluccan Protestants were the converse. Just 38% chose modern language, while 60% said power is in the hands of God. This sharp difference suggests that in this case, ethnic and geographical factors may be more influential than religious factors.

These figures do not represent absolute beliefs, but rather, which is the most cogent symbol system for representing Indonesian imaginations of power. It is quite possible to "believe" in all three answers. A good example is Siti Syamsiyatun in our interview with her in the previous chapter. Atun said the modern answer was her primary response to the question about power. Power is relational and structural. However she also affirmed the traditional response. She believes it is possible to get power through ascetic exercises, magic or sacred objects which contain an unseen being. While she thinks it is possible, she cautions that it is unwise. According to Atun, power from magical sources is usually just physical power and may be evil. It's better to stay away from such sources of power. She also affirms that power is from God. God is sovereign in determining who holds positions of authority. I suspect that this synthetic understanding of power is very widespread in Indonesia. Most Indonesians are fluent in using more than one symbol system depending on the situation and context. Many respondents may have been influenced by the fact that they were in the academic context of a university when they filled out the questionnaire.

Although our research does not show the absolute beliefs of Indonesians about power, it does demonstrate that the majority of educated Indonesians prefer modern, social scientific imaginations of power over traditional or religious terminology. The vast majority steer away from magical or substantive language about power. This may indicate growing disenchantment and might support the thesis of an evolutionary development from traditional magic to modern sociological explanations of power. It does show that most of these Indonesians are comfortable with abstract theoretical language about power as a relationship. But, as we have seen in the answers to other questions, it does not indicate that Indonesians no longer believe in an unseen world.

Anderson's ideal-type theory of ancient Javanese conceptions of power is not "wrong." Even his four ideal types of Javanese conceptions may reflect how some ancient and modern Javanese think about power. But it is certainly not the primary way in which most Indonesians imagine power today.

Traditional Imaginations of a Powerful Leader

Most Indonesians imagine power as invested in a leader. Power as a concept is abstract, but leaders are concrete. Indonesian imaginations of a good and powerful leader are shaped by their ethnic cultures. Most Indonesians would resent an assumption that all ethnic groups think like Javanese. Traditional *adat* for selecting and empowering a leader differ widely from group to group. For many, their ethnic identification with Aceh, Arab, Asmat, Bali, Banjar, Banten, Batak, Betawi, Biak, Bugis, Chinese, Dyak, Flores, Gayo, Gorontalo, Indian, Java, Lampung, Madura, Makassar, Manggarai, Minahasa, Minang Kabau, Nias, Papua, Poso, Riau, Sasak, Sumba, Sunda, Toraja, Wamena, West Timor, and so on, determines what qualities are necessary to become a leader. Many of these groups, especially the Papuans and Dyaks, have many different tribes within them, each with its own distinctive traditions of leadership.

Some groups are strongly patriarchal and patrilineal, like the Balinese and Bataks. Some are patriarchal and matrilineal, like the Minang Kabau. Some have ancient traditions of female leadership, like the Acehnese. Many have elaborate, traditional requirements for leadership. I recall a student explaining that in his ethnic community to be selected leader a person had to complete twelve *adat* rituals. Preparation for the rituals was so time consuming and expensive that for most people it would take their entire lifetime. This ensured that leaders would be old. It also ensured that not only would they be rich but they would also be willing to spend all their wealth on rituals, which redistributed their resources to the whole group.

Competition for leadership is very intense in Indonesia. It sometimes seems that power struggles for leadership are a constant reality at every level of society. Most political parties have split at one time or another, usually because of a power struggle for leadership. Some continue to have rival claimants to power. Muslim, Protestant, Catholic, Hindu, Buddhist, and Confucian organizations often are weakened or split by continual jockeying for power. Universities split or lose faculty over the election of rectors (presidents). Even very local, small-scale leadership changes can trigger a crisis. Once a group of Christian students from one ethnic group who were studying in Yogyakarta gathered at our home to plan Christmas celebrations. The meeting bogged down when they tried to select the head of the Christmas Committee (Panitia Natal). After hours of heated debate between factions supporting rival candidates, I finally went to bed at midnight while the conflict raged on into the wee hours.

Part of the problem is related to ancient Indonesian traditions of selecting leaders by discussion and consensus (*musyawarah mufakat*). This is the traditional way of choosing leaders in many villages throughout Indonesia. Ideally it is very democratic since everyone has the opportunity to express an opinion. A wise leader discerns when the group is in agreement and states the decision of the group. Even if there are a few who don't agree, they will submit to the decision of the group and declare their support so that there will be unanimity. For President Soeharto, this process was a convenient way to consolidate power. Before a major decision, he would privately lobby the key parties involved and elicit their agreement with his plan. When they held the discussion to reach consensus, no one would dare speak out against his opinion since everyone knew the decision had already been made. There was always consensus because it was too dangerous to oppose him. Since the fall of Soeharto, democratic processes have been instituted at every level of society, replacing earlier top-down appointments or consensus mechanisms. Rapid urbanization and social mobility mean that more and more communities are no longer monoethnic. Large and small organizations still hold meetings for discussion to reach consensus, but if they do not achieve clear results, they hold an election with secret ballots. Many Indonesians are dissatisfied with democracy, especially because of the widespread practice of "money politics." Vote buying is very common. But even those who are dissatisfied are unable to suggest an alternative system.

Even though Indonesians are very aware of sharp differences in their ethnic cultures of leadership, there are certain commonalities in traditional imaginations of a powerful leader with which most Indonesians would agree. Indonesians are more alike than they realize. Three characteristics stand out. The first is that a powerful leader is refined and subtle (*halus*) in his or her use of language. This characteristic is well known for Central Javanese. But even Indonesian ethnic groups that are famous for being very outspoken and crude compared to the people from the *kraton* cultures of Central Java are refined and subtle in their use of language in comparison with most of the world. A Batak, Bugis, or Moluccan is a paragon of subtlety and refined restraint compared to an Italian or Brazilian. Indonesian leaders are supposed to be able to control their tongues, to be patient and polite. Ahok was not reelected as the governor of Jakarta not only because of his religion, ethnicity, or alleged blasphemy but because of a lack of refinement and subtlety in his speech. On the other hand, the fact that he was such a popular governor (in spite of being a Chinese Christian) indicates that traditional imaginations of leadership are being modified by awareness that someone who makes serious progress tackling complex modern problems may also be a good leader.

A second traditional characteristic is that ideal Indonesian leaders have an inner charisma, which attracts, guides, and controls their followers. Anderson was correct in asserting that charisma and inner power are fundamental elements in Javanese traditional imaginations of power.[7] This is true not only in Java but throughout Indonesia. Indonesians from many different ethnic groups believe that the use of inner power or charisma to control social reality is a fundamental characteristic of a powerful leader. For some Indonesians, huge demonstrations (e.g., against Trump or Ahok) indicate that a leader lacks the inner charisma to control the people. This is one reason why many people feared that massive demonstrations in Jakarta could lead to the fall of the national government. President Jokowi may have botched his handling of the first mass demonstration in November 2016, but he handled the second with elegant skill.

The third characteristic of an ideal powerful leader is virtue. A powerful leader should be without self-interest or ambition. In Indonesia candidates for leadership positions routinely deny that they want to be picked. They say they will run or accept leadership positions only if they are compelled to do so by their followers. Whereas many people in the West regard ambition as a virtue characteristic of people willing to strive for excellence, in Indonesia most people think of ambition as a vice indicative of a selfish person who puts his or her interests above those of others. A powerful leader in Indonesia should be *ikhlas*, willing to give up his or her own ego and accept the will of the group. The ideal leader can then lead by example.

Good leaders show their followers how to live in the world by being examples of patience, piety, calmness, benevolence, refinement, simplicity, and courage.

Ahok was often criticized for his displays of negative emotions such as anger and disappointment. His decision not to appeal his two-year blasphemy conviction seems to have been motivated by his belief that it was God's will for him to lose the election and he should accept the court's decision, however unjust, with patience and courage. President Soeharto was a popular leader for most of his thirty-two years in power in part because he studiously projected the virtues of patience, calmness, and benevolence (real or imagined) while eliminating all opposition.

In traditional Indonesian shadow puppet theater the heroes are thin, delicate, and highly refined.[8] They move slowly and speak in very polite high Javanese. When they go to battle, they hardly move, repelling and defeating their enemies by means of their inner power not superior muscle. Their enemies are huge, strong, and monstrous. But they are no match for the inner power of the heroes. The ideal traditional leader rules by means of inner authority (*wibawa*) backed by virtue and the power to guide and control the people through example and inner strength. According to Ward Keeler, "In contrast to a less powerful person, who must exert himself strenuously to attain any end, such a king need do very little. Should he need to exert himself obviously, he demonstrates a lack of potency. So his power must always be in a sense absent: evident in the condition of the kingdom but never demonstrated in coercive action" (1987:85: see also Anderson 1990).

Joko Widodo (Jokowi) won the 2014 Indonesian presidential election in part because he appealed to these traditional qualities of a leader. Jokowi is thin and seems gentle, like a typical traditional Javanese. His persona fit well with the traditional ideal ethics of Java. He appeared attentive and focused (*waspada*), calm (*tenang*), humble (*rendah hati*), simple (*sederhana*), harmonious (*rukun*), honest (*jujur*), patient (*sabar*), and ready to work with whoever was willing (*gotong royong*). Compared to his opponent, Prabowo, who seemed ambitious, Jokowi appeared to be almost without self-interest (*tanpa pamrih*) and willing to give of himself in service (*ikhlas*) (see Magnis-Suseno 1984). These traditional marks of Javanese virtue are highly regarded throughout Indonesia. In spite of an extremely vicious campaign attacking his character, Jokowi won the election by more than six percentage points, in part because of his image as a virtuous Javanese leader.[9] To the disappointment of many activists, since his election Jokowi has been somewhat passive and has failed to vigorously combat various social evils. But this, too, is in keeping with the traditional imagination of a powerful leader.

In Indonesia the myth of a Just King/Queen (Ratu Adil) has reoccurred over the centuries up to the present. Many Indonesians believe that a just ruler will have power to bring all things into balance so that harmony and prosperity will reign in both nature and society. There are high stakes in having a powerful, virtuous leader. In our city of Yogyakarta, many residents believe that the harmony of the city is caused by the inner power of the sultan, who maintains a balance between the male power of the volcano Mount Merapi and the female power of the ocean (the Queen of the South).

The three characteristics of an ideal traditional leader, subtle language, inner charisma and virtue, can be summarized in the word *dignity* (*bermartabat*). Someone who is *bermartabat* is not only dignified. He or she has an inner quality of nobility, which shows in outward signs, such as refined speech and dress, but also includes a character of authority (*berwibawa*), which compels loyalty (*kesetiaan*). Leaders who have dignity do not have to compel obedience by force or violence. Their inner strength (*kekuatan*) controls the people by the force of their character. Their example of virtue and honor guides the people.

Peter Berger suggests that dignity and honor were the fundamental social values of traditional premodern people (Berger 1983). Dignity and honor were not the personal attributes of an individual. Rather they were contingent on a person's role in society. One had dignity when one performed with honor the tasks associated with one's role and position in the community. Honor and dignity were inner qualities but also relational and dependent on the acknowledgment of the community. Even the most lowly farmers, had dignity if they performed their farming duties with honor. But if a farmer tried to pretend that he was a knight, people would just laugh at him. The highest dignity was reserved for the high born, who had much heavier responsibilities to the community. In contrast, Berger suggests that modern people have a social ethic of authenticity. Authenticity is part of an individual's personal identity. Authenticity is what you have when all your social roles are stripped away and you decide who you want to be regardless of what anyone else may think.

Berger's ideal types illuminate the intense communality of leadership in Indonesia. However, I wondered if this traditional imagination of leadership is still widespread or is passing away under the onslaught of cynical power politics, corruption, technocratic bureaucracies, and religious conservatism. Is it isolated in some traditional communities or widespread throughout Indonesia? Are traditional concepts of a powerful leader part of a contemporary imagination of a sacred cosmos? On our questionnaire we looked for statistical evidence to help explore these issues by asking the following question.

Questionnaire Question IV.F on characteristics of a good leader

Which statement is most appropriate to describe a good leader for the people of Indonesia?

1. An educated, scientific leader who solves social problems by rational means.

2. A pious leader who counsels the people in accordance with the commandments of God.

3. A leader whose dignity controls and guides the people wisely by example.[10]

The first answer uses the modern vocabulary of education, science, rationality, and social problems. The focus is on solving social problems by rational means. According to this answer, the ideal leader has the intelligence, education, and scientific understanding to tackle the complex problems of society. The second answer uses religious language of piety and the commandments of God. The focus is on counseling and guiding (*membimbing*) in accordance with God's law. The ideal leader is a guide and mediator between the people and God. The third answer uses traditional language of dignity (*bermartabat*), inner character, and wisdom. The focus is on setting an example and controlling (*mengendalikan*) people in order to keep them on the right path. The ideal leader is a person of virtue and inner power who has the inner strength to create balance and control the people by his or her example.

The responses to this question for all groups were strongly in favor of the traditional language. Sixty percent of all Indonesians chose the traditional symbol system, including 58 percent of Muslims, 60 percent of Protestants, 65 percent of Catholics, 72 percent of Hindus, and 100 percent of Buddhists. The Muslims slightly preferred religious language (23 percent) over modern language (19 percent), while for Protestants the religious preference was stronger (religious 28 vs. modern 12 percent). Catholics and Hindus preferred modern language over religious (Catholics 29 to 6 percent, Hindus 21 to 7 percent). However, a strong majority in all groups imagined a good leader in traditional language. Table 7.2 shows a strong resemblance between the statistical preferences of Muslims and Protestants, whereas Catholics and Hindus resemble each other.

Table 7.2 *Responses to Question IV.F on the Qualities of a Good Leader*

Group	Traditional Dignity, Control Example	Modern Reason, Solve Problems Science	Religious Piety, Counsel, Mediate God's Commands
Muslim	58%	19%	23%
Protestant	60%	12%	28%
Catholic	65%	29%	6%
Hindu	72%	21%	7%
Buddhist	100%	0%	0%
All Indonesians	60%	18%	22%
Java	62%	16%	22%
Sunda	59%	14%	27%
Makassar	64%	18%	18%
Minang	55%	17%	28%
Aceh	58%	25%	22%
Toraja	67%	9%	24%
Minahasa	65%	13%	22%
Molucca	56%	15%	29%
Flores	65%	31%	4%
Bali	67%	25%	8%
Dyak	73%	12%	15%

The table enables a comparison of the statistical responses by different ethno-religious groups. There are five ethnic groups that are predominantly Muslim, three that are predominantly Protestant, one that is predominantly Catholic, and two that are predominantly Hindu.[11] From this selection, the majority in every ethnic group and religion preferred the traditional characterization of leadership. The statistics for the ethnic groups are generally consistent with the totals for their religious communities. There are a couple of minor anomalies. For example, the statistics for Minang and Molucca are virtually identical. This may have been influenced by the fact that the Moluccans include both Muslims and Protestants. Aceh was the only Muslim majority group that slightly preferred modern over religious language. However, their preference for the traditional language matched the total for all Muslims (58 percent).

The three responses are not incompatible. Most Indonesians would agree with all three answers. Nevertheless, the strong preference for the traditional language may shed light on why so few Indonesians vote for religious political parties. In spite of increasing piety, religious political parties have declined in influence over the past few elections. The three strictly Islamic parties garnered less than 15 percent of the total national legislative vote in 2014, which was less than in the previous election.[12] This does not mean that Indonesians don't care about the religion of politicians. In elections political candidates from nonreligious parties vie with each other to demonstrate their piety. Ironically, candidates from Muslim parties sometimes do the opposite. They try to show how secular and tolerant they are.

Traditional Imaginations of Good Government

Our questionnaire included a related question about the respondent's imagination of what constitutes a good government.

Questionnaire Question III.C on the characteristics of a good government

Of the following, which is the most important characterization of a good government?

1. The government is like parents, who should guarantee the safety, peace, harmony, and prosperity of society.

2. The government is the representative of God on Earth and should guide its citizens to obey God's laws and live moral and good lives.

3. The government is formed by the people and must protect the freedom and human rights of all the citizens of Indonesia.

The first answer to this question uses traditional paternalistic/maternalistic language about government. This answer imagines government parents whose job it is to take care of their children, the people. Government has the heavy responsibility of taking care of the family and ensuring that all is well with it. The second, religious answer imagines government as God's representative. Government has the essentially religious task of creating a people who obey God's laws and live good moral lives. The third answer employs modern, liberal-democratic imaginations of government as responsible to the people and responsible for protecting the freedom and human rights of all citizens.

The statistical responses to this question are much more evenly balanced. Thirty percent of Indonesians chose the traditional answer, which employs the familial language of government as parents. This included 35 percent of Muslims, 19 percent of Protestants, 31 percent of Catholics, 39 percent of Hindus, and all of the Buddhists.

The largest group of Indonesians, 41 percent, chose the modern answer, which employs democratic, social contract language about government as responsible for protecting the freedom and human rights of citizens. This included 40 percent of Muslims, 33 percent of Protestants, 56 percent of Catholics, and 55 percent of Hindus.

Twenty-nine percent of Indonesians chose the religious language, which imagines government as representing of God on Earth. This included 25 percent of Muslims, 48 percent of Protestants, 13 percent of Catholics, and just 6 percent of Hindus. The high percentage of Protestants is notable. It's a little surprising that the Protestants had such a relatively high preference for the religious language, especially since they are a minority in the largest Muslim nation in the world. We might have expected them to prefer modern language about the protection of human rights. They may have been influenced by a strong Calvinist interpretation of the Apostle Paul's exhortation in Romans 13 to submit to government because it is God's representative on Earth. The low percentage of Muslims choosing religious language is also notable. If the influence of Islamic modernism were stronger, we would expect the percentage of Muslims choosing the religious answer (government as Kalifah—God's representative on earth) to be higher. As it stands, 75 percent of Muslims preferred traditional paternalist language or modern democratic language. This reflects the fact that most Indonesian Muslims do not want Indonesia to become an Islamic state.[13]

If we compare four ethnic groups that are predominantly Hindu (Bali), Catholic (Flores), Protestant (Toraja), and Muslim (Makassar/Bugis), we see that, although the ethnic group percentages for the different choices all differ from their dominant religious percentages, the proportions are

Table 7.3 *Responses to Question III.C on the Characteristics of Good Government*

Group	Traditional	Modern	Religious
Muslim	35%	40%	25%
Protestant	19%	33%	48%
Catholic	31%	56%	13%
Hindu	39%	55%	6%
Buddhist	100%	0%	0%
All Indonesians	30%	41%	29%
Makassar/Bugis	36%	36%	28%
Toraja	21%	24%	55%
Flores	30%	60%	10%
Balinese	33%	52%	15%

roughly the same. This suggests that religion is a stronger variable than ethnicity in people's imagination of a good government.

Traditional Imaginations of a Good Society

The goal of a good government is to produce a good society. Indonesians use different symbol systems in their imaginations of what constitutes a good society. Power should be used to help a society fulfill certain aims. Therefore we formulated the following question to try to see what kind of language people used to imagine the aims of their lives together.

Questionnaire Question II.C on the characteristics of a good society

Which of the following societies is most noble ("paling mulia")?

1. A society which obeys the commands of God and implements religious requirements.[14]

2. A society which uses science, reason and common sense to solve life's problems.

3. A society which maintains harmony, honors the ancestors and follows tradition.

In light of the response to the question about the aims of government and the qualities of a good leader, the response to this question was a little surprising. Seventy-two percent of all Indonesians chose the religious answer. An admirable society is one that obeys God and carries out its religious duties faithfully. This included 77 percent of Muslims, 73 percent of Protestants, 46 percent of Catholics, and 59 percent of Hindus. The fact that most Indonesians do not think that religious piety is the primary qualification of a good leader, or that government should act as God's representative, is not an indication that they do not want to have a deeply religious society. Their ideal society may be deeply religious, but they don't want the government to tell them how to do it.

There is quite a sharp difference between the Muslim and Hindu imaginations of a good society. Thirty-one percent of Hindus chose the traditional answer, compared to just 7 percent of Muslims. Twenty percent of Catholics preferred language about harmony and honoring ancestors, while Protestants, with just 10 percent choosing traditional values, were more similar to Muslims. Only the Catholics had a minority who chose religious language (46 percent), but even for them it was the most popular of the three choices.

There are some interesting ethnic variations. Eighty-one percent of indigenous West Papuan respondents, who were all Protestant or Catholic Christians, chose religious language. Only the Minang of West Sumatra had a higher percentage (85 percent) of those whose ideal society is obedient to God. In contrast, their fellow Muslims in nearby Aceh preferred religious language by only 67 percent. Only 58 percent of the Dyak respondents, who were mostly Hindu Kaharingan, favored religious language.

Indonesian imaginations of power are complex and hybrid. All Indonesians are influenced by the rituals, beliefs, traditions, and stories of their ethnic group. But none is purely "traditional." In this chapter we have seen that very few Indonesians primarily imagine power as a magical energy that a person can own. But that doesn't mean they don't believe that such powers exist. A strong majority from all groups favored traditional language about leaders whose inner character of authority controls the people wisely by example. But that doesn't mean they don't care if their leaders are educated or pious. About a third of Indonesians imagined government in

Table 7.4 *Responses to Question II.C on the Characteristics of a Good Society*

Group	Traditional Harmony, Respect for Ancestors, *Adat*	Modern Reason and Science	Religious Obey God, Implement Religion
Muslim	7%	16%	77%
Protestant	10%	17%	73%
Catholic	20%	34%	46%
Hindu	31%	10%	59%
Buddhist	0%	100%	0%
All Indonesians	11%	17%	72%
Minang/West Sumatra	3%	12%	85%
Aceh	14%	19%	67%
West Papua	9%	10%	81%
Dyak/Kalimantan	33%	9%	58%

traditional terms as like a parent who should take care of them. But most want their government to be democratically elected and to defend their human rights. They also expect their government to act like God's representative and protect public morality. A strong majority imagined a good society as one that obeys God and fulfills its religious duties. But that doesn't mean they don't care whether or not their society is harmonious or characterized by well-educated, intelligent people.

Of the four questions considered in this chapter, the results were evenly divided. Indonesians strongly favored a modern answer to the first question. They strongly favored a traditional answer to the second question, and they strongly favored a religious answer to the fourth question. On the third question they were fairly evenly divided (30 percent traditional, 40 percent modern, and 29 percent religious). I did not plan this even division between the four questions, but it nicely supports my thesis that Indonesians shift back and forth between different vocabularies and symbol systems. Indonesians live in a sacred cosmos that is infused with meaning from supernatural sources, but their imagination of reality is also informed by modern and religious imaginations.

8

Modern Indonesian Imaginations of Power

"Power and violence are opposites; where the one rules absolutely, the other is absent. Violence appears where power is in jeopardy, but left to its own course it ends in power's disappearance."

—Hannah Arendt

IN 1998 INDONESIA WAS SHAKEN to the bone by a political, economic, social, and cultural crisis. As the thirty-two-year-old regime of President Soeharto collapsed under massive protests, the country began a process of democratization that has fundamentally changed the exercise of power and government in Indonesia. The end of an authoritarian regime, delegitimation of the military, decentralization of power, and euphoria of "Reformasi" (Reformation) raised great expectations. Activists called for the "total reformation" of all aspects of government, including the institution of truly democratic processes; freedom of expression; and end to corruption, collusion, and nepotism (nicknamed "Korupsi, Kolusi, Neopotisme" or KKN); the rule of law; and vigorous protection of basic human rights (known as "Hak Asasi Manusia" or HAM). Many radical and serious changes were made in the structures of power in Indonesia.

Unfortunately, all the substantial changes introduced did not usher in a golden age of freedom and prosperity but rather a period of serious conflict between races, tribes, villages, religious communities, political groups, regions, and international economic interests. The transition crisis, which lasted from 1998 to 2002, was a period of power struggles, which were the inevitable result of the power vacuum that followed the fall of Soeharto. Conflicts that had been repressed for decades under a militaristic regime roared into life under the banner of democracy. Most were struggles over economic and political power under conditions in which the future direction of Indonesia was still uncertain. In a few places, there was mass violence amounting to virtual civil war. By 2002 there were no more outbreaks of mass violence, although isolated incidents of ethno-religious conflict continued to occur until 2004. In 2004 the reformist military general Susilo Bambang Yudhoyono (known as SBY) was directly elected president by a large majority of Indonesians in what was internationally lauded as an open and fair election.

Now, after more than fifteen years of political stability and economic growth, democracy is well entrenched, but corruption and the rise of radicalism lead some to question whether decentralized democratic institutions are able to effectively address Indonesia's many problems. In late 2016, just after the election of US president Donald Trump, Indonesia was rocked by huge demonstrations organized by Islamic radicals.[1] Hundreds of thousands of Muslims flocked to Jakarta, demanding that Basuki Tjahaja Purnama (Ahok), the Chinese Christian governor of the capital province, be imprisoned for blaspheming Islam.[2] There were even fears that the massive demonstrations might bring down the government of President Joko Widodo (Jokowi), who is a friend of Ahok. The crisis was averted due to adept political maneuvering by President Jokowi and the military. But questions remain about the stability of democracy and the growth of radicalism in Indonesia.

This chapter explores how prominent western social theorists can help explain the dynamics of power in Indonesia. Can democratic institutions bridge the huge differences between different interest groups in Indonesia? How can Indonesians navigate extremely rapid social and economic change? How does the capitalist world economy oppress Indonesians? What is the positive relevance of religion? Is there a way to resolve the tensions between hierarchical power conceived as domination and democratic aspirations that locate power in the people? How can the public sphere be shaped to promote rational discourse? How do knowledge/power regimes control and guide Indonesians to govern themselves? And how do cultural elites use symbolic violence to dominate society?

The Division and Limitations of Power

Power is not whole or monolithic. Rather it is divided into many different kinds of power held by different groups for different purposes. These groups are rarely unified, or united with each other, except when facing some large outside threat to them all. Even then they may not unite because they hold different goals and have different interests. They are just as likely to compete with each other as to cooperate. Each group believes that it holds the key to unlock the gate leading to the right path for the welfare and salvation of all. Similarly, each group also seeks the welfare and prosperity of its own primordial group based on ethnicity, religion, tribe, or ideology. Each is afraid of being subjugated by another group. The basic goals of each group may be idealistic and universal or egoistic and narrow. As often as not, they are both.

For example, one group wants to build an Indonesia that is more democratic and safe from the abuse of basic human rights. Another group believes that Indonesia should become more Islamic and obedient to the commandments of Allah in the Sharia. A third group is concerned that power is too centralized in Java and wants to overcome the tendency for wealth to flow from the outer provinces into Jakarta, where it serves the interests of a small elite. It wants decentralization. Another group feels that foreign investment is the key to Indonesia's economic prosperity. Therefore it presses for legislation that will liberalize trade and support the interests of big businesses. Another group represents a particular ethnic group or tribe that feels the government has discriminated against it for too long. It wants to gain access and power in the government for the sake of its tribe or province. Meanwhile, another group, representing the interests of the military, is very concerned over the erosion of its authority and honor. Above all it wants to defend the unitary integrity of the Republic of Indonesia. At the same time it wants to protect the considerable economic interests of the military, which provide the funds needed to carry out its job since the national military budget for the military is so small. Another group of civil servants experiences hardship because its members' salaries have not kept pace with the rising cost of living. Since corruption is the only way they can get the funds necessary to meet their basic needs, they want to deflect attention from the fight against corruption while at the same time strengthening their position in the bureaucracy. Another group feels that, on the contrary, corruption is the worst problem facing Indonesia and that its elimination should be the first priority of government. In a country as large and diverse as Indonesia, this hypothetical list of competing interests could go on and on.

Even if most of the people in Indonesia agree on Pancasila as the national ideology, there still remain sharp differences between groups based on their ideologies, goals, and interests. These differences are not caused by a conflict between good and evil. They are not the result of particular evil groups (terrorists, radicals, Soeharto, communists, Jews, the CIA, capitalists, neoliberals, etc.).[3] Every group has its own legitimate interests and goals. But each group finds it very difficult to understand the legitimate interests and goals of other groups. Each group has a particular kind of power but is limited by the power and interests of competing groups. Power within society is divided. Democracy does not eliminate differences. Often it seems to intensify them. Democratic institutions provide a means for the negotiation of differences in order to find a tolerable balance between competing interests.

Power is ambiguous and necessitates negotiating to find a meeting place between different prejudices. A democratic society somehow manages to "extract a measure of truth from our contrasting errors" (Niebuhr 1932:14). According to Niebuhr, democracy "provides for checks and balances upon the pretensions of men as well as upon their lust for power; it thereby prevents truth from turning into falsehood when the modicum of error in truth is not challenged and the modicum of truth in error is not rescued and cherished" (20). According to this democratic ideal, the power that exists within a society is not grounded in either a powerful leader or some natural harmony of interests but rather in structures that enable society to negotiate between competing differences.

Seven western social theorists provide useful tools for analyzing power and change in Indonesia. Durkheim, Marx, Weber, Arendt, Habermas, Foucault, and Bourdieu pop up with amazing regularity in Indonesian books, articles, papers, theses, and dissertations.[4] While there are many differences between them, each provides a useful theoretic framework to interpret how power works in the midst of rapid social change in Indonesia.

Most modern Indonesians have never read these theorists. Modern views of power for most Indonesians are shaped by mass media, including movies, the internet, social media, newspapers, and magazines. Nevertheless, these figures have profoundly influenced how some modern Indonesian intellectuals imagine power in their own society. They contribute language and symbol systems, which complement and contradict other imaginations of power drawn from tradition and religion.

Émile Durkheim: Power, Urbanization, and Symbolic Representation

Émile Durkheim shows how economic change alters the structures of power and social relations in society. In his classic *The Division of Labor in Society* ([1893] 1933), Durkheim examines how population growth, the Industrial Revolution, and urbanization changed the way people relate to each other. In traditional Indonesian agrarian communities, people relate to each other on the basis of similarity. According to Durkheim, in villages most of the people work together, doing the same thing, whether it is farming, fishing, or some other occupation. They have a "mechanical solidarity" based on working together toward the same goals. In the village they are linked by kinship and inherited values like tradition (*adat*) and religion. Not only are there only a few different kinds of work, but each family or village is basically self-sufficient. Each unit performs all the tasks it needs to survive.

When they move to the city, villagers have to compete with each other and there is a dramatic division of labor. Instead of doing the same basic tasks together, they work separately in thousands of different professions. The city is pluralistic, with many different ethnic groups, religions, and traditions. Each individual or family is dependent on many other people in order to survive. Urbanites no longer grow their own food, make their own clothes, educate their children, provide their own entertainment, and make their tools. Instead, they depend on professionals: markets, stores, gas stations, garbage collectors, teachers, religious professionals, doctors, mechanics, government bureaucrats, schools, sports facilities, internet cafés, and on and on. This interdependence creates "organic solidarity." The city is more like an organism with many living parts doing different things but depending on each other.

Indonesia has the highest rate of urbanization in Asia, surpassing India and China. When I first came to Indonesia, the great majority of people lived in villages and were small farmers. Today more than 54 percent live in cities, and this figure is growing at a rate of 2.69 percent a year, also the highest urban growth rate in Asia.[5] Rapid urbanization has created many social problems and changed the dynamics of power in Indonesia. Power no longer resides in a few community leaders, who traditionally make decisions by means of consultation and consensus (*musyawarah mufakat*), but rather is dispersed throughout society, often centered in large impersonal institutions and bureaucracies. Durkheim was very concerned about anomie, a condition that occurs in society when norms break down, leading to alienation and social chaos. Anomie leads to crime and social conflict.

Durkheim's theory helps us understand the process of economic and social change that affects the structures of power in Indonesia. The growth of radicalism may not primarily be due the attractiveness of radical Islamist ideas or the export of elite Muslim power struggles in the Middle East, as suggested by Syafi'i Ma'arif, but rather the breakdown of norms in the urban jungle. Radical groups provide a sense of community, an income, and a violent outlet for the frustrations of competitive life and poverty in the city. Radical groups can effectively recruit members from all socioeconomic classes, since anomie is not just the result of poverty but results from a large gap between expectations (media dreams) and realistic prospects. The problem of anomie is exacerbated by high unemployment among young people, many of whom have migrated to cities to look for work. Half the population of Indonesia is under 28.6 years old.[6]

Durkheim's later work, *The Elementary Forms of the Religious Life* ([1912] 1915), also provides insights into power relations in Indonesia. Reversing his earlier assessment that religion is destined to fade away in an organic society, Durkheim argued that religion provides the transcendent symbols that make society possible. Religion is the glue that holds everything together. Religion is the symbolic representation of society. Rituals provide an experience of "collective effervescence," when sacred, transcendent symbols give meaning to mundane life and the legitimate the order of society. Without symbols to legitimize order by linking transcendent meanings to mundane life, organic society is always threatened with disintegration (see Berger 1967).

Durkheim's theory of religion helps explain why the overwhelming majority of Indonesians in our survey imagined a good society as one in which the people obey God and follow His commandments. The power of religion is imagined as being greater than the power of the government. It may also explain why many Indonesians who are afflicted with anomie turn to religion as a source of values. Most Indonesians also believe in democratic values, but the few who turn to radicalism do not find democratic values as cogent as the transcendent values of submission to God.

Karl Marx: Power, Capitalism, Resistance, and Religion

Karl Marx has a dangerous but powerful attraction for Indonesian intellectuals. Prior to 1965, Indonesia had the largest communist party in the world outside the Soviet Union and China. All that changed with President Soeharto's campaign to eliminate communism in Indonesia. According to Indonesian ideology, Marxism is atheist and in diametrical conflict with Pancasila and a moral, religious society. Many Indonesians equate atheism with immorality and anarchy since religion is the assumed basis for social order and ethics. Therefore it might seem surprising that many Muslim intellectuals, including Islamist radicals, freely use Marxist ideas. Outside the context of universities, they seldom attribute their ideas to Marx, even though they use his language. Indonesians often reference three constellations of Marxist ideas.

The first is Marx's critique of the links among capitalism, imperialism, and colonialism. The Netherlands and other western powers exploited and enslaved Indonesians for "350 years." According to President Sukarno, the basic structural cause of this imperialism was the capitalist system.[7] There are many who practice capitalism in Indonesia but few who would dare openly defend it. According to many Indonesians, capitalism creates insatiable greed for natural resources and markets. "Neoliberalism" is just a new form of this exploitation, also known as neocolonialism. In our brave new modern world, the most dominant form of power is capital. Capital may be productive for the wealth of the few, but it leads to impoverishment for the many. For example, Indonesian factory workers who make Nike shoes may be paid 5 US dollars per pair for their labor, whereas the shoes sell for more than 180 dollars in the West.[8]

Class conflict and radical resistance is the second commonly cited Marxist idea. Corrupt capitalist elites seem to run the country, but there are literally hundreds of nongovernmental organizations (NGOs) dedicated to opposing them. Indonesia has a very vibrant civil society. While the language of class conflict is a little risky in this communist-phobic country, resistance by workers and the people against the exploitation of capitalists is perfectly acceptable. Resistance is not only against the capitalists in Indonesia but more broadly against the hegemony of the West. These ideas are often linked to Islamic militancy since western capitalists are portrayed as Christian imperialists who are the enemies of Islam. For some Indonesians, the so-called clash of civilizations is just another word for the class struggle between rich capitalists and the poor Muslim communities they exploit.

The third "dangerous" constellation of Marxist ideas is his critique of religion. Some of my students argue that Marx did not really critique religion as such but only its misuse. Marx said that religion is the opium of the people, but in his day opium was more akin to medicine than narcotics (Mckinnon 2006). Opium dulled pain in the absence of modern pain killers. Marx also said that religion was the cry of the people in a heartless world. Thus religion is a potent force for mobilizing resistance to capitalist oppression. Marx critiqued the way capitalist elites use religion to deflect people's attention from their exploitation. The people should resist the misuse of religion to legitimate unjust power structures. Some Indonesians say that Marx teaches them to pay attention to the way global capitalism enriches the 1 percent while many people suffer.

The widespread valiancy of Marxist ideas (but not communism) in Indonesia helps explain why a large majority of Indonesians selected the modern language of structures and relationships to describe their imagination of power rather than religious or mystical symbol systems. Even those who know nothing about Marx are aware that power is exercised through economic and political structures that determine how people relate to each other.

Max Weber: Power as Domination and Religion as Creative

Two main ideas from Max Weber are helpful for understanding power in Indonesia. The first is that power is domination. The ultimate form of domination is violence. Leaders, kings, sultans, and presidents all possess power in order to dominate the people. Weber writes, "The state is a relation of men dominating men, a relation supported by means of legitimate (i.e., considered to be legitimate) violence." Weber defines the modern nation state as, "a human community that (successfully) claims the monopoly of the legitimate use of physical force within a given territory."[9] From this viewpoint, it appears that power means the ability to force the people to obey the will of the powerful, if necessary by using violence. Domination is power. The supreme form of power is violence because violence enforces absolute obedience.

President Soeharto was an exemplar of Weber's view of power. He brought an end to the chaos of 1965–66 by monopolizing violence in Indonesia. He tolerated no opposition and brutally imprisoned or annihilated those who opposed his will. He also brought order, safety, education, health care, and dramatic economic growth to the majority of Indonesians who accepted his authority. Even today there are many who openly long for a return to his relatively benevolent kind of dictatorship.[10]

President Jokowi is also aware of the importance of monopolizing the use of violence in Indonesia. In late 2016, when confronted with hundreds of thousands of Muslim demonstrators against Ahok, Jokowi made highly publicized visits to all branches of the armed forces. He also arrested prominent figures accused of plotting treason and mobilized tens of thousands of law enforcement officers to demonstrate his resolve not to allow the demonstrations to turn violent. One reason why Islamic radicals are much more powerful than their numbers would indicate is that they are willing to use violence. Many Indonesians submit to radical demands that violate human rights, rather than opposing them, because of the very real possibility that opposition will lead to violence (see Adeney-Risakotta 2009b).

Max Weber's idea that religion is a powerful force for bringing social change is also a useful tool for analyzing power in Indonesia. Over against Marx, who considered religion not a cause but an effect of material economic relations, Weber argued in *The Protestant Ethic and the Spirit of Capitalism* that religion is a creative force for social change. Some Indonesians misread Weber to mean that Christianity is the cause and defining ideology of capitalism.[11] They suggest that Weber was right, that religion can transform the economic and political structures of the world. Islam, they believe, through Sharia economics, will bring about the just and equitable changes that Protestantism failed to produce in the capitalist West. Or, conversely, they suggest that Islam has the same ability as Christianity to stimulate hard work, frugality, and honesty, leading to effective capitalist structures for creating wealth. A Protestant pastor from Sumba showed the same misreading of Weber when he proposed a thesis asking why Christians in Sumba are still among the poorest people in Indonesia after more than a hundred years of Reformed Protestant Christianity. He thought Weber's argument meant that Reformed Protestants should become rich capitalists! A more nuanced reading of Weber suggests that religions can be a powerful and creative force for social change, but that does not imply that the changes stimulated by religion will necessarily bring prosperity or justice.

Hannah Arendt: Power as Different from Domination and Located in the People

Hannah Arendt questions the predominant tradition that does not distinguish *power* from *violence*. If power is the same as domination, then what is the basis of democracy and the sovereignty of the people?[12] Arendt points out that most writers do not clearly distinguish between the meanings of power, strength, force, and authority (1970:44–45). The confusion of meanings, according to Arendt, stems from the belief that only one political question is ultimately important: Who rules whom? If this is the only question that really matters, then power, strength, force, authority, and violence are all means for determining who rules and who follows. They are all just tools for domination.

Arendt suggests that power should be defined as the ability of society to act together in concert. Power is not possessed by the leader but rather is owned by the people. Power may be delegated by the people to a leader to act in their name. But power still originates in the people and is dependent on them. In contrast with Weber, Arendt argues that power is different from strength or force.

According to Arendt, *force* is a kind of energy that may be released by a social movement (e.g., a revolution) or nature (e.g., an earthquake). *Authority* may be connected to either a structural position (e.g., the office of president) or the character of a particular individual (e.g., Mahatma Gandhi). In some cases authority is linked to both character and position (e.g., President Nelson Mandela). A person with authority is honored and obeyed by other people just because of his or her authority. Force, coercion, or even persuasion is unnecessary. If persons in authority try to coerce or persuade their followers to obey, they will probably lose some of their authority. *Violence* is different from power, strength, force, or authority. Arendt says that violence magnifies the strength of a person by using weapons or tools intended to cause pain. Violence is closely connected to domination. Modern nation-states monopolize the tools of violence through the police and military. Therefore the state is expert in using violence to force the people into submission. Nevertheless, Arendt argues that violence is not the same as power.

Arendt's explanation of the differences among power, strength, force, authority, and violence have different nuances than similar terms in Indonesian. For example, strength (*kekuatan*) is different from power (*kekuasaan*), but strength need not be thought of as just the possession of an individual. In Indonesian *kekuatan* (strength) may be either individual or social. For example, a hunter may be physically strong, but he will become even stronger if he can convince others to cooperate in a hunting expedition. In a group their strength is multiplied. Arendt's theory does not address supernatural power such as *kesaktian*, which assumes that there are unseen spiritual elements in power. Many Indonesians assume that any major struggle involves unseen forces that are beyond human control.

Koentjaraningrat argues that strength (both individual and social) is just one of the factors that contributes to a leader's power (1984). Other elements of power include authority (*wibawa*), responsibility/legitimacy (*wewenang*), magical powers (*kesaktian*), and charisma. Koentjaraningrat's approach contrasts with that of Anderson, who dichotomizes supernatural or spiritual conceptions from rational, material conceptions. Koentjaraningrat conceptualizes power as supported by various "gifts," both inner (*batin*) and outer (*lahir*). His theory includes mythical narrative elements as inseparable from social science. He only pays attention to the kind of power wielded by leaders and shows little awareness of the power that is located in the people.

In Indonesia many people believe that if society is in crisis it is because there are no great leaders. The people are waiting for the Just Ruler (Ratu Adil) who will come and restore the people to virtue and prosperity. The Just Ruler will ensure the well-being of the whole cosmos by mediating God's power to the people. This recalls the result of our question about a good leader. The great majority chose the traditional language of a leader with the inner power to guide the people by example. It doesn't so much matter what they do but rather whether or not they have that inner charisma, a gift from God.

According to Arendt, the power (or impotence) of leaders comes from the power (or impotence) of the people. A weak people allows a corrupt leader to flourish. In some sense the people deserve the leader they have. Therefore passively waiting for a good leader to fix everything is futile. This imagination of power is in tension with older, theocentric ideas that power devolves directly from God to the king, who is God's viceroy or *kalifah*. According to democratic theory, a ruler is the representative of the people, not the representative of God. All people are God's *kalifah* on earth, not just the ruler. This is different from the assumption of many Indonesians that people are powerless to change anything unless a Just Ruler shows them the way.

According to Arendt, violence destroys power. Violence may strengthen the domination of a tyrant. But domination is not power. Violence can subjugate, hurt, and even destroy the people's power. But violence cannot empower either the people or their leaders. The more the leaders use violence the more powerless they are. Arendt explains, "Violence can always destroy power; out of the barrel of a gun grows the most effective command, resulting in the most instant and perfect obedience. What never can grow out of it is power" (1970, 53). Violence may destroy but also stimulate the growth of power in the people. "Where there is power, there is resistance" (Foucault 1978:95). State-sponsored violence provokes resistance. Resistance multiplies the strength of people to oppose their rulers.

Before Soeharto was forced out of office in May 1998, the people of Indonesia experienced more and more incidents of state-sponsored violence. Ironically, the more the government used violence, including kidnapping, torture, and extrajudicial executions, the more people rebelled and the weaker the government became. Violence was met with violence, and both the government and the people seemed powerless to stop the spiral of bloodshed. The country seemed to be headed for either one-sided slaughter or a civil war. In the end it was not violence or bloodshed that forced Soeharto out of office. Rather it was the unified action of the people, including the students, the "little people" (*wong cilik*), the political elite, and even the military, which finally withdrew its support for the unpopular president. On May 20, 1998, half a million people marched in Yogyakarta in a peaceful demonstration demanding that Soeharto step down.[13]

A similar process can be seen in the events that led to East Timor's independence. For decades the Indonesian government used violence to pacify the people of East Timor. Thousands died, and the military dominated the lives of th people. Both sides used horrific violence, but neither side was safe and neither the government nor the people could reach their goals. Both sides seemed powerless. After the fall of Soeharto, President Habibie initiated a UN-sponsored referendum, which opened a peaceful path for the people of East Timor, and the pro-independence side laid down its arms. Anti-independence (pro-Indonesia) East Timorese militias increased their use of violence and intimidation, with support from the military. However, the more the militias used violence the less power they had. As the people suffered, they grew in power. If they had continued to respond to violence with violence, the Indonesian military probably would have invaded to bring "law and order," canceling the referendum in the process, and East Timor would still be part of Indonesia. In Indonesia the government is weakest in precisely the areas of the country where the military has used the most violence. There is a direct correlation between state-sponsored violence in East Timor, Aceh, the Moluccas, and West Papua and the powerlessness of the government and the people in those same areas.[14]

Jürgen Habermas: Power, Reason, and the Colonialization of Life Worlds

Jürgen Habermas is one of the most quoted social theorists in Indonesia.[15] From his prolific pen flowed many ideas that Indonesian intellectuals and activists found useful. Two related ideas connected to power are very influential. The first is universal rationality, rooted in human communication, which should operate in the public sphere. Over against postmodern skepticism, Habermas provides a theoretical argument for holding on to the Enlightenment ideal of a universal rationality capable of describing both the natural world and human social life. He suggests that freedom of expression in the public sphere is a basic requirement of a democratic society. He provides ammunition for activists who insist that the second principle of Pancasila, that is, one just and civilized humanity, implies that discourse about human rights must be tolerated in the public sphere.

This idea was important as a basis for opposing President Soeharto's oft-repeated Indonesian exceptionalism. Soeharto frequently fended off international criticism of human rights abuses by stating that western discourse about human rights was not appropriate for Indonesia. According to him, the nation-state of Indonesia is not based on the western idea of a social contract but rather is a family. In social contract theory, rights are based on a contract guaranteeing individual citizens rights in exchange for protection by the government. On the contrary, according to Soeharto Indonesian citizens are members of a family and should submit to their government as children do to their parents.

Indonesian activists cite Habermas in support of their criticism of the government based on universal human values. According to Habermas, human rights are based on the structure of ideal communication. If human beings communicate freely, without fear, they will agree that all their basic human rights should be defended. This is not based on culture or time but is fundamental to what it means to be human. While Indonesia was formally bound by the Universal Declaration on Human Rights (ratified by the UN in 1948), under Soeharto it refused to sign various UN human rights declarations. The strongest opposition to Soeharto's position came from the Indonesian National Commission for Human Rights, founded in 1993. This commission enjoyed extraordinary legitimacy, both in Indonesia and abroad, because of the integrity and international reputation of its members. It succeeded in drawing attention to many human rights abuses in Indonesia and undermining the legitimacy of the New Order government. In 1999, just after the fall of Soeharto, Indonesia passed a wide-ranging law guaranteeing human rights throughout the country.[16] Unlike many Indonesians, Habermas does not ground human rationality and freedom in the order of a moral cosmos founded by God but rather in the structure of human communication.

A second, related Habermasian idea is that rational communication and action are undermined by the colonialization of the life world by money and violence. Both political coercion and economic pressure undermine rationality. According to Habermas, rational communication does not operate on a Platonic level of pure ideas but always within concrete material contexts. When people are subjected to threats of violence or financial pressure, rational communication is undermined. The overwhelming power of a global capitalist economy and the expanding powers of the nation-state render rational communicative action impotent. Habermas's ideas about the colonization of human life worlds are doubly attractive, not only because they describe the experience of many Indonesians but also because he holds out hope that the public sphere can be reformed to empower people. Habermas's ideas provide fuel for a radical critique of the state and the capitalist economy, as well as hope for positive change.

Michel Foucault: Power/Knowledge Truth Regimes and the Creativity of Power

When I first started teaching at UIN, I was surprised to find that there were extracurricular study groups made up of "traditionalist" (NU) Muslim students who were reading Michel Foucault together. In fact students from all religious and ideological communities find Foucault interesting. Like Habermas, Foucault is frequently quoted, not only in academic publications but also in the popular press.[17]

Foucault constructed a theory of knowledge as power and power as knowledge, or "power/knowledge." He suggested that power is created, re-created, and disseminated through "truth regimes." Power is wielded by those who determine what is true (Foucault 1980, 1997). During the Soeharto era, the New Order government constructed a powerful truth regime based on its own interpretation of Pancasila. In 1982 every institution in Indonesia, including religious organizations, was required to commit to accepting Pancasila as its single foundation and basis for all activities (*asas tunggal*). Pancasila is very broad and open to many interpretations. However, the government insisted on a single interpretation, which was disseminated through a mandatory education program (known as P4) with required classes for students from kindergarten through university. The government interpreted Pancasila as supporting its programs for "development" (*pembangunan*) and "progress" (*kemajuan*). It also entailed a monolithic reading of Indonesian history. History could only be taught or written in a way that legitimized the New Order regime. Foucault's analysis gave power to those who resisted this truth regime. Part of the reason for the fall of Soeharto was the delegitimation of his truth regime, which was undercut by corruption, lies, and violations of basic human rights.

According to Foucault, those who are powerful create institutions that discipline the people to submit to a particular definition of what it means to be normal, rational, healthy, good, and upright. More than that, truth regimes create people who discipline themselves in line with the dominant knowledge of the time. *Governmentality* implies that the government does not have to maintain surveillance over everyone all the time (panopticon) because people have been conditioned to watch, discipline, and govern themselves (Foucault 1997).

After the fall of Soeharto in 1998, the Reformasi government initiated radical decentralization of political and economic power. Structures were democratized and the government lost its monopoly on truth/knowledge. Consequently it also lost its control over power. This created a power vacuum into which Islam stepped to expand its power. Initially, the massive "moderate" Islamic organizations of NU and Muhammadiyah enjoyed tremendous prestige, not only for their many educational, economic, and health care institutions but also because they had led the resistance against Soeharto. Abdurrahman Wahid (Gus Dur), the head of NU, was elected president, and Amien Rais, the head of Muhammadiyah, became the speaker of the national legislature. However, after Gus Dur's impeachment and the relative failure of Amien Rais's political party, Partai Amanat Nasional (PAN, National Mandate Party), some people feared that the influence of NU and Muhammadiyah was in decline.[18] Both are too large and diverse to articulate a unified truth regime. They not only differ on many things, but they also are unable to enforce a unified vision within their own membership, let alone in the whole society.

Indonesian imaginations of truth are very complex, but it is arguable that the strongest truth regime in Indonesia today is Islam. The most significant barrier to creating a truth regime based on Islam in Indonesia is the diversity within the Indonesian community. Indonesians take their religions very seriously, but they are wary of authoritarian commands about what they can or cannot do based on their religion. The Majelis Ulama Indonesia, which is meant to supply a unified voice to Islam in Indonesia, issues many fatwas (rulings) on a plethora of subjects, but no one pays much attention to them.[19] Islamist radicals insist that they represent the one true voice of Islam. Some fear that they are well on their way to establishing a Foucauldian truth regime based on their narrow interpretation of Islam. No one knows the future, but my guess is that even among the minority of radicals there is too much diversity of opinion to form a very effective truth regime.

Through his archaeological method, Foucault uncovered the arbitrary discontinuity between different conceptions of what is abnormal, insane, criminal, sick, or perverted that were held in different times and places. In contrast, his genealogical method shows how different exercises of power/ knowledge developed over time. In Indonesia the discontinuity between definitions of what is normal and good is illustrated by the head scarf (*jilbab*). From 1982 to 1991, students were forbidden to wear *jilbabs* in public schools.[20] Under Soeharto's truth regime, conservative Islam was seen as a threat to national integration. Students had to all wear the same uniform without displaying their ethnic or religious identity. Today *jilbabs* are part of the required dress code, even for non-Muslims, in some public schools. Another example is the attitude toward LGBT people. Conservative Muslims portray homo- and transsexuality as a social disease imported from the decadent West. But in traditional Indonesian communities, there are many ancient art forms and institutions that celebrated homo- and transsexuality as a special gift. Even today in Yogyakarta there are several active LGBT organizations and institutions in spite of threats by Islamic radicals.[21]

In his later work, Foucault expanded his understanding of power to include not just political, economic, religious, and professional elites and institutions but also power as it is disseminated throughout society (1980). Power is everywhere. It is not just oppressive, it is creative. Wherever there is oppressive power, there is also resistance. After reading his earlier work, one might be forgiven for becoming depressed. The power of large impersonal institutions, which carry out massive amounts of surveillance and condition people to discipline themselves in accordance with oppressive truth regimes, seems overwhelming. Indonesians gained new hope from Foucault's later insight that power is creative and diffused throughout society. As suggested by Wening, in Indonesia most people cannot be bothered to enter into confrontations with Islamic radicals, but that doesn't mean they accept their views. Wening suggested that there is power in the majority of tolerant Indonesian Muslims, who will stand up and express themselves when the time is right.

Pierre Bourdieu: Habitus, Cultural Capital, and Symbolic Violence

Pierre Bourdieu, the renowned French sociologist and anthropologist, is another influential social theorist among Indonesian intellectuals.[22] Bourdieu's primary focus is on how power works in society. One idea is the way language shapes power relations. In Indonesia this is most obvious in the Javanese language. Javanese children are conditioned from birth to have dispositions that pay attention to status levels in language. There are different grammatical structures, vocabularies, intonations, and bodily practices that indicate dominance or submission and are integral to speaking good Javanese. According to Bourdieu, these are shaped by a habitus, which combines social structures, subjective feelings, and bodily practices to create dispositions that determine power relations. These dispositions are not fixed or invariable relationships based on rigid structural categories such as age, wealth, sex, birth position, social status, ethnicity, race, family connections, education, or position in a bureaucracy. They include all these things but are internalized and modified by subjective dispositions, which are shaped by the personality and psychology of each person. A habitus is neither wholly subjective nor the objective result of a structure, but rather it is constantly negotiated through time.

In our monthly neighborhood meetings, there is an appearance of radical equality. We all sit on mats on the floor so that we are at the same level. No one would think of sitting on a chair, even though there are chairs available. The head of my neighborhood is actually one of the poorest and least educated of my neighbors. He is a Muslim but not obviously religious. He delegates introductions and Islamic prayers to another neighbor who speaks good formal Javanese and can speak better Arabic. Almost all who attend are men, apart from one or two older widows. Women may serve food, but they will crawl across the floor to do it, making sure to keep their heads lower than everyone else's. If men serve, they do the same. Subtle differences in language and demeanor are evident when a professor or other person of high status speaks or is addressed. According to Bourdieu, even in apparently egalitarian societies, language, attitude, and bodily practices are unconscious dispositions that produce and reproduce power relations. An individual's habitus is both structured and structuring. It is not fixed but is always responding to new situations and personalities.

According to one story, two Javanese brothers, one the governor of a province and the other a Catholic bishop, would never speak their mother tongue to each other because it was too difficult to determine which status level of Javanese they should use in speaking. Instead they used Indonesian, which is much more egalitarian. Nevertheless, even Indonesian is full of subtle status markers and ways to show respect and dominance. It is easy to learn basic communication in Indonesian, but it takes great skill to learn to speak politely and appropriately in multiple social situations. As we might expect from Bourdieu's theory, this includes not only verbal skill but also body language, intonation, and disposition. In chapter 7, I suggested that the first characteristic of a traditional Indonesian imagination of a powerful leader is the ability to use language in a refined and subtle way. Bourdieu's theory explains why this so important in power relations and how it is shaped by lifelong interactions that combine subjective feelings, interpersonal negotiations, and social structures. In the previous chapter I suggested that Ahok's decline in popularity was partly due to his often harsh and unsubtle speech. But compared to many western politicians, Ahok is a model of subtle, refined speech. He may not speak like a Javanese aristocrat, but most of the time he shows remarkable sensitivity to the perceptions of his listeners. If he didn't, he would never have reached the governor's office in Jakarta.

Another influential idea from Bourdieu is that of "cultural capital." While economic capital, social capital, political capital, and all kinds of other capital are important, Bourdieu suggests that cultural capital is the most important. Within a habitus, all these other kinds of capital are united in dispositions that constitute your cultural capital. Your cultural capital is conditioned by social structures, which are legitimized and reproduced in a person's subjectivity. Your cultural capital also has the potential to change your position within power relations. Cultural capital, like the ability to speak appropriately or show "class" through sophisticated taste in art, food, music, clothing, and so on, can lead to increasing objective enhancements to cultural capital, including educational degrees, higher positions, the right husband or wife, or the place where you live. Thus cultural capital, which is shaped by social structures, is also "structuring." It shapes and changes your power position in society.

Cultural capital (not just money or family) enables one person to dominate another. This idea helps explain the second characteristic of a traditional ideal leader in Indonesia: dignity (*bermartabat*). Dignity is shaped by your habitus. It is an inner quality that enables one person to dominate another. While traditional Javanese might explain this charisma in mystical terms as a substantive power to control others, Bourdieu offers a complex sociological explanation that does not refer to the supernatural. Of course cultural capital is sufficiently subtle and complex to be quite mysterious. Bourdieu uses the modern symbol systems of sociology, anthropology, psychology, and philosophy to explain things that could also be explained using traditional or religious symbol systems.

Another of Bourdieu's many rich ideas is "symbolic violence." Bourdieu was a public intellectual who did not just offer an abstract description of the way power works. In many different ways during his lifetime, he took a moral stance against symbolic violence. Bourdieu said symbolic violence occurs when one person dominates another by symbolic means, that is, through the symbols that are part of a powerful person's cultural capital. Symbolic violence is most effective either when it legitimizes an unjust power structure in the eyes of the victims or when they don't even notice that they are being dominated. Symbolic violence eliminates or reduces resistance. If one person uses religious, political, economic, or other symbols in such a way that dominated people feel that it is right and proper for them to be dominated, then an unjust structure is reproduced and legitimized. If people don't even know that they are being dominated by symbols, then it is just as bad. In either case, Bourdieu calls this violence. He says it is even worse than physical violence because it does not provoke resistance but only passive submission.

The idea of symbolic violence enables Indonesian intellectuals and activists to understand how Islamic radicals use religious symbols to dominate people who are their real victims. Many people have died in Indonesia because of the manipulation of religious symbols, often for the very material ends of enhancing the power of small elites. Charges of blasphemy, separatism (lack of nationalism), communism, speaking to Jews, Christianization, Islamization, immorality, neoliberalism, homosexuality, drug use, disrespect for the flag, insulting Pancasila, dishonoring the Koran, planning to overthrow the government, being an atheist, or disrespecting the president are all very recent examples of symbolic violence in Indonesia. These elites use religious, racial, political, economic, social, and moral symbols that are so powerful that people don't even realize they are being manipulated, often for very cynical purposes. Elites that control the media and care nothing about the true meaning of the symbols they invoke use their cultural capital as a symbolic weapon against their rivals for power. Bourdieu's moral fire against injustice, oppression, and domination strikes a chord with Indonesians that goes well beyond simple respect for an academic social theorist.

This chapter opened with a discussion of how democratic theories and practices raised high hopes for the post-Soeharto reformation period. However, democracy is a messy process for negotiating difference. Some

Indonesians have raised doubts about the relevance of democracy as a political sytstem for addressing Indonesia's many problems, especially in the light of intense competition for power between people and groups with competing interests. Some even wonder if Indonesia needs a strong-arm ruler like Soeharto, who sacrificed democratic freedoms for stability and economic growth.

The seven modern social scientists discussed in this chapter offer perspectives on what is going on in Indonesia. None of them offers a master theory for solving Indonesia's problems, but all of them provide insights into what is happening. Their theories lend perspectives on the rapid process of social change in the modern world. Durkheim clarifies the radical social change brought about by urbanization and the transformation from traditional to modern economic structures. He shows the power of religion to define a society and create solidarity. Marx shows how capitalist economic structures oppress those who are marginalized and how religion sometimes functions as legitimation for oppression, as well as the expression of suffering. Weber shows the creative force of religion in transforming the ethos of society so as to bring about radical change. Arendt suggests a transformed understanding of power, not as domination but as the power of people to act and reach their aspirations. Violence undermines the power of both the government and the people. Habermas clarifies that rational discourse in the public sphere is still possible between people of different interests when it is not subverted by violence or money. The common good is still relevant for building a just society. Foucault shows us how power creates knowledge and vice versa. Knowledge/power is diffused throughout society and is creative. Oppression produces resistance, which is an alternative means of attaining knowledge/power. Bourdieu uncovers many sources of "capital." Economic capital is often eclipsed by cultural capital, which may be a source of violence. But human beings are not controlled by their habitus; they also have agency to shape the social space in which they live.

The next chapter explores the relationship between Islam and power in Indonesia.

9

Muslim Imaginations of Power in Indonesia

Every religious practice will only have meaning if we are not too focused on just the formal aspect, but rather comprehend the content and spirit behind it.

—Nurcholis Madjid

Islam came, not to change the culture of our ancestors into Arab culture. ... We must defend what is ours and filter out the culture, not the teaching.

—Abdurrahman Wahid

THIS CHAPTER EXPLORES THE NATURE of religious power in Indonesia. It considers how Indonesians imagine an ideal relationship between religion and political power. There is no sharp division between religion and the state in Indonesia, but there are many differences in how Indonesians imagine religion should influence law, how the government should regulate religion, how religious imaginations shapes society, and the power of religion in controlling the people. The chapter also explores how Islam empowers people through mimetic rituals, meaningful narratives, moral guidance, and theoretical reflection.

Islam and Law in Indonesia

For many Muslims, the most important locus of power is law. Laws and rules are central to Islam. Even the smallest details of daily life are regulated, for example, how you greet another person, how you respond to the greeting, and proper relations between men and women. There are many Muslim interpretations of Islamic law. That is why Sharia is such a contentious issue. Muslim scholars distinguish between Sharia, *fiqh*, and *usul al-fiqh*. Sharia is the way or law of God as revealed in the Koran and

Sunnah. *Fiqh* is the interpretation of Sharia and its application in the form of positive law. *Usul al-fiqh* are the principles for the interpretation of Sharia.

Since Indonesia is not an Islamic state, Sharia as *fiqh* is not the law of the land, with the special exception of the province of Aceh. Since Indonesia's founding, there have been repeated attempts to make Sharia mandatory for Muslims. However, they have been opposed by the great majority of Indonesians. Since Sharia is normative for all Muslims according to Islamic teaching, the important issue is not whether Muslims should follow Sharia but rather whether or not the state should be involved in enforcing Sharia or implementing it by inserting *fiqh* into national law. Muslims are certainly free to follow Sharia in their communities. Many Indonesian Muslims believe that the substance of Sharia, for example, justice, mercy and equality, should be implemented in national positive law but that *fiqh* from many centuries ago should not be the law of modern Indonesia.

Many Islamic schools (*madh'hab*) of interpretation have grown up over the centuries. The divisions and variety in Islam are as complex and confusing as they are in Christianity and all major religions. It is not my purpose to discuss the different schools or the normative debates about Islamic jurisprudence. Most Indonesians are Sunni Muslims who follow the Shafi'i school for the interpretation of *fiqh*.[1] But even within this apparent uniformity there are many substreams with vast differences. The following figure 9.1 sketches out some of the most important schools and branches of Islamic interpretation.[2]

Indonesia recognizes three different systems of law: *adat* traditional law, which differs from ethnic community to ethnic community; Islamic law, which only applies to Muslims; and national law. In theory national law takes precedence over religious and *adat* law. There is one national Supreme Court, which has jurisdiction over all three systems. However, local courts often defer to *adat* or religious law, which may have more legitimacy than national law in the eyes of the community. A large body of national law was inherited from Dutch colonialism. Needless to say, this law has been revised extensively since independence was declared in 1945. In addition to the national judicial system, there are Islamic courts that have jurisdiction over family law for Muslims. This primarily involves questions of marriage, divorce, and inheritance (see Bowen 2003; and Adeney-Risakotta 2016b).

Figure 9.1 *Islamic schools and branches of interpretation*

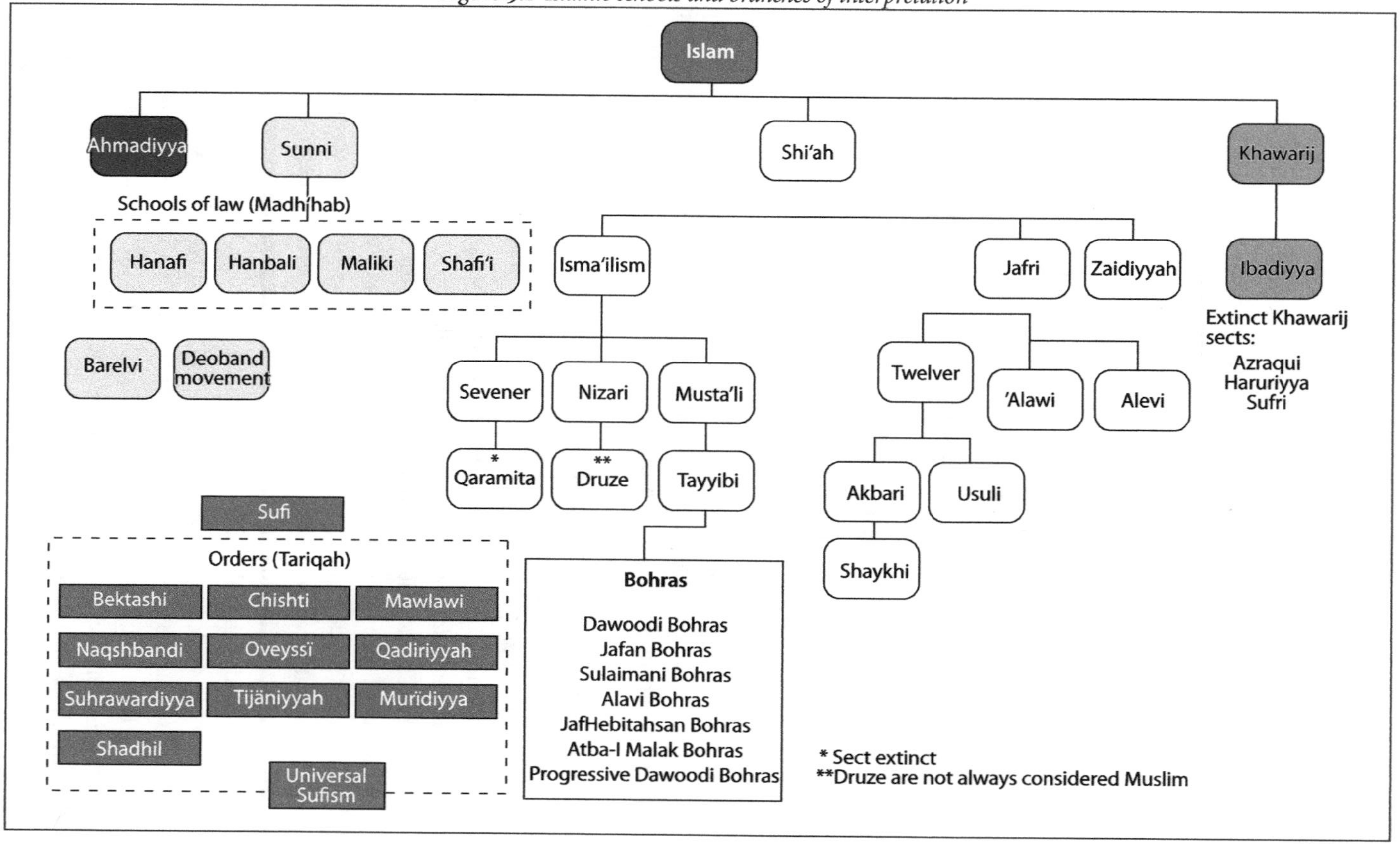

In our questionnaire, we asked two questions about the respondents' views on law. The first asked a normative question about what they thought should be the basis of law. The second asked a practical question about to which kind of law they felt were most obedient.

Questionnaire Question III.E on the basis of law

Which of the following is the most important basis of law?

1. Tradition, *adat*, the will of the ancestors, loyalty to my ethnic community.

2. Reason, science, discussion and consensus, equality before the law.

3. The Scriptures (Koran, Bible, etc.), religious teachings, God's commandments.

The first answer locates law in the ethnic community. Law is passed down from the ancestors and establishes an order and identity based on membership in an *adat* community. Under the Dutch, there were separate *adat*, religious, and national courts. With independence, the nationalists did away with *adat* courts because they believed the colonialists had used *adat* and the differences between different ethnic groups as a tool of division: divide and conquer. The ideal was for all Indonesians to be united under one national law. However, the nationalists knew they had to respect traditional *adat* law and Islamic law as well.

The second, modern answer stipulates that the basis of law is in reason, achieved through discussion and consensus (*musyawarah mufakat*). This phrase is modern, not only for the emphasis on reason and science but also because it incorporates the idea of a public sphere for discussion and establishment of a broad consensus. The phrase *musyawarah mufakat* is part of the fourth principle of Pancasila, is derived from Arabic, and has Islamic roots as well. It can also be considered traditional since discussion and consensus are the traditional way Indonesian villagers make decisions.

The third, religious response identifies divine revelation as the basic source of law. God's law should be the basis of human law. For many Muslims, this is part of their normative religious beliefs. It implies that Sharia should be the basis of human law. However, how Sharia should be interpreted and implemented in Indonesian national law is a subject of great controversy. There are even serious differences between activist conservative Muslims. Some years ago I interviewed Yusril Ihza Mahendra, the national head of the conservative Islamic Partai Bulan Bintang (Crescent Star Party, PBB). I asked him if Sharia law should apply just to Muslims or to all Indonesians. He replied, to all Indonesians. Later I interviewed a provincial leader of the same political party and asked the same question. He replied, only to Muslims.

On another occasion, when I met him in Amsterdam, I had a long conversation with Hidayat Nur Wahid, the head of the Partai Keadilan Sejahtera (Prosperous Justice Party, PKS) and former speaker of the People's Consultative Assembly (MPR-RI). The Partai Keadilan Sejahtera is the most conservative of the Islamic political parties in Indonesia and reportedly has ties to the Muslim Brotherhood in Egypt. I asked Wahid how his party differed from Amien Rais and PAN, which is formally a secular nationalist party but is loosely associated with Muhammadiyah and widely perceived as having an Islamic agenda. Wahid responded that PKS and PAN were not much different in their desire to build an Islamic society; however, PKS wants to build a big house with separate sections for each religion, whereas PAN wants to build one house with no divisions. This might be interpreted to mean that PKS would apply a stricter interpretation of Sharia, though only for Muslims, whereas PAN would apply a broader interpretation of Sharia to all Indonesians.

The first question, on the foundation of law, is a normative question about the respondents' beliefs. The second is a practical question about which form of law is most effective in eliciting their obedience. Research on cross-cultural ethics has shown that there is sometimes a substantial gap between ascribed values and actual practices. In other words, what people say are their values is not necessarily an accurate description of the way they live (Adeney 1995). We have no way of knowing if the respondents were really obedient to the system of law they indicated. But the statistical responses to the question reveal which legal system they said they most often obeyed.

Questionnaire Question II.B on obedience to law

To which system of law are you most obedient?

1. National law.

2. Traditional (*adat*) law, the law of my ethnic or tribal group.

3. Religious law.

The first, modern answer is legally binding under the government of Indonesia. It is nonpartisan and in theory treats all Indonesians equally. Indonesians often express their respect for the rule of law without regard to religion, ethnicity, sex, wealth, or ideology. However, the rule of national law is often disregarded. Traditional, *adat* law, in contrast, has a sacred character and is linked to the ancestors and local unseen powers. *Adat* law is enforced by means of material penalties such as fines and is cited in rulings of the "secular" judicial system. *Adat* law is also enforced by means of supernatural sanctions such as sickness and death imposed by the ancestors or other unseen powers on those who violate taboos. It is binding on those within an *adat* community and constitutive of their identity. The Bataks have a saying: those who do not follow *adat* are worse than those who don't follow their religion. Rapid urbanization and increasing mobility pose a serious threat to traditional *adat* laws, which were often shaped by agrarian village life. Religious law is contested in Indonesia. Attempts to integrate Sharia into national and provincial law have failed, except in Aceh. But political decentralization has allowed Islamic conservatives to introduce Sharia laws in some districts at the local level.

Table 9.1 *Responses to Questions III.E on the Basis of Law and II.B on Obedience to Law*

Group	Traditional Law		Modern Law		Religious Law	
	III.E Basis	II.B Obedience	III.E Basis	II.B Obedience	III.E Basis	II.B Obedience
Muslim	6%	6%	18%	31%	76%	63%
Protestant	8%	6%	29%	45%	63%	49%
Catholic	25%	22%	43%	49%	32%	29%
Hindu	27%	19%	44%	62%	29%	19%
All Indonesians	10%	9%	26%	39%	64%	52%

Table 9.1 lays out the percentages of preferred languages for both questions by major religious communities, followed by a comparison of Muslims from six different ethnic groups. It facilitates comparing the statistics between what people thought should be the foundation of law and to which kind of law they felt they were most obedient.

In this table we can see an emerging pattern: the Muslims and Protestants are very close in their choice of preferred symbol systems, whereas the Catholics and Hindus resemble each other. None of the groups preferred the traditional language, which imagines law as located in the ethnic community. This indicates a victory of both the nationalists and the religious communities at the expense of traditional communities. A strong majority of both Muslims (76 percent) and Protestants (63 percent) imagined God's revelation and commandments in the Scriptures as the foundation of law. Both groups had a lower level of obedience to religious law than their affirmation of its divine origin might suggest. But both groups said they were more obedient to religious law than to national or traditional law (Muslims 63 percent, Protestants 49 percent).

In contrast, only 32 percent of Catholics and 29 percent of Hindus chose Scripture as the basis of law and even fewer said they were most obedient to the laws their religion. That may be because both groups put less emphasis on Scripture than the Muslims and Protestants do. Not many Muslims (18 percent) and Protestants (29 percent) thought that rational discourse and consensus should be the basis of law. But more of them (31 and 45 percent) said they were more obedient to national law than any other law. The Catholics (43 percent) and Hindus (44 percent) chose rational discourse and science as their first choice as the basis of law, and even more of them (49 and 62 percent), said they were more obedient to national law than to *adat* or religious law. Overall, most Indonesian respondents chose Scripture as the basis of law (64 percent) and also indicated that they were most obedient to religious law (52 percent).[3]

The statistical results from these two questions indicate the respondents' preferred social imaginary for understanding and obeying law. The three possible answers to both questions are not mutually exclusive. Most Indonesians agree with all three answers. Nevertheless, these statistics confirm that religion is a dominant part of the imagination of most Indonesians. Modern language about law based on rational discourse, science, and consensus is also strong, especially among Catholics and Hindus. However, most Indonesians would rather obey God's law than the national law of Indonesia.

A little more nuance can be added to these statistics by comparing them with a 2015 Pew Foundation survey of attitudes in ten Muslim majority nations on how the Koran should be applied to national law. Ninety-one percent of the respondents from Indonesia were Muslims, but just 22 percent said that national law should be strictly based on the Koran. Another 52 percent said that Indonesia's laws should follow the values and principles of Islam but should not strictly follow the teachings of the Koran. Sixteen percent said that Indonesia's laws should not be influenced by the teachings of the Koran. Of the ten Muslim majority countries, only Turkey had a lower level of support (13 percent) among Muslims for strictly basing law on the Koran. In our research, 64 percent of all religious communities

Figure 9.2 *How much should the Quran influence our country's laws?*

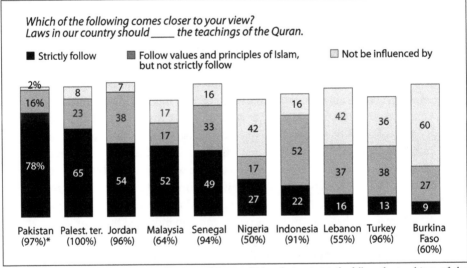

* Percentages in parentheses represent the share of the sample in each country who identify as Muslim.

Note: Results include full country sample, including Muslims and non-Muslims.

Question wording: "Which of the following three statements comes closer to your view — laws in our country should strictly follow the teachings of the Quran, laws in our country should follow the values and principles of Islam but not strictly follow the teachings of the Quran, or laws in our country should not be influenced by the teachings of the Quran?"

Source: Spring 2015 *Global Attitudes Survey*. 124.

"The Divide Over Islam and National Laws in the Muslim World,"

Pew Research Center.

and 76 percent of Muslims thought law should be based on Scripture. The Pew research suggests that many Muslims among that 76 percent, believe that law should follow the values and principles of their religion but should not follow the detailed laws or teachings of the Koran. Note the large number of Indonesians (52 percent), compared to other Muslim countries, who chose the medium-shaded response in figure 9.2 ("Laws in our country should follow the values and principles of Islam but not strictly follow the teachings of the Quran").

Government Regulation of Religions

There is no official legal definition of religion in Indonesia. The Constitution and positive law remain silent on what religion is, even though it is a key issue in the polemics over the obligation to state one's religion on the national identification card, as well as about the constitutionality and meaning of the law against "blasphemy and the defamation of religion." Nevertheless there is a popular understanding of religion that is taught to schoolchildren, that is, that religion includes belief in one God, who is revealed by a prophet, through Holy Scriptures, which stipulate a law about how to live and rituals for worship. An implication of this popular definition is that teachings and practices that do not include all five of these elements (God, prophet, Scriptures, law, and rituals) are not considered true religions.

The state affirms six religions. In order of their size, these are Islam, Protestantism, Catholicism, Hinduism, Buddhism, and Confucianism. All of these groups receive state funding, representation in government, publicly funded religious institutions, and legal protection. The amount of funding is in proportion to the official size of the group in a particular locale.[4] Other "world religions" are, in principle, protected as well. They don't receive funding, support, or acknowledgment from the government, but their right to meet and worship is guaranteed by the Constitution, which says that freedom of religion is an inalienable human right.

Most Indonesians do not recognize indigenous tribal religions (*agama suku*) as religions. They are protected by law as cultural beliefs (*aliran keper-cayaan*) and may receive modest state funding from the Department of Tourism, but their members have not been able use their religious beliefs as a basis for obtaining legal documents such as identification cards, school registrations, and birth, marriage, or death certificates, all of which require applicants to list their religion. In the government, indigenous religions are regulated by the Ministry of Education and Culture rather than the Ministry of Religion. In November 2017 the Indonesian Constitutional Court issued a landmark ruling that members of indigenous religious groups have a constitutional right to list their group in the "religion" column of their national identity card. The ruling is final and cannot be appealed. It is controversial, however, and its enforcement and ramifications for the legal definition of *religion* are uncertain.

Atheism is not officially against the law in Indonesia, but the law against blasphemy and defamation of religion means that atheists cannot freely express their beliefs without risking arrest for defamation. The same applies to various sects that are considered heretical versions of one of the six

Figure 9.3 *The legality of religions in Indonesia*

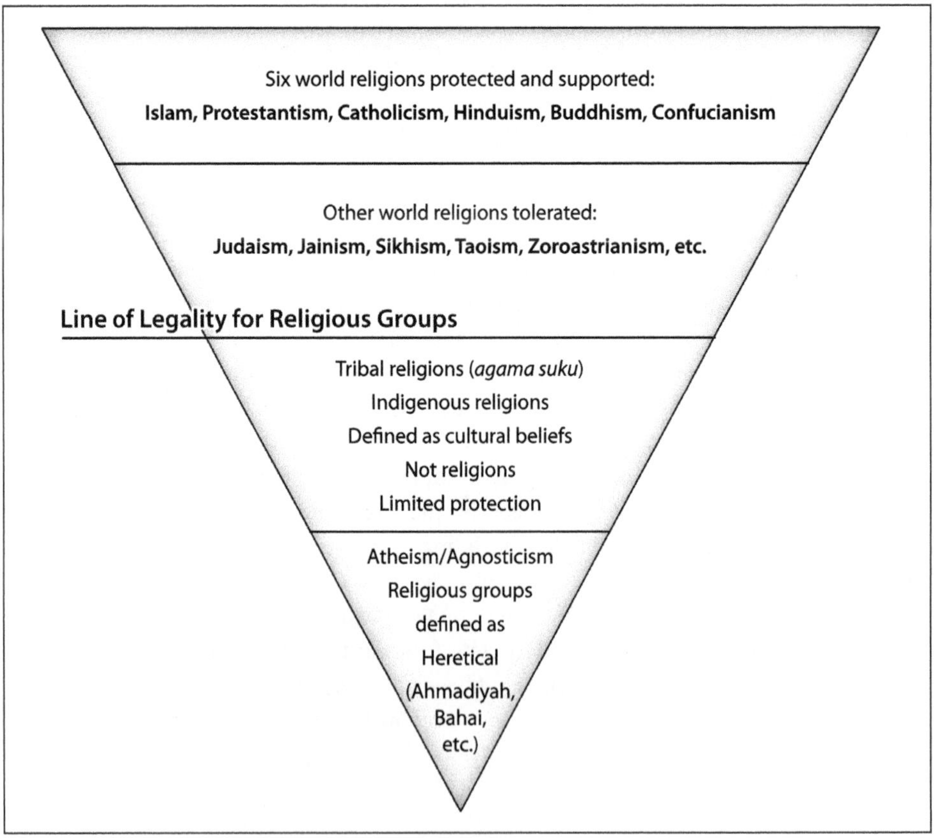

recognized religions. The largest group in this category is Ahmadiyah. Ahmadis are not forbidden to practice their version of Islam, but they are forbidden to teach or spread it. They lack legal protection, and their members have been killed and their mosques burned without adequate government action to protect them. Figure 9.3 summarizes the legal status of religions in Indonesia.

In our questionnaire, we asked respondents to indicate how they thought the government should regulate religions. The question and answers are as follows.

Questionnaire Question IV.B on government regulation of religion

How should government manage religious diversity?

1. The government should support the six religions recognized by the state and suppress groups that are teaching or practicing beliefs that are heretical.

2. The government should protect the fundamental human right to freedom of worship for all groups without considering their teachings as long as they don't break the law.

3 The government should maintain harmony. If there is conflict, the government should find a solution that can be accepted by all sides in the dispute.

The first answer is "religious" in the sense that it prioritizes the six religions recognized by the government and mandates that the government suppress heretical beliefs. This response supports the law on blasphemy and defamation of religion, which has been a tool for denying basic rights to groups such as Ahmadiyah, Baha'i, Shia, Jehovah's Witnesses, and various others. These are not considered religions but rather heretical sects that threaten the main religions. The blasphemy and defamation law also legitimizes the denial of full rights to the religions of indigenous groups, including tribal religions and nonorthodox mystical movements.[5]

The second answer uses the modern vocabulary of human rights and religious freedom. This answer reflects the imaginary of a social contract that protects all people equally, without regard to their personal beliefs or practices, as long as they stay within the rule of law. This answer is consistent with the Indonesian Constitution and the country's ratification of a range of international human rights protocols.

The third answer uses the traditional vocabulary of government and its mandate to maintain balance and harmony in the community. The government is like parents who must mediate fairly between the interests of their "children." If there is conflict, the government should find a solution that is acceptable for all. There are hints in this answer of the ruler who maintains harmony in society by ensuring balance in the cosmos. Indonesians distinguish between solving problems through law courts and solving them through a "family process" (*cara kekeluargaan*). The latter is an approach that considers the relative power, authority, and morality of all parties in a dispute and mediates a solution that prioritizes harmony over human rights or legal freedoms.

In response to these choices, most Indonesians (52 percent) chose the modern response, that the government should protect human rights and freedom of religion regardless of the beliefs of the group. This included 49 percent of Muslims, 57 percent of Protestants, 50 percent of Catholics, 47 percent of Hindus and all the Buddhists. The second most popular answer (34 percent) was the traditional one, that the government should maintain harmony and mediate conflict. This included 34 percent of Muslims, 33 percent of Protestants, 39 percent of Catholics, and 44 percent of Hindus. Relatively few Indonesians (14 percent) chose the religious response of supporting the six religions and suppressing heretical groups. Seventeen percent of Muslims, 10 percent of Protestants, 11 percent of Catholics, and 9 percent of Hindus chose the religious answer. Since the blasphemy law is exclusively

Table 9.2 *Responses to Question IV.B Government Regulation of Religions*

Group	Traditional Maintain Harmony and Mediate Conflict	Modern Protect Religious Freedom and Rights	Religious Support six Religions and Suppress Heresy
Muslim	34%	49%	17%
Protestant	33%	57%	10%
Catholic	39%	50%	11%
Hindu	44%	47%	9%
All Indonesians	34%	52%	14%

used against nonorthodox Islamic groups and non-Muslims, it is not surprising that more Muslims supported the religious response than the other groups did. However, even among Muslims, only 17 percent chose the religious answer.

Ideal Characteristics of the Nation-State of Indonesia

The power of religion in society is not only a matter of the implementation of religious law or the role of government in regulating religions; it is also the power to create the kind of society that conforms to the ideals of religion. In Indonesia this certainly includes concern for electing religious leaders. However, in chapter 7 we saw that relatively few Indonesians chose religious piety as the primary requirement of a religious leader. Most Indonesians from all religious groups chose traditional qualities of dignity, inner power, and moral example as the primary qualities of leadership. In this section we examine what kind of society Indonesians hope will be realized in their nation-state. In our survey we asked the following question.

Questionnaire Question III.D on ideals for the nation-state of indonesia

Which of the following ideal characteristics do you most hope will be realized in the nation-state of Indonesia?

1. God's people, who are good, orderly, obedient to God, and religious.[6]

2. A just democracy in which all citizens are equal and the human rights of all members are protected.

3. A harmonious family that honors its elders and is wholehearted and safe.[7]

This is a normative question that explores Indonesian imaginations of an ideal national political community. The first answer is based on a social imaginary that understands religion as the most important foundation of a good society. This answer envisages not only the theoretical foundations of the community but also the normative results. People who are religious will also be good, orderly, and obedient to God. The order of society is located in commitment to God.

The modern social imaginary in the second answer also assumes a normative result, namely, that in a society characterized by justice and democracy all citizens will be equal and everyone's rights will be protected. In this second answer, a political structure, that is, a just democracy, will produce a political, economic, and social order in which all citizens are treated equally and protected from the violation of their basic human rights.

The traditional answer is based on the metaphor of society as a family. If Indonesian society is like an ideal family, it will be harmonious and show honor to the elders. The people will be wholehearted in the sense of giving up their selfish interests and acting for the good of the family (*ikhlas*). A harmonious family is safe. When I first came to Indonesia people often asked me how I liked Indonesia. When I responded that I really liked it, an elderly man nodded his head wisely and commented, "It is safe here. It is safe." For him, "safe" (*aman*) was the most important characteristic of a good society. Most Indonesians agree with all three of the answers. But their preferred symbol system indicates which answer is the most vivid part of their imagination of a good society.

Out of these three choices, most of our respondents (57%) preferred the modern response, which uses the language of democracy, justice, equality and human rights. This included 53% of Muslims, 56% of Protestants, 78% of Catholics and 68% of Hindus. Only 9% preferred the traditional language of a harmonious family (10% for Muslims). This indicates that most Indone-

Table 9.3 *Responses to Question III.D on Ideals for the Nation-State of Indonesia*

Ideal Characteristics for the Nation-State of Indonesia	Traditional Harmonious Family Honors Elders *Ikhlas* and Safe	Modern Democratic Community Justice, Equality, and Rights	Religious God's People Good, Orderly, and Obedient to God
Muslim	10%	53%	37%
Protestant	8%	56%	36%
Catholic	7%	78%	15%
Hindu	9%	68%	23%
All Indonesians	9%	57%	34%

sians have been deeply affected by modern social imaginaries and political structures. They may still want society to be like a harmonious family, but they think a just and democratic society is the best way to get there. Older respondents may shy away from the familial language because they remember its misuse for the violation of human rights under the militaristic New Order government.

A substantial minority of Indonesians (34 percent) chose the religious imagination of a good society. Muslims and Protestants had similar statistics (37 and 36 percent) for those who imagined obedience to God as the most important characteristic of a good society. Catholics (15 percent) and Hindus (23 percent) were less attracted to the religious language. However, all religious groups showed a strong preference for the democratic language of justice, equality, and human rights.

The Power of Religion to Control Society

Most Indonesians consider social control (*kontrol sosial, pengendalian sosial*) to be a positive thing. The term is often used, and I have seldom heard it used with negative connotations. In contrast, in the West social control often has bad connotations connected to illegitimate limitations on a person's freedom through social pressure or authoritarian intervention. Indonesians often say they have a "shame culture" (*budaya malu*) whereas westerners have a "guilt culture" (see Adeney 1995). According to this ideal-type theory, westerners are taught from infancy to control themselves and follow their own personal consciences (guilt) whereas Indonesians are controlled by the community (shame). In Indonesia, if you do something wrong, you have not failed yourself or some objective standard (guilt); you have failed the community (shame).[8] Indonesians complain that politicians know no shame. They no longer are controlled by *budaya malu*.

These are overgeneralized ideal types, which have been much criticized since Ruth Benedict's influential study of Japanese shame culture ([1946] 1989). All cultures and people suffer shame and guilt, which are not separated into distinctly different or contrasting things in human experience (Adeney 1995). Indonesia is no exception. I have no idea whether or not Indonesians experience more shame and less guilt than westerners. However, the ideal types help us understand why Indonesians generally interpret social control and a shame culture in such a positive light. In a highly communal culture the community is more important than the individual. Sometimes transgressions are ignored by the community because if they are revealed everyone close to the transgressor will feel shame.

In Indonesia religion is a powerful agent of social control. It is a "field" that overlaps and interacts with many other fields, such as politics, education, television, economics, and fashion. Together these fields shape a person's habitus.[9] A habitus structures people's experience and controls their behavior, even down to little things like what food they eat, how they walk, and so on (Bourdieu 1984). Religions control people's behavior by shaping their habitus.

In Indonesia community control of people's behavior is exercised by many fields. I would not care to speculate which field exercises the strongest control: religion, government, a capitalist economy, education, media, internet, the family, or some other field. As Bourdieu says, they are all overlapping and interpenetrating. But religion, especially Islam, is one of the strongest fields shaping peoples' habitus and thus structuring their lives. The power of religion in Indonesia is not primarily exercised through the coercive power of government or through any other single field, but it is in all of them.

Foucault uses the term *panopticon* to indicate the surveillance power of the modern state (1997).[10] Islam certainly exercises a panopticon-type function in Indonesian society. Everyone knows who is praying five times a day, who attends the Friday prayers, who goes to koranic readings, and so on. One of my Javanese neighbors is one of the few Christians in the village. He told me that young people from the mosque started to visit him regularly at his home. They talked to him about the teachings of Islam and why it was so important to pray five times a day, fast during Ramadan, and attend the Friday prayers and sermon. They wondered why they never saw him at the mosque, which was just down the street. The man is quite old and a very traditional Javanese, so he was too polite to tell them he was not a Muslim. He just listened politely, uttering noncommittal Javanese affirmations. Eventually they learned that he was a Christian and stopped the visits after apologizing for bothering him.

Most religious social control is exercised peacefully by means of social pressure within tight-knit communities rather than by force. In 1996 I stayed for a few days with a well-known Javanese shadow puppet master (*dalang wayang kulit*). I learned that he was an expert in Javanese mysticism (*kebatinan*). I asked him to teach me, and he was very willing. We had many conversations about his esoteric knowledge and practices. But he warned me not to tell anyone that I was learning Javanese mysticism from him. He said there were many Islamic conservatives in his village and he could get in trouble. He suggested that if we were talking about Javanese mysticism and any of his neighbors came near, we should immediately switch to the subject of *wayang kulit*. Since people often stopped by to look at the *bule* (white man), we had many abruptly interrupted conversations! Radical groups gain a lot of publicity and wield disproportionate power in society because of their willingness to use violence (see chapter 12). But they are not the main force for religious social control in Indonesia. Social control through religion is usually much more subtle.

The main power of religion in Indonesia is that people control themselves in conformance with the teachings of their religion. One aspect of this self-disciplining is explained by Foucault's concept of governmentality, which is developed in Bourdieu's concept of the habitus. Governmentality is the extension of power over people by persuading them to control themselves. A panopticon is unnecessary if people watch themselves and discipline their own bodies. Bourdieu emphasizes that a habitus is shaped by interactions between a person (agent) and the surrounding structured and structuring fields. It is neither the willful creation of an agent nor the inevitable result of overpowering structures. Rather a habitus is created through interactions between the agent and structured and structuring fields. In other words, we are involved in the creation of our own habitus, even though we are largely unconscious of the process.

Foucault says that power is distributed throughout society. Everyone has power, and power is creative. We use our power/knowledge to achieve the ends for which we hope (Foucault 1970). Arendt emphasizes that true power lies in the ability of people to work together to achieve their ends (1970). Using these perspectives, we can view the power of religion in Indonesian society as a positive phenomenon. Islam is not an outside foreign power forcing people to do what they don't want to do. Islam is inside the people. It is part of their core identity and shapes their deepest convictions. It is not external to Indonesian society. Consistent with Durkheim, religion creates Indonesian society. For most Indonesians, Islam is the transcendent symbolic representation of Indonesia as the most populous Muslim country.

Islam tells them who they are and who they want to be.[11] As mentioned above, 72 percent of Indonesians said that the noblest society was one that obeyed God and implemented in society the teachings of their religion. Islam and nationalism are overlapping fields that together create strong solidarity among Indonesians. Islam and the constructed category of "religion" are the glue that holds Indonesia together.

The Power of Religion in Indonesian Society

The power of religions works within Indonesian society through mimetic rituals, mythical stories, ethical teaching, and theoretical reflection. If the last section suggested that religions play a coercive and/or manipulative role in controlling society, this section considers the role religions play in shaping people's lives in ways they consider positive.

The power of religious mimetic rituals

Virtually all Indonesians structure their lives with mimetic rituals.[12] Muslims prostrate themselves five times a day to imitate with their bodies an order in the cosmos in which they are completely dependent on God. During Ramadan they fast together from early morning till sunset to practice what it means to go without and control their desires. Then on Idul Fitri they feast together and gather with their families to celebrate their victory and solidarity. They give *zakat* (a tithe of their wealth) as a sign of their solidarity with the poor and an expression of thanksgiving. At Idul Adha, they shed blood and sacrifice a living animal to share the meat with the whole community and imitate the sacrifice of Abraham, who was willing to sacrifice his own son in submission to God. They go on the *Haj* to imitate the trials and tribulations of the Prophet and to be mimetically cleansed of their sins.

Indonesian Christians order their lives with daily prayers, practicing the skill of living a life of thanksgiving to God. Every Sunday they gather to express their solidarity and worship. Most Protestants use an ancient liturgy in the Dutch Reformed tradition, but the meaning they give the forms is quite different from that of western churches. Both Protestants and Catholics use ancient liturgies that establish a moral order within a sacred cosmos.

They take Communion and attend Mass to vicariously experience the sacrificial death of Christ and their unity with him in one body. On Ash Wednesday, at the beginning of Lent, they put ashes on their foreheads to express mourning for their sins and begin a cleansing fast.

Hindus give daily offerings of fruit, flowers, and incense to imitate their dependence on the ancestors and unseen powers that surround them. Almost every day of the year there are special festivals, dances, music, and other rituals intended to maintain mimetic balance with the unseen world. Before the holy day of Nyepi, they parade around with huge scary monsters to mimetically evict evil beings from their community before burning them on the beach. On Nyepi, the whole of Bali is completely silent. There is no electricity allowed and no motor vehicles. They even shut down the international airport. They practice what it means to be empty and willing to listen to the voices inside their hearts.

Buddhists, Confucianists, and the devotees of hundreds of local indigenous religions all have equally elaborate mimetic rituals, which structure their lives and imitate a sacred order in the cosmos. Religions are powerful in shaping people's lives in Indonesia in large part because people know the meanings of their spiritual faith through their bodily actions. Mimetic rituals create bodily knowledge in a community of common practice (see de Certeau 1984). When you learn to ride a bike or play a musical instrument, you have to do it with your body. You cannot learn it by reading about it in a book or memorizing a list of skills and rules. You have to practice. When you learn something with your body, by doing it over and over again, it changes you. Like knowing how to ride a bike, you cannot forget it even if you want to. Similarly, religions are powerful in ordering the lives of Indonesians because they learn them with their bodies through repeated mimetic rituals. Two of the people interviewed in chapter 5 (Syafi'i and Zainal), mentioned that they always *bersholat* (worship) five times a day because if they miss one of their prayer times they feel like something is missing from their lives. I've heard the same comment many times from Muslim students. Many do not pray because they have to, or because someone is watching, but rather because it gives them the power to know things with their bodies that they might otherwise miss.[13]

Naturally, whether all these mimetic forms of bodily knowledge empower the people or curtail their ability to know other things through other ways of knowing is a matter of perspective. What we see can hide what we ought to see. Sometimes those accused of corruption, murder, or other crimes are the most prominent in displaying their piety through mimetic rituals. If so, it may be that the power of religion is being used as a narcotic to deflect attention away from their crimes. Arendt commented that there is good in everyone, but only the hypocrites are rotten to the core.

The power of religious stories

Indonesians tell stories to give meaning to their lives. In fact narratives are the primary way all human beings think. We remember in narrative, hope in narrative, dream in narrative, and relate to each other in narrative (Hauerwas and Jones 1997). All the religious mimetic rituals mentioned above gain their meaning and power from stories. The power of religions to shape life lies in their stories. Sacred stories are paradigms through which Indonesians interpret their lives. For Muslims, Scripture does not just mean the Koran but also the Sunnah. The Sunnah includes stories about what the Prophet said, did, thought, intended, approved, and so on. It also includes the biography of the Prophet and stories about the practices of his close companions and the people of Medina. These stories are considered models that Muslims should imitate.

The power of religion through stories does not just include stories from sacred texts but also stories about heroes. Many of these Indonesian heroes were religious leaders who resisted or rebelled against the Dutch colonialists. Their stories are retold not only as religious narratives of Muslim struggles against oppressors but also as nationalist stories about the struggle for independence and the defeat of western imperialism and colonialism. This is one of many ways the fields of religion and nationalism are intertwined (see Carey 2008).

In 1995 I attended an evening of blessing for a village leader who was going on the *Haj* to Mecca. He invited a prominent Muslim leader (*kyai*) to address the village. I was amazed at his performance. For almost three hours the *kyai* held the whole village spellbound. Like a puppet master (*dalang*), he told stories using different accents and voices for different characters. He sang songs, recited poems, and switched effortlessly among Indonesian, Javanese, and Arabic, including different dialects in Indonesian and Javanese for comic effect. He kept his audience in stiches of laughter but also brought them to tears. His power lay in the ways he wove together stories from the Koran and Sunnah, from everyday life in Java, from the Ramayana Hindu Javanese myths, and from current political events. His skill in weaving many different narrative strands together was astonishing.

While stories can be used to empower the people, they can also be used to deceive, manipulate, and trivialize religion. In any case, stories are powerful. Once I was invited to the dedication of a mosque that had just been renovated. Another Muslim leader also told stories, but they were stories that demonized non-Muslims and promised automatic forgiveness of sins and a path to paradise in exchange for performing certain mechanical mimetic rituals. Conversely, if the people were not faithful in their rituals, they would burn in hell. In this case, stories were used to manipulate and compel obedience.

The power of ethical moral guidance from religion

Many Indonesians believe that the power of religion lies in its ability to give detailed moral instructions on how to live. In an age of precipitous urbanization, bewildering social change, and the invasion of Indonesia by globalized media, religions offer belief that there are norms, rules, and practices mandated by God. In 1993 I happened to be in a Javanese mountain village on a Monday morning when the US football Super Bowl was being broadcast on live TV. American sports were almost never on Indonesian TV, so I asked my host if there was a TV in the village where I could watch. There was one TV in the village, and the owner was happy to invite me to watch the game. Lots of Javanese villagers crowded into the room, to watch with me, or to watch me. The cultural disconnect in that small mountain village was quite intense. On the little screen, huge, monstrous men in armor and helmets were seemingly trying to kill each other while half-naked Dallas Cowboys cheerleaders pranced on the sidelines and Michael Jackson performed at halftime. The village Javanese watching in disbelief were small, gentle people who dressed modestly and avoided conflict of any kind. One gentle man politely commented, "It seems such a rude game!"

Today everyone has a TV and access to internet. In spite of government attempts to censor the internet, extreme pornography is readily available. With rapid urbanization, anomie (the breakdown of norms and values) is common, and many people turn to religion to find meaning and direction. In Pew Foundation polling, 99 percent of Indonesians said religion was important or very important to them personally. Indonesians often claim that religion is the source of ethics (*akhlak*) and order in society.

In the story related above about the celebration put on by a village to send one of its leaders on the *Haj*, all the villagers participated. They donated food and other resources, cooked together for days, rented huge tents and sound systems, and worked around the clock to prepare for the big event. The man going on the *Haj* asked me if in America a whole village would donate its resources and work together like this to celebrate someone going to Mecca. I had to admit it was unlikely. The ethics of communal cooperation (*gotong royong*) is inspired by religious sentiments, but it is not all derived from religion. In part it is rooted in traditional practices of village solidarity that predate the coming of Islam. Religious ethics in Indonesia is always mixed with traditional practices and modern ideas.

This mixture of religion and other sources of ethics is illustrated by the responses to our Question III.B about economic ethics.

Questionnaire Question III.B on economic ethics

> *Which of the following statements do you think is most important?*
>
> 1. We should use moral and clean/*halal* means in seeking wealth.
>
> 2. Be part of the community. Live simply and honestly, serving others without self-interest.
>
> 3. Develop the soul of an entrepreneur. Learn to compete in a healthy manner in the free market era.

The first answer uses the religious markers "moral" and "clean/*halal*." Indonesians often affirm that they are committed to working hard as long as the work is moral and *halal*, that is, not forbidden or against the teachings of religion. The second answer uses the traditional language of village ethics. "Be part of the community" (*bermasyarakat*) is a term commonly used to judge whether or not someone is good. It is in contrast to someone who is aloof, arrogant, or seldom participates in neighborhood functions. The terms "simple" (*sederhana*), "honest" (*jujur*), "serving" (*ikhlas*), and "without self-interest" (*tanpa pamrih*) are all traditional moral values throughout Indonesia. Of course they are also linked to more overtly religious ethics and are reinforced with stories from many different sources. The third response is thoroughly modern. The term "soul of an entrepreneur" (*jiwa enterpreneur*) is quite popular in Indonesia. Traditionally, Indonesians avoid overt competition. But in the era of a global free market, new virtues are required, and competition is acceptable as long it is conducted "in a healthy manner" (*bersaing secara sehat*).

Most Indonesians preferred the answer that used the vocabulary of traditional Indonesian values (58 percent). This included 55 percent of Muslims, 69 percent of Protestants, 43 percent of Catholics, 54 percent of Hindus, and all the Buddhists. Most Indonesians would argue that these values are not just traditional but also the essence of the teachings of their religion. The preferences don't tell us if the respondents really live according to these values, but they affirm that they think they ought to live that way. Twenty-five percent of Indonesians selected the religious language of using moral and clean/*halal* means of seeking wealth. Only 17 percent chose the language of healthy competition in a free market era.

Even though these results do not indicate a direct connection between religious moral teachings and economic ideals, they do indicate a strong correlation between morality and economic ethics. Most Indonesians of all religions consider that the "traditional values" of living simply, honestly, and without self-interest and putting the community first are religious values ordered by God. Whether or not they actually live up to them is another matter.

Table 9.4 *Responses to Question III.B on Economic Ethics*

Groups	Traditional Community, Live Simply, Serve without Self-Interest	Modern Entrepreneur Healthy Competition Free Market Era	Religious Moral Clean/*Halal* Seek Wealth
Muslim	55%	18%	27%
Protestant	69%	13%	18%
Catholic	43%	22%	35%
Hindu	54%	20%	26%
Buddhist	100%	0%	0%
All	58%	17%	25%

Most Indonesians do not imagine their religion as a private matter or something to be kept in the private sphere of personal experience. Muslims, especially, are adamant that religion should affect all areas of life, including politics, economics, social relations, media, culture, family life, and education. In order to integrate religion with all areas of human life, Indonesians are constantly engaged in theory building. Some of this theory building goes on in universities, including public universities that are not religiously affiliated.

For example, at UGM, the largest national university in Indonesia and the most highly rated in the social sciences and humanities, there are many programs, study centers, and research projects dedicated to the study of Islamic perspectives on various academic fields. Programs in Sharia economics are particularly popular, spurred by the prospect of careers in government or banking. The national government now has a department for Sharia economics, and most banks have Sharia divisions. At UGM there is also a program in Islamic psychology. Many faculty members and students are publishing articles and books on such topics as Islamic physics, Islamic medicine, Islam and gender, Islamic literature, Islam and law, Islam and politics, Islam and social theory, Islam and religion, Islam and astrophysics, and so on.[14] Hundreds of books and thousands of articles are published every year on almost everything under the sun and its relation to Islam. Christians (both Catholic and Protestant) also have a thriving publishing industry driven by hundreds of educational institutions with a hunger for books in Indonesian.

There is a wide range of epistemologies associated with people who are writing on religion in relation to traditionally secular disciplines. Some are informed by an agenda of naive apologetics, for example, anachronistic interpretations of ancient texts intended to prove that all the theories of modern science were already revealed in the Scriptures. There are also highly sophisticated dialogues between the latest complex theories and religious perspectives informed by postmodern and postcolonial philosophy. Naturally, most of what is published lies somewhere in between the extremes of academic excellence and naive apologetics. Unfortunately, most of even the best publications will never be read outside Indonesia because they are published in Indonesian.

This chapter explored the power of religions in Indonesia by considering Islam and law, government definition and regulation of religion, religion and the ideal nation-state, the power of religion to control the people, and how religions influence people's lives through mimetic rituals, religious narratives, ethical norms, and theoretical reflection. In all these areas, religions do not operate as autonomous actors. Rather religion is a field that interpenetrates and interacts with other fields to shape the habitus of people as they continue to create a unique, traditional, religious, and modern civilization.

The last section of the book explores how social imaginaries of a sacred cosmos shape Indonesians' views of nature, women, and conflict. The next chapter focuses on imaginations of nature and how Indonesians experience the tragedy of natural disasters.

Part IV
Nature, Women, and Conflict
in a Sacred Cosmos

PART IV EXPLORES how living in a traditional, religious, and modern sacred cosmos shapes how Indonesians' view nature, women, and religious conflict. First, how do complex social imaginaries shape their understanding of nature and the environment? How does it help them interpret frequent natural disasters? Second, how does living in a sacred cosmos affect their understanding and regulation of gender relations in an Islamic society? Third, how do Indonesians use traditional, modern, and religious strategies to deal with religious conflict?

10

Imaginations of Nature and Natural Disasters

> One must still have chaos in oneself to be able to give birth to a dancing star.
>
> —Friedrich Nietzsche

INDONESIA IS A VERY BEAUTIFUL country.[1] It boasts abundant natural resources; rich, fertile soils; warm weather; and bountiful rainfall. In some parts of Java and Bali, farmers can harvest crops four times a year. All kinds of fruit trees grow like weeds in their profusion.[2] Indonesia ranks third in the world (after Brazil and Congo) in the amount of area covered by tropical rain forests, which are filled with unimaginably diverse wildlife and flora. Among the seventeen thousand islands are pristine beaches, lush jungles, soaring mountains, and oceans full of all kinds of sea life. Yogyakarta is not far from the ocean, but from my home I can see two beautiful mountains, both of which are around three thousand meters (ten thousand feet) high.

Indonesia is also extremely prone to natural disasters. It is part of the Pacific "Ring of Fire," which accounts for 90 percent of the world's earthquakes and volcanic eruptions. There are at least 129 active volcanoes in Indonesia. One of the most active in the world is Mount Merapi (Burning Mountain), one of the two mountains I can see from my house. It is usually smoking and erupts every two or three years with larger eruptions every ten to fifteen. Huge eruptions occurred in 1006, 1786, 1822, 1872, and 1930. In addition to earthquakes and volcanoes, destructive floods and landslides occur on a yearly basis, especially affecting large coastal cities such as Jakarta, Surabaya, and Semarang. Global warming has brought a rising ocean with increasing flooding, extreme storms, and the inundation of islands.

On December 26, 2004 a 9.3 magnitude earthquake off the northern tip of Sumatra caused a tsunami that killed more than 250,000 people in fourteen countries, including around 200,000 in Aceh, Indonesia. This was the largest natural disaster in recorded history. On May 27, 2006, a devastating earthquake hit my city of Yogyakarta, killing more than 5,700 people, injuring tens of thousands, destroying more than 154,000 homes, and damaging more than 260,000 additional homes and buildings. In 2010 Mount Merapi erupted again, killing close to 400 people and covering the city of Yogyakarta in volcanic ash.

How Do Indonesians Feel about Nature?

Indonesians traditionally view nature as dangerous. Wild places, such as mountains, jungles and the ocean, are viewed as the abode of spirits and dangerous invisible beings. In the ever popular *Ramayana* stories, the heroes have to face their most harrowing adventures in the jungle. In the jungle there are monsters. While Indonesians certainly appreciate natural beauty, many feel that wildness has to be tamed and ordered to make it safe. Places of great beauty may be also places of supernatural power (*tempat keramat*). Indonesians make pilgrimages to such places, sometimes in the middle of the night, to meditate and pray for blessing or power. But as far as possible such places are avoided. If a place becomes a popular tourist or pilgrimage destination, neat paths with flowers, cement benches, and artificial landscaping are built around the site. The wildness is ordered to assert human control over nature and make it safe.

I used to live in a mountain town in Central Java on the slopes of beautiful Mount Merbabu. The nicest hotel in town could have had unobstructed views of the mountain, but all the windows and balconies faced a courtyard. None of the walls facing the beautiful mountain had windows. The manager explained to me that people would be scared if they looked directly at the mountain. It would not be polite or wise to gaze directly at it. The mountain is a place of power.[3]

Traditional Indonesian tribal peoples such as the Samin (wong Sikep) in Java, the Dyak Kaharingan in Kalimantan, and the Dani in West Papua are known for their ecological lifestyle. They make everything they need from natural organic materials. Since they live simply on the margins of subsistence, there is no waste. Everything is recycled until it decomposes. The land, the trees, and all of nature are treated as sacred. Large trees may not be cut down except to meet urgent needs of the people. Before cutting a tree there must be consensus of the elders, who will perform rituals to ask forgiveness and permission from the life of the tree to be sacrificed. The elders politely invite the spirits who inhabit the tree to move for the sake of the people. Mountains, rocks, rivers, and jungles are all viewed as agents who can communicate with and affect the well-being of the people. They must be treated with honor and respect.

Indigenous tribal peoples do not make a sharp distinction between human life and nature. There is one community in a sacred cosmos, which includes unseen beings, natural forces, the ancestors, and living humans. Before we romanticize this life of oneness with nature, it is good to remember that in such communities life expectancy is short and life is fragile. Even the most remote tribes are now adopting the fruits of modern technology. Their lives are made easier by plastic bags, modern medical clinics, and even chemical fertilizers. As modern "development" encroaches on their lands and further marginalizes their traditional way of life, many are adopting modern ways to increase their comfort, health, and safety. Unfortunately, at the same time they are losing indigenous knowledge of nature and ecological ways of life that are needed, more than ever, to ensure the future of our planet.

There is a strong environmental movement in Indonesia that is powered by many NGOs. The movement transcends religious, political, and ethnic boundaries. Most environmental NGOs are multireligious.[4] During an interreligious dialogue on globalization, which included radical Islamists, I was surprised to learn that these radical Islamists were also radical environmentalists. They were very critical of capitalist development and wanted to save the forests. The Islamists initiated a project to make a contract with villagers to not cut down their trees. For many villagers, trees are their money in the bank. Whenever they need cash, they cut down a tree and sell the wood. As a result, the trees of poor villagers seldom grow very large. They need the money so their children can go to school. These creative students paid villagers the value of the wood in their trees if they promised to not cut them down for twenty years.

Different Ways of Imagining our Relation to Nature

Educated Indonesians are all aware of the ecological crisis and believe that we should preserve the environment. In our research, we framed a question to discover whether Indonesians favored traditional, religious, or scientific language as their primary symbol system for imagining their relation to nature.

Questionnaire Question III.G on relation to nature

What should the relationship between Indonesian people and nature or the environment be?

1. Honor the earth of our ancestors. We are an indivisible part of the natural world.

2. As God's representatives on earth, the people should protect and preserve nature.

3. We should use science to build a sustainable economy that is gentle on the environment.

The first answer uses language that corresponds to traditional Indonesian concepts of nature in two ways. First, it links the earth with the ancestors, who should be honored. Honoring the earth is a way to honor the ancestors. Both the earth and the ancestors give us life. Second, it locates the human community as part of nature, indeed indivisible from nature. This implies that humans are not above or apart from nature but rather are part of Mother Earth (Ibu Tiwi). Thus the answer can be seen as cosmoscentric.

The second, religious answer is theocentric (God centered). God is above both us and nature. Human beings are located over and above nature, as God's stewards. We are God's agents to protect nature. Nature is imagined as separate from the human community. Since God is over both humans and nature, our responsibility to preserve the earth is fundamentally a matter of obedience to God.

The third answer is anthropocentric. The environmental crisis threatens the long-term sustainability of the human community. Science and technology contribute to the environmental crisis. Both must be harnessed to ameliorate the uncontrolled destruction of the natural world for the sake of the long term-survival of the human community.

From interviews it was clear that many participants agreed with all three of the possible answers and had difficulty choosing among them.[5] Nevertheless, most respondents chose one of these symbol systems, the one that felt most appropriate for them.

These results indicate that religious communities have a considerable influence on which of the three symbol systems feels right to a respondent. Catholics had the highest percentage of people choosing the traditional language, with 56 percent. They are closely followed by the Hindus, of whom 49 percent chose the cosmos-centered language. Muslims had the lowest figures for choosing the traditional language, with 26 percent. Protestants had just a little more, with 30 percent choosing the cosmoscentric language. Muslims and Protestants were quite close to each other, while Catholics, Hindus, and Buddhists were close to each other in their preferred choice of traditional language. There is a large gap of 30 percent difference between Muslims (26 percent) and Catholics (56 percent).

Another difference is that most Muslims and Protestants strongly preferred religious language over both modern and traditional language. Muslims preferred theocentric language by 41 percent, which is more than the 33 percent who chosen modern, anthropocentric language. Fifty-one percent of Protestants chose theocentric language, while only 19 percent preferred the language of science. In comparison, most Catholics, Hindus, and Buddhists did not prefer religious language. Only 22 percent of Hindus and Catholics and none of the Buddhists chose the language of protecting nature because we are God's agents on earth.

Table 10.1 *Responses to Question III.G on Relation to Nature*

Groups	Traditional Mother Earth	Modern Sustainability	Religious God's Agents
Muslim	26%	33%	41%
Protestant	30%	19%	51%
Catholic	56%	22%	22%
Hindu	49%	29%	22%
All Indonesians	32%	28%	40%

According to Lynn White's well-known thesis, the environmental crisis has philosophical roots in monotheism and the Abrahamic religions (White 1967). According to the Abrahamic religions, at creation God gave human beings dominion over nature, thereby leading to the imagination of nature as separate from humans. Humans may dominate nature to serve their own needs. White's argument recalls Hegel's discussion of "bad infinity." According to him, when God is imagined as utterly transcendent and all powerful over humanity and nature, it leads to alienation from God, alienation from other people, and alienation from nature. Human beings imitate God's domination by seeking power over each other and nature (see Placher 1989).

White's and Hegel's arguments are useful tools with which to interpret these statistics. Buddhists, Hindus, and Catholics all conceive of transcendence as also immanent. God is close. Buddhism and Hinduism both tend toward pantheism, in which God and nature are infused with each other. Catholic Christianity has a sacramental view of nature, rooted in natural law. Nature is to be revered as revelatory of God's glory. In contrast, Muslims and Protestants emphasize the transcendence of God. God is all powerful and far above us. The Calvinist belief in natural depravity means that nature is unreliable as a source of revelation. Muslim prayers (*sholat*) enact a bodily imitation of our relation to God as absolute surrender. This recalls a self-depreciating joke once told by Abdurrahman Wahid. Gus Dur joked that Buddhists were closest to God because they encountered the Divine through silence and meditation. Christians were also close because they prayed to God with a soft voice. Muslims were farthest from God because they had to use loudspeakers!

Most of the Protestant respondents to our questionnaire were from the Reformed tradition of Calvin and Luther. As already noted, the Protestant Reformation was a modernist movement that championed reason, science, and devotion to God alone. In contrast, Catholics have historically been much more accommodating of local beliefs and practices. Both Islamic modernism and Protestant Reformed theology influence attitudes toward nature in Indonesia.[6]

The preceding attempts to explain the statistical findings through theological reflection should not obscure the reality that none of these religious groups is a monolith. Each community includes a great variety of beliefs, practices, and imaginations. Many Muslims and Protestants experience

God as very near. For Muslims the ideal is to worship five times a day in order to be engrossed in the presence of God. For some Protestants the ideal is to pray without ceasing, to make one's whole life a prayer. On the other hand, some Catholics, Hindus, and Buddhists experience God as utterly transcendent and distant. Theological reflection is a helpful tool for explaining statistical trends, but it should not be used for stereotyping, let alone as a normative description of the essential teachings of the religious communities.

The Meaning of Natural Disasters

How do Indonesians give meaning to natural disasters? Beauty, bounty, danger, and disaster are not abnormal, unusual events but almost daily experiences. The following section explores how mimetic, mythic, ethical, and theoretic ways of knowing inform Indonesian experiences of natural disasters. Indonesians use mimetic, cosmic rituals to guard a balance in nature and their relation to God. They use mythic stories to lend meaning to both the abundance of nature and its periodic deadly destruction. They interpret "blessing" and judgment through the lens of moral introspection. And they use modern science to understand natural causation and find ways to enhance the benefits and mitigate the destruction they receive from Mother Earth and Ocean (Ibu Tiwi and Tanah Air). For most Indonesians, these four ways of knowing are not mutually exclusive choices but rather alternative symbol systems that complement each other.

Human tragedies do not have a single, fixed ontological meaning such as "the real reason this occurred is X." The meaning of a tragedy changes in relation to human responses. We create the meaning. This does not mean that the meaning is just subjective or arbitrary. We are not free to create any meaning we wish. Rather the meaning is intersubjective, substantive, and social. The meaning is "intersubjective" and evolving because it is the result of a social process. Many people, thinking and acting in relation to each other, interpret the meaning of the natural disaster. New meanings are suggested all the time. Some meanings are superficial, self-deceiving, or wrong. Meanings that are convincing and accepted by a community change both the meaning of the remembered event and the future of the community that is shaped by its memories.

Some meanings are substantive because they endure in the real world. They are not just a fleeting thought in an individual mind. They change social reality. Some meanings create institutions and are linked with other meanings to form networks that shape culture. Meanings determine social relations between people. Social meanings create justice and injustice, hope and despair, life and death, beauty and ugliness, good and evil. The same events (e.g., the tsunami in Aceh) mean different things at different times and in different places. September 11 meant something different in the United States than it did in Indonesia (Adeney-Risakotta 2004).

Different questions confront different people in a disaster and result in different responses. The differences are not only in the questions they ask but also in the different sources to which people turn for answers. In *Habits of the Heart*, Robert Bellah and his associates analyzed the languages Americans use to describe their actions (Bellah et al. 1985). The book concludes that most Americans are heavily influenced by utilitarian and emotive individualism. Their language appeals to what they feel is right for them personally based on emotional, aesthetic, or practical considerations. The authors suggest that in the past Americans had a richer vocabulary, drawn from the Bible, and a republican, liberal philosophy. However, these rich languages are being forgotten and replaced with a much more superficial, individualistic language that Alistair MacIntyre calls "emotivism" (1984). People act on the basis of what "feels" right emotionally without much consciousness of the rich symbols and traditions that have shaped centuries of reflection about the meaning of life.

Indonesians are not much influenced by emotive individualism, but they are pulled between overlapping and competing symbol systems. These symbolic vocabularies are not individual choices but integral parts of their historical consciousness. In response to tragedy, Indonesians find resources for creating meaning in all these ways of knowing.

Stanley Hauerwas wrote that our challenge is to build a "community of character" that is capable of facing tragedy without resorting to self-deceiving explanations (1991). Natural disasters are "tragedies," in the Greek sense, because they create great human suffering caused by powers that are far beyond human control. Building a community of character depends on our habitual practices.

Mimetic Practices and Rituals Create Order and Safety amid Chaos

On the day of the earthquake in Yogyakarta, May 27, 2006, I saw a family of Muslims praying in the ruins of their house. Even though the house was just a pile of rubble, the women had somehow managed to find clean white prayer robes. The father, mother, and their three children were on their knees with their heads in the dirt, then up on their feet with their arms outstretched to God, calling out "Allahu Akbar! Allahu Akbar!" (God is Great! God is Great!). It reminded me of a woman I saw after the tsunami in Aceh. She had lost her entire family and was standing among the ruins with tears streaming down her face, crying out "Allahu Akbar! Allahu Akbar!" In the face of tragedy, performing a familiar ritual that expresses a deep link with the ground of our being is a "precognitive" way to create meaning. It is a mimetic, communal ritual that re-creates a sacred cosmos and imitates our place within it.

On the day of the earthquake in 2006, I drove around Yogyakarta on my motorcycle. I saw a lot of death and suffering, but no one was alone. Everyone was part of a community of practice. They were performing familiar communal practices of *gotong royong* (mutual assistance) and *sholat* (worship). These acts created order and meaning even when the very earth under our feet was not stable.[7]

One of my graduate students at Duta Wacana Christian University was a pastor who was born and raised in Aceh. At the time of the tsunami his father had recently died, and the whole family was planning a Christmas reunion at his mother's house near the beach in Banda Aceh. The family reunion was a mimetic ritual to express and re-create the unity of the family in the face of death. Elisa was two days late because he had to finish a research paper. He was on his way to Banda Aceh and called me when he heard news of the tsunami, asking what he should do. He went on to search for his family. After climbing for hours through rubble and around bloated corpses he finally made it to his mother's house. As he stood on the wall of the ruins he saw desolation in all directions. Fifteen members of his immediate family were swept away and never seen again. In his heart he felt an overwhelming conviction that God had deserted them. He was alone. All the sermons that he had preached about God's loving kindness returned to him empty. He explained to me that the problem was not just that all his family members were dead but the way they died. Tens of thousands of corpses could not be identified as they were bloated and disfigured beyond recognition by the water and debris. He could not perform the mimetic rituals of lovingly washing their bodies and clothing them in white to prepare them for burial. They were not only dead; they were violated. The sacredness of his cosmos seemed shattered.

Elisa faced four major questions.

1. How do I go on living? What do I have to do?
2. Why did God allow this to happen? Why didn't God save us? Why did I survive?
3. What have we done to deserve this? Who did this? Who is to blame?
4. What were the natural causes of the earthquake and tsunami? What can we do to prevent or mitigate this tragedy if it happens again?

These four questions cannot all be answered by one form of knowing. The first is best addressed by mimetic practices, which express "habits of the heart." We just continue to do what we have practiced doing for many years: we imitate an order that makes sense of our lives, even when we feel no sense. We practice kindness to our neighbors and worship, performing rituals that create meaning even in the face of appalling grief. The second question is best addressed through a narrative to make sense of the question. We tell stories that make some kind of sense out of tragedy. The third question is a moral one about the nature of good and evil and the ways we might have been complicit in the tragedy. This question leads to both personal and communal introspection. The fourth question begs for a scientific answer. We create theories to explain what happened and why.

Practices and rituals give order and meaning to life, even when our intellectual and emotional resources are taxed beyond all reason. Following the tragedy, Elisa spent a lot of time in prayer to a God who seemed to be absent. He gathered members of his community so they could weep together, tell each other their stories, and pray and worship together. I will not easily forget the experience of gathering in a living room with Elisa and other survivors, some of whom had lost most of their families. One young Christian woman told of how her Muslim neighbor grabbed her by the hair as she was being swept away, saving her life. Since Elisa was well educated and spoke Indonesian, Acehnese, and English, several international relief agencies offered him large salaries to help lead their humanitarian aid programs.

But Elisa refused. He told me he just wanted to concentrate on helping his only surviving nephew, who was having a very difficult time. For Elisa his family had boiled down to one person, and he just wanted to practice being a family with this troubled teenager.

Myths and Narratives Rescue Meaning from Despair

Several weeks after the tsunami, Elisa returned to Yogyakarta to continue his graduate studies. His Christian university held a service of remembrance for his family, and the whole community gathered around to support him. During the service, Elisa talked about his experience. He was already beginning to construct a story to give meaning to his loss. Human meaning always requires a narrative structure. Even meaninglessness or nihilism is experienced as a narrative. Elisa was trying to construct a story that had meaning. I was struck by his vehemence when he said, "God did not do this! God did not do this!" Who did *not* do this was more important to him than who did. Elisa was already constructing a story about what his tragedy meant. It might take him a long time to come to terms with the difficulty of answering the questions "Why me?" or "Why didn't God save us?" or "Why did I survive?" But if he can say "God did *not* do this!" then at least his basic faith in the goodness of God can give him the strength to go on.

The example of Elisa is in contrast with that of my "grandmother," the oldest living relative on my wife's Javanese Muslim side of the family.[8] The 2006 earthquake near Yogyakarta destroyed my family's village of Tajih, near Prambanan. When the earthquake hit, our grandmother had just finished morning worship (*sholat subuh*) and was going for her daily walk. Because she could not stand up on the heaving earth, she just sat down. Her adult son was frantic, searching for her and calling her name. Finally he found her and cried out that their old teak home was destroyed, level with the ground. She looked at him calmly and said, "Let it go. Let it go" (Biarin. Biarin.). Grandma was *pasrah*, submitted to the will of God. In contrast to Elisa, Grandma believed that God did it. According to her story, if the house was destroyed, then it was God's will. The only thing to do was let it go and entrust all things to the hands of God. Her strength gave hope to the rest of the family.

The differences between Elisa and Grandma were not determined by the differences in their religions but rather by the stories they constructed. Reformed Christian Elisa and Muslim Grandma are not too far apart in their faith in the sovereignty of God. But their stories were different because their personal experiences of tragedy were different. Grandma "only" lost her home, and she was already submitted to God and ready to face her approaching death as a very old woman. Elisa not only lost most of his closest family, but he was also relatively young with his whole life ahead of him. He too became *pasrah* (submitted to the will of God) in time. But he could not go there easily without cheapening the magnitude of his loss. The magnitude of his grief demanded that he construct a narrative that somehow reconciled his religious faith with his experience of abandonment.

In contrast, Grandma's narrative never questions whether God was responsible for her loss. She knows God was responsible. She was not that concerned with questions of why. For her the burning questions were more concerned with how she could strengthen her family to help it face its loss. Mimetic practices and a narrative of submission to God were more important than philosophical or ethical reflection. As the matriarch of a large extended family, Grandma provided a model for the rest to follow. Neither Elisa nor Grandma offered cheap "self-deceiving explanations" of the tragedy. In his narrative, Elisa said, "God did not do this!" while Grandma said in effect, "God did it, so let it go!" Neither answer rings false. Religious people have been struggling for millennia with the meaning of God's involvement in tragedy without finding an answer. Elisa's faith in God's goodness implied that God did not curse his family or predestine it for destruction. For Grandma it meant that even if her family lost all it had built, God was good and her relatives could rebuild.

The difference in their narratives is not only related to differences in their age and experience of tragedy. It is also affected by their education, gender and class. Elisa is a highly educated, male, ordained Christian minister (*pendeta*). Grandma is without formal education, a Muslim woman from a relatively poor family.[9] As a highly educated, male minister, Elisa is trained to construct theological narratives that provide answers to pastoral dilemmas. Grandma's role is more practically oriented. She's not expected to ask ultimate philosophical questions but rather to help her clan survive in difficult times. In Indonesia women are frequently entrusted with financial management and most of the practical details of running the household. In contrast men are responsible for symbolic spiritual leadership in the community. Men are socialized to be more spiritual and abstract, while women are expected to ensure the family's practical survival on a day-to-day basis.

These are socialized gender roles rather than essential characteristics of men and women. Nevertheless, they profoundly influence the kinds of stories women and men construct in response to natural disasters. In Lawrence Kohlberg's well-known theory, the highest stage of moral reasoning is a Kantian commitment to universal, abstract, ethical principles. Carol Gilligan points out that this is a very white and male perspective. Women are far more likely to focus on narratives that impact the practical well-being of the people around them rather than on a narrative that answers ultimate philosophical questions (1982). According to her, there is no inherent reason why a narrative that serves the needs of the community should be considered inferior to a narrative that answers abstract philosophical questions. Commitment to abstract moral principles is not a higher stage of moral consciousness than practical action on behalf of the people around you.

In the book *Perempuan dan Bencana* (Women and Disaster), the Indonesian women authors are overwhelmingly oriented toward stories of how they responded in practical ways to the suffering of the victims the earthquake (F. Adeney-Risakotta 2007). The book includes narratives that address more abstract questions, but that is not the major focus. The question "Why" is just not as important as the question "What must we do?" In contrast, many of the essays by male authors in the book *Teologi Bencana* (A Theology of Disaster) struggle to shape narratives that address more abstract questions about why the disaster happened. In particular their narratives struggle with the goodness or justice of God in a world of suffering (theodicy) (Ngelow 2006).[10]

Most Indonesians believe in invisible powers, which reside all around them. These powers may be malignant, benevolent, demonic, neutral, ambivalent, or glorious. For some people, these local invisible powers are to be cultivated, placated, feared, served, revered, or even worshiped. For others these powers should be avoided, cast out, ignored, or cursed. For many they are just ignored as irrelevant to the practicalities of everyday life. But only a few Indonesians disbelieve in them all together.

Sindhunata relates that Javanese villagers who live on the slopes of Mount Merapi believe in a male deity referred to as Grandfather Merapi

(Singgih 2006:253–69; Sindhunata 1998). Eruptions of the volcano are part of the everyday lives of the villagers. From the volcano comes the amazing fertility of the land but also the threat of death. The volcano is beautiful but also dangerous and awesome. A villager relates:

> Grandfather Merapi is frightening but also full of love for [us] villagers. Grandfather Merapi is far from the palace and cannot be reached by human beings, but Grandfather Merapi also comes near to humans and gives fertility and life to us. With his lava and eruptions that kill, Grandfather Merapi demands human victims, but Grandfather Merapi also pays us back with the overflowing richness of nature. We hear again the roaring from Mount Merapi. And we feel that God is like Grandfather Merapi. This God is overwhelmingly powerful but beautiful (*dahsyat tetapi indah*). He kills, but He also gives life. He is far away but always close. He demands much, but He also gives with generosity. He is extremely rich but also simple. (Sindhunata 1998:175; see also Singgih 2006:254).

This quotation uses an ancient language passed down through stories from generation to generation. Death and tragedy are not trivialized but are seen as integrally related to life. This is the kind of worldview that led Grandma to say, "Let it go. Let it go." There is a balance: today comes death, tomorrow comes life. We need to accept our fate (*pasrah*) because Grandfather Merapi, like God, is really much too strong for us, and in any case he knows best. He is terrible but beautiful, and He loves as well as kills.

John Campbell-Nelson relates that some villagers on the island of Alor believed that the devastating earthquake that occurred there on November 12, 2004, was caused by government drilling in search of thermal energy in a place known for its sulfur and hot springs. The site of the drilling was close to the epicenter of the earthquake, and the sulfur springs were believed to be the place where one of the ancestors, a powerful shaman, was buried. She was the one who created the sulfur springs, and she was furious about the drilling into her home. Therefore she caused the devastating earthquake. The villagers were upset with both the government for drilling in a sacred place and the spiritual elders who did not ask proper permission of the ancestors before allowing the drilling (Campbell-Nelson 2006:99). Another version of the story drew on the ancient belief that the island of Alor was built on the back of a great dragon. The drilling pricked the dragon, which shook itself and instantly destroyed thousands of homes.

The stories of Grandfather Merapi, a buried shaman ancestor, and a sleeping dragon are all narratives that demand reverence for the earth and a relationship with nature of honor and respect. If they are discarded as superstitious myths, the truths embodied in them may simply be replaced with modern myths of progress and capitalist development, which provide few resources for either reverencing the earth or facing the tragedy of natural disasters. One of the challenges for the creation of meaning in a natural disaster is to integrate mimetic rituals, traditional myths, ethical reflection, and modern scientific understanding in a convincing account of the cosmos. Of course we cannot believe in what we do not believe. I have my doubts about the existence of a dragon under the island of Alor. But the stories people tell may contain more wisdom than Enlightenment myths about the power of science to solve all human problems. Indonesians learn things through stories of which others may be blind. Their stories challenge us to honor the natural world and resist unrestrained exploitation of the earth. Retelling the stories, honoring the ancestors, and following the traditions, can lead to a wisdom that promotes reverence towards the earth.

The stories Indonesians tell are not all drawn from the traditions of their ancestors. Powerful stories are drawn from their Scriptures. Stories of the Prophet's oppression and flight to Medina, the death and resurrection of Christ, the dialogue between Arjuna and Krishna, and the Buddha's enlightenment, are potent frames through which experience, including the experience of tragedy, is given meaning.

Tragedies Interrupt Normality and Stimulate Moral Reflection

Natural disasters almost inevitably stimulate profound ethical reflection. Suffering is the handmaiden of soul searching. When all goes well, it is easy to assume that prosperity is normal and what we deserve. But when disaster strikes, we may cry out, Why me? The massive earthquake and tsunami in Aceh stimulated not only moral introspection but also profound social change. Decades of civil war had brutalized the population, leading to hopelessness, cynicism, and casual cruelty on a daily basis. Then, in a matter of hours, the earthquake and tsunami wiped out more people than decades of war. No one would choose such a stimulus. But it sparked a new perspective on human community. The whole world came to the aid of Aceh. In the face of tragedy, your religion, ideology, or nationality no longer mattered. Ethical reflection was not primarily an exercise engaged in by individuals. Tragedy changed the orientation of a whole society.

Ethical reflection depends on the narrative constructed to give meaning to an event. Immediately after the tsunami in Aceh, I asked a tough, hard-living Muslim truck driver what he thought had caused it. When the tsunami hit he was driving down the western coastal road in Aceh. He was ripped from his truck and all his clothes were stripped away by the tsunami. As he was flung up by the raging water and debris, he grabbed the top of a coconut palm. That saved his life. He clung there bleeding for thirty-six hours before descending into mud and water that rose to his neck. For two days he slogged through swampy water to his village, only to find it gone. He stayed a night with a friend who lived up the mountain, then walked for another two days through mud and jungle to reach the city of Meulaboh. Meulaboh looked like the ruins at Hiroshima, but miraculously he found his wife and two small children still alive. Hearing his story and seeing the way he drove us through the jungle muck only few days after the tsunami, made me think, "This guy is not easy to kill."

His explanation was that the tsunami was God's punishment because he and his people had not been living according to God's law (Shari'a). I spent three days with this rough man, trying to reach survivors who had no food, and I never saw him *bersholat* (pray), which is a basic requirement of Shari'a. Perhaps he hadn't followed Shari'a for so long that he didn't know where to start. In any case, the urgency of trying to save lives in the midst of a crisis absorbed all his time, energy, and attention. His obviously sincere explanation that the tsunami was God's punishment was addressed to himself. Essentially he thought, "I and my people are sinners. We need to repent." Whether or not his explanation was "true," it was not a self-serving rationalization. It expressed his existential experience of feeling he had been punished by God. This Acehnese truck driver gave meaning to his experience through an ethical language of judgment not so different from that of a Balinese Hindu who told me that the Bali terrorist bomb was the people's karma because they had become too materialistic and failed to guard a balance with nature. Both the Acehnese Muslim and the Balinese Hindu used an ethical symbol system as a tool for introspection and moral self-critique.

The case is different if a theology of God's punishment is used to accuse another group (scapegoating) or used as a tool of domination over others. If an ulama seeks political power by preaching God's terrible punishment on all who do not follow his own narrow understanding of Shari'a, then we may suspect that "self-deceiving explanations" are at work. Self-interest transmutes theological reflection into an ideological tool of domination. The Acehnese truck driver told me that some religious teachers said the tsunami was God's punishment for a Christmas party on the beach at which people wore bathing suits and drank alcohol. I asked him if he thought Christians were then to blame for the tsunami. "No," he said. "Some Muslims are much worse than the Christians."

Similarly, some Christians said the tsunami was God's punishment of Muslim Acehenese for oppressing the Church. In both cases, a natural disaster was used as a weapon against those who are perceived as "the enemy." One characteristic of self-deceiving explanations is that they are a weapon of self-justification wielded against the "other." After a great earthquake in Lisbon in 1755, members of the clergy went around the city looking for "sinners" to burn at the stake in order to appease the wrath of God. Such actions may be motivated by a desperate attempt to blame the suffering on someone else. If the only interpretive option is to blame someone for the tragedy, then punishing the "real sinners" is a means of absolving yourself of guilt.

Scientific Constructions of Natural Disasters Create Hope

Scientific theories that describe the physical reasons why a natural disaster took place are always subject to change. Old paradigms are overturned when they fail to answer pressing questions. New paradigms are accepted because they offer a more convincing narrative that answers new questions (Kuhn 2012). One relatively recent example is the theory of plate tectonics as a cause of earthquakes. According to this theory, the surface crust of the earth is covered with huge plates that are slowly moving in different directions. Even if the plates only move a few centimeters per year, the edges grind against each other and create enormous pressures. Earthquakes occur where two or three of these plates meet. When the pressure becomes too enormous, there is a sudden "slip." This elegantly simple theory explains many things that were heretofore mysterious. When two plates "collide," one may be forced down into the molten core of the earth, while the other is forced up, creating cliffs and mountains.[11]

John Campbell-Nelson (2006) points out that if it were not for plate tectonics, eventually the whole earth would lie below the ocean. Rain and wind, rivers and floods, and freezing and thawing are constantly breaking up the land and carrying it to the sea. But thanks to plate tectonics, new dry land is constantly being raised up out of the sea. Just as the old land is worn down to below sea level, new land is raised by the movement of plates. Some of the highest mountains in the world, including Mount Everest, have sea fossils buried in their peaks. At one time, Mount Everest was beneath the ocean. Plate tectonics raised it up to become the highest mountain on earth. Plate tectonics and their consequent earthquakes make life on earth possible. According to the theory, without earthquakes, only fish would have a chance to live.

The theory of plate tectonics aids our understanding of earthquakes in four ways. First, the theory provides a much longer *time perspective* for the causes and meanings of a major earthquake. A devastating earthquake is not primarily caused by something that occurred in my lifetime or even during the past hundred years, but is a recurring action that results from millions of years of subterranean geologic activity. The idea that such an event can be caused by some person's or group's sin is hard to maintain. The theory of plate tectonic activity over millions of years provides the perspective of a natural process occurring over a long period of time. It is consistent with the mythical exclamation, "Mbah Merapi itu dahsyat tetapi indah!" (Grandfather Merapi is terribly powerful but also beautiful!). God's judgment is not the only explanation available. An earthquake may be imagined as God's blessing as well.

Second, the theory of plate tectonics offers religious people an alternative perspective on how God is creating the world. The theory suggests that without earthquakes there would be no life on earth. Therefore the overall "purpose" of earthquakes can be interpreted as part of God's gracious provision for life on earth. If, in the process, I, my house, my city, or my family have to die, it need not be understood as an act of random carnage but rather as part of a larger gracious purpose. God is creating the world through earthquakes, tsunamis, and hurricanes. Devastating natural phenomena are not normally directed at particularly wicked people. Rather than simply accepting these events as fated or "deserved," we may focus on how to avoid them when possible and survive them if we must.

Third, scientific knowledge helps explain how human activities influence or cause natural disasters. The most outstanding example of this is the theory of climate change. There is overwhelming evidence that humanly caused greenhouse gases are thinning the ozone layer, leading to gradual worldwide warming and extreme weather activity. We do not yet know of any direct connection between humanly influenced ecological conditions and earthquakes. However, in time we may find that there is a connection. We do know that drilling in search of thermal energy caused a devastating mud eruption near Sidoarjo, which continues to rob thousands of people of their homes and land.

Fourth, scientific wisdom tells us how to avoid natural disasters or survive their worst effects. As a result of the tsunami in Aceh, a scientific monitoring and warning system was set up in particularly hazardous areas of Indonesia. Students and professionals competed to create new architectural models that showed local people how to build earthquake-resistant homes using local materials. City planning included detailed plans for evacuation in case of an earthquake or tsunami. Science stimulated new institutions to more effectively serve people in the midst of tragedy.

How Do Indonesians Comprehend Natural Disasters?

In our empirical research on Indonesian social imaginaries we asked the following question.

Questionnaire Question IV.E on natural disasters

> *Which of the following best expresses your understanding of natural disasters?*
>
> 1. Natural disasters are a warning, a test, and a judgment from God.
>
> 2. Natural disasters are a sign that society is not in balance or in harmony with nature. Social evils may have offended the ancestors and the spirits.

3. Natural disasters are the result of impersonal natural laws and
   don't have any particular meaning. Sometimes disasters are caused
   by human beings.

The first answer is a religious response, which uses ethical language to
make sense of a natural disaster. God allows disasters for a purpose. This
theocentric answer includes a moral imperative to heed the warning, pass
the test, and accept the judgment. Syafi'i Ma'arif affirms that everything
happens for a purpose and God is sovereign in all that happens. In discussing
the death of his children, he views his family's disaster as a severe test of his
faith and character. But he passed the test without compromising his faith
in God's goodness.

The second response reflects a traditional, cosmos-centered imagination
in which disharmony with nature creates the chaos of a disaster. This is not
the result of impersonal causation but rather is connected with the anger of
unseen powers over human greed. Nature is a subject, not an object.[12]
Syamsiyatun chose this cosmos-centered response. She believes we need to
maintain a balance between human needs and the imperative to honor the
earth and not offend the unseen powers. Iqbal also chose this response,
consistent with his conviction that the powers of the unseen world are
active in bringing blessing or disaster.

The third answer attributes natural disasters to impersonal processes of
nature. This modern, anthropocentric response recognizes human agency
in creating the conditions that bring on natural disasters, but it does not
attribute any meaning to disasters beyond natural causation. Both Machasin
and Wening are good examples of this perspective. Machasin's primary
imagination is that disasters are impersonal events without meaning. His
choice includes pragmatic reasons. Reason and science are more effective

Table 10.2 *Responses to Question IV.E on Meaning in Natural Disasters*

Groups	Traditional Disharmony	Modern Cause and Effect	Religious God's Test
Muslim	15%	39%	46%
Protestant	8%	52%	40%
Catholic	8%	28%	64%
Hindu and Buddhist	24%	39%	37%
All Indonesians	13%	42%	45%

means of facing disasters than attributing them to unseen beings. Science helps us understand and reduce the devastation of disaster. Even if the religious or mystical answers are true, according to Machasin they are much less productive.

Wening adds the element of deconstructing stories intended to support dominant power structures. According to Wening, theological and mythical symbolic constructions of the meaning of disasters are often created by those who want to bolster their position within a power structure. Mythical stories have a social meaning. It is better to understand disasters through science and show a healthy skepticism toward those who create narratives that support their own self-interest.

Zainal is a bridge figure between the three perspectives. He believes in natural causation of disasters but also acknowledges the need for human beings to find and construct meaning in disasters. He is impressed with the fantastic growth of sophisticated tools for the scientific understanding of nature. He says his son can access amazing knowledge on the internet that no one knew just a few years ago. However, ethical, theological, and mythical narratives construct meanings and are methods of "reenchantment." They are legitimate, creative human activities that can construct meaning.

According to our research, not many Indonesians prefer the traditional, cosmos-centered language about natural disasters. Only 13 percent of all Indonesians chose this language (Muslims, 15 percent).[13] Forty-five percent of all Indonesians chose religious language about a test imposed by God.[14] Forty-two percent preferred the impersonal scientific language of natural causation.[15] The majority of Catholics (64 percent) and Muslims (46 percent) preferred the religious language of God's agency over the modern language of natural causation. However, Protestants (52 percent) strongly preferred the language of science over theocentric explanations. This recalls Elisa's vehemence in declaring "God did not do this!" Hindus were divided fairly evenly between religious (37 percent) and scientific (39 percent) explanations.

These statistics could be interpreted to mean that disenchantment is very strong when it comes to explaining natural disasters. Not many Indonesians prefer the kind of language used by Abdurrahman Wahid when he and his friends discussed the meaning of an eruption of Mount Merapi. Traditional ways of knowing are pushed aside by religious and modern interpretations. On the other hand, the lens of mimetic, mythic, ethical, and theoretical ways of knowing suggest that the meaning of these statistics is more complex.

First, the three symbol systems of tradition, science, and religion are not mutually exclusive. Most of the respondents who chose the religious or modern interpretation believe there are unseen powers around us that affect both the natural world and human affairs. They do not find the traditional answer as powerful as religious and scientific meaning systems. This may be attributed to both modern education and increasing orthodox piety.

Of the 42 percent of respondents who chose natural causation, 59 percent chose religious or traditional answers to the question about their experience of the unseen world (II.D), 61 percent believe in the reality of spirit possession (II.F), and 85 percent believe that God or spirits are involved in sickness or accidents (II.G). Most of those who chose natural (and human) causation of disasters did not assume that the physical world is closed to spiritual influences.

Second, belief in a sacred cosmos where nature and human social life interpenetrate is encompassed by both the traditional and religious language. A majority of Indonesians (58 percent), believe that there is meaning in natural disasters and that disasters are influenced by unseen supernatural powers. That figure includes 72 percent of Catholics, 61 percent of Muslims, and 61 percent of Hindus. Only the Protestants are in a minority, as just 48 percent chose cosmos-centered or theocentric language. Most Indonesians have shifted from language about spirits and ancestors to language about God. They still believe there is meaning in natural events. Muslims did not have a higher percentage for the use of theological language than non-Muslims, raising questions about how far this trend is influenced by Islamic modernism.

Third, there are mimetic ways to experience the world embedded in all three symbol systems. In the traditional answer, balance and harmony are maintained through daily practices and rituals. The theocentric language of warning, testing, and judgment is also infused with many mimetic elements. The high percentage of Hindus who chose traditional or religious language (61 percent) is not surprising. Their countless daily offerings of food, flowers, and incense give meaning to all aspects of daily life through mimetic rituals.

The modern scientific response also includes mimetic elements. "Impersonal natural laws" seem to indicate "without agency or meaning," but they are part of a rational order that we should guard. Human activities can upset this order and thus cause chaos. We should imitate the ecological balance of nature in order to prevent disasters.

Fourth, the three responses all have a narrative, mythic structure. The traditional response tells a story of unseen powers that must be honored by preventing injustice and upholding the *adat* laws of the ancestors. Similarly, the religious response tells a story of God's agency and sovereignty. God is at work in all we experience. The modern explanation tells a story about a natural order that can only be maintained through respect for the laws of nature. These three narratives may be in tension or understood as complementary. For example, earthquakes can be imagined as the work of unseen beings, a warning, a test and judgment of God, or a complex result of essentially mechanistic processes. For some Indonesians, it is all three. The three stories interpenetrate and complement each other.

Fifth, while the theocentric story appears to be the most salient for most Indonesians, all three narratives are also infused with ethical reflection. The traditional response suggests that human social evils upset a delicate balance. Similarly, the theocentric language of warning, test, and judgment, is an ethical narrative. God is warning us, testing us, and judging us for not living according to His Way. The scientific language is also ethical. It implies that we should use reason to stop doing things that upset ecological balance.

Sixth, all three answers are theory laden. One suggests a theory that disasters are caused by social evil and the anger of unseen powers. The second is based on a theory that God knows the meaning of disasters and uses them for the good of the human community. The third is based on the latest scientific theories about the causes of disasters, whether they are global warming, plate tectonics, or El Niño climate patterns. None of the theories embedded in the three responses can be proved. They all depend on certain assumptions and beliefs. That does not mean that they are equally true or persuasive. A test of their "truth" lies in what kind of practices they inspire that impact the life of the earth.

Conclusion

This trembling land of seventeen thousand islands, volcanoes, and ancient civilizations is like a great dancing star, full of movement, beauty, and mystery. Yet it is also well acquainted with tragedy. Indonesians have resources for facing natural disasters in four different kinds of knowledge: mimetic, mythic, ethical, and theoretic. These are not dichotomous categories such as subjective-objective, rational-irrational, factual-moral, or symbolic-real. Mimetic rituals, narrative meaning, ethical reflection, and scientific theory are all symbol systems based on assumptions that cannot be proved. This doesn't mean that all are equally convincing or useful. Indonesians experience a dialogue between different ways of knowing that yields new insights based on multiple ways of experiencing the world. Traditional rituals engage a world enchanted by spiritual powers. They can teach us reverence for greater powers that share the earth. Narratives and myths tells us where we came from and where we should be going. Ethical reflection stimulates introspection and moral responsibility. Modern science helps explain natural causation and an ecological order of which we are a part rather than the center. Natural disasters are not just puzzles to solve but rather challenges for human communities that face tragedy, without self-deceiving explanations, in ways that lead to life and healing.

The following chapter explores the complexity of Indonesian social imaginaries about women. Indonesian gender relations are shaped by mimetic rituals, stories, moral regulations, and legal theory. The chapter examines the ways in which tensions among tradition, religion, and modernity are institutionalized in Indonesian law.

11

Imaginations of Women in Law and Practice

> Even if I am not fortunate enough to make it to the end of the road, even if
> I'm forced to return from halfway there, I will die feeling happy because the
> road is now open and I have helped create the road that leads to the place
> where the daughters of our soil are free and independent.
>
> —Raden Adjeng Kartini

Equality, Patriarchy, and Heterarchy in Indonesia

HOW DO INDONESIANS IMAGINE ideal relations between women and
men?[1] The answer is complicated. After independence in 1945, Indonesia's
Constitution guaranteed equality before the law to all citizens, male and
female. Indonesia has a vigorous movement for gender justice, with women's
study centers spread all over the country, especially in Muslim institutions.
There are hundreds of women's advocacy groups and NGOs, from national
organizations to local groups in every province and city. As a result of their
lobbying, the national legislature passed an affirmative action law requiring
all political parties to nominate women as at least one-third of their candidates for political office.

In 1984 Indonesia legally ratified the international Convention to
Eliminate All Kinds of Discrimination against Women (abbreviated as
CEDAW, Law No. 7, 1984). Strong women leaders are prominent in modern
life, and Megawati was elected the first woman president in 2001. In the
same year, the government Ministry for the Empowerment of Women
announced a national, "Zero Tolerance Policy" to completely eliminate
violence against women. In turn the Department of Religion appointed a
team of Islamic law experts to review Islamic law and remove aspects that

could contribute to violence against women. In 2004 Indonesia passed a strong law to Eliminate Domestic Violence (Penghapusan Kekerasan Dalam Rumah Tangga, or PKDRT, Law 23, 2004). The civil code of Indonesian law clearly favors gender equality.

In light of all this, one might conclude that Indonesia is one of the most egalitarian countries in the world regarding gender. However, Indonesia also has many patriarchal structures and practices that discriminate against women. I can still recall my shock when I first attended a neighborhood meeting in Java and realized that all the "heads of households" present were men. We sat in a circle on the floor, making decisions for the village while women served snacks, crawling around the room to make sure their heads were lower than ours.

This chapter asks how we can make sense of the egalitarian and patriarchal aspects of gender in Indonesia. What are the roles of tradition, religion, and modern institutions in shaping Indonesian social imaginaries of women and their relation to men? The chapter suggests that mimetic practices, stories, law, and theory continually re-create complex gender relations that are best characterized by the term *heterarchy*. In contrast to the terms *patriarchy* and *matriarchy*, *heterarchy* suggests a society in which there are different gender hierarchies in some spheres and/or no fixed hierarchy between men and women in others. There is no single Indonesian social imaginary about women and men. Rather there are contrasting, competing, and sometimes complementary social imaginaries.

Mimetic Practices That Shape Gender Relations

Imaginations are shaped by habitual practices. No matter what a person may think on a normative or theoretical level, gender relations within their own families and villages create most people's imagination of proper relations between men and women. Gender practices in Indonesia are constantly evolving through a dialectic among traditional modes of acceptable behavior, religious structures, and modern institutions.

Many ethnic groups have elaborate rules (*adat*) that shape relations between the sexes. For example, Farsijana Adeney-Risakotta relates that in northern Halmahera one *adat* rule forbade a man to touch an unmarried woman without her permission. According to the rule, a man had to pay a fine if he touched such a woman (F. Adeney-Risakotta 2005). However, changes in technology and economic structures made the rule difficult to enforce. When the people lost their land to a large international agribusiness that grew bananas for export, men and women went to work on the plantation and were picked up each day by a large truck. On the rough roads, standing in the back of the truck, it was impossible for men and women not to be jostled against each other. The rule had to be modified. In this case, the women proved far better at adapting to disciplined wage labor on the plantation. Many of the men lost their jobs and became depressed. This changed the dynamics between women and men because the women were the sole source of support for their families. Prior to the advent of agribusiness, men traditionally took care of the coconut palms and long-term crops while the women tended the vegetable gardens. Loss of their land and changes in the economy not only changed sexual power relations but also contributed to the outbreak of violence within the community (F. Adeney-Risakotta 2005).

The relative equality of women in some Indonesian communities is not a new phenomenon or the result of modern feminist movements. In 1820 Crawfurd, a European traveler to Java, observed the following.

> [Javanese] women are not treated with contempt or disdain. They eat with the men, and associate with them in all respects on terms of equality, as surprised us in such a condition of society. ... Women appear in public without any scandal .... They take an active concern in all the business of life; they are consulted by men on all public affairs, and are frequently raised to the throne, and that too when the monarchy is elective. ... At public festivals, women appear among the men; and those invested with authority sit in their councils when affairs of state are discussed, possessing, it is often alleged, even more than their due share in the deliberations. ... The Javanese women are industrious and laborious beyond all those of the archipelago, but their labor, instead of being imposed upon them by the men, becomes through its utility to the latter, a source of distinction. (quoted in Winzeler 1982:178)

This rather idealized account may have been prompted by the comparatively low status of women in Europe at the time. Raden Adjeng Kartini's letters in the late nineteenth century record the oppression of an intelligent Javanese court woman who died in childbirth in 1904 at the age of twenty-five. However, Javanese women who were not confined to the court or forced into polygamous marriages had much more freedom.

Anthony Reid suggests that a significant reason why Indonesians did not adapt well to the economic opportunities of early modernity, which allowed them to be dominated by Chinese, Indians, Arabs, and Europeans, is that they were introduced at the height of European patriarchal society (2014a, b). The early structure of modernity and global economics was overwhelmingly dominated by men. Women were expected to stay at home and learn to serve their husbands and families. They were excluded from the new marketplace. However, economic practices in Indonesia, and Southeast Asia generally, had long been dominated by women. Men had little experience of or inclination to deal with finance and trade. They were ready to accept the patriarchal structures and ideology imported from Europe (and also China, India, and the Middle East), but they did not have the skills to enter the global marketplace. The women were the ones used to taking care of business.

According to Reid, there is an irony in the perception that feminism and women's empowerment are an import from the West. From a longer historical perspective, patriarchy was the western export to Southeast Asia, which traditionally enjoyed far more egalitarian gender relations than the West. In terms of the practices of daily life, even today Indonesian women are often the ones who ensure that their families have enough to survive. Javanese *adat* follows bilineal inheritance laws, under which wealth is inherited equally by men and women. But women often control the purse strings. Many Javanese men are expected to turn over all their earnings to their wives, who are responsible for managing household finances. An amusing example of this dynamic occurred when I gave a raise to our Javanese repairman and gardener. Pak Sungkana asked me not to give him a raise in his official salary but only an equivalent "bonus" every month. When I asked why, he explained that his wife took all his earnings and gave him only a tiny allowance for personal needs. If his salary remained the same, he would not have to tell his wife about the bonus and would have more cash. Of course he also asked me not to tell her about the bonus!

Javanese culture has been called matrifocal because the mother is the center of responsible authority in the family (Geertz [1961] 1989; see also Magnis-Suseno 1984). In the Javanese Muslim village (in the city of Yogyakarta) where I live, social structures are clearly patriarchal, with men defined as heads of the family and holding all important village leadership positions. However, many men are unemployed while their wives work.

The head of the village confirmed that the wives are the principle sources of income for most of the traditional Javanese households in the village, despite the fact that Islamic marriage law defines the husband as responsible for supporting his family. Since Javanese tradition constructs women as more practical and "earthy" than men, in a postagrarian community the mothers go out and create work to feed and educate their families.[2] This gives men more time for religious activities, which bring God's blessing. Most mosque and other ritual activities are only attended by men. The exception to this rule is widows, who may attend village events as the heads of their households. Some very old women pray frequently in the mosque as they prepare for the next life.

Even without attending, women are involved behind the scenes in village rituals, cooking and blessing the ritual foods. Bianca J. Smith shows that women play a vital role in Kejawen (Muslim village rituals).[3]. They not only prepare the necessary foods and offerings, but they also play a key role in performing behind-the-scenes prayers and rituals, which ensure that there is a balance between male and female principles in the ritual (Smith 2008).

Nevertheless, most "public" positions of recognition and power are in the hands of men, while women remain leaders in the domestic sphere. As most Indonesians transition from family-centered, agrarian village economies to complex urban economies where most of the functions traditionally carried out by the family are taken over by male-dominated institutions, women are further marginalized from communal authority (Adeney 1995). Nevertheless, gender practices in Indonesia do not easily fit into binary categories of "oppressed" and "oppressor." In some spheres assumptions may be patriarchal, but in practice Indonesians are used to depending on strong and independent women.

One of my graduate students who did research on attitudes toward women's leadership in Java found that in poor villages the ideology was very patriarchal. There was wide consensus among both men and women that men should be the leaders. However, in practice village men and women worked together, both in the fields and in the home. Men participated in housework, child care, and cooking. In contrast, in the cities, among better educated, middle-class Javanese, the ideology was far more egalitarian, with both women and men agreeing that women should have equal opportunities for education, professional work, and leadership.

However, the practices in domestic life were more patriarchal than in the villages. Women were expected to do all the housework, child care, and cooking, regardless of whether or not they had salaried positions outside the home.

Traditional practices vary widely from ethnic group to ethnic group. For example, inheritance practices in some groups are patrilineal (inheritance is from father to son, e.g., Batak, Balinese), in some others matrilineal (property passed down from mother to daughter, e.g., Minangkabau, Kerinci), and in still others bilateral (both sons and daughters inherit equally, e.g., Javanese, Dayak). Even within a single ethnic region, there may be different *adat* systems. For example, Riau includes both patrilineal and matrilineal traditions of inheritance. This adds a further element of complexity to courtship since young people from different villages need to know if their prospective spouses are from villages that practice matrilineal or patrilineal inheritance! Which practice applies may be determined by where they live. For example, a lad from a poor family in a patrilineal village may find it advantageous to marry a lass and live with her more prosperous family in a matrilineal village (and vice versa).

Many ethnic groups are proud of traditions that empower women, including women in positions of top cultural, religious, and political leadership. For example, four queens (sultanas) in a row ruled in Aceh from about 1640 to 1700. Among the three hundred or so *adat* traditions there are matrilineal and matrifocal societies where women exercise power and responsibility. However most ethnic groups are patrilineal or bilineal, and all are patriarchal. For example, Minangkabau culture is famously matrilineal. Women own most property and pass it down to their daughters. A Minang professor shared that a Minang man does not dare mistreat his wife because if he does he can be kicked out of his wife's house. However, men are still the leaders in political and religious affairs.

Patriarchal religious practices undoubtedly have an impact on mimetic social imaginaries. Religious leaders (ulamas) are all men, and women are not required to pray at the mosque. When they do, they are placed at the back or in a separate space. All major world religions perpetuate ritual practices that discriminate against women (see Gross 2014). However, in spite of patriarchal religions, women in Indonesia are used to being powerful members of society. Practices sometime subvert patriarchal bias. In patrilineal contexts or communities ruled by Islamic inheritance law, under which sisters are entitled to only 50 percent of the inheritance assigned to their brothers, some families subvert the gender bias by giving gifts to their daughters before death so that the inheritance will be equal.

The Minangkabau have produced some famously powerful women and are proud of a reputation as being fiercely committed to Islam. One such woman is Dewi Fortuna Anwar, who said about the relationship between Islamic law and matrilineal Minangkabau *adat*, "Islam was put at the top, the highest body of law, to which the *adat* would be subordinated. The saying is: 'The *adat* would lean on the sharia and the *sharia* on the *Kitab* [Scriptures]'. ... Practices explicitly violating Islam were to be forbidden—drinking, gambling, cockfighting, marrying more than four wives. But other aspects are considered O.K., because there is nothing in the Koran or in the sayings of the Prophet against the matrilineal system" (quoted in Naipaul 1998).

Habitual practices are part of a person's habitus. They are not just the application of ideology to life but are continually reproduced through imitation. Ideologies of gender complementarity, equality, and women's subordination are all shaped by habitual practices, which in turn form long-lasting social imaginaries. The rich variety of Indonesians' practices contributes to the complexity of their imaginations of women.

Stories that Shape the Imagination

Social imaginaries are nourished by stories. The stories that shape Indonesian social imaginaries are drawn from ethnic traditions, religious texts, and modern media. The complexity of women's position in Indonesia is well illustrated by a myth from the island of Pura in Alor, NTT (Nusa Tenggara Timur), Indonesia.[4] It is the story of Bui Hangi, a young woman who became the wife of a god. The villagers believe the story is true because it reflects their own social reality.

Bui's father, Olangki, went to borrow some rice from the village of Reta because his people were hungry during the long dry season. On his way home, while near the summit of Mount Maru, he saw a huge wild boar. He tried to hunt it, and chased it for a long time, but without success. Finally, exhausted and almost perishing from thirst, he thrust an arrow into the ground and vowed that if the god of the mountain would give him water to drink and to irrigate the crops of the village, he would give his daughter to be the mountain god's wife. Immediately water bubbled up from the ground pierced by his arrow and rain began pouring down. Regretting his rash promise, he returned home. The rain poured down so hard that landslides threatened to bury the village. Olangki figured that he had better fulfill his promise to the god or his village might drown. So he commanded his wife to take their daughter to the top of the mountain. There the mother watched her daughter disappear into the mist.

After crying and singing her grief, the mother saw a bamboo pole suddenly float to the surface of a nearby lake. She decided to use it as a walking stick to help her descend the slippery path. That night she tossed the bamboo under the house and went to bed. Olangki dreamed that his wife brought home a bamboo stick and it turned into a sacred sword. Sure enough, in the morning he found a sacred sword where his wife had left the bamboo. Anytime he thrust the sword into the ground, water would gush forth, and if he did it again the water would stop. This became a key to the prosperity of the village. Olangki knew from his dream that it was a bridal gift (*mas kawin*) from the god.

A year later the villagers held a festival to celebrate their good harvest. Olangki sent an invitation up the mountain to his daughter Bui. She came, bringing her newborn baby, but kept it wrapped up and forbade anyone to look at it. While Bui was dancing with the other women, the "baby" made some strange noises and Bui's mother opened the wrappings. In fact the baby was a large red fish with big luscious eyes. The mother was hungry and popped one of the fish's eyes into her mouth and ate it. Bui felt her baby's pain and rushed back. She left the village immediately and told her family she would never be able to return. However, the village continued to prosper with plenty of food and water.

The social imaginaries associated with women in this myth are complex. The story portrays a painful reality in the people's past. According to Rodemeier, old women in the village still recall times during periods of famine when families traded their daughters for food. The father in story is portrayed as having complete control over both his daughter and his wife. The mother may weep, but she has no power to oppose the decision of her husband. Bui has no choice but to obey her father. Although Olangki may feel bad about trading his daughter for prosperity, there is no hint of moral reproach. In fact it seems to turn out well for all involved, apart from the baby fish who lost an eye! Nonetheless, women appear to be powerless before the wishes of men, be they human or god. In one sense the bride is like a slave, sold to the god in exchange for his blessings. She is a sacrificial victim who is later divinized (see Girard 1972).

On the other hand, Bui is very valuable. The god delivers a priceless bridal gift in exchange for her. She is the key to the villagers' prosperity. Without her they might all die. She is desired by a god and brings rain and fertility. Even Bui's mother plays a powerful role in singing her sorrow and discovering the bridal gift (*mas kawin*): a bamboo stick that becomes a magic sword. Perhaps if her mother had not foolishly eaten her grand-daughter's eyeball, Bui could have been an ongoing mediator between the villagers and the god. But instead the direct connection is broken and Bui achieves semidivine status. The mother is imagined as a weak woman, lacking in proper control over her appetite.

The villagers who recounted the story were sure that the huge wild boar was the mountain god, associated with rain, maleness, and potency. Mean-while they associated the large fish with the feminine power of the ocean, another source of food and fertility. Both are needed to bring prosperity. There is little in the story to encourage an imagination of gender equality. But the story does embody elements of gender complementarity that are common to many *adat* cultures in Indonesia. Women are not autonomous individuals but rather a valuable part of the family unit. They may be pow-erful, but their power is controlled by men. They need the men to manage their power, while the men need them to make up for their own deficiencies.

In the Special Province of Yogyakarta (DIY), Javanese myths associate Mount Merapi with a male god, Grandfather Merapi (Mbah Merapi), while the ocean is associated with the female goddess Queen of the South Sea (Kanjeng Ratu Kidul). Javanese believe that the sultan plays a critical role in maintaining a balance between Grandfather Merapi and the Queen of the South Sea. Only if there is a balance between male and female power will there be peace and prosperity. The sun, the sky, and the rain represent male power, while the earth and the plants are female, represented by Dewi Sri, the rice goddess. The fertile earth is impregnated by the male sky to bring forth new life. Various versions of this myth occur throughout Java and more widely throughout Southeast Asia (see Headley 2004).[5]

These stories give rise to many rules that affect gender roles, especially with regard to the rituals associated with planting and harvesting. For example, in some places, men go first, thrusting sticks into the earth to make holes. The women follow behind, dropping seeds into the holes (Tsing 1993). Only men are allowed to plow the land, preparing it for the planting, in mimetic imitation of their role in procreation. However, men and women participate equally in planting and harvesting. Usually the women work together in one group while the men work together in another.

The portrayal of women in stories in Indonesia is the subject of an extensive literature (see, e.g., Hellwig 1994). Since 1998 a whole new generation of modern women authors have become prominent.[6] They are sometimes called *sastrawangi* (fragrant literati) because of their frank portrayal of women's sexuality in the context of modern urban life.

Stories of women are drawn from many sources, including religion. One of the most popular names for women in Indonesia is Aisyah, after the wife of the Prophet. Aisyah wrote many stories about the Prophet (*hadiths*) and was one of Islam's greatest early intellectuals. She is credited with having produced about 25 percent of early Muslim laws (Ahmed 1986). In some *hadiths* she defends the rights of women against patriarchal norms. According to some sources, she also went to war against Ali in the power struggle that followed the death of the Prophet.

Stories of women in Indonesia do not always portray them in a positive light. One of the most popular stock characters in Indonesian horror movies is the beautiful ghost. Ghosts are almost always beautiful women, who are powerful and dangerous. They lure men to their deaths. This recalls the "myth of Lubang Buaya" in the New Order propaganda film *Pengkhianatan G30S/PKI*, which used to be shown every year to all schoolchildren. According to this story, young communist women of Gerwani danced naked and sexually mutilated the corpses of the generals they had helped kidnap and murder in 1965.[7] This salacious story not only directly stimulated sexual crimes against women in 1965–66, but it also effectively stamped out a vigorous movement for women's empowerment and equality.[8]

The complexity of Indonesian social imaginaries about women is illustrated by the phenomenal popularity of President Jokowi's minister of oceans and marine resources, Susi Pujiastuti. According to stories widely reported in the media, she is hardworking, honest, effective, courageous, frank, and tough. A fellow minister in Jokowi's Cabinet commented that if we had just a few more people like Susi we could solve all of Indonesia's problems! Susi breaks all the normal stereotypes of a good Javanese Muslim woman. The press revels in showing shocking pictures of her smoking, riding a man's motorcycle, revealing a tattoo, blowing up illegal fishing boats, telling jokes about taboo topics such as corruption, and so on. Susi dropped out of high school because of her political activism against Soeharto and went on to become a highly successful businesswoman in the fishing industry, as well as founding her own airline company. She is twice divorced and a single mother. Stories of Susi deconstruct traditional images of a "good woman" and expands the Indonesian social imaginary of women. She is frequently referred to as a national hero and is the most popular minister in the Cabinet of President Jokowi.

Powerful stories shape imaginations of women in unpredictable ways. Many gender ideologies are assumed in traditional, religious, and modern stories that do not follow rigid types. Many powerful stories are drawn from modern movies. Movies from Hollywood, Bollywood, and Hong Kong are all popular. These stories do not advocate a consistent image of women and men but contribute to the complexity of gendered imaginations in Indonesia.

Morality and Legal Pluralism Affecting Women in Indonesia

As in all countries, relations between women and men are regulated by law. Indonesia has multiple, complex, overlapping legal systems that interpenetrate, complement, influence, and compete with each other. Indonesian state law seeks to incorporate religious and traditional law. Islamic law is modified by incorporation of both *adat* and modern legal principles. *Adat* adjusts itself to modern legal conditions and Islamic or other religious law (Lukito 1997; see also Bowen 2003; Minhaji 2008).[9]

Of course there are conflicts and contradictions among the three systems. There are also conflicts and contradictions *within* each of them: among different *adat* systems, different Islamic interpretations, and different modern legal approaches. In principle the three traditions of legal discourse are seen as three branches that coexist within one legal system.[10] *Adat* and religious law have a sacred character based on cosmic, supernatural, and divine references. In contrast, state law is viewed as a purely human creation, including many elements taken from colonial Dutch jurisprudence. In the eyes of some Indonesians, *adat* and religious (Islamic) law have much greater authority than state law. In order to increase its authority, the state often appeals to religious and *adat* law to legitimize national law (Bowen 2003; see also Minhaji 2008).

Islamic *fiqh* has a special legal status in Indonesia because it governs family relations for all Muslims. Islamic law may also be inserted into the civil code (e.g., regarding Sharia banking), but for family law all Muslims have a right to be judged by Islamic law. In marriage and divorce Muslims must use Islamic institutions, whereas in other areas they may appeal to either religious or civil courts. Non-Muslims are only governed by the civil courts. Both religious and civil courts are under one Supreme Court, so that matters decided in either religious or civil courts can be appealed to the Supreme Court.

Legal diversity runs against the grain of modern western concepts of law, which "regards law as an autonomous, uniform, exclusive, and systematic, hierarchical ordering of normative propositions" (Lukito 2013:3). The ideal of modern western law is consistent, universal application of the same laws to all persons without regard to their ethnic, religious, sexual, racial, cultural, social, political, or economic identity. Law is oriented toward human rights and based on the imagination of the law as a clear boundary between what an individual may or may not do legally. If you step over the line and do something that is illegal, there are clear punishments. Many activists lament the "flexibility" of Indonesian law and hope that the Constitution and international conventions, which have been ratified into Indonesian national law, will become absolute standards such that all local laws must be made to conform to them. Ironically, conservative Muslim scholars, who advocate Islamic law as absolute, believe it should be the universal standard to which all other laws should conform. To both groups, the discursive character of Indonesian law is a problem that needs to be overcome. In practice, Indonesian law is a tradition of discourse for solving disputes and seeking harmony for the whole community. It is local and contextual rather than universal. The abstract rights of individuals are often compromised in favor of the perceived common good of a particular community.[11]

The rights of women before the law are no exception. Since there are multiple sources of law, multiple legal institutions, and multiple cultures to consult in making decisions, the actual impact of public policy on women is deeply influenced by the social imaginaries of women in a particular context. For example, in Banjarmasin we talked with a Muslim judge who appeared very committed to decreasing the high number of child marriages in South Kalimantan. Marriages of girls under the age of sixteen are illegal but can be permitted if a judge agrees. This judge normally refused to marry girls under sixteen. However, the families often appealed to him by confiding that the girl was already pregnant, often by a much older man. Rather than prosecute the man for statutory rape, the judge would permit the child marriage for the sake of the family's honor and communal harmony.

Since judges can appeal to different legal discourses, their decisions may be based on their own conscience in how they frame the evidence. Bowen suggests that in the Gayo highlands of Aceh *adat* law appears to be more egalitarian than Islamic law. However, the great majority of decisions in the cases brought to the religious courts favor women, often overturning civil court decisions that were based on *adat*. Islamic courts have generally acted to restore to women the shares of inheritance denied them in village settlement processes even though on the surface the Islamic legal principles appear to be less favorable to women than do the principles of Gayo *adat* (Bowen 2003:200).

Indonesian law is not a single unified code but rather three legal systems in dialogue with each other, as illustrated by the following story. Two Muslim sisters in the Gayo highlands of Aceh, in northern Sumatra, were given land by their mother, who received the land from her father (their grandfather).[12] The women were born on the land, built houses there, and worked the land for many years. Years later an army officer came to the village and claimed that he was the rightful owner of the land. He was the cousin of the two sisters, the son of their mother's older brother. According to him, their common grandfather had only loaned the land to their mother, and so when he died the land should have been inherited by his father as the oldest son. If so, then his father's oldest son (the army officer) had a right to inherit the land. In Gayo *adat* the oldest son inherits the land. This is reinforced by Islamic law (*fiqh*), which assigns male heirs double the inheritance of their sisters. National law, while favoring gender equality in inheritance cases, defers to the local inheritance laws of *adat* and religion.

Traditional law also recognizes gifts of land, so if the grandfather truly gave the land to his daughter, his eldest son would have no legal claim to it. Violating the authentic wishes of a patriarch (such as a grandfather) can have serious consequences for a whole community. A grandfather is a powerful ancestor who can bring sickness, disaster, or death if his wishes and promises are set aside. In this case, each party produced a land certificate and brought conflicting witnesses to testify whether the land was given to the patriarch's daughter as a gift or a loan. It was difficult to prove the competing claims.

The courts decided the case by negotiating between three different sources of legal authority: *adat*, religion, and the state. While the court was clearly sympathetic to the claims of the sisters, in the end the land reverted to the patrilineal line of inheritance. According to Bowen, Gayo *adat* strongly favors inheritance through the male line that is native to the village. "Sons and their families exert a greater control over resources than do daughters and their families and this inequality can be represented as sanctioned by *adat*" (Bowen 2003:43). The decision was not the result of the impersonal, deductive application of *adat*, *fiqh*, or national law but rather of consideration of the relative merits, power, and influence of all three forms of legal discourse in the context of a local, patriarchal social imagination.

For many ethnic groups, women are traditionally imagined as a complementary part of a family unit whose head is the father. Islamic law (*fiqh*) is the area where religious law has the most impact on women. Since the marriage law was passed in 1974,[13] the Islamic courts have been granted broad powers and greatly increased resources for implementing *fiqh* for Muslims in the area of marriage and family law. The interpretation of the marriage law for Muslims is governed by the Compilation of Islamic Law (CIL), which was issued by Soeharto in 1991 as a Presidential Instruction. It is not a law but rather "a guide to applicable law for Judges within the jurisdiction of the Institutions of Religious Justice in solving the cases submitted to them" (Elucidation 5, cited in Hooker 2003, 23). The intent of the CIL is to promote the modern agenda of legal uniformity across all the Islamic courts in Indonesia. Prior to the CIL, Muslim judges were free to draw from diverse texts and schools of Islamic law to support their own interpretations of *fiqh*. Now the CIL supplies one set of guidelines for all the judges in the religious courts.

On many points the CIL is more progressive than traditional *fiqh*. Among the improvements, CIL limits child marriages, imposes heavy conditions on permissible polygamy, and gives wives greater rights within marriage and divorce. Nevertheless, the CIL is not gender neutral and conflicts with the Constitution and ratified international conventions that guarantee equal rights for women. For example, under the CIL, women do not have the right to marry themselves but must be represented by a male legal guardian (Adeney-Risakotta 2016b).

In 2003 the Department of Religion appointed a team of Islamic law experts, led by Dr. Siti Musdah Mulia, to revise the CIL in line with Muslim jurisprudence and the constitutional mandate for gender equality. The committee produced a thorough revision based on Islamic theological reasoning called the Counter Legal Draft (CLD). The CLD caused such a storm of protest from conservative and mainline Muslim organizations that the government withdrew it in 2005 before it was deliberated in the legislature.[14]

The CIL is hard to revise is because it encapsules the social imaginaries of many Indonesian Muslims regarding the proper relationship between men and women. During his thirty-two years in power, President Soeharto depoliticized everyone but especially women. Much of the nationalist women's movement was wiped out with the purge of communists. Most women's organizations were disbanded, and the government supported only one (Dharma Wanita), whose main agenda was to teach women to be good modern housewives whose primary purpose in life is to support their husbands and care for their children. This social construction was presented as women's *kodrat* (natural law or essential nature). According to Soeharto, opposition to *kodrat* undermined development. He believed that an orderly family was also the foundation of economic prosperity.

Bookstores are flooded with guidebooks (*panduan*) for women, most of which provide Islamic religious justification for women to dedicate their lives to pleasing God, their husbands, and their children. The largest bookstore in Yogyakarta (which is Catholic owned) has a large section in the Religion area with Islamic guidebooks for women. I wondered why the guides are only addressed to women. Is there no need for such instruction for men? One book suggests an answer. Its title is *Why the Majority of People in Hell Will be Women: How to Keep Women out of Hell.* The book claims that many women will go to Hell because they are weak and cannot control their desires. They cannot fulfill the *kodrat* of dedicating their whole lives to God, their husbands, and their families.[15] Apparently to keep out of Hell women need to do a better job of obeying and pleasing their husbands.

Similar messages are projected through TV programs, advertisements, movies, the internet, computer games, and social media. "Dakwahtainment," Islam's answer to Christian televangelism, has become a big business (Sofjan 2014). Local Sharia laws (Perda), are overwhelming focused on controlling and restricting the behavior of women. Sharia legislation that restricts women has been rejected at both the regional and national levels.[16] Most Indonesians do not accept messages advocating women's extreme subordination to men. The vitality of gender-conscious Islamic women's movements from the grass roots all the way up to the highest positions of government point to a different social imaginary.

Social Imaginations and Theories of Ideal Gender Relations

Riaz Hassan has surveyed attitudes about women and society in the Muslim majority countries of Indonesia, Pakistan, Egypt, and Kazakhstan. Not unexpectedly, Indonesia scored by far the highest in terms of percentages of men (65 percent) and women (78 percent) who hold "modern" views on the role of women in society (Hassan 2002:180). Unlike in the other countries, most Indonesian men and women agree that women may work outside the home, earn more than men, get as much education as men, and become leaders. Similarly, Indonesia scored significantly higher than other Muslim countries on the Gender Empowerment Index of the UN Human Development Report. (Hassan 2002:203). The Gender Empowerment Measure (GEM) calculates the relative empowerment of women in various aspects of public life compared to that of men. Indonesia received the highest GEM score of any Muslim country.

It is apparent to even casual observation that Indonesian women are more active and visible in public life than, for example, women in Pakistan. When I visited Islamabad and Rawalpindi, my impression was of cities with no women. Only 10 percent of the people in public spaces were women.[17] All were veiled from head to foot in black chadors that covered the face. Some even covered their eyes with black gauze. Public transportation was gender segregated, and all the buyers and sellers in the marketplace were men.[18] Most women seemed to be confined to their homes. The absence of women was startling to me since I had just come from Indonesia, where women in brightly colored clothing seemed to dominate the markets and public spaces.

Therefore it came as a surprise that according to Hassan's research Indonesian men and women scored higher than those in other countries, including Pakistan, in agreeing that women should be veiled and segregated from men. The attitudes of Indonesian men and women were overwhelmingly (80 percent) in favor of women wearing Muslim dress and being separated from men. The measurement of this attitude was based on the percentage of men and women who agreed with the sentence "Women are sexually attractive, and segregation and veiling are necessary for male protection" (Hassan 2002:195). Why would Indonesians favor women's equal participation in public life while also agreeing with veiling and segregation?

A simple explanation is that Indonesian Muslims imagine "veiling" and "segregation" quite differently from Muslims in Pakistan and the Middle East. Veiling and sexual segregation evoke different feelings for Pakistanis, whose daily practices embody far more restrictive control of women in the public sphere. For Pakistanis veiling and segregation are mandatory, whereas in Indonesia they are voluntary. Many Indonesian women imagine Muslim dress as a means of empowerment rather than a restriction. It may be imagined as a restriction on men's right to look rather than a restriction on what women may wear. Muslim dress serves as protection from male harassment.

Most Indonesian men and women would agree that women are beautiful, sexually powerful, and attractive. The dangerous power of women is the subject of many myths, ghost stories, and soap operas. Some Indonesian men would agree that they need protection from the dangerous sexual power of women. The danger posed by beautiful women is part of their attraction. Women are also aware of their power. Some women feel that they are even more attractive and powerful when they wear a Muslim head covering. Relatively few see their head covering as part of their duty to their husband so that only he can see his wife's beauty.

Head coverings have a long history in many of the traditional cultures of Indonesia, including for non-Muslims. They are part of flamboyant local styles that serve a variety of practical purposes in a tropical climate. Distinctively Muslim dress for women is a more recent trend, whose meaning keeps evolving. Most women wear colorful *jilbabs* in a rapidly expanding repertoire of attractive styles. The so-called "veil" does not cover the face and is often coupled with the latest fashion styles. One of my students coined the phrase "*jilbab* Britney Spears" to describe the common practice of students wearing head coverings along with tight and sexy clothing. *Jilbabs* have changed in their political meaning. At one time they were a sign of opposition to the Soeharto government. But they also serve as markers of pride in a Muslim identity and resistance to western domination of fashion. Protecting men from temptation may be one reason why some women wear a head covering, but it is probably not the dominant reason for most women (Doorn-Harder 2006; Hooker 2003).[19]

For hundreds of years, most traditional and religious practices in Indonesia have separated the sexes. In village meetings, worship in the mosque, parties, ritual meals, chanting of the Koran, and work in the fields, women and men tend to group together with others of their own sex. Many children go to Islamic schools (*pesantren*) where boys and girls are separated. In some Indonesian churches the men sit on one side and women on the other. Separation of the sexes is customary and habitual in everyday life. Even in some university classes the women students tend to sit on one side while the men sit on the other, although the separation is not fixed or rigid. Separation does not imply that women are excluded from access to public space. They are certainly not confined to their homes. Separate spaces for men and women evoke a social imaginary different from that of gender segregation in Pakistan.

Hassan's research suggests that most Indonesian men (68 percent) and women (70 percent) believe that men should be the head of their families and that women need men's leadership (Hassan 2002:201). Approval of this expression of patriarchy among Indonesians appears to be much higher than among Pakistani men (62 percent) and women (44 percent). Statistics can lie, and survey questions may lead people astray. However, it is interesting that 70 percent of Indonesian women appear to approve of patriarchy while only 44 percent of Pakistani women do so. In contrast, much higher percentages of Indonesians have egalitarian views of women's role in society and all areas of public life.

A possible explanation for this anomaly is that patriarchy is more "benign" in Indonesia than it is in Pakistan. In Pakistan women experience more restrictions on their access to public life, education, and advancement. Literacy levels for women in Pakistan are much lower than for men (males 69.6 vs. females 42.7 percent), whereas in Indonesia the gap is much less (males 96.3 vs. females 91.5 percent).[20] Indonesian women do not feel as oppressed by male leadership of the family (*kepala keluarga*) because they are the mother of the family (*ibu rumah tangga*) who effectively rules the household. Formal male leadership of the family does not preclude women becoming leaders in other areas, including business, home, and politics.

"Patriarchy" is a one-dimensional oversimplification when it comes to a complex society like that of Indonesia. "Heterarchy" may hint at more of the complexity. Carole Crumley defines *heterarchy* as "the relation of elements to one another when they are unranked or when they possess the potential for being ranked in a number of different ways" (1995). Heterarchy does not deny the reality of patriarchy in some dimensions of life, but patriarchy is not the only form of social organization. In some dimensions of life there may be matriarchy or no particular hierarchy. It is not unusual in Indonesia to meet a woman who is a feminist and activist for gender equality but imagines her husband as the head of the family. At the same time she rules her household and manages her husband, children, servants, and finances, all the while teaching full time and earning the bulk of the household income.

How do Indonesians imagine ideal relations between women and men? In our questionnaire on Indonesian social imaginaries, we asked respondents to choose between three contrasting "theories" of the proper relationship between women and men.

Question IV.D on relations between women and men

What are good and true relations between men and women?

1. Women and men are equal and enjoy the same rights. Both men and women can become leaders.

2. Women should submit to men. Women can be a temptation to men and should be separated from men. Women should wear a head covering and modest clothing.

3. Men and women have different complementary roles, which balance each other. Women are the mothers of their households while the father is the head of the family.

The first answer uses the modern language of equal human rights for women and men. It asserts that men and women are equally fitted for leadership. The second answer says that women should be subordinate to men and that they are a temptation to men and should be separate and wear modest clothing. This is the "religious" answer insofar as it is the position taken by religious conservatives. Of course many religious people do not agree with this theory. The third answer is "traditional" in the sense that it emphasizes complementarity. Traditional cosmologies emphasize balance between male and female principles. Men and women are considered different but complementary. Each has a function, and the proper balance between female and male (yin and yang) principles is what creates a prosperous and harmonious society.

A few people chose all three answers, indicating that they saw no contradiction among them. A few more (12) chose a combination of the religious and traditional answers, indicating that they thought female subordination and complementarity were both true. Many more (66 or 3.1

Table 11.1 *Responses to Question IV.D on Ideal Relations between Women and Men*

	Traditional (3) Complementary	Modern (1) Equality	Religious (2) Subordination	Combined 1 and 3 Traditional/ Modern
Muslim Men	51%	30%	17%	2%
Muslim Women	48%	36%	12%	4%
All Muslims	49%	33%	14%	4%
Protestant Men	33%	59%	3%	5%
Protestant Women	34%	60%	3%	3%
All Protestants	34%	59%	3%	4%
Catholic Men	13%	81%	1%	5%
Catholic Women	25%	74%	1%	0%
All Catholics	20%	77%	1%	2%
Hindu Men	36%	55%	5%	4%
Hindu Women	40%	56%	2%	2%
All Hindus	38%	56%	3%	3%
Indonesian Men	40%	46%	10%	4%
Indonesian Women	41%	48%	7%	4%
All Indonesians	41%	47%	9%	3%

percent) chose a combination of modern and traditional answers, indicating that they believed in both equality and complementarity. Nevertheless, the largest group (1,004, or 47 percent) chose the modern answer of equal human rights between men and women. A few less (887 or 41 percent) chose the traditional answer of gender complementarity. Only 181 respondents, or 8.4 percent, chose the conservative religious answer of strict subordination and separation of women from men.

Ninety-one percent of Indonesians did not imagine women's subordination to men as their primary perspective on male-female relations. Less than 9 percent chose the "religious" response of clear subordination of women to men. There was not a large gender gap. Men and women from the same religious communities expressed quite similar perspectives on gender. In most communities women had slightly higher preferences than men for equality or complementarity. The one exception is Catholic men, who appear even more egalitarian than Catholic women. The gender gap was widest between Muslim men and women. Seventeen percent of Muslim men chose the language of female subordination compared to 12 percent of Muslim women. Thirty-six percent of Muslim women preferred the language of equal rights compared to 30 percent of Muslim men.

The differences between religious communities is more striking. Muslims chose female subordination at a significantly higher rate (14 percent overall, 17 percent for Muslim men) than non-Muslims did (1 vs. 3 percent). Unlike the other groups, Muslims also preferred the language of complementarity (49 percent) over equality (33 percent). Nevertheless, it should be noted that 86 percent of Indonesian Muslims did not primarily imagine women as subordinate to men but preferred the language of complementarity or equality. These statistics confirm my impression from teaching that non-Muslim students tend to hold more egalitarian theories of gender relations than Muslims do. Among my graduate students in Muslim universities, the great majority are male, but most Muslim female graduate students tend to be strongly committed to empowering women.

Conclusions

How do mimetic practices, powerful stories, legal structures, and theories of gender relations shape Indonesian social imaginaries about women and men? First, there is great diversity. Rituals, myths, laws, and theories range from patriarchy and/or misogyny to matriarchy and/or complete equality. There is no uniform view.

Second, Indonesia has a long history of gender practices in which women play leading roles in society. Movements to empower women were not imported from the West. Rather, patriarchy was imported into societies in which women traditionally wielded significant power in economic and other spheres while men more frequently held positions of symbolic leadership. Powerful women are common in many spheres of modern Indonesian life.

Third, many traditional ethnic myths assume that there must be a cosmic balance between male and female principles in both nature and society. Traditional narratives of complementarity between the sexes are common. In many such narratives, there is an assumption of male leadership but women are understood to be powerful and necessary for communal well-being.

Fourth, since Indonesian independence in 1945, the language of gender equality and human rights has been enshrined in the Constitution and laws of the country. The language of gender equality has become the preferred symbol system for most Indonesians. However, there is an uneasy tension between the language of women's rights and the common practices of differentiated gender roles and complementarity.

Fifth, all Indonesians are subject to the marriage law of 1974; however, the interpretation of the law for Muslims has been granted to Islamic courts. These courts have the jurisdiction and authority to draw from various sources of law, including *adat*, civil law, and Islamic law (*fiqh*) to decide cases for Muslims. The CIL was mandated by the president in 1991. Some aspects of it give religious legitimacy to legal discrimination against women (Adeney-Risakotta 2016b). Since law is more of a discourse than a fixed boundary, there is continuing hope for negotiation and reform.

Sixth, according to surveys, Indonesian Muslims hold more egalitarian views of women's full participation in society than do people in other Muslim majority countries. Indonesian Muslim women also participate more vigorously in the public sphere. Nevertheless, Indonesian Muslims have significantly less egalitarian views about relations between women and men than do Indonesian non-Muslims.

Seventh, the great majority of Indonesians reject gender theories that place women in a subordinate position compared to men. More than 90 percent of Indonesians prefer to think of gender relations as based on either equality (47 percent), complementarity (41 percent) or a combination of the two (3 percent).

Eighth, patriarchy is entrenched in some aspects of Indonesian public policy, especially as it is influenced by religion and ethnic traditions. However, the widely documented power of women in Indonesian society suggests that patriarchy is not the defining characteristic of all social relationships. *Heterarchy* is a more helpful term, one that points to the great diversity of gender relations in Indonesia. The complexity of gender relations there is unlikely to resolve itself into either full gender equality or male domination. Nevertheless, rapid social change will continue to put pressure on the ongoing process of negotiations for harmonious relations between men and women.

Ninth, as in most countries, there are dark currents of misogyny in Indonesia's collective historical memories. These are especially revealed in the brutal suppression of the Gerwani woman's movement in the name of anticommunism in 1965–66, the mass rapes in Jakarta in 1998, and ongoing attempts to limit the rights of women through localized Sharia regulations. Indonesians need to face these dark memories in order to neutralize their power. Increasing conservative pietism gives religious legitimation to misogynist views of women.

Finally, this chapter argues that social imaginaries deeply influence public policy concerning women. Habitual practices and rituals, myths and stories, ethical reflection, and law and gender theories all shape Indonesian social imaginaries about gender. Indonesian social imaginaries tend to stress complementarity as well as equality. Women are powerful in Indonesian society, and I expect that power will only increase as time goes by.

The final chapter of this book addresses how Indonesians deal with conflict. It assesses the evidence for rising intolerance and draws conclusions regarding the major questions of the book.

12

Conflict, Intolerance, and Hope

Ring the bells that still can ring.
Forget your perfect offering.
There is a crack, a crack in everything.
That's how the light gets in.
That's how the light gets in.

—Leonard Cohen

Global Circulations of Fear and Hatred

CONFLICT RESULTS FROM competing interests. It is an ordinary part of everyday life. The tremendous ethnic, religious, racial, and ideological diversity of Indonesia does not in itself create conflict. However, when difference and otherness are allied with competing political or economic interests, they intensify conflicts. Religion is a particularly powerful as a tool for rallying support for political and economic interests. Religions employ transcendent symbols and rituals that create social solidarity. Religions invoke ultimate concerns. When deeply religious people feel that their religious community is under attack, they experience apocalyptic emotions. They feel it as an attack on what is most precious in their existence.

Societies, like people, have repertoires for dealing with conflicts. Repertoires are patterns we follow when feeling threatened or attacked. They are the different possibilities that we can imagine or feel are possible responses to a situation of conflict. Nation-states have broad strategies for managing diversity, but individuals and communities employ tactics that sometimes resist the strategies of powerful elites. In this chapter I examine repertoires that are used in Indonesia not only to prevent conflict but also to intensify it and heal it when the time is right.

Indonesia's contemporary repertoire for dealing with conflict and diversity is shaped by its history of internal struggles and external interactions with multiple civilizations. In other words, it is reproducing relationships and conflicts that have been going on for centuries. It is also in a symbiotic relationship with what is going on around the world right now. The present in Indonesia influences and has been influenced by the Syrian refugee crisis, the election of Donald Trump, Brexit, the Islamic State of Iraq and Syria (ISIS), Palestine, the French election, resistance to Trump, and so on. In other words, the habitus in which Indonesians live is not just the sum of different fields of influence within Indonesia. It is also a product of the circulation of influences from around the world. Just days after Trump was elected president of the United States, half a million people showed up in Jakarta for a massive demonstration asserting their Muslim identity. With his anti-Muslim rhetoric, Trump symbolizes a globalized western attack on Islam. One result has been a much more aggressive assertion of Muslim identity in Indonesia. In light of global circulations of fear, hatred, bigotry, and intolerance, how likely is Indonesia to overcome its own radical divisions and exert a positive influence on the future of Muslim relations with the rest of the world?

Is Religious Intolerance Increasing in Indonesia?

Under President Joko Widodo's (Jokowi) leadership, Indonesia has consolidated democratic institutions and is seriously addressing many of its pressing problems. But Jokowi is cautious about confronting intolerance and violations of the rights of minorities. According to the watchdog Setara Institute, there was a sharp increase in intolerance and attacks on minorities in Indonesia in 2017.[1] In 2014 there were 134 reported violations of religious freedom. The number rose to 197 in 2015 and 208 in 2016. Meanwhile reported acts of religious intolerance rose from 177 in 2014 to 236 in 2015 and 270 in 2016. Of the 270 cases of religious intolerance reported in 2016, reportedly 140 were perpetrated by government actors, including police and local administrations. Some were discriminatory local laws. In 2016 there were acts of violence and discrimination against Ahmadiyah, Shia, Christians, Gafatar (a new religious movement), and various indigenous religious groups.

For example, in 2016, Gafatar was declared heretical (*tersesat*) by MUI and illegal by the government, even though it declared that it was not part of Islam.[2] In a discussion that took place at the Ministry of Religion in 2012, a high-ranking government official emphasized that discrimination against Ahmadiyah would stop if it would admit that it is not part of Islam. As a non-Islamic religion, it would be protected by the guarantee of freedom of religion in the Constitution. However, since it does claim to be part of Islam, Ahmadiyah is vulnerable to being charged with defaming religion. Evidently this logic was not applied to the Gafatar group when it denied that it is Muslim. Some members were attacked and driven from their homes while the police did nothing to protect them.

In another typical example, the local government in Bandung canceled a Christmas celebration, to be held by a church in a local park because of threats from a hardline Islamic group. Even though the parishioners had a permit, the police stood by and did nothing to protect them from physical attack by radicals when they tried to hold their service. Leaders of NU, Muhammadiyah, and MUI later condemned the religious intolerance, but by then it was too late. On February 24, 2017, the local government sealed (*disegel*) an Ahmadiyah mosque in Depok, West Java, for the sixth time.[3] Seven hundred police and military personnel guarded the mosque from a mob demanding that it be closed permanently.

Massive demonstrations in November and December 2016 against the Chinese Christian governor of Jakarta, Basuki Tjahaja Purnama (Ahok), demanding that he be imprisoned for blasphemy and defaming Islam, are a more disturbing sign of increasing intolerance. Ahok publicly questioned interpretations of a verse from the Koran that was used to imply that Muslims should not vote for non-Muslim leaders. The demonstrations brought hundreds of thousands to the capital city and included more than a million in various parts of the country. The charges and demonstrations led to Ahok losing the election by a significant margin after a campaign that prominently featured the mobilization of religious sentiment against him. Ironically, even up to the day of the election, Ahok's approval rating among Jakarta residents remained very high. Seventy-six percent of Jakartans had a positive view of what Ahok had achieved in office, but he still lost the election by a margin of 42 to 58 percent. Apparently, many of those who approved of his performance did not vote for him because of his religion or ethnicity. Even more alarming was his later conviction for blasphemy and sentence to two years in prison.

It is hard to measure something like increasing levels of religious intolerance. There are many more incidents of religious or ethnic discrimination, intimidation, and violence throughout Indonesia than the Setara Institute numbers indicate. It is a huge country, and many incidents go unreported, unpublicized, and unknown, especially to a relatively small NGO located in Jakarta. Most of the cases the institute reported were from West Java, Jakarta, and East Java, which are closest to its base. Officials avoid reporting incidents in their own self-interest. Some victims are also loath to publicize their oppression for fear of retaliation, especially if they have negotiated a tolerable solution. Minority groups don't want publicity but would rather resist in hidden ways (Scott 1985, 2012).

Some acts of religious intimidation are little more than criminal protection rackets. In one unreported incident a local pastor told me that his small church had purchased land and received permission to build a church from the local community. An outside, hardline Islamist group got word of it and threatened to burn the church down if the congregation did not pay it a very large sum of money. The group promised to guarantee the church's safety if it was paid. The church refused to pay but decided to search for a different, more remote location. If the Setara Institute's numbers are just the tip of the iceberg, then we cannot know whether or not the increasing numbers indicate a rise in incidents. It may simply reflect the increased effectiveness of human rights groups in locating and reporting intolerance. The phenomenal growth of social media means that many things that were kept secret in the past are now revealed.[4]

Public officials prioritize public safety over protection of human rights. For example, several years ago, the progressive rector (president) of Gadjah Mada University forced my Muslim colleagues to cancel a lecture by a controversial Canadian Muslim lesbian following threats by a radical group. The rector prioritized preventing violence on campus over academic freedom.[5] Confrontation with the small minority of radicals who are committed to using violence not only endangers innocent victims but also risks escalating the situation to a more dangerous level, which may ultimately benefit the radicals through increasing polarization and publicity. It is easier and less risky to just give in to their demands and avoid confrontation or escalation of the conflict. In this case, the lecture was moved off campus to the offices of a progressive Muslim publisher. The courageous publisher paid the price because it was attacked by the radicals, who vandalized its offices and destroyed its computers.

An ideal of Javanese power is for a leader to create harmony with minimum apparent effort. Confrontation, conflict, and violence are indications that the leader lacks the inner strength (*kekuatan*), authority (*wibawa*), and dignity (*martabat*) to maintain harmony and peace. Rather than risking the shame of a public spectacle of disorder, Indonesian leaders often give in to illegal demands in exchange for an apparently peaceful solution.[6]

The government is aware of the increasing strength of Islamic conservatism in Indonesia and is anxious not to appear to be un-Islamic or on the side of non-Muslim or other groups perceived as heretical by many Muslims. The Setara Institute's deputy chairman, Bonar Tigor Naipospos, said, "The President has to always be careful in policy-making so that he will not lose the popular vote. Any political actor in Indonesia always tries to look like he's supportive of Islam."[7]

If acts of intolerance, violations of religious freedom, and violence are increasing in Indonesia, then it is part of a worldwide phenomenon. In the United States after the election of Donald Trump there occurred a sharp increase in hate crimes, including acts of violence against Muslims and other minority groups. For example, in February 2017, one hundred Jewish gravestones were desecrated in Philadelphia.[8] The black lives matter movement has dramatized the ongoing problem of police violence against African Americans.[9] Europe has also seen a sharp increase in hate crimes. Sectarian violence in other parts of Asia, Europe, Latin America, Africa, and the Middle East has become a daily part of the news. Religious oppression, forced migration, terrorism, racism, increasing gaps between the rich and the poor, social media, the overwhelming power of capitalist consumerism, the destruction of the environment, and the rise of neofascism are all interrelated.

Religious persecution of minorities in Indonesia is connected to racism and violence against Muslims in America and Europe. Racial, religious, and gender discrimination is against the law and the Constitution in Indonesia, just as it is in most western countries. But outlawing intolerance and preventing it are two different things, especially when a group feels it is under attack by the "other." Just as Trump's anti-immigration stand and anti-Islamic rhetoric cannot be understood apart from global acts of radical

Islamic terrorism, so discrimination against minorities in Indonesia cannot be understood apart from worldwide anti-Islamic rhetoric and actions.

Putting Things in Perspective: Islam and Violence in Indonesia

Indonesia is one of the safest countries in the world, at least as measured by the danger of violent attack. Non-Muslims whose only association with Islam involves terrorism or the civil wars in the Middle East sometimes assume that the largest Muslim country in the world is likely to be a dangerous place. This is not the case. Most Indonesians live side by side with different ethnic and religious groups in relative harmony and peace, as they have done for centuries. As in any large, diverse democratic country, there will always be ethnic, religious, and political tensions. But they seldom result in violence.

It is possible to travel all around Indonesia without worrying about violent attack.[10] In the greater Yogyakarta area of over a million residents, most of whom are Muslims, I can walk alone in safety throughout the city anytime, day or night. This is in stark contrast to most large cities in the West. Women are also relatively safe from assault, although they may be harassed through aggressive flirting by young men if they go out alone at night.[11] Strangers are not only relatively safe, but in most places they are welcomed into homes with smiles and warm hospitality. Sometimes there is reverse racism combined with respect for age and social status. As an older, white-skinned professor, I am often accorded undo respect and unwarranted preferential treatment. The story might be less sanguine if I were a dark-skinned man from West Papua, a Chinese, or openly gay.[12] Nevertheless, the relative safety of Indonesian cities is remarkable. Indonesia has one of the lowest rates of violent crime in the world.[13] Indonesians like to think of themselves as hospitable people who like to smile.

These considerations provide perspective on reports of ongoing discrimination against minorities in Indonesia. They do not prove that religious intolerance is not increasing. Many Indonesians were shocked by the massive demonstrations against Ahok in Jakarta and saw them as a wake-up call to take a more aggressive stance against intolerance.[14] Since then there have been many large counterdemonstrations in support of diversity (kebhinekaan), though none on the scale of the massive anti-Ahok demonstrations on November 4 and December 2, 2016. Even if religious intolerance is seen as part of a global phenomenon, that does not make it any less disturbing. It should, however, warn us against stereotyping Islam as the source of the problem.[15] It is impossible to know for certain if intolerance is increasing or just taking a more public shape due to geopolitical influences from around the world. But whether it is increasing or just an ancient, persistent problem, it sets the stage for the question of how a highly religious country like Indonesia manages cultural and religious diversity.

In a country as large and complex as Indonesia, management of diversity is not primarily the task of government but rather of the whole population. Certainly government is crucial for providing structures, laws, and institutions that encourage people to live in harmony regardless of their religious, cultural, ethnic, or ideological differences. Politics is the art of compromise between competing legitimate interests. A government is expected to legislate and maintain a tolerable balance between sometimes irreconcilable differences. It not only provides structures but also leadership and example.

Nevertheless, throughout the long history of the Indonesian archipelago, governments have as often been the source of oppression and disharmony as they have been the means of resolving conflict. Even as recently as 1998, it took a massive people power movement to remove a dysfunctional government. From 1997 to 2002, political structures broke down, and government agents, including the military, participated in intensifying horizontal conflict and violence in many parts of Indonesia. Reconciliation, peace, and relative harmony returned, both through the popular election of a strong government and through the massive efforts of a myriad of civil society organizations. The people legitimized a strong government, and many NGOs worked tirelessly to create the conditions necessary for justice, peace, and reconciliation. One reason for Soeharto's downfall was that he was unable to prevent the growth and proliferation of civil organizations at all levels of society. Indonesia's vibrant, diverse, and active civil society helped stimulate radical, social, political, and economic change.

Governments both manage and intensify conflicts. The same is true of civil society. "The people" are not always a force for peace but sometimes the reverse, especially when they are manipulated by the sectarian interests of political elites (F. Adeney-Risakotta 2005). In Indonesia, both government and civil society use mimetic, mythic, ethical, and theoretical means to both intensify conflict and bring peace.

Mimetic Strategies for Intensifying Conflict and Creating Peace

In the struggle between political elites for the governorship of Jakarta, opponents of the incumbent governor Ahok found a powerful tool in the accusation that he had denigrated Islam (*penodaan agama*). Prior to the charge of "denigrating religion," Ahok had appeared unassailable in the polls. In spite of his Chinese Christian heritage, he was widely popular due to his vigorous exposure of corruption and practical effectiveness in addressing many of the problems of Jakarta. Ahok, who is typically knowledgeable and respectful toward Islam, unwisely referenced a verse in the Koran (Al Maidah 51), which states that Muslims should not choose a Jew or a Christian as their *wali*. *Wali* can mean a custodian, protector, friend, or ally. Some Muslims interpret it as including a leader. In a public speech, Ahok suggested that some of his opponents had used this verse to deceive people into thinking they should not vote for him because he is a Christian. The accusation of blasphemy was based on the assumption that Ahok was saying that a verse in the Koran was deceptive or wrong. Regardless of the merits of various interpretations of this verse by Islamic scholars, Ahok's political opponents found in it a powerful mimetic tool with which to attack his suitability to be governor of Indonesia's largest Muslim majority city.

The accusation of defaming religion tapped into a long history of scapegoating Chinese and Christians for injustice. Effective scapegoating is usually based on elements of truth. The long struggle for independence from the Dutch was widely construed as opposition to "Christianization" and exploitation by Dutch and European Christians. In 1997–98, Chinese were scapegoated as the partners of Soeharto in the economic exploitation of the nation (Suryadinata 2007). According to René Girard, a fundamental function of religion is to limit violence by mimetically sacrificing a scapegoat to atone for the sins of the people ([1972] 2005). The accusation of blasphemy stimulated huge emotions, which resulted in massive demonstrations against Ahok in many parts of Indonesia, including the "Super Peaceful Demonstration" held in Jakarta on December 2, 2017, which included hundreds of thousands of demonstrators.[16] Most Indonesians are very tolerant of religious difference. It is part of their self-identity.[17] The significant number of those who are less tolerant found a convenient scapegoat in the blasphemy charges against Ahok.

Whenever there is a major disturbance or violence in Indonesia, many people look for a *dalang* (puppet master) who is the cause of the violence.[18] A person or group is singled out as the evil cause of what happened. This is a mimetic strategy that can both create and limit violence. Scapegoating can create violence toward "the evil party" who is considered the cause of the tragedy, as it did when many Chinese businesses were burned and Chinese women raped in the riots leading up to the fall of Soeharto. But it can also limit violence by deflecting the guilt of both parties in a conflict. For example, Muslims and Christians in the Moluccas reconciled after a bloody conflict in part because they blamed the killing on a *dalang* in Jakarta. Depending on the parties' ideology, such a puppet master might be identified as the Soeharto family, the military, the CIA, the Taliban, ISIS, Jews, Javanese, Chinese, western capitalists, neoliberals, the Church, America, communists, separatists, and so on. A mysterious all-powerful scapegoat subdues violence because there is no way to attack such a distant enemy, on whom all the guilt is heaped.

Shortly after the tragedy of September 11, 2001, a progressive, feminist Muslim activist from NU who had lived in our household for several years passionately defended her conviction that the 9/11 attacks must have been planned by the CIA to discredit Islam. She could not believe that Muslims had carried out such a brutal act of mass murder. At the time, I recall thinking ruefully that perhaps she had watched too many Hollywood spy thriller movies and overrated the CIA. Since the Bali bombings, the rise of ISIS, and many other terrorist acts, not many Indonesians think Muslims are incapable of such violence.

Apart from creating conflict or deflecting guilt, Indonesians often use mimetic rituals to mitigate conflict. The massive demonstration against Ahok in Jakarta on December 2, 2016, was billed as a peaceful ritual of prayer (*sholat*) for the welfare of the nation. The government prepared more than 20,000 police officers to ensure peace and arrested some ringleaders, who were accused of plotting treason. However, when the police faced the demonstrators on both November 4 and December 2, they began the day with an unusual strategy. Carrying no weapons, dressed in white, and wearing haji turbans, 499 police officers sat on the ground before the demonstrators and recited the ninety-nine beautiful names of God.[19] Members of this "Beautiful Names of God Team" (Tim Asmaul Husna) were chosen from various provinces for their skill in reciting the Koran and *zikir* (prayers to remember God). They used mimetic rituals, which called on the mercy of God and physically enacted their unity with the Muslim community. They repositioned the government, not as opponents but as fellow Muslims who also prayed for the salvation of the nation. Similarly, President Jokowi joined the demonstrators for the Friday prayers in the rain. He asserted his solidarity with the demonstrators in praying for the nation. Wearing traditional Muslim dress, he bowed to the ground in *sholat*, showing humility, solidarity with the *umat*, and submission to the will of God. Mimetic rituals reduced polarization and affirmed the oneness of the nation. Mimetic rituals (combined with a strong show of force!) helped diffuse a volatile situation and prevent violence.

During a violent conflict in the North Moluccas in 1999–2002, both sides used mimetic rituals to gain power and ensure their purity (F. Adeney-Risakotta 2005). For example, Muslims placed white-clad, virgin girls on the front line to mimic the purity of their jihad. Christians refused to eat, wash, or have sex before battle to express their suffering and sincerity before God. When the violence came to an end, Muslims and Christians used mimetic rituals to create possibilities for peace. For example, they reenacted an ancient ritual to establish peaceful boundaries between the communities. When Christians fled the area, their Muslim neighbors refused to allow their lands to be appropriated by outsider Laskar Jihad troops on the grounds that the Christians were part of their family. They reproduced kinship rituals describing how each family came to own the land and thereby paved the way for reconciliation with their former enemies.

Mimetic rituals do not only draw from traditional imaginations of reality. In Joshua Oppenheimer's film *The Act of Killing*, about the mass killings in 1965–66, one of the death squad members relates his confusion about why the killings were wrong. He says they were influenced by American gangster films. They were just imitating the actions of the heroes of these films, who killed their enemies without remorse.

In 1965–66, Indonesians dealt with increasing conflict between ideological movements by physically and politically eliminating a major portion of Indonesian society. In a sense, this strategy was successful. Indonesians, who were construed as atheist-communists were annihilated as a recognizable group. Citizenship in the Republic was redefined to exclude them from public life. Political, economic, social, educational, religious, and cultural institutions banned them (and their offspring) from participation as full citizens. In the collective memory of Indonesians they were redefined through thirty-two years of New Order public discourse as the embodiment of evil and a dangerous threat to the meaning and identity of Indonesian society.

In the repertoire of Indonesian social responses to apocalyptic fear of the other, the strategy of annihilating the enemy is still a live option. The dramatic end to the New Order regime of Soeharto was followed by the extreme brutality of the ethnoreligious mass violence that broke out in Kalimantan, Java, Ambon, North Moluccas, and Sulawesi (especially Poso). The violent aftermath of Reformasi witnesses to the fact that this strategy is still a live option in Indonesia. Unsuccessful attempts to militarily annihilate separatists in East Timor, West Papua, and Aceh provide further examples. Even the brutal killing of petty thieves by villagers provides evidence that physical annihilation of the common social enemy is part of Indonesia's imagination (Colombijn and Lindblad 2002). It is part of the repertoire of social responses to painful diversity or threat. The inability of many Indonesians to face and condemn the massive killings of 1965–66 keeps these events alive as a dangerous memory and contributes to the willingness of some groups to use violence against those whom they define as radically evil.

On the other hand, unlike the massacres of 1965–66, none of the outbreaks of mass ethnoreligious violence in the transition period of 1998–2002 succeeded in eliminating the other. In every case, the mass violence yielded no clear winner and both sides sustained agonizing losses. In every case, to a greater or lesser extent, substantial progress has been made in achieving reconciliation through mimetic rituals, negotiation, and compromise. After a cataclysmic earthquake and tsunami, even Aceh ended a decades-old violent conflict and began the difficult process of peacefully negotiating power sharing between formerly irreconcilable groups. The fact that ethnoreligious conflicts remained relatively localized (in time and place) and Indonesia succeeded in forming a stable, democratically elected government that includes almost all sectors of society provides strong grounds for optimism that mass violence to eliminate diversity is less and less likely. Radical groups still use or threaten violence to attack groups that infringe on their conception of an ideal community. Their activities are constrained by a lack of public support or governmental tolerance. Most Indonesian communities recognize that the attempt to eliminate another substantial group through violence is just not worth the cost. However, their success in mobilizing religious and ethnic sentiments to defeat Ahok is a dangerous threat to the quality of Indonesian democracy. Future elections are likely to include the same tactics, with parties appealing to religion and ethnicity to gain popular support.[20]

Mimetic rituals by people who live in a sacred cosmos are no guarantee of peace or reconciliation between groups who experience reality through the lens of radically different social imaginaries. Sometimes mimetic rituals are weapons of attack or the means to create solidarity and intensify conflict with those perceived as enemies. Nonetheless, mimetic rituals are also an indispensable part of the Indonesian repertoire for limiting violence. Sometimes they are a means of creating lasting peace. After Ahok was defeated in the Jakarta election, thousands of his admirers sent elaborate flower displays to the City Hall. The area around the government buildings was a huge sea of flowers. The startling outflow of support mimetically elevated him from loser to victim. In mimetic theory, scapegoat victims are often elevated to the status of heroes or deities.

Competing Narratives for Dealing with Diversity

During the Indonesian war for independence from 1945 to 1949, and in the following years, several different narratives competed to shape the imagination of the emerging nation-state. According to one narrative, Indonesia was the largest Muslim nation in the world and independence from the Dutch should mean the establishment of an Islamic nation-state. According to this narrative, for centuries the Muslim community (*umat*) has struggled against Christian colonialists, often in the name of Islam. A prominent institutionalization of this narrative was Darul Islam Indonesia (DII), which fought the Sukarno-led nationalist forces and sought to establish an Indonesian Islamic State (Negara Islam Indonesia). One of the background narratives of this movement was the struggle over President Sukarno's ideology of Pancasila. An early draft of Pancasila was a compromise document between those who wanted an explicitly Islamic state and those who favored a more inclusive, religiously plural nation-state. The compromise formulation, called the Jakarta Charter, based the nation on the great unity of God but included the requirement that Muslims must obey Sharia.

However non-Muslims were supported by Muslim nationalists and communists in rejecting the Jakarta Charter. In the final version the first principle of
Pancasila eliminated special mention of Islam and Sharia.

Another competing narrative imagined the Indonesian revolution as
the rise of the proletariat against capitalist imperialists and colonialists. In
1948 the communists (Partai Komunis Indonesia, PKI) rallied the poor at
Madium against "Sukarno/Hatta, the slaves of the Japanese and America"
(Friend 2003:32).

Another competing narrative imagined Sukarno's nationalist revolution
as a new instance of Javanese imperialism in which Muslims from Java
would seize control over the Christian majority areas of eastern Indonesia.
They supported the struggle for independence from the Dutch but wanted
to establish their own nation-state, the Republik Maluku Selatan (Republic
of the Southern Moluccas, RMS).[21] After bloody fighting, the DII, PKI, and
RMS were all defeated by Sukarno. Their leaders were killed or fled the
country. But the narratives that inspired these alternative visions of Indonesia are still alive.

Sukarno's narrative of a unified Indonesia was victorious at great cost.
Forty-five to 100,000 Indonesians lost their lives in fighting during the
revolution, along with 25 to 100,000 civilians, compared to around 7,000
Dutch and allied troops (Kahin 1952; Reid 1974). Many Indonesians lost
their lives fighting each other over competing narratives about the future of
Indonesia.[22] Sukarno tried to mimetically unify the different narratives in
his own charismatic persona. He suggested that there were three main
groups of Indonesians: nationalists, religionists (Islamists), and communists,
known by the acronym NASAKOM (Nasionalisme, Agama, Komunisme).
The nationalists prioritized unity. The religionists prioritized Islam. The
communists prioritized social justice. Sukarno believed Indonesia needed
all three and that he himself was all three. After years of conflict, struggle,
and social, political, and economic chaos, this great vision of unifying conflicting narratives came crashing down on September 30, 1965. It was the
height of the cold war, and not only Indonesia but all the world was
polarized over communism.

In 1965–66 the communists in Indonesia were demonized and slaugh-
tered. In 1965, as many as twenty-three million Indonesians were connected
in some way to the Communist Party (PKI) or its affiliates. Half a million or
more were killed and many more sent to prison. Sukarno was forced out of

office, and Soeharto took the reins of government. During his thirty-two years in power, he created a new narrative of stability, investment, exploitation of rich natural resources, development, and progress. Conflicts among competing narratives of ethnicity, religion, race, and political ideology were silenced by a militaristic government that prioritized stability and unity. Soeharto presided over years of rapid economic growth and proclaimed himself the Father of Development (Bapak Pembangunan). Soeharto's Golkar Party overwhelmingly won the sham legislative elections of 1997, but his government was unraveling under the weight of rampant corruption, serious human rights abuses, environmental destruction, and blatant electoral fraud. This precipitated the delegitimation of Soeharto's government and the collapse of the economy.

Soeharto was forced out of office amid massive demonstrations calling for an end to corruption, collusion, and nepotism. In the heady days before and after Soeharto resigned, an Indonesian colleague argued passionately that we needed "total reformation." Just as we were facing a total crisis (KRISTAL, Krisis Total), so we needed total reformation in every area of life. But total reformation is never possible. There is always both continuity and discontinuity. New narratives are constructed out of the old. Apparently defeated narratives resurface in new forms. The narratives of nationalist unity, Islamic state, Marxist struggle, separatist resistance, developmental progress, western neocolonialism, tolerant diversity, and corruption-free government are all still well and thriving in Indonesia.[23]

The atrocities of 9/11, the war on terror, Brexit, and the election of Trump all helped revive a bipolar narrative in which Islam is construed as under violent attack by the West (apocalyptic fear). This view is supplemented by the conviction that only in Islam is there hope of building a just and moral society (utopian hope). The hopes and fears of this imagination are sustained by a particular narrative of the global situation.

Muslims who follow this narrative do not justify it only on the basis of the concrete situation in Indonesia but rather with reference to Palestine, Iraq, Afghanistan, Iran, Syria, and the United States. They participate in what Prasenjit Duara calls circulatory histories (2015:54). Ideas and practices circulate in a stream without a discernible beginning or end among the Middle East, India, Europe, Africa, the Americas, Russia, China, Indonesia, and so on. The story of Mahatma Gandhi is a good example of circulatory history. Gandhi influenced and was influenced by ideas that circulated among India (Hinduism), England (Christianity), South Africa (opposition to apartheid), the United States (Henry David Thoreau, civil disobedience, Martin Luther King, civil rights), and Russia (Tolstoy, pacifism).[24] A narrative of the global situation after 9/11 and the election of Trump informs some Indonesians of where they fit within a newly conceived bipolar world of Islam over against the west.

This narrative presents a new challenge to the discourse about religious violence and diversity in Indonesia. On the one hand, fears of globalization, western cultural hegemony, American militarism, capitalist neo-imperialism, and Christian proselytism can lead to violent attempts to protect the Muslim community from an outside enemy. Hopes for the rise of Islamic civilization can lead to vigorous efforts to purge society of non-Islamic, polluting influences such as churches, bars, nominal Muslims, LGBT persons, and heretical sects.

On the other hand, the majority of Muslims in Indonesia, even if they accept some elements of a post-9/11 bipolar worldview, do not believe that true Islamic civilization should be imposed through violence. In fact many believe that Indonesia's greatest contribution to global Islamic narratives is the creation of a unique Islamicate civilization that demonstrates the substantive Islamic values of peace, tolerance, human rights (and responsibilities), justice, and respect for diversity. On this reading, western civilizations have failed to live up to their own ideals. They believe it is time for Indonesian Muslims to demonstrate a different way of life, one that succeeds where the West has failed.

Strategies versus Tactics for Dealing with Diversity: Interreligious Marriage

One example of conflict between religious communities is interreligious marriage. Interreligious marriage threatens the clear division between religious communities and may result in one community losing a member. A government strategy for dealing with potential conflicts associated with interreligious marriage has been to give instructions that Muslims may not marry non-Muslims.[25] Since only religious leaders can perform marriages, there is no provision for a civil union. Many religious leaders will not perform marriages if both parties are not from their religious community.

This makes it difficult to marry someone from another religious community. In spite of many bureaucratic hurdles, many interreligious marriages take place in Indonesia, as they have for centuries. Individuals and communities have tactics for resisting the government's strategy.

In Banjarmasin, after attending a workshop at the UIN Pangeran Antasari, a Banjar Muslim driver took us into the Meratus Mountains to visit Kaharingan Dayak villages. After four days of driving and hiking together, he confided that his wife was a Christian. I asked how that worked. He replied that it was hard because both of their families and communities had strongly opposed the marriage. Government and religious elites make it difficult to marry across religious boundaries unless one party converts. But, our friend confided, he was sure that the marriage was right and willed by Allah. He explained that the Koran did not forbid marriages between a Muslim man and a woman who was one of the "People of the Book" (Christians and Jews).

He said that he and his wife respected each other's religion. During Ramadan, his wife faithfully fasted along with him and celebrated Idul Fitri with their extended Muslim family. During Christmas and Easter, he and his wife both celebrated along with their Christian family and attended church services. I asked about their children. He and his wife had agreed, before the wedding, that any boys would be raised as Muslims and girls would be raised as Christians. In fact they had one boy and one girl. The boy was Muslim and his sister was Christian. This reminded me of an agreement among villagers in northern Halmahera (Moluccan Islands) that if a Christian and Muslim married the bride had to convert to the religion of her husband. However, their first child (male or female) would be raised as a member of the wife's original religious community.

In both cases, the tactics for dealing with conflicts that might arise from interreligious marriage are dependent on a history of tolerance between religious communities. Without an underlying narrative that justifies practices of tolerance, the tactic of committing an unborn child to the community of a different religion would not work. The tactic includes mimetic elements; for example, both husband and wife participate in the rituals of their spouse's religion to enact their essential unity. The commitment of children to a different religious community mimetically maintains an assumed cosmic balance and mutual respect between different religious communities. In the case of the Banjar driver, both spouses remain loyal to their families' religions, allowing both parties to continue the story of their religious faith. Ethically, their strategy is based on the principle of reciprocity. Each honors his or her spouse by participating in the other's religious festivals. Theoretically the tactic is justified with reference to koranic teachings of respect for the People of the Book. In contrast, the Moluccan case assumes gender imbalance by requiring the wife to convert to her husband's religion, thereby easing the bureaucratic hurdles of interreligious marriage. However, respect is still maintained by committing the first child to the wife's original religious community. In both cases, mimesis, narrative, morality, and theory are used to enact and justify the union.

How a society deals with diversity is not just a matter of public policy or law. Indonesian laws discourage interreligious marriage for theological reasons and as a strategy for avoiding conflicts when volatile frontiers between religions are crossed. Not all Indonesians agree with government strategies for maintaining the boundaries between communities. Human beings are endlessly creative in devising ways to live according to their imagination of what is right. People such as this Banjar Muslim driver and his wife use their own "tactics" to resist the government paradigm for dealing with diversity.[26]

Sometimes family and societal pressures are much harder to overcome than legal barriers. There are many ways to overcome the legal hurdles of interreligious marriage.[27] Boundary maintenance, however, is not only a legal concern. Two of our dear friends who were students in Yogyakarta fell deeply in love. The Javanese artist was the son of a Muslim leader (*kya*), while his sweetheart was the daughter of a Christian minister (*pendeta*) from Poso. Poso was the site of bitter mass violence between Muslims and Christians. The couple wanted to marry, but both families adamantly opposed the union. In spite of the deep love between them, neither wanted to be cut off from his or her family or religious community. In deep anguish they broke off their relationship and moved far away from each other. In their case, the problem was not the law but adamant opposition from the families that gave them life. We visited the Javanese Muslim artist, who is now married to a lovely Muslim woman and has three children. We were startled to see a huge, more than life size painting in his living room of a Javanese Christ hanging in agony from a cross. He explained to us calmly that he knew it was not his fate to marry his former girlfriend. It was not the will of Allah. But that did not do away with the pain of a broken heart.

A Clash of Civilizations?

The following story illustrates the power of competing narratives.

I felt serious trepidation as I walked into the large auditorium at the Indonesian Islamic University (UII) in Yogyakarta. It was packed, with more than five hundred students filling every seat. Many sat on the floor in the aisles. The women, wearing colorful head scarves, sat on the left and the men on the right. I knew I was not the main attraction. A famous radical Muslim cleric, who had been in and out of jail, was one of the speakers. It was his students who set off the Bali bombs. Most of those who helped the suicide bombers were caught and executed. Another speaker was a younger Muslim intellectual. He was famous for his inflammatory, stridently anti-Christian, anti-western writings. Some of my Muslim colleagues and I had been the objects of his published attacks. I was the third speaker.

One of my former students from UIN Sunan Kalijaga was now a dean at UII. When his students requested permission to hold a panel discussion sponsored by two militant Islamist organizations (Majelis Mujahidin Indonesia and Hizbut Tahrir), the dean agreed but suggested they should invite me to be on the panel as well. The theme was "American Hegemony and the Future of Muslim Relations with the West." I suspect that I was chosen to represent American hegemony.

The younger firebrand spoke first. He used a sophisticated PowerPoint presentation to outline the greatest crimes the West and Christians had perpetrated against Islam and humanity over the past thirteen hundred years. With pictures and video clips, he told a story of oppression, cruelty, and injustice that stretched from the Crusades and the Spanish Inquisition up to and including the bombing of Iraq, the oppression of the Palestinians, and the war on terror. Also included was a fierce indictment of western capitalism, economic inequality, violence, racism, promiscuity, the massacre of native peoples, slavery, crime, pornography, war, homosexuality, destruction of the environment, human trafficking, abortion, and the sexual victimization of women and children. In contrast to this gruesome story, he presented the noble teachings of Islam, including justice for the poor, defense of the weak, racial equality, peace, respect for women, care of the environment, sexual morality, and an ordered, law-governed society.

My presentation was next, and I was caught off guard, unprepared for such a vivid wholesale attack on the West. Without using the term, his narrative had reprised Samuel Huntington's famous theory of the "clash of civilizations" between Islam and the West. But unlike Huntington, who generally portrays the West as the good guys, in this story the forces for good are in Islam while the West is the source of all evil. Compared to his sensational, inflammatory narrative, my presentation was analytic, gentle, reasonable, polite, and uninspiring. The last speaker continued the basic narrative of the first. What he lacked in technological sophistication, he made up for by coming across as a fatherly, wise, and pious man of God deeply grieved by the evils of the West.

During the question and answer period, I felt strong emotions rising within me. I knew I had not effectively addressed the historical narrative that the other speakers had presented so passionately. Those who observed closely could see smoke beginning to seep from my ears. The moderator invited me to speak again. For half a minute I was silent, just looking out over the hushed audience. Perhaps they sensed what I felt. Then I said quietly into the microphone:

> You know, brothers and sisters, America is much worse than you imagine. All the terrible things presented by the other speakers about the West are true. There are many other ugly realities that they did not mention. There is much in our history and present reality that grieves and shames me.
>
> But the West is also much better than you imagine. There is amazing goodness and beauty in the peoples, cultures, and civilizations of the West. The amazing achievements of science, literature, religion, art, education, civil society, law, and social institutions are all parts of "the West" that the other speakers failed to mention. The other speakers have only compared the worst crimes and problems of the West to the noble teachings of Islam. That is not fair.
>
> Are there no crimes and problems in Muslim societies? Does Pakistan, Iraq, Sudan, Saudi Arabia, Bangladesh, Afghanistan, or Indonesia embody the noble teachings of Islam? All countries have both beauty and ugliness in their history, including Indonesia. Every country does not live up to its brightest ideals nor sink to its lowest shame. If you must compare different countries, religious communities, and civilizations, you should compare teachings with teachings, ideals with ideals, crimes with crimes, social problems with social problems. It is not fair to compare the worst crimes of one to the best teachings of the other.
>
> The world is not divided into black and white, good and evil, the good guys and the bad guys. Rather there is good and evil in all of us, as well as in all of our histories. Islam is now part of the West, and the West is part of all of us in this room.

I paused for them to think about it. Then I concluded by saying quietly into the microphone:

Brothers and sisters, I am a Christian and an American. Am I your enemy?

I sat down. In that large hall, you could have heard a pin drop. Finally the old Muslim cleric broke the silence. He said, "No, Professor Bernie. You are not our enemy, only the enemies of Islam are our enemies."

Most Indonesian Muslims hate terrorism and the use of violence in the name of religion.[28] Nevertheless, they are also influenced by narratives that suggest that Islam is under attack. The election of Trump seemed to vindicate radical narratives of a bipolar world. Our research suggests that multiple narratives and symbol systems shape the social imaginaries of most Indonesians. Fortunately, most believe that religious and ethnic communities can and should live in peace in Indonesia.

Conclusion: Is Indonesian Islam a Source of Hope?

No one knows the future, and it is easy to imagine a wide range of scenarios. At one extreme is a very negative future. Indonesia may be sucked into an increasingly polarized world in which conflict, intolerance, and violence between different communities tear the nation apart or lead to authoritarian uniformity and/or religious radicalism. At the other extreme is the possibility that Indonesia could become a beacon of hope: a large, prosperous, democratic, tolerant, and creative Islamicate civilization in which diversity is valued, human rights for all religious and ethnic groups are respected, and the people live together in peace. Perhaps the reality will lie somewhere between these two extremes. Indonesia may continue to muddle along, known as an exotic tourist destination made somewhat risky by spectacular natural disasters, occasional civil disorder, environmental destruction, corruption, and conservative Islamic law. However, there are good reasons to believe that Indonesia is already a source of hope for creative, peaceful relations between Muslims and non-Muslims. The major question is whether it will continue to be a source of hope. The answer to that question doesn't just depend on Indonesia. Indonesia is part of a world system that continually shapes it, just as it shapes all nations.

If the dramatic changes that have occurred over the last fifty years are any indication, the only certainty is that the future will be different from anything we can currently imagine. No one could have predicted the impact of the internet and social media, the collapse of the communist bloc, the European Union, September 11, terrorism, the election of Obama and then Trump, ISIS, the economic transformation of China, the refugee crisis, Brexit, global warming, the fall of Soeharto, or the reformation era in Indonesia. In light of the speed of social change, any predictions about the future of Indonesia are risky. The future is unknown, not just because there are too many variables for anyone to fully grasp but also because it is open. The future is created out of the present and the past, and also by the actions and decisions of millions of human beings. Nature is also one of the actors, as witnessed by the major changes in the religious, social, and political structures of Aceh after the tsunami of 2004.

Indonesians are creating a unique modernity informed by overlapping, complementary, and competing symbol systems. Most Indonesians are deeply religious and inhabit a sacred cosmos. They integrate multiple ways of knowing, including mimesis, myth, morality, and modernity. Their social imaginaries constantly synthesize contributions from ongoing interactions with multiple civilizations. How is this relevant to the future of Islam?

Most Indonesian Muslims are committed to democracy, the rule of law, protection of human rights, gender equality, scientific rationality, social justice, clean government, and the urgency of the environmental crisis. They don't see these issues as in conflict with their traditional beliefs or religious practices. Most do not see any fundamental "clash" with the West on these points.

While most Indonesians agree on these admirable principles, there is endless diversity in opinions about how they should be implemented. It's easy to agree on "thin" principles such as democracy and social justice but hard to reach agreement on the "thick" task of fleshing them out in public policy and practice (Walzer 1994). Most Indonesians resent pressure to follow the lead of western or Middle Eastern countries in creating modern institutions. Many feel that both the West and the Middle East have failed to create truly democratic societies that guard the dignity of all. They hope that Indonesia may succeed in building a society that is closer to the Islamic values of justice, tolerance, and peace.

Indonesia faces rapid social change influenced by urbanization, social media, capitalism, global warming, terrorism, hate crimes, populism, and the global circulation of violence, fear, and hatred. It has a symbiotic relationship with the rest of the world. There is no way to predict how Indonesia will respond to the global circulation of social, political, economic, and cultural change. But Indonesia is not a passive recipient of global influences. As the largest Muslim country, it will influence the future of the world.

Indonesia does not represent the rest of the Muslim world. But Indonesian social imaginaries of a sacred cosmos are not foreign to other Muslim countries. Many Muslims all over the world feel alienated from western countries that ban religion from public life and refuse to acknowledge mimetic, mythic, or ethical cognition as forms of rationality. Indonesian social imaginaries not only illuminate other Muslim countries but also throw the light of contrast on western societies. Understanding Indonesian social imaginaries illuminates the peculiarity of western imaginations of reality.

There are many internal barriers to Indonesia asserting a positive influence on interreligious relations in the rest of the world. Indonesian history includes dangerous, suppressed communal memories waiting to awaken. Natural disasters, social injustice, corruption, and rampant power struggles all undermine Indonesian ambitions to become an exemplary Islamic "city on a hill." Nevertheless, Indonesia has rich social and cultural capital born of a long history of interreligious and interethnic harmony that provides hope for the future.

The great axial civilizations of China, India, the Middle East, and Europe are all part of Indonesia, but none is dominant. Just as with every other nation-state, there is no "essential" Indonesian civilization that can be distinguished from the circulation of influences from around the world. Indonesia has rich social and cultural resources for facing an uncertain future. But, like other great nations, there are skeletons in the closet. Not all historical circulations are positive. In this book we considered some of the factors that undermine Indonesia's ambition to be a Muslim city on a hill. We also considered Indonesia's rich cultural capital, which empowers this country to share its treasures with the world. Indonesia is not the savior of either Islam or the world. But it is a source of hope. It is a unique, modern,

Islamic civilization made up of people who live in a sacred cosmos and believe that their future lies in the hands of God.

Appendices

APPENDIX I

Confidential Questionnaire
on Indonesian Social Imaginaries in English

Instructions: In all the following questions, circle *only one* answer, the one you believe is the most important or the closest to what you believe is true. If you are unable to choose one answer as preferable, you may choose more than one or write your own answer below.

Part I. General

A. *Age (circle one):*

    1. 18–29 years

    2. 30–45 years

    3. 46–59 years

    4. 60 and over

B. *Income per month:*

    1. Less than Rp. 1 million

    2. Rp. 1–3 million

    3. Rp. 3–7 million

    4. More than Rp. 7 million

C. *Education:*

    1. No formal education

    2. Elementary or junior high

    3. High school

    4. University, undergrad, or grad

D. *Sex: Male Female*

E. *Religion:* _____

F. *Ethnicity:* _____

G. *Home: Rural Urban*

H. *Profession/work:*

    1. Student. Faculty: _____

    2. Full-time parent/homemaker

    3. Business/trade/economic activity

    4. Professional (doctor, academic, etc.)

    5. Farmer/fisherman/agriculture

    6. Civil servant/government/politics

    7. Other: _____

Part II. Identity and Experience

A. *Which of the following communities is most important to you (circle one)?*

    1. My ethnic group or tribe (*suku*).

    2. My religious community.

    3. My citizenship as an Indonesian.

B. *To which system of law are you most obedient?*

    1. National law.

    2. Traditional (*adat*) law, the law of my ethnic or tribal group.

    3. Religious law.

C. *Which of the following societies is most noble (paling mulia)?*

    1. A society that obeys the commands of God and the requirements of religion.

    2. A society that uses science, reason, and common sense to solve life's problems.

    3. A society that maintains harmony, honors the ancestors, and follows tradition.

D. *Which of the following best expresses your experience?*

    1. I often experience the presence of spiritual powers around me, such as spirits of ancestors, *jins*, ghosts, and other spirits.

2. Sometimes I experience miracles, angels, or God's supernatural protection.

3. I never experience supernatural, mystical events. I think it is better to use science and rationality to understand the mysteries of life.

E. *How do you think we should interpret dreams?*

1. Dreams are usually the product of our own, psychological processes. However, sometimes God or unseen powers speak to me in dreams.

2. Dreams are all in our head. They are simply psychological expression of our unconscious mind.

3. God and/or other spiritual powers often speak to me in dreams. Dreams are an important source of communication and knowledge about the real world.

F. *If all the students in a high school class lost normal consciousness and did not know who they were, how should such an event be interpreted and faced?*

1. This is possession by an evil spirit, which should be exorcised by a religious leader.

2. This is mass hysteria, and a doctor of psychology should be called.

3. This is spiritual possession, which can be controlled by a shaman or paranormal.

G. *If you experienced a serious accident or unusual illness, what might it mean?*

1. Accidents and sickness don't have any particular meaning. They happen by accident and just mean you are unlucky.

2. It may mean that I am under attack by an evil spirit or spiritual power.

3. Perhaps the suffering is God's way of speaking to me and warning me.

Part III. Social Imaginaries

A. *Which of the following sources of information is most valuable to you?*

1. My parents, teachers, community leaders, folktales, and other oral sources.

2. Sermons, religious programs on TV, religious websites, and religious books.

     3. Newspapers, popular TV programs, general websites, and popular films.

B. *Which of the following statements do you think is most important?*

     1. We should use moral and clean/*halal* means in seeking wealth.

     2. Be part of the community. Live simply and honestly, serving others without self-interest.

     3. Develop the soul of an entrepreneur. Learn to compete in a healthy manner in the free market era.

C. *Of the following, which is the most important characterization of a good government?*

     1. The government is like parents who should guarantee the safety, peace, harmony, and prosperity of society.

     2. The government is the representative of God on earth and should guide its citizens to obey God's laws and live moral and good lives.

     3. The government is formed by the people and must protect the freedom and human rights of all the citizens of Indonesia.

D. *Which of the following ideals do you most hope will be realized in the nation-state of Indonesia?*

     1. God's people, who are good, orderly, obedient to God, and practice their religion.

     2. A democratic community with justice and equality where the human rights of all members of the community are protected.

     3. A harmonious family that honors our elders is wholehearted and safe.

E. *Which of the following is the most important basis of law?*

     1. Tradition, *adat*, the will of the ancestors, loyalty to my ethnic community.

     2. Reason, science, discussion and consensus, equality before the law.

     3. The Scriptures (Koran, Bible, etc.), religious teachings, God's commandments.

F. *Which of the following statements most accurately describes the present Indonesian reality?*

1. Destiny, increasingly religious, ruled by the will of God; there will be a Day of Judgment.

2. An age of insanity, messed up, tragic, mysterious, fate, karma.

3. Progress, development, evolution, struggle for an uncertain future.

G. *What should be the relationship between Indonesian society and nature or the environment?*

1. Honor the earth of our ancestors. We are an indivisible part of the natural world.

2. As God's representatives on earth, the people should protect and preserve nature.

3. We should use science to build a sustainable economy that is gentle on the environment.

Part IV: Social Ethics

A. *Which of the following statements is the best description of power?*

1. Power can be obtained by fasting, by ascetic practices, or from a magical object such as a *keris*.

2. Power describes the relations between people. Anyone can exercise power over another person through use of superior knowledge, technology, or by holding a higher position in the structure.

3. Only the will of God determines who is given power.

B. *How should government manage religious diversity?*

1. The government should support the six religions recognized by the state and suppress groups that are teaching or practicing beliefs that are heretical.

2. The government should protect the fundamental human right to freedom of worship for every group without considering its teachings, as long as it doesn't break the law.

3. The government should maintain harmony. If there is conflict, the government should play the role of finding a solution that can be accepted by all sides in the dispute.

C. *What is the wisest policy for addressing corruption, collusion, and nepotism (KKN)?*

1. The people should be taught with the culture of shame. Our culture of gift exchange is good, but the people should also know shame so that they stay clean from corruption.

2. We must change the social structures that preserve corruption. We need economic, political, and legal structures that are transparent, rational, and clean from corruption.

3. Corruption is stealing. God hates stealing. Corruptors should be given heavy punishment.

D. *What are good and true relations between men and women?*

1. Women and men are equal and enjoy the same rights. Both men and women can become leaders.

2. Women should submit to men. Women can be a temptation to men and should be separated from men. Women should wear a head covering and modest clothing.

3. Men and women have different, complementary roles that balance each other. Women are the Mothers of their households while the Father is the head of the family.

E. *Which of the following best expresses your understanding of natural disasters?*

1. Natural disasters are a warning, a test, and a judgment of God.

2. Natural disasters are a sign that society is not in balance or harmony with nature. Social evil may have offended the ancestors and spirits.

3. Natural disasters are the result of impersonal natural laws and don't have any particular meaning. Sometimes disasters are caused by human beings.

F. *Which statement is most appropriate to describe a good leader for the people of Indonesia?*

1. An educated, scientific leader who solves social problems by rational means.

2. A pious leader who guides the people in accordance with the will of God.

3. A leader whose inner character of authority controls the people wisely through example.

G. *What is the most important purpose of media such as television, the internet, and newspapers?*

1. Preserve Indonesian culture, entertain and educate the people.

2. Serve as a forum for free expression where people who have different opinions can struggle for their ideas and influence public policy.

3. Educate the people so that they become increasingly pious, religious, and moral.

Confidential Questionnaire
on Indonesian Social Imaginaries in Indonesian

Petunjuk: Jawablah semua pertanyaan di bawah ini dengan melingkari satu pilihan saja yang paling sesuai atau paling mendekati keyakinan Anda. Kalau tidak bisa pilih yang paling sesuai, boleh pilih dua, atau menulis jawaban Anda di bawah pertanyaannya.

Bagian I: Informasi Umum

A. *Usia:*

    1. 18–29 tahun

    2. 30–45 tahun

    3. 46–59 tahun

    4. 60 tahun atau lebih

B. *Penghasilan per bulan:*

    1. Rp. 0–1 juta

    2. Rp. 1–3 juta

    3. Rp. 3–7 juta

    4. Di atas Rp. 7 juta

C. *Pendidikan Terakhir:*

    1. Tidak sekolah formal

    2. SD SMP

    3. SMA

    4. S1 S2 S3

D. *Jenis Kelamin: Laki-Laki Perempuan*

E. *Agama:* _____

F. *Suku:* _____

G. *Tinggal di: Desa Kota*

H. *Profesi/pekerjaan*

    1. Mahasiswa: Fakultas:_____

    2. Ibu/Kepala rumah tangga

    3. Bisnis/Dagang/Ekonomi

    4. Profesional (Dokter, Akademisi, dst.)

    5. Petani/Nelayan

    6. PNS/Pemerintahan/Politik

    7. Lainnya: _____

Bagian II: Identitas dan Pengalaman

A. *Identitas manakah yang paling penting bagi Anda?*

    1. Suku atau etnik saya (e.g. orang Jawa, Bali, Batak dllsb.)

    2. Umat keagamaan saya (beragama, Islam, Kristen dllsb.)

    3. Warga Negara Indonesia

B. *Anda lebih taat kepada sistim hukum yang mana di bawah ini?*

    1. Hukum negara Republik Indonesia

    2. Hukum adat suku/etnis saya

    3. Hukum agama saya

C. *Di antara pernyataan ini, manakah masyarakat yang paling mulia?*

    1. Masyarakat yang mematuhi perintah Tuhan dan mengamalkan kewajiban agama.

    2. Masyarakat yang menggunakan akal sehat, nalar dan ilmu pengetahuan modern.

    3. Masyarakat yang rukun, menghormati para leluhur dan taat kepada adat.

D. *Di antara pernyataan ini, manakah yang paling sesuai dengan pengalaman Anda?*

   1. Kehadiran roh leluhur, makhluk halus atau kekuatan gaib, sering saya rasakan.

   2. Kadang-kadang ada mujizat, malaikat atau kekuatan Tuhan yang melindungi saya.

   3. Saya tidak pernah mengalami kehadiran kekuatan gaib, roh atau makhluk halus. Sebaiknya kita pakai sains dan rasio untuk memahami misteri-misteri kehidupan.

E. *Bagaimana mimpi seharusnya ditafsirkan?*

   1. Mimpi biasanya lahir dari proses psikologis kita sendiri. Akan tetapi, Tuhan kadang berbicara kepada saya melalui mimpi.

   2. Mimpi hanyalah buah pikiran kita saja. Mimpi adalah ungkapan psikologis dari pikiran bawa sadar kita saja.

   3. Tuhan atau kekuatan spiritual lainnya, sering berbicara kepada saya melalui mimpi. Mimpi adalah media komunikasi yang penting tentang dunia nyata.

F. *Kalau semua anak pada suatu kelas SMA kehilangan kesadaran dan tidak tahu diri, bagaimana sebaiknya dihadapi?*

   1. Ini kesurupan dari roh jahat yang harus diusir oleh pemuka agama.

   2. Ini histeria masal dan sebaiknya dokter psikologi dipanggil.

   3. Ini kesurupan oleh makhluk halus yang bisa dikendalikan oleh orang pintar.

G. *Seandainya kecelakaan serius atau penyakit luar biasa menimpa Anda, apa artinya?*

   1. Penyakit atau kecelakaan tidak punya arti apa-apa. Hanya kebetulan dan tidak beruntung.

   2. Bisa saja saya diserang oleh roh jahat atau kekuatan gaib.

   3. Mungkin kesakitan ini adalah cara Allah mengingatkan dan berbicara dengan saya.

Bagian III: Imajinasi Sosial

A. *Sumber informasi yang paling berharga bagi Anda adalah yang mana?*

   1. Orang tua, guru, tokoh masyarakat, ceritera rakyat dan sumber lisan lain.

   2. Khotbah, program agama di TV, website agama dan buku-buku agama.

   3. Berita koran, program hiburan TV, website2 umum dan film2 popular.

B. *Di antara pernyataan ini, menurut Anda, manakah yang dirasakan paling penting?*

   1. Kita harus pakai cara yang moral dan bersih/halal dalam pencarian kekayaan.

   2. Bermasyarakatlah dan hidup jujur, sederhana, ikhlas dan tanpa pamrih.

   3. Bangunlah jiwa enterpreneur. Belajar bersaing secara sehat pada era pasar bebas.

C. *Di antara pernyataan ini, manakah yang paling penting untuk pemerintah yang baik?*

   1. Pemerintah adalah ibarat orang tua yang menjamin keamanan, perdamaian, kerukunan dan kesejahteraan masyarakat.

   2. Pemerintah adalah wakil Tuhan di muka bumi dan harus mengarahkan warganya untuk mematuhi hukum Allah dan menjalani kehidupan yang baik dan bermoral.

   3. Pemerintah dibentuk oleh masyarakat dan harus melindungi kebebasan dan hak asasi manusia bagi setiap warga negara Indonesia.

D. *Cita-cita yang paling diharapkan untuk diwujudkan oleh bangsa-negara Indonesia adalah:*

   1. Umat yang baik, tertib, taat kepada Tuhan dan beragama.

   2. Demokrasi yang adil, semua warga setara dan hak asasi manusia dilindungi.

   3. Keluarga yang rukun, menghormati orang tua, ikhlas dan aman.

E. *Di antara landasan hukum di bawah ini, manakah yang paling penting?*

　1. Tradisi, Adat, kehendak leluhur, kesetiaan pada suku bangsa saya.

　2. Akal budi, ilmu pengetahuan, sains, kesetaraan di muka hukum.

　3. Kitab Suci (Al-Qur'an, Alkitab, dst.), ajaran agama, perintah Tuhan.

F. *Di antara istilah ini, manakah yang paling menjelaskan kenyataan Indonesia sekarang?*

　1. Takdir, makin beragama, digariskan oleh kehendak Tuhan, akan ada Hari Pembalasan.

　2. Zaman edan, kacau, tragis, misterius, nasib, karma.

　3. Kemajuan, berkembang, evolusi, berjuang untuk masa depan yang tidak tentu.

G. *Bagaimana rakyat Indonesia sebaiknya berhubungan dengan alam dan lingkungan hidup?*

　1. Hormatilah bumi leluhur kita. Kita adalah bagian tak terpisah dari alam semesta.

　2. Sebagai wakil Tuhan di bumi, rakyat harus menjaga dan melestarikan alam.

　3. Melalui sains kita membangun ekonomi yang berkelanjutan dan ramah lingkungan.

Bagian IV: Etika Sosial

A. *Di antara pernyataan ini, manakah yang paling benar tentang kekuasaan?*

　1. Kekuatan tertentu bisa diperoleh melalui bertapa atau dari pusaka seperti keris.

　2. Kekuasaan adalah hubungan antara manusia. Siapapun bisa berkuasa atas orang lain melalui pengetahuan, teknologi atau dengan menempati jabatan struktural.

　3. Kekuasaan diberi kepada seseorang atas kehendak Tuhan semata.

B. *Bagaimana seharusnya pemerintah mengelola keberagaman agama?*

　1. Pemerintah harus mendukung keenam agama resmi negara dan menekan kelompok yang mengajarkan atau mengamalkan keyakinan yang sesat.

　2. Pemerintah harus melindungi hak asasi setiap kelompok untuk beribadah, tanpa memandang ajaran mereka, selama mereka tidak melanggar hukum.

　3. Pemerintah harus memelihara kerukunan. Kalau ada konflik, pemerintah harus berperan menemukan solusi yang bisa diterima oleh semua kalangan yang berbeda.

C. *Bagaimana sikap yang paling bijaksana terhadap korupsi, kolusi dan nepotisme (KKN)?*

　1. Rakyat harus dididik dalam budaya malu. Budaya tukar-menukar (hadiah) adalah baik, tetapi rakyat harus juga malu supaya bersih dari korupsi.

　2. Struktur masyarakat yang melestarikan korupsi harus diubah. Kita perlu struktur ekonomi, politik dan hukum yang transparan, rasional dan bersih dari korupsi.

　3. Korupsi adalah pencurian. Tuhan membenci pencurian. Koruptor harus dihukum berat.

D. *Bagaimana hubungan yang baik dan benar di antara laki-laki dan perempuan?*

　1. Perempuan dan laki-laki adalah setara dan hak-hak mereka sama. Baik laki-laki maupun perempuan boleh menjadi pemimpin.

　2. Perempuan harus tunduk kepada laki-laki. Perempuan bisa menjadi godaan bagi laki-laki dan sebaiknya dipisahkan dari laki-laki dan berpakaian jilbab/sopan.

　3. Laki-laki dan perempuan mempunyai peran yang berbeda dan saling melengkapi secara seimbang. Perempuan yang Ibu rumah tangga dan Bapak yang kepala keluarga.

E. *Pernyataan manakah yang paling tepat mengenai bencana alam?*

　1. Bencana alam adalah peringatan, ujian dan hukuman Tuhan.

2. Bencana alam adalah tanda bahwa alam semesta dan manusia tidak seimbang atau selaras. Kejahatan masyarakat membuat murka para leluhur dan kekuatan gaib.

3. Bencana alam terjadi secara alamiah dan tidak punya maksud tertentu. Bencana alam kadang terjadi karena ulah manusia.

F. *Pernyataan manakah yang paling tepat tentang kepemimpinan masyarakat Indonesia?*

1. Pemimpin yang ilmiah mengatasi masalah-masalah rakyat dengan cara rasional.

2. Pemimpin yang saleh membimbing rakyat sesuai dengan perintah Tuhan.

3. Pemimpin yang bermartabat meneladani dan mengendalikan rakyat secara bijaksana.

G. *Tugas paling penting dari media seperti televisi, internet dan koran adalah:*

1. Melestarikan budaya Indonesia, menghibur dan mendidik masyarakat.

2. Menjadi forum bebas di mana orang yang beda pendapat bisa memperjuangkan ide-ide mereka dan memengaruhi kebijaksanaan umum.

3. Mendidik rakyat supaya mereka menjadi makin saleh, beragama dan bermoral.

APPENDIX III

Statistical Analysis of Questionnaire Responses regarding the Supernatural, Dreams, Spirits, and Accidents or Illness

This appendix presents the methods and reasoning that lie behind the conclusions I draw in chapter 5. It provides a more detailed analysis of the statistics from our questionnaire (see the "Introduction") and suggests whether or not there is a correlation between Islamic modernism and disenchantment.

The Unseen World and Scientific Reason (Question II.D)

Questionnaire Question II.D on experience of the unseen world

Which of the following best expresses your experience?

1. I often experience the presence of spiritual powers around me, such as spirits of ancestors, *jins*, ghosts, and other spirits.

2. Sometimes I experience miracles, angels, or God's supernatural protection.

3. I never experience supernatural, mystical events. I think it is better to use science and rationality to understand the mysteries of life.

In order to simplify the analysis, I suggested "null hypotheses" for each of the questions. These hypotheses express what should be seen in a statistical analysis of the respondents if there is significant disenchantment happening in Indonesia and if religion is the dominant factor in it. Analysis of the statistics of the questionnaires shows whether there is a significant correlation supporting the null hypotheses or not.

Null hypotheses are propositions, which the statistics should demonstrate if disenchantment is taking place and if there are strong correlations between disenchantment and religion. The most interesting results may be where the hypotheses are proved wrong because the correlations hypothesized are not supported by the statistics. Whether or not the null hypotheses are proven correct, our interpretation of why or why not the hypotheses are supported by significant correlations is more important than the actual null hypotheses.

The first null hypothesis is a simple test of whether or not most Indonesians prefer scientific and rational language over traditional or religious language to describe their experience of the mysteries of life. The null hypothesis is as follows.

1. The majority of Indonesians will choose #3, indicating that they have no experience of an unseen world. This would indicate that disenchantment regarding the mysteries of life is a general phenomenon in Indonesia.

According to this hypothesis, if most Indonesians think mysterious phenomena should be interpreted primarily through the language of modern science and reason, rather than through religious or traditional symbols, this would indicate that disenchantment regarding the unseen world (*gaib*) is a general phenomenon. In fact this null hypothesis is proved wrong because only 36 percent of all respondents chose modern scientific language to express their understanding of the unseen world. Fifty-two percent chose religious language, and 12 percent chose traditional language. Thus 64 percent used language that includes symbols of the unseen world (God, ancestors, and unseen beings or powers). The fact that only 12 percent indicated that they frequently experienced the presence of unseen beings might indicate that traditional perceptions of many different spiritual powers that influence their lives is growing weaker. If so, for most Indonesians it is replaced with religious language about God and God's agents (52 percent) rather than a more scientific perspective. Another possible interpretation is that, although only 12 percent have frequent experience of the unseen world, this does not imply that the others don't believe that an unseen world surrounds them. In traditional societies only a small minority, such as shamans and religious leaders, have special abilities to perceive the unseen world. Most people rely on these religious experts to mediate their experience of the sacred.

The second null hypothesis is a little more complicated. It assumes the converse, which is a classic logical fallacy. The hypothesis is as follows.

2. The choice of #3 indicates that the person does not believe in the existence of spirits or the unseen world. This hypothesis assumes the converse and requires further testing. Those who believe reason and science are the most effective ways to address the mysteries of life may show by their answers to questions II.E, II.F, II.G, IV.A, or IV.E that they also believe that God and/or the spirits are important factors in their experience of the mysteries of life.

For the 36 percent who chose the language of modern science with regard to the mysteries of the unseen world, most indicated by their answers to other questions that they also believe in God and spiritual beings. Thirty-three percent of those who said they had no experience of the unseen world (*gaib*) had experienced communication through dreams, 60 percent believe in spirit possession, 84 percent believe that God or other beings are involved in sickness and accidents, 33 percent believe that power comes from God or other beings, and 56 percent perceive a link between natural disasters and the work of God or other unseen beings. This implies that very few of the 36 percent who say they have had no experience of the unseen world indicate that they do not believe in its existence. Thus the second null hypothesis is proved false. We cannot assume the converse in the case of this question.

It may be that the anomaly of people rejecting language of an unseen world but then indicating that they believe that spirit possession is real, or that God or other beings communicate with them through phenomena such as dreams, sickness, accidents, or natural disasters, is a result of Islamic modernism. As we saw in the interviews with Ma'arif and Syamsiyatun, believing in the existence of the unseen world is part of Islamic teaching. But Muslim modernists believe we are forbidden to pay attention to it. The beings are there, but we should not glorify (*memuliakan*) them in any way. This could lead some to reject language that might imply interacting with *gaib*, even though they show by their answers to other questions that they don't doubt its existence.

The third null hypothesis assumes that Islamic modernism would influence Muslims to choose either the modern, rational language (#2) or the religious language (#3) about the unseen world. If Islamic modernism is a major factor in disenchantment, we might expect there to be a higher percentage of Muslims than non-Muslims who would choose #2 or #3. Here is the null hypothesis.

3. As a result of Islamic modernism, a higher percentage of Muslims than non-Muslims will choose #2 or #3. If proven, this hypothesis will show that Muslims, more than non-Muslims, prefer religious language about God, or scientific language about natural processes, over mystical language about spirits, ancestors, and unseen beings. This would suggest that disenchantment is stronger among Indonesian Muslims than non-Muslims.

The null hypothesis is proved false. Eighty-eight percent of Muslims and 88 percent of non-Muslims chose the modern (#2) or the religious (#3) answer. For both Protestants and Catholics, the percentage was even higher than for Muslims; 90 percent of Protestants and 90 percent of Catholics chose religious or scientific language. Only Hindus, at 81 percent, had a lower rate of choice than Muslims for religious or modern language. For all religious communities, the traditional answer expressing frequent interaction with the unseen world was chosen by a minority. Only 12 percent of Muslims, 10 percent of Protestants, 10 percent of Catholics and 19 percent of Hindus chose the traditional answer over religious or scientific language.

There are two opposite ways to interpret these data. The first is that Islamic modernism has very little impact on Muslim responses to questions about the unseen world. The percentage of Muslims choosing religious or scientific language to express their experience of the unseen world is high but actually lower than that of Protestants and Catholics. This suggests that that there are other factors, such as modern education and the media, that may have a greater influence than religious affiliation or belief. Such factors influence all religious communities. An alternative interpretation is that Islamic modernism indeed influences members of the Muslim community to shy away from explicitly expressing their belief in *gaib*. However, other religious communities, especially Protestant and Catholic Christians, have modernist movements that are equally strong. They may not be influenced by Islamic modernism, but "demythologization" and secular currents in mainstream Protestantism and Catholicism are equally strong.

The fourth null hypothesis compares the relative influences of religion and ethnicity on disenchantment. For example, are Muslims and non-Muslims within one ethnic group more similar than Muslims and Muslims from different ethnic groups? The null hypothesis is as follows.

4. The correlation between Islam and the choice of answers #2 or #3 is stronger than the correlation between ethnicity and the choice of #2 or #3. This hypothesis is meant to show whether religion or ethnicity is the stronger factor in influencing those who choose religious or modern scientific responses. The hypothesis is tested in two ways: (1) by comparing Muslims and non-Muslims from two ethnic groups from which we have a substantial sample of both Muslims and non-Muslims (on Java and the Moluccas); and (2) by comparing five different ethnic groups that are predominantly Muslim (from Java, Sunda, Makasar/Bugis, Minang, and Aceh).

The results of the first test indicate that ethnicity is a significant factor. If we compare Javanese Muslims with Moluccan Muslims, there is a significant difference. Ninety-two percent of Javanese Muslims chose religious or scientific answers compared to 81 percent of Moluccan Muslims, an 11 percent difference. This might indicate that the impact of Islamic modernism is stronger in Java than in the Moluccas. However the difference could just as well be caused by stronger educational institutions in Java or the stronger influence of traditional ethnic culture in the Moluccas. Nineteen percent of Moluccan Muslims chose traditional language compared with just 8 percent of Javanese Muslims.

If we compare the difference between Muslims and non-Muslims in these two places, there are significant differences. The Muslims in Java prefer religious or modern language (92 percent) compared to Javanese non-Muslims (88 percent). In the Moluccas, the results are the reverse: 86 percent of Moluccan non-Muslims prefer religious or modern language compared to 81 percent of Moluccan Muslims. A higher percentage of Moluccan Muslims prefer traditional language (19 percent) compared to Moluccan non-Muslims (14 percent), and a lower percentage of Moluccan Muslims prefer religious language (36 percent) compared to Moluccan non-Muslims (42 percent). In their preference for religious language, the difference between Javanese Muslims (50 percent) and Moluccan Muslims (36 percent) is significant (14 percent difference). In all, the Javanese Muslims are more religious/modern by 4 percent compared to Javanese non-Muslims, whereas the Moluccan non-Muslims are more religious/modern by 5 percent over Moluccan Muslims.

Measured by their choice of religious or modern language, the Javanese Muslims are 4 percent more affected by Islamic modernism (92 percent) than the national average (88 percent). In comparison, by the same measure, the Moluccan Muslims are 7 percent less affected by Islamic modernism (81 percent) than the national average (88 percent). Interestingly, the national average for both Muslims and non-Muslims is 88 percent of all respondents who preferred religious or modern language in their answers to question II. D. regarding the unseen world. According to this data, all Javanese, including Muslims and non-Muslims, equal or exceed the national average for selecting religious or scientific language to describe their experience of the unseen world. Conversely, all Moluccans, Muslim and non-Muslim are lower than the national average.

The fourth null hypothesis is incorrect according to the first method of testing. The correlation between ethnicity and choice of religious or modern language is stronger than the correlation between religion and the religious modernist response. The statistics are listed in chapter 5 (tables 5.1–5.9).

A base line for the second test of the fourth null hypothesis is that the national average for all Muslims, all non-Muslims, and all Indonesians who chose modern or religious language in response to the question about their experience of the unseen world is 88 percent. This remarkable convergence for most ethnic groups across Indonesia lends significance to the test of differences among Muslims from different ethnic groups. For the overall percentages by ethnic group, of those who chose religious or modern symbol systems to explain their experience of the unseen world, the range is 12 percent, from 80 to 92 percent: Aceh 80 percent, Minang 86, Sunda 90, Makassar 92, and Java 92. It is interesting that Aceh and Minang have the lowest figures. Both groups are deeply committed to Islam but also known for their strong local traditions. For those who chose the traditional language of spirits and unseen beings, the range of difference is likewise 12 percent: Aceh 20 percent, Minang 14, Sunda 10, Makassar 8, and Java 8.

Of these five groups, three preferred religious over modern language: Makassar, 54 percent religious and 38 percent modern; Java, 50 percent religious and 43 percent modern; and Aceh, 42 percent religious and 38 percent modern. The other two preferred modern language over religious language: Sunda, 51 percent modern and 39 percent religious; and Minang, 44 percent modern and 42 percent religious. It is interesting that Java and Makassar scored the highest for religious language, the highest for either religious or modern, and the lowest for traditional language. These figures may indicate that Islamic modernism is more powerful among people in Java/Madura and Makassar/Bugis.

The second test of the null hypothesis confirms the findings of the first test. The statistics do not support the hypothesis that religion is stronger than ethnicity in determining whether people will choose the modern or religious response to the question about the unseen world. The null hypothesis is not supported. Ethnicity has a significant impact on responses to this question. For some ethnic groups, such as those in Java and Makassar, Muslims have a higher percentage for the religious modernist response than the national average. For other groups, like those in Aceh and Minang, the percentage for the religious modernist response is lower than the national average. The statistics are laid out in table 5.2.

The Meaning of Dreams

Questionnaire Question II.E on the meaning of dreams

  How do you think we should interpret dreams?

  1. Dreams are usually the product of our own psychological processes. However, sometimes God or unseen powers speak to me in dreams.

  2. Dreams are all in our head. They are simply psychological expressions of our unconscious mind.

  3. God and/or other spiritual powers often speak to me in dreams. Dreams are an important source of communication and knowledge about the real world.

The following are my null hypotheses regarding dreams.

  1. The majority of Indonesians will choose answer #2, indicating that they believe dreams are simply the result of a psychological process. This would

indicate that most Indonesians have no experience of communication from outside their minds through dreams.

The statistics for answers to this question support the first null hypothesis. Fifty-four percent of all respondents to this question on our questionnaire chose #2, that dreams are purely a psychological process that goes on within our own minds. The statistics are as follows.

Muslims had the highest proportion of purely rationalistic answers with 60 percent. Protestants had the highest percentage (46 percent) who believe that God speaks to them in dreams and was the only group with less than 50 percent of respondents who chose the modern psychological explanation. Catholics had the highest percentage (22 percent) of people who often receive information from outside their minds through dreams. However, the overall total of 54 percent indicates that modern psychological explanations of dreams is dominant for most Indonesians. The null hypothesis is supported by these data.

The second null hypothesis seeks to find out if those who do not believe that dreams are a source of communication from outside our minds thereby indicate that they don't believe that God or spirits or unseen beings can communicate with human beings.

2. The choice of #2 indicates that the respondent has a "buffered mind" and believes that there is no external, supernatural agency that can communicate directly to his or her mind. This null hypothesis assumes the contrary and requires further verification. Those who believe that dreams are a purely psychological process may show by their answers to questions II.D, II.F, II.G, or IV.E that they also believe that God and/or the spirits may communicate with people through other means.

For the 54 percent who chose the language of modern psychology with regard to the meaning of dreams, most indicated by their answers to other questions that they also believe that God or other spiritual beings can communicate with us by means other than dreams. Of those who gave a psychological answer regarding dreams (54 percent), 53 percent said they occasionally or often experience the presence of God or other unseen beings, 62 percent believe in spirit possession, 83 percent believe that God or other beings are involved in sickness and accidents, and 56 percent perceive a link between natural disasters and the work of God or other unseen beings.

This implies that very few of those who do not believe in supernatural communication through dreams thereby indicate that they do not believe in communication from the unseen world. Thus the second null hypothesis is proved false. We should not assume the converse in the case of this question. It does not appear that most Indonesians have "buffered minds."

The third null hypothesis tests whether Islamic modernism is a major factor that influences people's interpretation of the meaning of dreams.

3. As a result of Islamic modernism, a higher percentage of Muslims than non-Muslims will choose #1 (religious) or #2 (psychological). If proven, this hypothesis would show that, in comparison with non-Muslims, Muslims are more comfortable with language about God and psychology rather than mystical language about messages from spirits, ancestors, and unseen beings. This might suggest that because of Islamic modernism, disenchantment regarding dreams is stronger among Indonesian Muslims than non-Muslims.

The statistics from the question regarding dreams on our questionnaire suggest that this null hypothesis is formally correct. A total of 1,168 out of 1,273, or 92 percent of Muslim respondents, chose either the modern or religious answer to this question. In comparison 1,026 out of 1,180 non-Muslim respondents, or 87 percent, chose the modern or religious answer. The null hypothesis is proved correct, but whether or not the cause is Islamic modernism may be questioned. There was considerable variation within the different non-Muslim groups. Protestant Christians were very similar to Muslims in their total percentage. Ninety-one percent of Protestants chose religious or modern responses compared to 92 percent of Muslims. However, the proportions were different. Forty-five percent of Protestants, compared to 60 percent of Muslims, chose the modern answer, and 46 percent of Protestants, compared to just 32 percent of Muslims, chose the religious answer. Only 9 percent of Protestants and 8 percent of Muslims chose the traditional answer, indicating that they frequently receive communications from the unseen world through dreams.

Catholics were quite different from both Protestants and Muslims. Twenty-three percent of Catholics said they frequently receive communications through dreams. However, 53 percent of Catholics chose the modern psychological response, which is closer to the Muslims (60 percent) than the Protestants (45 percent). Only 24 percent of Catholics said they occasionally received messages from God through dreams. Overall, 77 percent of Catholics chose the modern or religious response compared to 92 percent of Muslims and 91 percent of Protestants. Hindus were closer to Catholics than to either Muslims or Protestants. Seventeen percent of Hindus frequently receive communication through dreams. However, 55 percent of Hindus said dreams are purely psychological compared to 60 percent of Muslims and 53 percent of Catholics. Twenty-eight percent of Hindus said God speaks to them occasionally through dreams. Thus their overall modernist religious total was 83 percent. The Buddhist respondents were too few to be meaningful, but all of them chose the religious response (see table 5.3).

From these statistics it is clear that Muslims and Protestants are equally skeptical that spirits or powers from the unseen world frequently communicate with them through dreams. However, almost half the Protestants experience God speaking to them occasionally through dreams, while a clear majority of Muslims believe that dreams are just a psychological process. A significantly larger percentage of Catholics and Hindus frequently receive messages from unseen beings through dreams. However, more than double their percentages believe dreams are a purely psychological process that takes place within our own minds. The similarities between Protestants and Muslims may be because both have experienced strong religious modernist movements. Both may be influenced by beliefs that it is wrong to communicate with any beings other than God and/or are suspicious of mystical any experience that is not focused on God. In contrast, Catholics and Hindus are more tolerant of praying to or communicating with beings other than God (e.g., saints, the Virgin Mary, or local deities).

The fourth null hypothesis explores whether religion is the dominant influence on people's interpretation of dreams or whether ethnicity is equally influential. The fourth null hypothesis is as follows.

4. The correlation between Islam and the choice of #1 or #2 is stronger than the correlation between ethnicity and the choice of #1 or #2. This hypothesis is meant to show whether religion or ethnicity is a stronger factor in influencing those who choose #1 or #2. The hypothesis is tested in two ways: (1) by comparing Muslims and non-Muslims from two ethnic groups for which we have a substantial sample of both Muslims and non-Muslims (from Java and the Moluccas); and (2) Comparing five different ethnic groups that are predominantly Muslim (from Java, Sunda, Makasar/Bugis, Minang, and Aceh).

According to the first test, religion has a slightly higher correlation with the religious modernist response than ethnicity does, and therefore the null hypothesis is marginally supported. Ninety-three percent of Javanese Muslims chose psychological or religious language to describe their experience of dreams compared to 89 percent of Javanese non-Muslims. In the Moluccas, the Muslims had a marginally higher percentage of religious modernist responses (89 percent) compared to Moluccan non-Muslims (88 percent). In both ethnic groups, Muslims chose the religious modernist responses at a higher percentage than non-Muslims did. However, the fact that Javanese Muslims and non-Muslims both have a higher percentage than Moluccan Muslims and non-Muslims indicates that ethnicity is still a factor in their choice.

Both Javanese Muslims and non-Muslims preferred psychological over religious language. Javanese Muslims preferred psychological language over religious language by 58 to 35 percent. For Javanese non-Muslims, the figure was 48 to 41 percent. Similarly, Moluccan Muslims preferred psychological over religious language by 48 to 46 percent. However Moluccan non-Muslims preferred both languages equally, 44 to 44 percent. If we compare the preference for psychological over religious language of the Moluccan Muslims (48 to 46 percent) to that of the Javanese Muslims (58 to 35 percent) or to the national average for Muslims (60 to 31 percent), there is considerable difference. This indicates that Moluccan ethnicity has a significant impact on how people interpret dreams. Eighty percent of Javanese non-Muslim respondents were Protestants but also included were Catholics, Hindus, and Buddhists. Most of the non-Muslim respondents in the Moluccas were also Protestant Christians. Therefore the figures for non-Muslims in these two ethnic groups can be read as meaning primarily Protestants.

Spirit Possession and Psychology

Questionnaire Question II.F on spirit possession

If all the students in a high school class lost normal consciousness and did not know who they were, how should such an event be interpreted and faced?

1. This is possession by an evil spirit, which should be exorcised by a religious leader.

2. This is mass hysteria, and a doctor of psychology should be called.

3. This is spiritual possession, which can be controlled by a shaman or paranormal.

The religious answer (#1, evil spirit possession) and the traditional answer (#3, spirit possession) equally indicate belief in spirit possession. The difference is in whether or not the spirit is labeled evil and whether a paranormal/shaman or a religious leader should handle it.

1. The majority of Indonesians chose #2, indicating that they think mass possession of children by spirits is a purely psychological phenomenon. This would indicate that disenchantment regarding spirit possession is a general phenomenon in Indonesia.

The null hypothesis is not supported by the statistics. Sixty-five percent of Indonesians chose one of the two answers, which indicates that they believe spirit possession is real. Just 35 percent indicated that they think mass possession of children is a psychological phenomenon. A majority of all religious groups in Indonesia indicated that they regard human possession by spirits as real.

2. The choice of #2 implies that respondents do not believe in an unseen world of spiritual beings or forces that are capable of possessing humans or affecting human beings in other ways. This null hypothesis assumes the converse, which requires further investigation.

An interesting anomaly in the statistics is that of those who said they have frequent experiences of the presence of spirits and unseen beings (Question II.D, traditional answer), 25 percent chose the modern psychological answer to the question about spirit possession (II.F). This indicates that even for those who have frequent communication with the unseen world, a significant number have doubts about the mass spiritual possession of children. The second null hypothesis is incorrect. Even though 35 percent of Indonesians chose the modern psychological explanation for mass spirit possession, it does not mean that they do not believe in spirits or the possession of individuals by spirits.

3. As a result of Islamic modernism, a higher percentage of Muslims will choose #2 than non-Muslims will.

This null hypothesis is proved wrong. Just 34 percent of Muslims chose the psychological explanation for spirit possession compared to 49 percent of Catholics and 42 percent of Protestants. Only Hindus, at 26 percent, were lower than Muslims for the modern scientific explanation. However, Muslims were lower than the overall choice of the modern psychological explanation (35 percent). There is no statistical evidence that Islamic modernism causes more Muslims than non-Muslims to choose a "disenchanted" perspective on spirit possession. By this evidence, the null hypothesis is not supported.

4. The correlation between Islam and choice of psychological language is greater than the correlation between ethnicity and this choice (#2). As with the other cases, we will test this null hypothesis by comparing Javanese and Moluccans and by comparing five majority Muslim ethnic groups.

The results of the first test suggest that the null hypothesis is incorrect, but the results are complicated. There is a significant difference between Javanese and Moluccan responses to the question about spirit possession. Forty percent of Javanese Muslims chose the modern psychological language compared to 69 percent of Javanese non-Muslims, demonstrating that religion is a very significant factor influencing the preferred language chosen by Javanese. However, Islamic modernism is not the cause because the figure for non-Muslims is much higher than for Muslims. For Moluccans religion is much less of a factor. Thirty-three percent of Muslims and 34 percent of non-Muslims in the Moluccas chose modern psychological language.

Sixty percent of Javanese Muslims indicated that they believe in spirit possession by choosing religious (22 percent) or traditional language (38 percent). Only 31 percent of Javanese non-Muslims indicated that they believe in mass spirit possession of children by choosing religious (13 percent) or traditional (18 percent) language. A full 67 percent of Moluccan Muslims indicated belief in spirit possession by choosing religious (34 percent) or traditional (33 percent) language. Moluccan non-Muslims showed an almost identical belief in possession. Fifty-three percent of them chose traditional and 13 percent chose religious language for a total of 66 percent who expressed belief in possession.

What stands out in these statistics is the big difference between Javanese Muslims and non-Muslims, whereas Moluccan Muslims and non-Muslims believe in possession equally. A substantial majority (60 percent) of Javanese Muslims believe, whereas almost 70 percent of Javanese non-Muslims say they are skeptics, at least about the mass possession of schoolchildren. Clearly Islamic modernism is not a significant factor in beliefs about spirit possession in Java. Javanese non-Muslims are almost twice as disenchanted regarding spirit possession as Muslims are.

Both Moluccan Muslims (67 percent) and non-Muslims (66 percent) believe in spirit possession at a higher percentage than the Javanese Muslims do. The only difference is that the Moluccan non-Muslims strongly prefer traditional language, which does not label the spirits as evil, whereas the Muslims are equally divided between traditional and religious language.

How do we account for the big difference in belief between non-Muslims in Java (only 31 percent) and Molucca (66 percent)? Most Javanese non-Muslims come from families that converted out of Islam during the past hundred years. Since 90 percent of Javanese are Muslims, those who left Islam took a radical step, which may have included rejecting the spirit beliefs of the Islamic majority. This is especially true of those who became Reformed Protestants. European Reformed Christianity is classically rationalist. The empirical results for Java might include a much higher rate of belief among non-Muslims if we had a higher proportion of Catholics and Charismatic Christians.

In contrast to the relatively recent age of the Javanese Church, the Moluccan Protestant Church was founded in 1605. Most Moluccan non-Muslims are from families that never converted from Islam and share many Moluccan *adat* traditions with their Muslim neighbors. Similarities between Muslims and Christians in the Moluccas led Frank Cooley to coin the term Ambonese Religion (Agama Ambon), which encompasses both Christians and Muslims (1966).

Javanese Muslim belief in spirit possession (60 percent) is lower than the national average for Muslims (66 percent), possibly due to the influence of Islamic modernism in Java. However, that could also be due to better access to modern education. In contrast, both Moluccan Muslims and non-Muslims believe in possession at a higher rate than the national average. In Java the distinction between shamans and religious leaders is not always clear. As we saw in the interview with Iqbal, Islamic leaders, especially leaders of Islamic boarding schools (*kyai*) in East Java, are often also paranormals or shamans. The same is true in the Moluccas. Islamic leaders are expected to be able to carry out healing and other magical duties, as well as leading prayers.

A comparison of Muslims from five Muslim majority ethnic groups reveals more commonalities than differences. A clear majority of Muslims in all these groups believe in spirit possession. All prefer traditional over religious language, albeit by different margins. In light of the possible Java bias of the question, it is interesting that Java and Sunda have the lowest percentage of people who believe in possession based on this question, that is, 60 percent. The highest percentage of belief is in Minang, where 72 percent of respondents said they believe in possession. Not far behind was Aceh, with 68 percent, and Makassar with 67 percent.

Minang and Makassar both strongly preferred traditional over religious language (Minang, 51 to 21 percent; Makassar, 49 to 18 percent). This indicates that a large majority do not view possession as a necessarily bad thing since the spirits are not labeled evil. It may also indicate a larger role in those societies for paranormals or shamans. The other three groups also preferred traditional over religious language by significant margins: Aceh, 41 to 27 percent; Java, 38 to 22 percent; and Sunda, 36 to 24 percent.

Java and Sunda both had 40 percent of respondents who chose a psychological explanation for spirit possession, thereby suggesting that geography is as important as ethnicity. The Sunda and Java ethnic groups are both on the island of Java but speak different languages and have different customs. However, both have access to better educational resources on Java than are available outside it. Java is also the center of the Muhammadiyah Islamic modernist movement.

The national average for Muslims who believe in possession is 66 percent. Java and Sunda are well below this average, whereas Minang, Aceh, and Makassar exceed the average. Therefore I conclude that the fourth null hypothesis is not supported by the second test. This confirms the first test and suggests that ethnicity is an important factor that influences belief in spirit possession, perhaps as much or more than religion.

Meaning in Sickness or Accidents and Natural Causation

Questionnaire Question II.G on the meaning of accidents or illness

If you experienced a serious accident or unusual illness, what might it mean?

1. Accidents and sickness don't have any particular meaning. They happen by accident and just mean you are unlucky.

2. It may mean that I am under attack by an evil spirit or spiritual power.

3. Perhaps the suffering is God's way of speaking to me and reminding me.

1. The majority of Indonesians will choose #1, indicating that they do not believe there is any particular meaning in sickness or accidents.

The first null hypothesis is proved wrong. Only 5 percent of Indonesians said they thought that serious accidents or illness have no meaning other than chance. The overwhelming favorite answer for this question was the religious answer. Eighty-one percent of Indonesians indicated that God speaks to them through accidents or illness. Only 14 percent thought it might be because they are under attack by a spiritual being. Thus 95 percent of Indonesians believe there is a supernatural meaning associated with serious sickness or accidents. Not all of those who said that God speaks to them through sickness or accidents believe that God causes the illness or accidents.

2. The choice of #1 indicates that those who choose this answer do not believe that illness is ever the result of chance or a spiritual attack. This null hypothesis assumes the converse and requires further investigation.

Even though the religious answer is dominant, what people mean by it is quite varied. For example, some believe that nothing happens by chance. As we saw in the interview with Syamsiyatun, she believes that God orders everything that happens to us. Nothing happens by chance. Although Atun's first response was to say that God speaks to her through suffering, she also believes that some illnesses or accidents are caused by satanic or spiritual attack.

This argument is confirmed by the statistics of the relatively small percentage who chose the modern answer of natural causation for illness or accidents. Of this group of only 5 percent of respondents, many chose religious or traditional answers for other questions that relate to the unseen world. This includes 57 percent who said they frequently or occasionally sense the presence of unseen powers, 36 percent who experience communication through dreams, 50 percent who believe in spirit possession, 58 percent who think there is meaning in natural disasters, and 27 percent who think God or unseen beings affect the possession of power. These statistics and examples demonstrate that the second null hypothesis is false. We should not assume the converse in relation to this question.

3. As a result of Islamic modernism, a higher percentage of Muslims will choose #1 (modern) or #3 (religious) than non-Muslims in their interpretation of sickness or accidents.

This null hypothesis is incorrect. Islam does not correlate with a higher percentage of those who chose modern or religious language to describe their experience of suffering due to illness or accidents. Ninety-five percent of Muslims and 96 percent of non-Muslims chose #1 (modern) or #3 (religious). Muslims had the highest percentage of religious answers (85 percent), indicating that they believe God speaks to them through phenomena such as serious illness or accidents. This compares with 81 percent for Protestants, 70 percent for Catholics, and 72 percent for Hindus. Of these four groups, the language choices of the Muslims and Protestants are closest to each other, whereas the Catholics and Hindus are more similar in their statistics. This may be because Muslims and Protestants are both influenced by religious modernism and both are more individuated religions. In both Islam and Protestant Christianity, there is a strong desire to have a personal experience of God. In contrast, Catholic Christianity and Hinduism have a greater emphasis on communal cosmic rituals in which a priest mediates for the entire community.

Protestants had the lowest percentage (3 percent) who believe that their suffering might be caused by a spiritual attack (compared to 5 percent for Muslims, 6 percent for Catholics, and 7 percent for Hindus). However, the very low Protestant percentage might have been higher if respondents had included more Pentecostals or Charismatic Christians. On the other hand, as we saw with the previous null hypothesis, the religious response to this question is probably the default choice of most religious people and does not rule out the likelihood that they also believe in both natural causation and spiritual attack.

4. The correlation between Islam and the choice of #1 or #3 is greater than the correlation between ethnicity and the choice of #1 or #3.

For the first test, the statistics comparing Javanese and Moluccans confirms the trend we have seen with other questions. There is a significant difference based on ethnicity, indicating that the null hypothesis is incorrect. Only 3 percent of Javanese Muslims chose traditional language, indicating that they believe sickness or accidents may be caused by a spiritual attack by unseen beings, whereas 16 percent of Moluccan Muslims chose traditional language. Ninety-seven percent of Javanese Muslims chose religious (89 percent) or modern (8 percent) language. In comparison, 84 percent of Moluccan Muslims chose religious (73 percent) or modern (11 percent) language.

Remarkably, none of the Javanese non-Muslims chose the traditional language of spiritual attack compared to 4 percent of Moluccan non-Muslims. The Javanese non-Muslims were the most "secular" of the ethnoreligious groups on this question. Twenty-six percent indicated that they thought accidents and sickness are purely the result of chance or natural causes. This compares with 8 percent of Javanese Muslims and 11 percent of both Moluccan Muslims and non-Muslims. The difference between Moluccan Muslims (16 percent) and non-Muslims (4 percent) was significant regarding belief in physical attack by unseen beings; however, they were identical in the percentage who saw illness as only the result of natural causes (11 percent).

More Javanese Muslims (89 percent) than non-Muslims (74 percent) chose religious language about God speaking through suffering. However, this comparison was reversed in the Moluccas. More Moluccan non-Muslims preferred religious language (85 percent) than Moluccan Muslims did (73 percent).

The second test comparing Muslims in five different ethnic groups shows a remarkable convergence for four of the five groups. Java, Sunda, Makassar, and Minang produced very similar statistics. Not all of them favored the traditional language of attack by spirits: Java 3 percent, Sunda 1, Makassar 3, and Minang 4. A few more chose the modern language of natural causes, but the percentages are still low: Java 8 percent, Sunda 11, Makassar 7, and Minang 7. They all much preferred the religious language indicating that God is involved in sickness and accidents: Java 89 percent, Sunda 88, Makassar 90, and Minang 89. As a result, all four had strong religious modernist scores for choosing either modern or religious language: Java 97 percent, Sunda 99, Makassar 97, and Minang 96. These figures suggest that for these four groups ethnicity is not as strong a factor as religion in the interpretation of sickness and accidents.

The one exception to this unanimity was Aceh. Eleven percent of Acehnese chose the traditional language of spirits (compared to 1 percent of Sundanese), and 21 percent of Acehnese chose the modern language of natural causation (compared to 7 percent of those from Makassar and Minang). Just 68 percent of Acehnese chose religious language (compared to 88 to 90 percent of the others). The Acehnese exception, in combination with the first test, which shows significant differences between Javanese and Moluccans, leads to the conclusion that the null hypothesis is not supported by the statistics. For some groups, ethnicity is a significant factor in respondents' views of illness and accidents.

APPENDIX IV

Ethnic Variations in Muslim Views of Religion and Power

The Basis of Law

Questionnaire Question III.E on the basis of law

Which of the following is the most important basis of law?

1. Tradition, *adat*, the will of the ancestors, loyalty to my ethnic community.

2. Reason, science, discussion and consensus, equality before the law.

3. The Scriptures (Koran, Bible, etc.), religious teachings, God's commandments.

Questionnaire Question II.B on obedience to law

To which system of law are you most obedient?

1. National law.

2. Traditional (adat) law, the law of my ethnic or tribal group.

3. Religious law.

Table IV.1 presents statistics for Muslims from six different ethnic/ geographic groupings. I wanted to see if ethnicity and geography made any difference in their imagination of the basis of law and obedience to it. Java, Sunda, Makassar, and Minang Muslims show very similar views of the basis of law, with only 2 to 4 percent choosing the traditional language and 78 to 82 percent basing law on divine revelation. Just 14 to 18 percent indicated that reason, discussion, and consensus should be the basis of law. Moluccan Muslims and Acehnese are a little different. Nine percent of the Moluccans chose *adat* law, and 31 percent preferred reason and consensus as the foundation of law. That is more than any other Muslim group and even more than the Protestants. The majority still favored religious language (60 percent), but that was lower than any other Muslim group. As usual, Acehnese favored traditional language (17 percent), more than any other Muslim group, but their preference for religious language was strong (68 percent) even though it was less than the national

Table IV.1 *Responses to Questions III.E on the Basis of Law
and II.B on Obedience to Law*

Groups	Traditional Law		Modern Law		Religious Law	
	III.E Basis	II.B Obedience	III.E Basis	II.B Obedience	III.E Basis	II.B Obedience
Islamic	6%	6%	18%	31%	76%	63%
Protestant	8%	6%	29%	45%	63%	49%
Catholic	25%	22%	43%	49%	32%	29%
Hindu	27%	19%	44%	62%	29%	19%
All Indonesians	10%	9%	26%	39%	64%	52%
Java Muslims	4%	4%	14%	34%	82%	62%
Sunda Muslims	3%	4%	18%	35%	79%	61%
Makassar Muslims	2%	5%	18%	34%	80%	61%
Moluccas Muslims	9%	15%	31%	32%	60%	53%
Minang Muslims	5%	6%	17%	26%	78%	68%
Aceh Muslims	17%	8%	15%	27%	68%	65%
Dyak Hindus	29%	19%	42%	62%	29%	19%

average for Muslims (76 percent). Only 15 percent thought reason and consensus should be the basis of law.

The last line of table IV.1 shows the results from Dyak, Hindu Kaharingan, from Central Kalimantan, as a comparison with Muslim ethnic groups. I expected the Dyaks to be the most traditional of all the groups. Although more Hindu Dyaks (29 percent) chose *adat* as the basis of law, modern language was their primary choice (42 percent). In that they resembled Hindus generally, as well as Catholics. Their state-influenced construction of Kaharingan as a Hindu religion led 29 percent to choose Scripture as their description of choice for the basis of law.[1]

Government Regulation of Religion

Questionnaire Question IV.B on government regulation of religion

How should government manage religious diversity?

1. The government should support the six religions recognized by the state and suppress groups that are teaching or practicing beliefs that are heretical.

2. The government should protect the fundamental human right to freedom of worship for every group without considering its teachings as long as it doesn't break the law.

3. The government should maintain harmony. If there is conflict, the government should play the role of finding a solution that can be accepted by all sides in the dispute.

Table IV.2 compares statistics for religious groups from nine ethnic communities. Moluccan and Minang Muslims differ somewhat from the figures for all Indonesian Muslims. A relatively higher percentage of Moluccan Muslims (27 percent) chose the religious response, and relatively few chose the modern response (33 percent). Forty percent of Moluccan Muslims chose the traditional response that the government should maintain harmony and mediate conflict. The Moluccas (Molucca and North Molucca provinces) are relatively evenly divided between Muslims and Christians and have a recent history of violent conflict. This insecurity

Table IV.2 *Responses to Question IV.B on Government Regulation of Religion*

Groups	Traditional Maintain Harmony Mediate Conflict	Modern Protect Religious Freedom and Rights	Religious Support Six Religions and Suppress Heresy
Islamic	34%	49%	17%
Protestant	33%	57%	10%
Catholic	39%	50%	11%
Hindu	44%	47%	9%
All Indonesians	34%	52%	14%
Java Muslims	36%	48%	16%
Java Protestants	35%	58%	7%
Molucca Muslims	40%	33%	27%
Molucca Protestants	47%	45%	8%
Minang Muslims	33%	56%	11%
Aceh Muslims	40%	40%	20%
Manado Protestants	31%	65%	4%
NTT Protestants	31%	66%	3%
Papuan Protestants	32%	48%	20%
Flores Catholics	38%	50%	12%
Bali Hindus	45%	45%	10%

encourages a desire for the government to mediate conflict and actively support the mainstream groups. In contrast, very few Moluccan Protestants (8 percent) thought the main role of government was to support the mainstream and suppress heresy. Most Moluccan Protestants thought the government should concentrate on mediating conflict (47 percent) or protecting human rights (45 percent).

Minang Muslims had a high percentage (56 percent) who chose the modern human rights answer. Relatively few (11 percent) chose the religious response of suppressing heresy. This reflects the reality that West Sumatra and Minang Muslims are a strong and confident majority in their own areas. They face little competition from nonmainstream or non-Muslim groups.

Manado/Minahasa (North Sulawesi) and NTT (East Southeastern Islands) Protestants are virtually identical.[2] They have a very low percentage (3–4 percent) who chose the religious response. Surprisingly, 20 percent of Papuan Protestants chose the religious answer. This may reflect Papuan Christians feeling threatened by the Muslim majority in Indonesia and hoping that the government will protect and support Christians in Papua. Most Christians in all ethnic groups chose the modern human rights perspective on the role of government in regulating religions.

Ideals for the Nation-State of Indonesia

Questionnaire Question III.D on Ideals for the nation-state of indonesia

Which of the following ideal characteristics do you most hope will be realized in the nation-state of Indonesia?

1. God's people, who are good, orderly, obedient to God, and religious.[3]

2. A just democracy, where all citizens are equal and the human rights of all members are protected.

3. A harmonious family that honors our elders is wholehearted and safe.[4]

In table IV.3, we compare different religious communities in six ethnic groups. In the case of Java, Bali, and NTT, there is a strong majority-minority element. Java is 90 percent Muslim, Bali is 84 percent Hindu, and NTT is 90 percent Christian.[5] However, among Dyaks (Kalimantan), Bataks (North Sumatra), and Moluccans (North Moluccas and Moluccas) the communities are more evenly balanced between the religious communities. I wondered if being a minority in an area dominated by another religious community would affect the statistical results of their preferred answers.

In the case of Java, it appears that the non-Muslim minority has a significantly higher preference for the modern democratic response than the religious answer in comparison with the Muslim majority. This reflects the reality that non-Muslims are aware that the ideal of a society based on religion will be dominated by Muslims in Java. However, Javanese Muslims and non-Muslims both still prefer the modern, democratic imagination of a good society.

Table IV.3 *Responses to Question III.D on Ideals for the Nation State of Indonesia*

Groups	Traditional Harmonious Family Honors Elders *Ikhlas* and Safe	Modern Democratic Community Justice, Equality, Human Rights	Religious God's People Good, Orderly, Obedient to God
Islamic	10%	53%	37%
Protestant	8%	56%	36%
Catholic	7%	78%	15%
Hindu	9%	68%	23%
All Indonesians	9%	57%	34%
Java Muslims	9%	55%	36%
Java Catholics	13%	87%	0%
Java Protestants	7%	76%	17%
Bali Hindus	7%	69%	24%
Bali Protestants	5%	60%	35%
NTT Catholics	7%	77%	16%
NTT Protestants	0%	74%	26%
NTT Hindus	19%	52%	29%
Dyak Hindus	12%	69%	19%
Dyak Muslims	9%	73%	18%
Dyak Protestants	0%	75%	25%
Batak Protestants	10%	72%	18%
Batak Muslims	14%	72%	14%
Molucca Muslims	9%	49%	42%
Molucca Protestants	8%	47%	45%

In the case of Bali, the responses from Hindus and non-Hindus are very similar. In fact the non-Hindus have an even greater preference for the religious answer than their Hindu neighbors do. This reflects the reality that non-Hindus are less threatened by the hegemony of Hindus in Bali. While they sometimes face discrimination, they are anxious to accommodate the Hindu majority and emphasize their cultural commonality with Balinese Hindus.[6]

In NTT, as might be suspected, the Hindu minority has a higher regard for the traditional imagination of society and also a higher preference for a religious understanding of a good society.[7] Although a majority (52 percent) also preferred the language of a just democratic society, the fact that 48 percent chose traditional or religious social imaginaries, in comparison with just 23 percent for Catholics and 26 percent for Protestants, indicates that the Hindus have not assimilated to the dominant Christian majority in NTT. The Christian majority strongly prefers democratic language (77 and 74 percent in comparison with the Hindu minority at 52 percent). Democracy is more attractive if you feel you are part of the majority.

In contrast to NTT, Dyak Hindus, Muslims, and Protestants have very similar statistics for their choice between the three answers. Since they are more evenly balanced, at least in the cities of Kalimantan, this may reflect their primary desire to assimilate with each other. They all show a high preference for modern democratic language (69, 73, and 75 percent).

Batak Christians and Muslims have almost identical statistics. This reflects not only their numerical balance but also the strong cultural ties between Batak Christians and Muslims. Bataks are more likely to fight with members of their own religious community than they are to fight with members of an opposing one. Even though Bataks have a reputation for being pugnacious and stubborn, during the transition period after the fall of Soeharto, when ethnic and religious conflicts broke out all over Indonesia (1998–2002), there were no significant conflicts between Batak Christians and Muslims. This is a reflection of their cultural solidarity. My Batak students tell me that being Batak is more important to their identity than their religious affiliation. Bataks were also well aware that if there were Christian-Muslim conflicts in North Sumatra it would be disastrous for both sides. Seventy-two percent of both Batak Protestants and Muslims chose a modern democratic structure as their ideal society.

Moluccan Muslims and Protestants were also virtually identical in their choices of social imaginaries. Like other groups, they were not much attracted by the traditional language (9 and 8 percent). However, unlike other groups, they were almost evenly divided between modern democratic and religious imaginations of an ideal society. Forty-nine percent of Moluccan Muslims and 47 percent of Moluccan Protestants chose the democratic symbol systems of an ideal society. Forty-two percent of Moluccan Muslims and 45 percent of Moluccan Christians chose religious symbols. This reflects the highly religious character of both communities. It also suggests that cultural commonalities may be more influential than religious differences in their choices. Both religious communities are closer to each other than they are to the national average for their respective religions.

In chapter 7 we analyzed the answers to a very similar question on our questionnaire:

Which of the following societies is most noble ("paling mulia")?

1. A society that obeys the commands of God and implements religious requirements.[8]

2. A society that uses science, reason, and common sense to solve life's problems.

3. A society that maintains harmony, honors the ancestors, and follows tradition.

The statistical responses to this quite similar question were significantly different. The percentage of Indonesians choosing the traditional answer was similar for both questions (9 and 11 percent). However, there was a large difference in the percentages of those who chose the modern response emphasizing reason and science (17 percent) and those who chose the modern symbol system emphasizing a just democracy, equality, and human rights (57 percent). This implies that there was also a large difference between those who chose the religious response that emphasizes obeying God and implementing (*mengamalkan*) religious requirements (72 percent) and those who chose the religious response that emphasizes being good, orderly, and religious (34 percent). What accounts for this large difference in response to similar questions, one of which is about a more noble society and the other about the ideal characteristics of the nation state of Indonesia?

The answer is located in the different language used in the three responses. While the statistics for those who chose the traditional response to each of these questions are almost the same, I expected the response that mentions honoring elders, safety, and *ikhlas* (giving up your ego) (9 percent) to be more popular than the response that mentions harmony, respecting ancestors, and *adat* (11 percent). In fact the latter is slightly more popular. Evidently language that mentions honoring ancestors and *adat* is not less strong than language that mentions elders and safety.

The large difference between the statistics of those who chose the modern answer mentioning reason, science, and common sense (17 percent) and those who chose the modern answer mentioning democracy, justice, equality, and human rights (57 percent) is more clear. It's not that Indonesians reject reason, science, and common sense but rather that these words are much weaker symbols of a good society compared to *justice, democracy, equality*, and *human rights*. Reason, science and common sense, are less cogent to those who live in a sacred cosmos.

A similar observation holds true about the large statistical difference between those who chose the religious response of obeying God and implementing religious requirements (72 percent) and those who chose the religious response that emphasized being good, orderly, and religious (34 percent). Virtually all Indonesians are religious, most are orderly, and many are good. But not so many implement religious requirements in their daily lives. The language of *mengamalkan* (implement in practice) is much stronger than the language of *beragama* (be religious). Many people from all religious groups wish that their highly religious society would better incarnate in social life the noble teachings of their religions.

A comparison of the differences in the responses to these two questions reinforces the thesis that Indonesians cannot be classified into discrete groups as traditional, modern, or religious. They are all three, and they use each of the

Table IV.4 *Comparing Language*

Which Society Is More Noble?	Traditional Harmony, Respect Ancestors, *Adat*	Modern Reason, Science, Common Sense	Religious Obey God, Implement Religious Requirements
All Indonesians	11%	17%	72%

Ideal Characteristics of the Nation-State of Indonesia	Traditional Harmonious Family Honors Elders *Ikhlas* and Safe	Modern Democracy, Justice, Equality, Human Rights	Religious Good, Orderly, Obedient to God Religious
All Indonesians	9%	57%	34%

different symbol systems of these types in different contexts, with subtle differences of symbolic language, for different purposes.

APPENDIX V

Indonesian Muslim Views of Nature and Ethnic Variations

Chapter 10 discussed Indonesian attitudes to nature by religion. The following takes the analysis further by considering the influence of ethnicity on views of nature.

Relation to Nature

Questionnaire Question III.G on relation to nature

What should the relationship between Indonesian people and nature or the environment be?

1. Honor the earth of our ancestors. We are an indivisible part of the natural world.

2. As God's representatives on earth, the people should protect and preserve nature.

3. We should use science to build a sustainable economy that is gentle on the environment.

Table 10.1 suggests that in some parts of Indonesia religion is the dominant influence on the imagination of nature. But in other parts ethnicity seems to be more significant than religion. For example, 72 percent of Javanese Muslims chose religious or scientific language to describe their relation to nature. In contrast, only 36 percent of Javanese non-Muslims chose religious or scientific answers to the question. Sixty-four percent of Javanese non-Muslims expressed themselves using traditional language about honoring the earth of our ancestors and being one with nature.

In the Moluccas, the results were quite different. Seventy-four percent of Muslims and 75 percent of non-Muslims chose religious or scientific language. Just 26 percent of Muslims and 25 percent of non-Muslims selected cosmos-centered language. This remarkable similarity between religious groups in the Moluccas suggests that ethnicity (being Moluccan), has a stronger impact on the people's attitude toward nature than differences in their religion. This cultural similarity is intensified by the fact that most of the non-Muslim Moluccans who filled out the questionnaire were Protestants. Moluccan Islam and

347

Table v.1 *Javanese and Moluccan Responses to Question III.G on Relation to Nature*

	Javanese Muslims	Javanese Non-Muslims	Moluccan Muslims	Moluccan Non-Muslims	Indonesian Muslims	Indonesian Non-Muslims
Traditional	28%	64%	26%	25%	26%	38%
Scientific	31%	11%	39%	14%	33%	22%
Religious	41%	25%	35%	61%	41%	40%
Religious or Scientific	72%	36%	74%	75%	74%	62%

Moluccan Protestantism inculcate remarkably similar views of our relation to nature.[1] A difference between the two groups is that the non-Muslims strongly preferred religious language (61 percent), while the Muslims showed a small preference for scientific language.

If we compare Muslim ethnic groups, for those who used scientific or religious language to talk about their relation to nature, Java's 72 percent compares with Makassar's 79 percent, Sunda's 83, Minang's 71, and Aceh's 65.

The only real surprise here is the relatively low percentage for the Acehnese. What accounts for the large gap between the Acehnese (65 percent) and the Sundanese (83 percent)? Both ethnic groups have a reputation for deep commitment to Islam and relative intolerance toward non-Muslim groups. Aceh is the only province in Indonesia with permission to enact and enforce Islamic law (Sharia). The reason for Aceh's relatively low percentage for those who use religious or modern language about our relation to nature suggests that Acehnese have complex imaginations of nature, perhaps related to their deep trauma following the earthquake and tsunami. Honoring the earth of their ancestors and affirming their oneness with nature may be an important part of their existential experience of life. Their practice of Islam is integrated with their commitment to Acehnese *adat* (see Bowen 2003).

Thirty-five percent of Acehnese chose the cosmos-centered language, whereas only 26 percent chose theocentric language and 39 percent chose anthropocentric modern language. Even though the largest group chose scientific language, I suspect that Islamic modernism is not the dominant factor in Acehnese imaginations of nature. In fact the relatively few who chose religious language may indicate a reaction among some Acehnese to the implementation of Shari'ah.

Table v.2 *Muslim Responses to Question III.G on Relation to Nature, by Ethnic Group*

Ethnic Groups	Traditional	Modern	Religious	Modern/Religious
Java/Madura	28%	31%	41%	72%
Sunda	17%	41%	42%	83%
Makassar/Bugis	20%	29%	51%	80%
Minang/West Sumatra	25%	29%	46%	75%
Aceh	35%	39%	26%	65%
All Indonesian Muslims	26%	33%	41%	74%
All Indonesian Non-Muslims	38%	22%	40%	62%
All Indonesians	32%	28%	40%	68%

Based on this research, it appears that ethnicity is a strong factor in views of nature in Aceh and the Moluccas, while religious difference is more influential in Java, Sunda, Makassar, and Minang. However, of these four, Java and Minang had significantly higher percentages of people choosing the traditional answer than for those from Sunda and Makassar. Ethnicity is an independent variable that influences all ethnic groups of Indonesians. But religion still shows the strongest correlation for most Indonesian Muslims in their choice of a preferred set of symbols with which to describe their relationship with nature.

Notes

Introduction

1 One writer accused virtually all Australian and American anthropology on Indonesia of orientalism, yet his own work only included one reference to an Indonesian thinker in the index. Ironically this Indonesian was a westernized, postmodern scholar who lived in Australia. See Elson 2008.

2 Many scholars overcome this difficulty by only writing about Java, Bali, or some other defined unit. Java itself contains more than half the population of Indonesia and can be crudely divided into Jakarta, Sunda (West Java), Central Java/Yogyakarta, East Java, and Madura.

3 The World Values Survey suggests that there is a direct correlation between education, income, and more conservative religious views in Indonesia. The lower the education and income, the more conservative the views. See van Klinken 2014. The World Values Survey takes periodic random samples in many countries. In 2001 and 2006 it took random samples of 1,000 respondents in Indonesia. See http://www.worldvaluessurvey.org.

1

Whither Islam? Whose Islam? Which Muslims?

1 I follow Marshall Hodgson (1974) in distinguishing between *Islamic* and *Islamicate*. To say that a civilization is Islamic implies a normative, religious claim that it conforms to the teachings of the Koran and Sunnah. In contrast, an Islamicate civilization is any civilization produced by Muslims or within cultures where Muslims are in the majority. There is no sharp dichotomy between Islamic and Islamicate since some Muslims consider elements of their Islamicate culture to be Islamic and vice versa. There is room for differences of interpretation.

However the distinction is important because it disavows making a normative, religious claim when using the term Islamicate.

2 This was a comment made by a librarian at Boston University who helped me check out a large number of books on Indonesia.

3 http://www.pewforum.org/2011/01/27/table-muslim-population-by-country/. accessed February 4, 2016,

4 An example of this bias is in the quote "Looking at the Middle East and its borderlands, it is difficult to find an exemplar of Islamic democracy. Indonesia, Malaysia and Bangladesh are all majority Muslim democracies, but their interactions with Middle Eastern states are too slight to qualify them as exemplars." *Washington Post*, June 2, 2015, accessed February 4, 2016, https://www. washingtonpost.com/blogs/monkey-cage/wp/2015/06/02/what-history-says-about-the-prospects-for-islamic-democracy. See also Owen 2014. Owen looks on Indonesia as just a borderland of the Islamic center.

5 For example, consider Donald Trump's proposal to ban Muslims from entering the United States.

6 The existence of national legal institutions guaranteeing human rights does not mean that there is no oppression of minority groups or women, especially as religious, traditional, and local laws sometimes are in tension with national laws. See especially chapters 11 and 12 of this volume.

7 In comparison, the United States had only 80 percent literacy, and less than 20 percent of Americans could read at a college undergraduate level. See Index-mundi, accessed February 4 2016. http://www.indexmundi.com/facts/indonesia /literacy-rate.

8 See Geobase, accessed February 4, 2016. http://www.geoba.se/population .php?pc=world&type=015&page=2.

9 Pew Foundation, accessed June 1, 2018, http://www.pewresearch.org/fact-tank/ 2017/04/06/why-muslims-are-the-worlds-fastest-growing-religious-group/.

10 History.com, accessed 4 February 4, 2016, http://www.history.com/topics/thirty-years-war. The Thirty Years' war was waged primarily between Protestant and Catholic Christians and recalls the current antipathy between Sunni and Syi'a Muslims. See *Washington Post*,June 2, 2015, accessed February 4, 2016, https:// www.washingtonpost.com/blogs/monkey-cage/wp/2015/06/02/what-history-says-about-the-prospects-for-islamic-democracy/.

11 I imagine this was a higher approval rating of the United States than that of Americans. It was certainly much higher than the views of Europeans.

12 The term *crusade* means "war of the crucifix." In Indonesian it is translated as *perang salib*, literally "war of the crucifix."

13 Pew Foundation, accessed February 4, 2016, http://www.pewglobal.org/2010/ 03/18/indonesia-the-obama-effect/.

14 Mass violence, in some areas amounting to civil war, was finished by 2002. However there were a few isolated incidents until 2004. In 2004 Indonesia held her first, direct election of a President. Susilo Bambang Yudhoyono won by a

large margin, putting to rest doubts about the legitimacy of the central government.

15 Pew Foundation, accessed February 4, 2016, http://www.pewglobal.org/2010/03/18/indonesia-the-obama-effect/.

16 Asia Foundation, accessed April 13, 2017, https://asiafoundation.org/resources/pdfs/IndonesiaElections.pdf.

17 Pew Foundation, accessed February 6 2016, http://www.pewforum.org/2005/05/03/the-global-spread-of-wahhabi-islam-how-great-a-threat/.Almost certainly the number of Wahabi/Salafi followers in Indonesia is much larger now, in part because of abundant spending by Saudi Arabia to support its understanding of Islam in Indonesia. See Kovacs 2014.

18 Membership numbers are uncertain, but NU is probably the largest religious organization in the world apart from the Catholic Church.

19 In 1965 there was a leftist coup attempt, and General Soeharto took control of the military, which presided over the wholesale massacre or imprisonment of people associated with the Communist Party. Many of the accused Communists were *abangan* Muslims. One way to escape suspicion of being a Communist was by displaying public religious piety. Many *abangan* Muslims converted to Christianity, Hinduism, Buddhism, or a more *santri* form of Islam.

20 The Padri Wars in West Sumatra, 1803–1837, were fought between Minangkabau aristocrats who defended the unique traditions of Minangkabau Islam and Arab-influenced Muslims who wanted to purify the Islamic community of all nonkoranic practices. The wars took place during the time of the mystic synthesis according to Ricklefs's periodization.

21 This story has also been attributed to Gandhi, but its historical accuracy is uncertain. If Zhou Enlai is the one who said it, he may have been referring to the French uprising of 1968 rather than the revolution of 1792. If so, he was being much more profound than he intended! See Dean Nichols, "Zhou Enlai's Famous Saying Debunked." History Today (blog), accessed March 17, 2018, http://www.historytoday.com/blog/news-blog/dean-nicholas/zhou-enlais-famous-saying-debunked.

22 The analysis of four axial civilizations does not exclude the possibility that similar cognitive breakthroughs may have occurred in other places as well, for example, in Egypt, Latin America, Africa, and so on. China, India, the Middle East, and Greece have the advantage of having left us ancient manuscripts that we can decipher.

23 The modern entertainment industry has taken ritual and myth creation to stunning levels of technological sophistication and, just occasionally, to the level of high art.

24 See Andrew Curry, "Gobekli Tepe: The World's First Temple?": *Smithsonian*, November 2008, accessed January 4, 2018, https://www.smithsonianmag.com/history/gobekli-tepe-the-worlds-first-temple-83613665/.

25 Monotheism, or belief in the Great Unity of Deity, is defined very loosely so as to encompass many religions that have some notion of a single transcendent

principle, even if they worship many gods (as in Hinduism) or no god (as in some forms of Buddhism).

26 An internet search for "Islam Yes, Politik Islam No" will produce a long list of Indonesian articles still debating Madjid's controversial slogan more than four decades after his original article appeared.

2

Social Imaginaries in Indonesia and the West

1 According to a recent survey, North Americans are more divided by differences of in political outlook than by religion. It is easier for an American to imagine marrying someone from a different religion than it is for a democratic liberal to imagine marrying a conservative Republican.

2 This roughly corresponds to Clifford Geertz's distinction between "symbol systems of" and "symbol systems for." See Geertz 1973.

3 "Intersubjective" contrasts with the dichotomy between objective and subjective. An intersubjective narrative is not based on individual subjectivity. It is held in common with many other subjects. It has an "objectivity" outside the subject. But neither is it objective in the sense of independence from human subjectivity. Rather it is a shared, intersubjective conception of the real. See Gadamer 1975.

4 Prior to his untimely death in July 2013, I had several long conversations with Robert Bellah about the nature of second naïveté. I wondered how it is possible to believe in something with a second naïveté that you do not believe with a first naïveté? I'm not sure if we ever reached full agreement. But he did convince me that first-order, unreflective faith in the unseen world is practically impossible for many modern westerners.

5 The comparative research on Charismatic Evangelicals in the USA, Ghana and India, is not yet published. Based on preliminary research Prof. Luhrmann expressed this difference between Americans, Africans and Asians in a private conversation on February 12, 2014 at Boston University.

6 Taylor lists four principle western social imaginaries. This list of fifteen elaborates on his conceptualization and adds some additional elements. See Taylor 2003, 2007.

7 This is not based simply on individualism over communalism. The foundation of society is imagined as a contract between individuals, but the goal of the social contract is communal (see Durkheim [1893] 1933).

8 Taylor writes, "Political society enables these individuals to serve each other for mutual benefit, both in providing security and in fostering exchange and prosperity" (2004:20).

9 The government is meant to protect the freedom of individuals to work together to further their own interests. Government may regulate and prevent abuses, but it is people, working together in a free marketplace, who are responsible for their own prosperity. There have always been exceptions to this moral imagination. Peter Maurin, the Catholic socialist who worked with Dorothy Day, argued that the proper goal of society was not to make people happy or prosperous but rather to make them good (Day 1952).

10 Society must protect each person's individual human rights and provide justice, otherwise they might withdraw their consent and cause the government to lack legitimacy. The consent of the governed is an ongoing necessity that implies that a particular segment of the nation has a right to withdraw if it feels it is no longer served by the state. This is what happened with the referendum in East Timor. After the fall of Soeharto, the Indonesian province of East Timor held a UN sponsored referendum to gain independence from Indonesia. In spite of violent intimidation sponsored by the Indonesian military, the people overwhelmingly voted for independence and formed a new nation-state: Timor Leste. East Timor was the only province in Indonesia that was never under Dutch control. It was a Catholic majority Portuguese colony, in contrast with West Timor, which has a Protestant majority and was under the Dutch until Indonesian independence in 1945. In recent years both Scotland and Quebec narrowly chose to remain part of their respective countries.

11 Discrimination on the basis of sexual preference is still hotly debated in some countries, especially the United States.

12 The theory of human biological evolution is embedded in the popular social imaginary of people all over the world and has spread into nonbiological fields of thought. Social evolution is a metaphor implying progressive change from lower, simpler forms to higher, more complex forms of human organization. Development and progress assume that changes should be in a positive direction. The dominant metaphor assumed by nineteenth-century social scientists like Marx, Weber, Durkheim, and Tönnies was of societies evolving from traditional to modern. Even with its dark side, progress was thought to be inevitable. Most social scientists have abandoned the typology of a transition from traditional to modern societies. However, the imagination of progress from traditional to modern life is still very influential. The social imaginary of progress and evolution is not always optimistic about the final outcome of evolution.

13 I deliberately constructed these fifteen types in contrast to the fifteen "western" types derived from Charles Taylor and others. The fifteen Indonesian types are not a description of how most Indonesians imagine reality. Rather they are constructed contrasts to the western types that illustrate alternative social imaginaries that I have often observed in Indonesia. For most of the fifteen types, I cite examples that illustrate how these imaginaries shape the perceptions of some Indonesians. For some of the types, I cite statistics based on my own empirical research. My hypothesis is that most Indonesians are shaped by some of these types. Most are also shaped by some of the western types. Very few imagine reality exclusively through the lens of either the "Indonesian" or "western" types.

14 The use of familial, hierarchical titles may be breaking down in urban areas. Recent research by Nancy Smith-Hefner (2007) on slang language used by young urban Indonesians suggests that such titles are no longer universal.

15 The law, passed under President Susilo Bambang Yudhoyono, is widely ignored, especially in places like Hindu majority Bali, Christian majority NTT (Nusa Tenggara Timur–Eastern Archipelego that includes the islands of Sumba, Flores and West Timor), and West Papua, where non-Muslims are also in the majority. The law provoked widespread opposition and went through radical revisions, which removed many of the provisions that were most objectionable to non-Muslims, progressive Muslims, and artists.

16 Of course this is not the perspective of minority groups that want to secede, such as some Papuans, Acehnese, and Moluccans.

17 For the text of the ruling, see the website of the Indonesian Constitutional Court http://www.mahkamahkonstitusi.go.id/index.php?page=website.Berita InternalLengkap&id=3941 (cited in Ricklefs 2012:448). Some of my Muslim colleagues were very disappointed at this ruling and in fact supplied expert testimony to the court in support of ruling that the Blasphemy Law was unconstitutional because it violates the constitutionally guaranteed right of freedom of religion. See Lindsay and Pausacker 2016 for a discussion of the tension between the Constitution and the Blasphemy law.

18 The figure was much higher for Muslims, 78 percent of whom thought law should be based on religion. But the overall figure was lower because only 32 percent of Catholics, 30 percent of Hindus, and 65 percent of Protestants agreed.

19 In Islam many Muslim bodies can issue fatwas, which are intended as authoritative rulings that will, in a sense, end a discussion. In Indonesia the Muslim body with the greatest influence on the government is the Majelis Ulama Indonesia (MUI). MUI is designed to represent all the major Muslim organizations in Indonesia. During the reign of President Soeharto it was widely seen as a rubber stamp organization for the President. Since his fall, it has gained increasing power and legitimacy. However it's fatwa's tend to the conservative side of Islam. Many Muslims prefer to listen to fatwas issued by NU or Muhammadiyah. Others ignore all the fatwas and just follow their own consciences.

20 I have exaggerated this contrast for effect. In reality many Muslims in all countries do not live in such an ordered and meaningful sacred cosmos. Muslim refugees, especially those fleeing war zones, may experience reality as chaotic, meaningless, violent, and arbitrary. In contrast, many people in western countries, including those who are not religious, experience human social life as closer to a sacred cosmos.

3

Cultures, Religions, and Modernities in Indonesia

1 See Sample, Ian "Flores Fossil Discovery Provides Clues to 'Hobbit' Ancestors" *The Guardian*, June 8, 2016, accessed June 8, 2016 https://www.theguardian.com/science/2016/jun/08/flores-fossil-discovery-provides-clues-to-hobbit-ancestors.

2 See Moore and Brumm 2007.

3 This dominant narrative about the peaceful spread of Islam is frequently repeated by Muslims in Indonesia. However, the spread of Islam was not free of force and violence, as evidenced by the flight of most Hindus to mountainous areas of Java and to Bali and the destruction of hundreds of Hindu and Buddhist temples. There is, however, no evidence that Islam spread through the invasion of foreign Islamic armies. Rather, as Islamic forces spread and established sultanates, they struggled for power, both with each other and with remaining Hindu and Buddhist centers of power (Ricklefs 2008; Reid 2000).

4 According to Bellah's theory of axial civilizations, the Hebrew prophets in the eighth to sixth centuries BCE epitomized the birth of theoretic thought based on ethical monotheism. The axial age preceded the birth of both Christianity and Islam. The phrase "Abrahamic prophetic religion" is intended to imply the continuity between the early Hebrew prophets, Jesus, and Muhammad, all of whom carried on the tradition of ethical prophetic monotheism.

5 Gus Dur said, "I am actually, genuinely Chinese, but yes, mixed with Arab and Indian. My ancestors were originally Chinese." (*Saya ini China tulen sebenarnya, tapi ya sudah nyampurlah dengan Arab dan India. Nenek moyang saya orang Tionghoa asli*). See "Saat Gus Dur Mengaku Keturunan Tionghoa Tulen" in *Merdeka*, accessed March 14, 2016, http://www.merdeka.com/peristiwa/saat-gus-dur-mengaku-keturunan-tionghoa-tulen.html.

6 China was not unique in holding these views. Many civilizations have considered themselves the center of the world, including those of Sultan Hamengkubuono (the protector of the earth) and the Paku Alam (the "nail of nature" or center of the cosmos). China was unique in uniting so many peoples and so much land under one authority.

7 "The History of Spices," McCormick Science Institute, accessed May 5, 2016, http://www.mccormicksҫienceinstitute.com/resources/history-of-spices.

8 The manuscript may have drawn from oral traditions that are much older than the late nineteenth century. Although the story cannot be traced to any particular Javanese or Malay sources, it contains many elements similar to the stories about Sunan Giri told in Java.

9 Garin Nugroho, whose films have been shown at the Cannes Film Festival, was commissioned to produce this work in celebration of the 250th anniversary of the birth of Mozart.

10 See, "Sejarah Musik Keroncong di Indonesia" Trioindra website, accessed 7-5-2016, https://trioindra.wordpress.com/tag/sejarah-musik-keroncong-di-indonesia/.

11 Even though there are ethnic Indian and Chinese Indonesians, the cultural influence of these civilizations is much deeper than the relatively small number of "pure" Indians or Chinese.

12 In western discourse, it is common to group Judaism and Christianity together, with Greco-Roman civilization as the foundation of western modernity and fundamentally different from Islam. To change the framing, I categorize Judeo-Christian-Islamic as Semitic or Middle Eastern civilization (in origin), in contrast to Greco-Roman (European) civilization. There is no one "correct" way to categorize civilizations. Different ways of categorizing allow us to see different things.

13 During the holy month of Ramadan, Muslims are required to fast from the end of darkness (usually before 4:00 AM) until sunset (around 6:00 PM). Fasting includes not drinking anything (including water), not eating anything, not smoking, not making love, controlling your emotions, and not sinning. Since many Javanese males smoke, the first thing many of them do at the end of the fast is light up a clove cigarette.

14 The five principles of Pancasila have the same status in the Indonesian nation-state as the Bill of Rights has in the United States. They bind the diverse regions of Indonesia together in common agreement. One reason why they are effective is because they are abstract enough to allow multiple interpretations of how they should guide public policy.

15 *Ketuhanan*, while also used by Muslims and Christians to refer to God, is more acceptable to Hindus, Buddhists and Confucianists, as it can be interpreted to mean that there is one transcendent power over all.

16 The ethical world of Islam is part of the same family as Christianity and Judaism. The Koran is peppered with stories taken from Jewish and Christian Scriptures, many of which include a moral element. The influence is not only one way. Arabic translations and commentaries on Greek texts (e.g., Aristotle's *Ethics*) strongly influenced the development of Christian ethical discourse in fourteenth- and fifteenth-century Europe.

17 Three years of Japanese occupation also had a profound influence on Indonesian conceptions of Asian modernity. See Mangunwijaya 1994.

18 I usually enjoy the call to prayer. It gives rhythm to the day and reminds one of the presence of the transcendent. When it is done well, in good Arabic, it is also beautiful, a true art form. However sometimes it can be disruptive, with a cacophony of competing, overamplified calls emanating from different mosques.

19 Charles Taylor suggests that powerful ideologies are not only theoretical constructs, but they also have the ability to construct a world that, to the extent that they are believed, shapes and changes social reality. See Taylor 1979.

20 Martha C. Nussbaum explores competing social imaginaries over the nature of Hinduism and Indian nationalism in *The Clash Within* (2007). She points out that some of the fiercest civilizational clashes occur within apparently unified civilizations.

21 See appendices I and II for English and Indonesian versions of the questionnaire.

4

Enchantment and a Sacred Cosmos

1 One of the mysteries of modernity is that this great disembedding no longer seems self-evident, even in modern western societies. "Reenchantment" or "desecularization" may be one of the surprising trends in modern western societies (Berger 1999). See chapter 5.

2 Stories reveal more than abstract analysis, but they don't show how widespread or common these experiences are discussed in chapter 6 and appendix III.

3 Gus Dur was an eccentric president, always startling people with his frank jokes, pranks, and humble style. He is probably the only major head of state, apart from Gandhi, who sometimes received guests barefoot and wearing a sarong.

4 Gus Dur passed away in 2009, but he is still revered as a saint by tens of thousands of Javanese, especially members of NU.

5 Conversion from either Islam to Christianity or Christianity to Islam, as between other religions, is not unusual in Indonesia. It is usually traumatic for both religious communities and a sensitive topic. The reasons for conversion include social, political, and economic factors, as well as religious experiences. See Hefner 1993.

6 The following story was related by an American anthropologist, Loraine V. Aragon. See Aragon 2000.

7 Langse cave is a sacred place of power where mystics from all over Indonesia come to meditate. Prince Diponegara and other famous figures of Javanese history claimed they met the Queen of the South there.

8 The original Javanese and an Indonesian translation of the poem are as follows.

amenangi zaman édan,	*menyaksikan zaman gila,*
éwuhaya ing pambudi,	*serba susah dalam bertindak,*
mélu ngédan nora tahan,	*ikut gila tidak akan tahan,*
yén tan mélu anglakoni,	*tapi kalau tidak mengikuti (gila),*
boya keduman mélik,	*tidak akan mendapat bagian,*
kaliren wekasanipun,	*kelaparan pada akhirnya,*
ndilalah kersa Allah,	*namun telah menjadi kehendak Allah,*
begja-begjaning kang lali,	*sebahagia-bahagianya orang yang lalai,*
luwih begja kang éling klawan	*akan lebih bahagia orang yang tetap*
waspada ingat dan waspada.	

9 Some villagers referred to him as a *dukun*. But, like most people so labeled, Embah Selamat rejects that label. *Dukun* has various negative connotations, ranging from the slightly disreputable (e.g. a dishonest magician or charlatan) to the seriously evil (e.g., a black magic worker, dukun santet) or the heretical polytheist. Selamat preferred to be called a *wong pintar* (clever person), paranormal, or an expert in *kebatinan* (mysticism).

10 Apparently his clients included members of the Soeharto family, as well as at least one powerful Cabinet member (Harmoko) and one or two generals during the New Order regime.

11 The good *jins* are sometimes referred to as Muslim *jins* and may be the souls of very pious people who have died (see Bowen 1993:136–38).

12 *lā 'ilāha 'illā-llāhu muḥammadun rasūlu-llāh* (لَا إِلَٰهَ إِلَّا الله مُحَمَّدٌ رَسُولُ الله).

13 *Santri* now usually refers to students in Muslim boarding schools (*pesantren*) and institutions, including both those associated with the traditionalist NU and modernist Muhammadiyah.

14 On Idul Adha, a national holiday in Indonesia, Muslims sacrifice goats in remembrance of Ibrahim's willingness to sacrifice his son on God's command.

15 Anderson 1990:24. Anderson mistakenly removes all ethical considerations from the metaphor of compensation and treats it like a purely economic exchange to gain power. See also Ricklefs 1998.

16 Some early social scientists saw this as a positive process, for example, Hobbes, Comte, Feuerbach, Marx, Durkheim, and Freud. Others, such as Tönnies and Rousseau, viewed the passing of traditional society as a great loss. Weber saw it as both progress toward rationality and loss of meaning. See Baum 1975.

17 There is a lot of variation in Dyak Kaharingan beliefs and practices. My Dyak Kaharingan informants in Central Kalimantan said that traditionally Dyak shamans (*pendita*) were all women. Male priests (*basir*) lead corporate worship and are believed to have supernatural powers, but shamans still practice spirit possession and are often women.

5

Islamic Modernism and Disenchantment

1 See, for example, the interviews with Syafi'i Ma'arif and Machasin in chapter 6.

2 This is according to a current account of the founding of Muhammadiyah on the Muhammadiyah website, accessed November 10, 2016, http://www. muhammadiyah.or.id/id/content-180-det-eksistensi-muhammadiyah.html.

3 Sunnah are the collected, interpreted and validated stories about the sayings, example and actions of the Prophet Mohammah and his close followers. Ahaddith (Arabic plural of hadith) are all the stories about the Prophet's and his followers' sayings and actions. Some Haddith are of doubtful historical validity. Others are contradictory or of doubtful meaning. Hadith must be individually evaluated for their authenticity and meaning and may not contradict the Koran.

4 I have no statistics to support this, but when I asked around seventy of my students in a philosophy of science class at UMY whether they came from

Muhammadiyah or NU backgrounds, I was surprised to learn that the majority were from NU backgrounds.

5 Not all respondents answered all the questions. That accounts for some small differences in the total number of answers to each question. There were only two Buddhist respondents. Therefore I have not included statistics on Buddhist respondents; however, they are included in the percentages for the total number of non-Muslim answers. For simplicity, some ethnic groups are grouped together, usually based on geography. Small groups from the same part of the same island are grouped with larger groups. Over 50 ethnic groups are included in the total number of ethnic groups noted on the questionnaires (twenty-eight).

6 See also the story related by Dr. Siti Syamsiyatun in the following chapter about the Indonesian Ambassador to India who was possessed by his Grandfather.

7 The campus military program is similar to the Reserve Officers' Training Corps (ROTC) in the United States. Students who want to join the military can take a training course designed to prepare them to become officers.

8 In 2017 in Yogyakarta, three students died in a military-style training program involving mountain climbing, as a result of violent bullying by other students. In this case the family did demand an investigation, and as a result the rector of the university resigned as an expression of his sorrow and responsibility for the accident. It is unlikely that this would have happened during the Soeharto regime and shows the increasing openness of Indonesian society. For more on this, see "Tiga Mahasiswa UII Meninggal" *Kompas*, accessed November 10, 2016. http://regional.kompas.com/read/2017/01/25/18120561/tiga.mahasiswa.uii .meninggal.21.saksi.diperiksa.

9 He made the claim repeatedly, including before three thousand ulamas at a conference on *dzikir* (chanting verses from the Koran to remember God and claim his protection). For a video of SBY's statement, see YouTube, accessed January 6, 2017, https://www.youtube.com/watch?v=KxpBFKQd8Ak.

10 See, for example, interviews with Siti Syamsiyatun, Syafi'i Ma'arif, and Zainal Abidin Bagir in chapter 6.

11 The figure of 84 percent is based on the fact that 64 percent of Indonesians said they have experienced the unseen world. The remaining 36 percent said they had no such experience and did not believe in it. However, of these, more than 55 percent revealed through a different question that they believed spirit possession is real. Fifty-five percent of 36 percent is almost 20 percent ($64 + 20 = 84$). On the basis of these two questions, it appears that only 16 percent of the 2,492 respondents did not believe that the world of spirits is real. Even among the 16 percent of skeptics, many believed in God's intervention in the world.

6

Islam and Enchantment: Six Leaders

1 Schlehe suggests that the construction of the festival as an economic strategy to draw tourists to Kota Gede was somewhat artificial since almost all the spectators were local people.

2 IAIN stands for Institute Agama Islam Negeri (National Institute for Islamic Religion). Some IAIN, including IAIN Sunan Kalijaga, converted into universities with the new name UIN (Universitas Islam Negeri, or State Islamic University-UIN Sunan Kalijaga).

3 "Mengkafirkan Sesama itu Termasuk Hate Speech," *Bimas Islam* Edisi 3/III/2015. Accessed November 28, 2016, https://kemenag.go.id/file//2016/09/1473220569934409771.pdf

4 Iqbal used the English term *guardian spirit*, but he also used the term *qodem* (his spelling). I have been unable to find the name *qodem* in any list of Javanese *makluk halus* (invisible beings).

5 The same stories are common in many parts of Indonesia, for example, among Catholics in Flores.

7

Traditional Indonesian Imaginations of Power

1 Weber felt that maybe the phenomenon of charismatic power was really independent of both ancient and modern social constructs. He wrote, "Charisma shall be understood to refer to an extraordinary quality of a person, regardless of whether this quality is actual, alleged or presumed" (1946:279). Weber is wistful about the possibility that the power of charisma, such as was seen in the ancient prophets, was a real power that somehow escaped the iron cage of rationality. His threefold typology is still popular with sociologists, not because they share Weber's hope for positive prophetic charisma but because the category of charisma might be helpful in explaining the extraordinary power of irrational demagogues such as Hitler (see Anderson 1990). "Charisma" is a convenient "black hole" into which we can throw all kinds of power phenomena that are difficult to explain rationally.

2 In a footnote to an Indonesian translation of his original essay on Javanese power (1972) Anderson writes, "My previous effort (in 1970, when I wrote this essay), was intended to show Western students how different their assumptions were from those of the Javanese and that Javanese assumptions are just as fundamental and just as logical as those of Western political science. In other

words, I intended to shake up the assumptions of those Western students" (Anderson 1984:127). This is my translation of Anderson's Indonesian.

3 Anderson's later groundbreaking work on imagined communities ([1983] 1991) is more nuanced, but it still displays his Weberian evolutionary assumptions. See the discussion below on evolution from traditional to modern.

4 Koentjaraningrat 1984. Koentjaraningrat gives a description of concepts of power during a period of transition between ancient and modern cultures. His description is much more accurate and balanced than Anderson's theory. But Anderson's theory is much more interesting! Anderson's essay is a classic because it stimulates so many ideas and provides a new way of looking at the phenomenon of power in Indonesia.

5 In my first book I show how the tradition of political realism, which eschews morality from political analysis, is itself based on many unstated moral values. Kenneth Waltz and Ernst Haas were my professors during my doctoral work at Berkeley. When I first started doctoral work in international relations and explained my interest in ethics and violence, Professor Haas stated flatly, "Well it's your funeral. There is no relation between international relations and ethics!" In spite of some differences, he became my valued mentor and friend.

6 There is irony in this ideal (*budaya malu*) because Indonesians seem to tolerate corruption in powerful people far more than the inhabitants of many other countries do. In a glaring example, Setya Novanto was reinstated as head of the Legislature (Dewan Perwakilan Rakyat [People's Representative Council]) even though he had previously been forced to resign because of a video showing him asking Ma'roef Sjamsoeddin, director of the Freeport Mining Company, for 20 percent of the shares of the company, reportedly worth billions of dollars, in exchange for extending the company's contract. He was cleared of all charges, based on a technicality (the video was deemed inadmissible because it violated his privacy). He was however subsequently re-arrested in connection with other corruption charges.

7 Anderson suggests that Weber was wrong in considering charisma a separate intermediate category between traditional authority and modern rational-legal authority. While I agree with him that charisma is part of traditional power, I think it is also part of modern power. The conceptual distinction between traditional and modern is helpful for some purposes, but it obscures the extent to which such concepts influence each other and are both part of the same reality.

8 The exceptions are the hero-clowns Semar and his brothers. They are short, fat, crude, and impolite. But secretly Semar is the incarnation of the highest god. He is hilarious because he breaks all the stereotypes of a Javanese hero.

9 Jokowi defeated Prabowo by a margin of 53.15 to 46.85 percent and more than eight million votes. http://indonesiasatu.kompas.com/read/2014/07/22/18235991/ ini.hasil.rekapitulasi.suara.pilpres.di.33.provinsi (accessed 7 September 2014).

10 The third, traditional answer was difficult to translate from Indonesian. I translated *bermartabat* as "dignity." The word refers to an inner quality which includes the idea of character. *Mengendalikan* is translated "controls and guides,"

but the word also includes the idea of steering and keeping people on the right path. For the original Indonesian question and answers, see appendix II.

11 Most Dyak participants in our research were Dyak Hindu Kaharingan (of which there are many varieties). Actually most Dyaks are not Hindu or Kaharingan. Many converted to Islam and are no longer called Dyaks but rather Malays, Banjars, and so forth. Relatively few Muslims in Kalimantan call themselves Dyaks, and, as there has been extensive immigration of Muslims from other parts of Indonesia, it is difficult to determine the statistics for those who were originally Dyaks but converted to Islam. In the twentieth century there were mass conversions of Dyaks to Christianity, both Protestant and Catholic. Those who converted to Christianity still call themselves Dyaks. Apparently Christianity is the largest religion among those who call themselves Dyaks, but they are not included in our research findings.

12 The three strictly Islamic parties are Partai Keadilan Sejahtera (PKS 6.79 percent), Partai Persatuan Pembangunan (PPP 6.53 percent), and Partai Bulan Bintang (PBB 1.46 percent). Altogether they garnered 14.78 percent of the vote. There is one other Muslim party, Partai Kebangkitan Bangsa (PKB), which is associated with NU but also fields non-Muslim candidates. The three strictly Islamic parties received 9.04 percent of the vote. Including PKB, Muslim parties received 23.82 percent. Asia Foundation, accessed January 16, 2017, https://asiafoundation.org/resources/pdfs/IndonesiaElections.pdf.

13 A whimsical example of this is in the English translation of Univeristas Islam Negeri (UIN). A natural translation of this into English might be Islamic State University. However the rector of the university cautioned me not to translate it that way. He said the English translation *must* be State Islamic University! He did not want anyone to think his university was in favor of an Islamic state.

14 In the Indonesian original, the first, religious answer is as follows: *Masyarakat yang mamatuhi perintah Tuhan dan mengamalkan kewajiban agama.* The word *mengamalkan* is difficult to translate into English. The most common translation is "practice." Instead I used the word "implement." The root word is *amal*, which means "charity." So *mengamalkan* means to practice or implement religious requirements, including carrying out your social ethical responsibilities to those less fortunate than you (*amal*). See further discussion in Chapter 9.

8

Modern Indonesian Imaginations of Power

1 The hundreds of thousands of demonstrators were not all "Islamic radicals," but they were Muslims who felt threatened by Jakarta's rule by a Chinese Christian governor who had been charged with defaming Islam.

2 The charge was based on a doctored video of one of Ahok's speeches, which went viral on the internet and gave some people the impression that he was advising people not to follow the Koran. He was campaigning for reelection as governor of Jakarta, so many believe it was a political attack, with religion just a tool. The two mass demonstrations in Jakarta in November and December 2016 recall the equally massive demonstrations in Washington, DC, and elsewhere following the election of Donald Trump.

3 Many Indonesians are attracted to conspiracy theories. Whenever there is a tragedy or a crisis, many people assume there is a *dalang* (puppet master) who orchestrated the crisis. The idea that there is an all-powerful "ruler" who controls events is one indication that "traditional" conceptions of power are widespread in Indonesia.

4 Many modern, nonwestern, Muslim intellectuals are more influential than these seven theorists. Some are Indonesians, such as Nurcholis Madjid, Abdurrahman Wahid, Syafi'i Ma'arif, and Amin Abdullah, while others are foreigners whose works have been translated into Indonesian, including Fazlur Rahman, Abdullahi An Na'im, Kahled Fadou El Fadl, and Tariq Ramadan. However, most of these writers are heavily normative and less helpful for descriptive theories. This chapter focuses on modern, nonreligious, social scientific writers who influence Indonesian intellectual discourse about power. Their ideas are a convenient mechanism for exploring religion and social change in Indonesia. Chapter 9 focuses mores specifically on Muslim perspectives on the power of religion in society.

5 These are figures for 2015. See CIA World Factbook. Accessed January 17, 2017, https://www.cia.gov/library/publications/the-world-factbook/fields/2212.html. Indonesia is projected to overtake the United States in population in 2043. See Shamim Adam, Berni Moestafa, and Novrida Manurung, "Indonesia Population Approaching U.S. Revives Birth Control." Bloomberg, January 28, 2014, accessed May 18, 2015, https://www.bloomberg.com/news/articles/2014-01-27/indonesia-facing-populace-larger-than-u-s-revives-birth-control.

6 This 2016 estimate is taken from Indonesian Investements. Accessed January 3, 2018, https://www.indonesia-investments.com/culture/population/item67.

7 Sukarno, the nationalist hero and first president of Indonesia, was never a communist, but he was sympathetic with communist goals of freedom from colonialist, imperialist, and capitalist exploitation. He freely used Marxist ideas to further Indonesia's struggle against Dutch colonialism. See Sukarno 1975.

8 Eric Lorrand "Nike's Track Record." Blog accessed January 3, 2018, http://www-personal.umich.edu/~lormand/poli/nike/nike101-4.htm.

9 Weber 1946:78. Weber continues the ideas of a long line of political realists, including Machiavelli, Hobbes, and Rousseau (see Adeney 1988). Thomas Hobbes argued that the essence of the state is founded on fear ([1651] 1952). Fear is the dominating condition of human beings in the "state of nature." According to Hobbes, the state of nature is the natural condition of human beings before the creation of government. In the state of nature there is no law, there is no morality, and there is no community. Human beings are in a state of

war of all against all. No one is safe because without law and order anyone, even the weakest, can kill the strongest, for example, when he or she is asleep. Therefore, in Hobbes's famous sentence, life in the state of nature is "continual fear and danger of violent death, and the life of man, solitary, poor, nasty, brutish, and short" (Chapter XIII:9).

10 I have no idea of how many there are, but bumper stickers showing a benevolent, smiling Soeharto are quite common. It is reasonable to assume that some of the 63 million people who voted for Prabowo in the 2014 presidential election were in part longing for the return of a strong-arm government similar to that of Soeharto.

11 Weber's argument is not normative but descriptive. He suggested that in seventeenth- and eighteenth-century Europe and North America a particular brand of Reformed Christianity (Puritan pietism) helped transform a feudalist social order in Europe into an ethos of "worldly asceticism," which nurtured the development of capitalism. That kind of Christianity hardly exists in the world today. A related misreading is to think that Weber was a Protestant who was making a normative correlation between his religion and economic prosperity. Weber was not a Christian and had grave reservations about capitalism (Weber [1930] 2001).

12 The sovereignty of the people (*kedaulatan rakyat*) is the fourth principle of Pancasila.

13 The military forbade the demonstration, and we did not know if a bloodbath would ensue. We loaned our white Toyota Kijang to activists to be used as an ambulance since we feared the military might open fire, as in Tiananmen Square in Beijing. We felt the power of the five hundred thousand people on the streets of Yogyakarta that day who did not seem to care if the soldiers came and opened fire. Soeharto could not survive this massive and peaceful rejection, even though he controlled a powerful military. If, on the other hand, he had faced a violent coup attempt, it is quite likely that the military would have come to his defense.

14 Bertrand de Jouvenel suggests that power is rooted in the people, not only in democratic societies but even more so in monarchies. He writes, "The King, who is but one solitary individual, stands far more in need of the general support of Society than any other form of government" (1952:98; see also Arendt 1970:41). In the fourth century BCE, Mencius (Meng-tse) asserted that the voice of the people should be considered the voice of God. According to him, if the people will not acknowledge and support the king, then he is no longer a king. See Weber 1946:249.

15 A few recent examples on the internet include: https://youngage.co/habermas-hikayat-kopi-dan-kehampaan-ruang; https://jurnalismekapurung.wordpress .com/.../teori-ruang-publik-1-; https://simangade.wordpress.com/tag/jurgen-habermas/; and www.komnasperempuan.go.id/dewi-candraningrum-peng-arusutam. There are several books about Habermas in Indonesian, and several of his works have been translated into Indonesian.

16 Republic of Indonesia, Legislation Number 39 of 1999 Concerning Human Rights.

17 For example, see http://teori-teori.blogspot.com/2009/01/foucault-speak-diskursus.html; http://badakimuka.blogspot.co.id/2012/04/teori-foucault.htm.

18 Gus Dur was impeached on trumped-up charges of corruption. He was among the cleanest of Indonesian politicians, but he made many enemies by removing the military from power, by attacking corruption, and through his own inept administration due to a serious stroke and blindness. Amien Rais hoped that his party, PAN, which is informally associated with Muhammadiyah, would win a large proportion of the votes in the 1999 legislative election. Instead it won just 7.12 percent. In the 2009 election its proportion of the vote declined to 6.01 percent. See Eric C. Thompson 2016 "Indonesia in Transition: The 1999 Presidential Elections." In *Understanding Strategic Cultures in the Asia Pacific*, edited by Ashley J. Tellis, Alison Szalwinski, and Michael Wills. Washington DC: The National Bureau of Asian Research. Accessed January 6, 2018, http://www.nbr.org/publications/briefing/pdf/brief9.pdf.

19 One year it issued a fatwa declaring that Muslims should not say Merry Christmas to Christians because it was against Islam. The following year I received far more Christmas cards from Muslims wishing me Merry Christmas than I did from Christians.

20 See Elanda Harviyata, "Kasus Jilbab di Sekolah-sekolah Negeri di Indonesia." Wordpress blog. Accessed January 20, 2017, https://elandaharviyata.wordpress.com/2013/04/01/kasus-jilbab-di-sekolah-sekolah-negeri-di-indonesia/.

21 Until recently there was even a transsexual (*waria*) *pesantren* (boarding school for study of Islam) led by a transsexual Muslim scholar. The school was shut down following threats by Muslim radicals. However, it continues to operate in a less public manner.

22 At least two of his seminal works have been translated into Indonesian, and several books about his thought by Indonesian authors have been published. Many Indonesian books and articles in the social sciences and philosophy discuss his work. See, for example, Haryatmoko. 2016. *Membongkar Rezim Kepastian: Pemikiran Kritis Post-Strukturalis*. Yogyakarta: Penerbit Kanisius. Irianto, Agus Maladi. 2015. *Interaksionalisme Simbolik–Pendekatan Antropologis Merespon Fenomena Keseharian*. Semarang: Gigih Pustaka Mandiri.

9

Muslim Imaginations of Power in Indonesia

1 The Shafi'i school of interpretation followed by Indonesian Sunni Muslims should not be confused with Salafi, which in Saudi Arabia is virtually indistinguishable from Wahhabi Islam and is bound by the Hanbali school. Salafis in other places

(notably Egypt) may follow one of the other four schools of interpretation or refuse to be bound by any of them. See "Syafii School of Law." Oxford Islamic Studies Online, accessed January 5, 2018, www.oxfordislamicstudies.com/article/opr/t125/e2148.

2 See "Islamic Schools and Branches." Wikipedia, accessed January 20, 2017, https://en.wikipedia.org/wiki/Islamic_schools_and_branches.

3 See appendix IV for statistical analysis of ethnic variations in Muslim views of religion and power.

4 This can make statistics a hot political topic. If the numbers are inflated for a particular group, it could be eligible for more funding.

5 The law on blasphemy and defamation of religion is very vague. As seen in the case of Ahok and the Ahmadiyah group, a person or group can be accused under this law for disagreeing with beliefs that some people consider central to their religion. It is not necessary to attack the Prophet or desecrate a Holy Book.

6 The original Indonesian answer was "Umat yang baik, tertib, taat kepada Tuhan dan beragama." I translated *umat* as "God's people." Often this word is used to mean the "followers of Islam." However it is also used to refer to followers of other religions, for example, *umat Hindu Bali*. In a private conversation, Gus Dur told me the word means "those who come from the womb." Thus it can refer to all humanity, as in *umat manusia*.

7 The original Indonesian answer was "Keluarga yang rukun, menghormati orang tua, ikhlas dan aman." I translated the word *ikhlas* as "wholehearted." This word is notoriously difficult to translate into English. It is also a Javanese word that has slightly different connotations from the way it is used in Indonesian in other parts of the country. Often it is translated as "sincere." In Java it includes the connotation of "letting go of your ego" in the sense of acting without compulsion or self-interest (see Magnis-Suseno 1984; and Heider 1991:69–70).

8 See the discussion in Adeney 1995.

9 A habitus is something like a social imaginary. Taylor's emphasizes that social imaginaries are the result of intersubjective practices, whereas Bourdieu says a habitus is not subjective, intersubjective, or objective. Rather it is created by interactions with all three (see chapter 8).

10 A panopticon was a tower in the center of a prison from which it was possible to see into every cell, twenty-four hours a day.

11 In comments regarding a *Guardian* article about an Indonesian thrash metal, Muslim girls band (Voice of Bracepot/Noise) in which the girls wear the *jilbab*, one reader suggested that the girls were oppressed because they were forced to wear Muslim head coverings. Another suggested that they could not be Muslims and play heavy metal music. I suspect that the girls wore the *jilbab* because they wanted to. It was part of their habitus. They saw no contradiction between thrash metal and Islam. A teenage spirit of rebellion, exemplified by metal rock music, is universal. See Kate Lamb. "The schoolgirl thrash metal band smashing stereotypes in Indonesia," *Guardian*, June 9, 2017, accessed June 12, 2017, https://

www.theguardian.com/global-development/2017/jun/09/the-schoolgirl-thrash-metal-band-smashing-stereotypes-java-indonesia-voice-baceprot.

12 Not all mimetic rituals are religious. Nor are they all fixed and invariable. Sometimes mimetic rituals are a flexible way to carry out complex negotiations. Farsijana Adeney-Risakotta suggests this is especially apparent in the many complex traditional rituals leading up to a marriage. See F. Adeney-Risakotta 2005.

13 Of course this is not true of all Indonesian Muslims. There are many who are not strict about praying five times a day or fasting at Ramadan (see the interview with Wening in chapter 5). Several Muslim students told me that when they lived in their villages they never missed the five daily prayers, but since moving to the city and attending the university they seldom pray. Even among those who do pray faithfully (*Muslim taat*), there are many who just go through the motions because of pressure from their families or peers.

14 See, for example, Supelli 2016a, b.

10

Imaginations of Nature and Natural Disasters

1 Parts of this chapter were included in Adeney-Risakotta 2016a.

2 For example, papaya and banana trees do grow like weeds and often sprout on their own. From a little sprout, they can be bearing luscious fruit in a few months.

3 This was the town of Salatiga on the slopes of Mount Merbabu (3,000 m. or 10,000 ft.) in Central Java. Some things have changed since I lived there, and there are now some newer hotels with views of the mountain.

4 An example is the House of Authentic Sense (Griya Jati Rasa), a multireligious foundation established by Farsijana Adeney-Risakotta. One of its projects was to establish a recycling store. Villagers who bring clean and sorted recyclable trash can exchange it for basic foodstuffs.

5 Almost 6 percent of respondents chose more than one answer, which is more than for any other question.

6 Another factor is the trajectory of these communities. Islam started out accommodating indigenous practices, but now it seems to be headed in a more rationalistic, God-centered direction. In contrast, Protestantism started out very intolerant of indigenous beliefs but is moving in a more contextualized, accommodating direction. Protestant theological students are very critical of their Calvinist missionary forbears' intolerance of local practices. Many are incorporating local traditions into their reinterpretation of Christian theology. If so, Protestants and Muslims may be heading in opposite directions.

7 As with most large earthquakes, there were many aftershocks of varying intensity. The earth was literally unstable for many days after the initial shock.

8 My wife Dr. Farsijana Adeney-Risakotta's father is Ambonese, and her mother is Javanese. Most of her Javanese relatives are Muslims from Prambanan.

9 Her family illustrates the complexity of the Javanese social structure since it includes, in one family, civil servants and teachers (*priayi*), farmers and crafts-people (*abangan*), and pious merchants (*santri*).

10 The difference between men and women should not be essentialized, let alone lead to the conclusion that women are incapable of abstract philosophical reasoning or that men are uninterested in practical action. Ngelow's book includes several women among the authors, some of whom are oriented toward abstract theological questions. Conversely some of the male authors are primarily oriented toward practical action.

11 Actually plate tectonics includes three main actions: plates collide, move away from each other, or slide alongside each other. Each of these actions can create seismic activity. See Oreskes 2003.

12 At the Council for Southeast Asian Studies at Yale University in April 2016, there was a seminar about the agency of nature in resisting colonial exploitation of the land in Vietnam. One paper suggested that when the French colonialists forcibly introduced rubber plantations at a higher than usual altitude in Vietnam, it unexpectedly facilitated the rapid breeding of malarial mosquitos. The work force was decimated by sickness. The author argued that this was an example of the agency of nature responding to human exploitation.

13 The highest figure was for Hindus, 24 percent of whom chose the traditional language. Only 8 percent of both Catholics and Protestants chose the language that attributes natural disasters to human social evil and the agency of ancestors or unseen powers. The biggest surprise was the Catholics, who had the highest percentage of those who chose the cosmos-centered language about their relation to nature (56 percent). A cosmos-centered understanding of our relation to nature does not necessarily correlate with similar language used to explain natural disasters.

14 That figure included 64 percent of Catholics, 46 percent of Muslims, 40 percent of Protestants, and 37 percent of Hindus.

15 This included 52 percent of Protestants, 39 percent of Muslims, 39 percent of Hindus, and 28 percent of Catholics.

11

Imaginations of Women in Law and Practice

1 Parts of this article were originally published in Adeney-Risakotta 2016b.

2 Women often work in the "informal sector," running food stalls, catering, trading in the marketplace, selling snacks, or providing services such as laundry to the many students who live in the area. Informal sector businesses are not registered or licensed, do not pay taxes, and are not included in the country's gross national product. They usually operate with a tiny profit margin and may be subject to extortion by local gangsters (*preman*).

3 Kejawen is often translated as "Javanese mysticism." It is a complex mixture of supernatural beliefs and practices handed down from the ancestors.

4 This story was reported by Susanne Rodemeier (2014:17–49). It is recounted in great detail and followed by an even more thorough analysis. For the sake of space, I am only giving a brief summary.

5 Interestingly, in the village of Keningar, which is less than seven kilometers from the peak of Mt. Merapi, people believe that Merapi is a goddess, "Mother Merapi," and the source of the fertility of the soil (Candraningrum 2014).

6 The fall of Soeharto in 1998 also marked the end of strict government censorship of literature.

7 Gerwani (the Gerakan Wanita or "Women's Movement") was an organization of mostly village women that campaigned against polygamy and for the equal rights of women. It was linked to the Communist Party.

8 See Rika Theo, "Lubang Buaya dan pola pemerkosaan massal yang berulang di Indonesia." In Rappler Indonesia, accessed June 1, 2017, http://www.rappler.com/indonesia/112531-lubang-buaya-pemerkosaan-massal-1965-indonesia; See also Ari Susanto, "Kisah Suti: Nenek 96 tahun, aktivis Gerwani penyintas tragedi 1965." In Rappler Indonesia. Accessed June 1, 2017. http://www.rappler.com/indonesia/121070-suti-aktivis-gerwani-penyintas-tragedi-1965. Both of these are stories of activist women who campaigned for women's rights and then experienced sexual violence in 1965–66 because of their association with Gerwani. The power of the myth of Lubang Buaya may have helped stimulate the mass rape of Chinese Indonesian women in Jakarta in 1998. There is good evidence that the myth of Lubang Buaya was fabricated.

9 Ratno Lukito suggests that "in the Indonesian setting, both Islamic and *adat* laws were able to coexist. ... [B]oth in theory and practice, the two sets of laws were complementary. Islamic law ... acknowledge(s) the efficacy of local custom in the legislative process, while *adat* law conceives of religious law as the culmination and perfection of the indigenous legal system. In practice, the role of local customary law was never marginal to the interplay between Islamic legal precepts and social realities" (1997:130).

10 The complexity, diversity, and pluralism of Indonesian law, especially as it relates to religion, public policy, and gender, have been explored in detail in Irianto 2008; Feener 2007; Feener and Cammack 2007; Bowen 1993, 2001, 2003; Hooker 2003; Lukito 1997, 2013; and Minhaji 2008.

11 Achille Mbembe suggests that in postcolonial societies there are "a plurality of 'spheres' and arenas, each having its own separate logic and yet nonetheless liable to be entangled with other logics when operating in specific contexts;

hence the postcolonial 'subject' has had to learn to continuously bargain ... and improvise" (1992:5; see also Ong and Peletz 1995:2)

12 This case study is taken from Bowen 2003. This chapter presents a highly compressed and simplified version of the story. For more details, see Bowen 2003:35–43.

13 This was Law 1, 1974, on Marriage. The Religious Judicature Act (Law 7) was passed in 1989.

14 The CLD is a major reference point for those seeking to reconstruct *fiqh* so that it is consistent with international protocols of human rights. However the CIL is still the effective law of the land in Muslim family courts.

15 This is reminiscent of the teachings of the Bill Gothard Institute on Basic Youth Conflicts, which were popular among Evangelical and fundamentalist Christians in the United States during the 1970s and 1980s.

16 An exception is Aceh, which has special autonomy and a limited right to impose Sharia law.

17 This percentage is based on a very rough personal survey taken during my visit in 1989. Because I was surprised by the lack of women in public spaces, I spent an hour in the middle of the day on a busy street in the center of Islamabad counting the number of men and women who passed by. In that time and space, approximately 90 percent of the people I saw were men. The situation was quite different in the Hunza valley in the Himalayan mountains of northern Pakistan. There the women seemed much more active in public spaces and much freer to interact with men in public.

18 I caused quite a stir when I mistakenly got into the rear portion of a bus that was reserved for women. The women thought it was hilarious, but I was terrified until I safely made it through a small opening into the male compartment in the front of the bus. I was afraid I'd be arrested!

19 For an interesting reflection on the evolving meaning of Muslim head coverings in Indonesia, see Darmawan 2014. This is an extended review of a recent film about an Indonesian woman in Europe who decides to wear a *jilbab*.

20 See CIA World Factbook. Accessed January 6, 2018, https://www.cia.gov/library/publications/the-world-factbook/fields/2103.html.

12

Conflict, Intolerance, and Hope

1 "Government Inaction Creates Space for Rising Intolerance in Indonesia." *Jakarta Post*, February 1, 2017, accessed February 4, 2017, http://www.thejakartapost.com/news/2017/02/01/government-inaction-creates-space-for-rising-intolerance-in-indonesia-.html.

2 "Fatwa MUI Nyatakan Gafatar Sesat." *BBC Indonesia*, February 3, 2016, accessed February 4, 2017, http://www.bbc.com/indonesia/berita_indonesia/2016/02/160202_indonesia_mui_gafatar_sesat.

3 "Satpol PP Depok Segel Masjid Ahmadiyah, Massa Minta Ditutup Selamanya" *Wartakota*, February 24, 2017, accessed February 27, 2017, http://wartakota.tribunnews.com/2017/02/24/satpol-pp-depok-segel-masjid-ahmadiyah-massa-minta-ditutup-selamanya. According to Indonesian law, Ahmadis have a right to worship according to their beliefs but the government says they do not have the right to spread their teachings, which some Sunni Muslims consider heretical.

4 Unfortunately, social media also spreads hoaxes and false news.

5 Recently the University of California canceled a lecture by a Far Right speaker because of massive protests on the Berkeley campus. It seemed an ironic coda on the "free speech movement" of the 1960s.

6 See chapter 8.

7 "Government Inaction Creates Space for Rising Intolerance in Indonesia." *Jakarta Post*, February 1, 2017, accessed February 4, 2017, http://www.thejakartapost.com/news/2017/02/01/government-inaction-creates-space-for-rising-intolerance-in-indonesia-.html.

8 See "Up to 100 gravestones vandalized at Jewish cemetery in Philadelphia." *The Guardian*, February 26, 2017, accessed February 27, 2017, https://www.the-guardian.com/us-news/2017/feb/26/jewish-cemetery-vandalized-philadelphia

9 "More Than 250 Black People Were Killed By Police In 2016" *Huffington Post*, July 7, 2016, Updated January 1, 2017, accessed February 4, 2017, . In 2016, 258 African Americans were fatally shot by police in the United States, 39 of whom were unarmed. Of course, the high numbers of black people killed by police in America does not necessarily mean these were hate crimes or even racist. Some black people were killed by black police officers, and some were killed because they used violence in resisting arrest while engaged in a crime. Nevertheless, the high numbers suggest institutionalized racism through racial profiling and prejudice.

10 Safety is, of course, relative. The greatest dangers in Indonesia are not violent assault or natural disasters but rather traffic accidents, overcrowded public transportation, and mosquito-borne disease.

11 Young, single white women, especially if they are dressed "immodestly" by Indonesian Muslim standards, sometimes are harassed through the aggressive flirting of young Indonesian males. A young woman alone at night sends a message that may not be intended by a non-Indonesian. Young Indonesian women usually travel in pairs, with a boyfriend, or in groups when they go out at night. Nevertheless, single, white women tourists often travel around Indonesia in safety. But, unless they like the sexualized attention (and most do not), they are more comfortable if they travel in groups of two or more (see Adeney 1995: chapter 8).

12 Homosexuals and transgender people (*waria*) have been a visible part of Indonesian cultures for centuries. Many traditional art forms relied on homosexuals and transgender people for their performances. Even today it is not unusual to see Indonesian men dressed as women, including on popular TV programs. However, Muslim conservatives have conducted a campaign to ban them from public space. Recent demonstrations and physical attacks have made LGBTQ identity much more dangerous than it used to be. Muslim conservatives construct LGBTQ as sinful contamination from the West. Ironically, until recently, tolerant acceptance of LGBTQ identity as part of ordinary society was much less problematic in Indonesia than in most western countries.

13 Out of 218 countries in the world, Indonesia is ranked ninth from the top for countries with the lowest number of homicides per hundred thousand people. Most of the 8 countries with less violent crime than Indonesia are very small island nations. Japan is the only large country in the world with a lower homicide rate than Indonesia. See "Intentional homicides (per 100,000 people) —Country Ranking." *Index Mundi*, accessed February 4, 2017, https://www.indexmundi.com/facts/indicators/VC.IHR.PSRC.P5/rankings

14 Even if the massive demonstrations calling for Ahok to be jailed for defaming the Koran were politically motivated and sponsored by political actors who care little about religion, the demonstrators were able to whip up support for their cause by appealing to religion.

15 To put Ahok's election loss in perspective, it is well to remember that he was elected to the governorship of the Special Province of Jakarta in spite of being a Chinese Christian. It is hard to imagine a Muslim being elected governor or mayor of any state or large city in the United States.

16 Estimates of the number of demonstrators varied widely. Based on analysis of aerial photos, experts have estimated the number as between five and seven hundred thousand, but some organizers claimed that there were more than seven million. See "Menyimak Perdebatan Soal Jumlah Peserta Aksi 2 Desember," *Solopost Digital Media*, December 4, 2016, accessed February 4, 2017, http://www.solopos.com/2016/12/04/menyimak-perdebatan-soal-jumlah-peserta-aksi-2-desember-773937.

17 The religious tolerance of most Indonesians is illustrated by the fact that Ahok won the first round of the elections on February 15, 2016, in spite of months of negative publicity as a Chinese Christian blasphemer against Islam.

18 When I googled *dalang kerusuhan* (puppet master of riots) on February 24, 2017, there were about 243,000 articles listed discussing who was the puppet master behind various violent conflicts.

19 Many of the ninety-nine names emphasize God's mercy, compassion, forgiveness, and gentleness.

20 See Sidney Jones's perspective analysis in Jones 2017.

21 The Darul Islam rebellion in South Sulawesi also played on regional sentiments, portraying Sukarno's nationalist government as an extension of Javanese imperialism, symbolized by the Majapahit Empire.

22 Many Indonesians of mixed race and from eastern Indonesia also lost their lives. See Rosalind Hewitt, "The Forgotton Killings." *Inside Indonesia*, August 1, 2016, accessed February 27, 2017, http://www.insideindonesia.org/the-forgotten-killings. According to the Indonesian historian Sri Margana, during the revolution, many more Indonesians lost their lives at the hands of other Indonesians than at the hands of the Dutch and their allies. This is a controversial claim because it contradicts the dominant narrative of a unified Indonesia fighting western imperialist colonialists (stated in a lecture on the history of religions in Indonesia at ICRS, Gadjah Mada University, in February 2014).

23 Some politicians make the ludicrous claim that latent communism is a serious threat to the Republic of Indonesia. There is no danger of a rise of the PKI in Indonesia. But the narrative of struggle for social justice and resistance to capitalist exploitation still retains power for many Indonesians. See chapter 9.

24 Gandhi grew up in a conservative Hindu family in India; studied law in England, where he had dialogues with Christians; practiced law in South Africa, where he became involved in the antiapartheid struggle; he read Tolstoy from Russia and Thoreau from the United States. He was not a passive recipient of ideas and practices from these different contexts. He absorbed and influenced practices and ideas that circulated around the globe.

25 The CIL, the presidential directive for Islamic family courts, states that Muslims may not marry non-Muslims. It is not, however, part of the 1974 marriage law. See Adeney-Risakotta 2016b.

26 Michel de Certeau contrasts "tactics," as used by the powerless to resist the hegemony of the powerful, with "strategies," which are used by the powerful to impose their will on society. See de Certeau 1984.

27 In some cases, the couple finds a "liberal" religious leader who will perform the marriage according to one religion but allowing both parties to remain true to their beliefs. In other cases, one party nominally converts but continues with the practices of his or her religion. Another possibility is to fly to nearby Singapore, where civil unions are performed that are legally accepted in Indonesia.

28 After 9/11, one of my Muslim neighbors donned a black t-shirt with stark white lettering reading "Fuck Terrorists!" Muslim demonstrators against radicalism held signs reading "Terrorists have no Religion" and "Terrorists are not Muslims".

APPENDIX IV

Ethnic Variations in Muslim Views of Religion and Power

1 Dyak Kaharingan tribes include two groups: those who construct their religion as Hindu Kaharingan and thus obtain state recognition and support, and those who insist that Kaharingan is unique and not part of Hinduism. Members of the latter, more traditional group are dispersed throughout the mountains and

jungles of Kalimantan. The former are more urbanized and modern. Most of those who filled out our questionnaire were from the Hindu Kaharingan group. Therefore these statistics do not reflect the social imaginaries of all Dyak Kaharingan people.

2 The islands of NTT are distinguished from those of NTB. There are more than five hundred islands in NTT,, the largest of which are Flores, Sumba, and West Timor. Flores is predominantly Catholic, while Sumba and West Timor are majority Protestant. As a whole, NTT is 90 percent Christian, including 54 percent Catholic (especially Flores) and 35 percent Protestant (especially Sumba and West Timor).

3 The original Indonesian answer was "Umat yang baik, tertib, taat kepada Tuhan dan beragama." I translated *umat* as "God's people." Often this word is used to mean the followers of Islam. However, it is also used to refer to followers of other religions, for example, *umat* Hindu Bali. In a private conversation, Gus Dur told me the word means "those who come from the womb." Thus it can refer to all humanity, as in *umat manusia*.

4 The Indonesian original of this answer was "Keluarga yang rukun, menghormati orang tua, ikhlas dan aman." I translated the word *ikhlas* as "wholehearted." This word is notoriously difficult to translate into English. It is also a Javanese word that has slightly different connotations than the way it is used in Indonesian in other parts of the country. Often it is translated as "sincere." In Java it includes the connotation of "letting go of your ego," in the sense of acting without compulsion or self-interest (see Magnis-Suseno 1984; Heider 1991: 69–70).

5 There is very little majority-minority dynamic between Catholics and Protestants in NTT because, although Catholics are a strong majority in Flores, Protestants are a strong majority in Sumba and West Timor. East Timor is 98 percent Catholic, but it is no longer part of Indonesia. Hindus, however, are a small minority in NTT.

6 This is reflected in Balinese Christian (Catholic and Protestant) imitation of Balinese sacred architecture in building their churches. They reinterpret the religious symbolism of the architecture from the perspective of Christian theology in order to emphasize their cultural unity with Balinese Hindus.

7 The majority of citizens in NTT are Christians, including Protestants and Catholics.

8 In the Indonesian original of the questionnaire, the first, religious answer is "Masyarakat yang mamatuhi perintah Tuhan dan mengamalkan kewajiban agama." The word *mengamalkan* is difficult to translate into English. The most common translation is "practice." Instead I chose the word *implement*. The root word is *amal*, which means "charity." So *mengamalkan* means to practice or implement religious requirements, including carrying out your social ethical responsibilities to those less fortunate than you (*amal*). See chapter 7.

APPENDIX V

Indonesian Muslim Views of Nature and Ethnic Variations

1 This might lend credence to the thesis that there is something in Ambonese religion, or Moluccan religion, that transcends the differences between Christians and Muslims (see Cooley 1966). There is irony in the cultural similarities between Moluccan Christians and Muslims in light of their history of conflict.

GLOSSARY

abangan common people; tolerant Muslims open to traditional, non-orthodox practices

adat tradition, customs, rules, structures and beliefs of a particular ethnic group

aliran stream, branch or denomination of a group

batin inner, hidden, inward, mystical

bermasyarakat belonging; identification with the people

bersih desa cleanse the village; rituals, often at harvest, to give thanks

bid'ah unauthorized innovation; doing things not approved by the Koran and Sunnah

Bhineka Tunggal Ika Indonesian national motto; out of many, one; unity in diversity

dalang shadow puppet master, the artist who performs wayang kulit shadow puppet plays

dukun shaman, paranormal, wise man, alternative medicine practicioner

edan crazy, mad, wild; a period when society is in moral chaos

gaib the unseen world, supernatural

gotong royong cooperation, mutual help, communal effort

haj; haji pilgrimage to Mecca; title of someone who completes the pilgrimage

hadiths reports of the sayings of the Prophet Muhammad, collected by his followers

hormat honor, respect

ikat hand woven cloth

ikhlas purity of heart in acting for the service of others

Islamicate civilization developed by Muslims and influenced by Islam but not normatively Islamic

jilbab, hijab Muslim head covering for women

jins spiritual beings created by God out of fire; they may be good, neutral or evil

khalifah vice-regent, leader, representative of God

kebatinan the science and practice of inwardness; Javanese mysticism

kebhinekaan diversity

kejawen Javanese mysticism; kebatinan

kekuasaan power

kekuatan strength

kepercayaan beliefs; distinguished from religion (agama)

keramat sacred; a powerful, holy object or place

keris a traditional curved Javanese dagger; some keris are believed to have mystical power

kodrat natural law; the essential nature of a person

kraton palace; Sultan's traditional residence

kyai charismatic Muslim leader of a pesantren or Islamic school

maju, kemajuan go forward; progress

makluk halus a "being," who cannot be perceived with ordinary senses

malas lazy, reluctant

malu; budaya malu shame, embarrassment; culture of shame

martabat, bermartabat dignity, authority, presence, honor

mengamalkan implement, practice, carry out your duty

mufakat consensus

musyawarah deliberation, discussion

nalar reason, rationality

pasrah submitted to the will of God; accepting of fate

pembangunan development, especially economic development

pencak silat traditional Indonesian martial arts

pendeta minister, religious leader

pesantren a traditional Muslim boarding school led by a kyai

priyai aristocratic class, leaders and civil servants

pusaka heirloom; any object believed to be inhabited by power

rasa feeling, taste, thinking, perceiving

rukun harmony

sabar patience

sakti mystical power, invulnerability, magical power

santri strictly observant Muslims; students at a Muslim school (pesantren)

sederhana simple, plain, honest, unpretentious

selamatan ritual meal of thanksgiving

Sharia the way of God; the regulations and laws that are taught in the Koran

sholat worship; prayer; a required set of rituals to be performed five times a day

Sunnah the way of life taught by the prophet and his companions

syirik polytheism, idolatry, heresy, worshiping something other than God

tanpa pamrih without self interest

tenang calm, peaceful

tirakat spiritual rituals, practices and prayers to bring one close to God

umat the congregation or people of God; literally womb

wali representative, leader

Wali Sanga nine legendary apostles who spread Islam in Java

waspada to be alert, careful, disciplined

wayang kulit leather shadow puppets and shadow puppet performance

wewenang sphere of authority and responsibility

wibawa, berwibawa authority, power, influence, dignity

References

Adeney, Bernard. 1988. *Just War, Political Realism, and Faith.* American Theological Library Association Monographs, no. 24. Metuchen, NJ: Scarecrow Press.

———. 1994. "Liberalism Protects Dignity of Indonesians." *Jakarta Post,* March 1.

———. 1995. *Strange Virtues: Ethics in a Multicultural World.* Downers Grove, IL: InterVarsity Press.

Adeney, Frances S. 2003. *Christian Women in Indonesia: A Narrative Study of Gender and Religion.* Syracuse, NY: Syracuse University Press.

Adeney-Risakotta, Bernard. 1998. "Reformasi Gereja dan HAM." *Orientasi Baru: Jurnal Filsafat dan Teologi* 11:60–75.

———. 2004. "The Impact of September 11 on Islam in Southeast Asia." In *Islam in Southeast Asia: Political, Social, and Strategic Challenges for the 21st Century,* edited by K. S. Nathan and M. Hashim Kamali. Singapore: Institute of Southeast Asian Studies.

———. 2005. "Power from Below: Deconstructing the Dominant Paradigm." *Asian Journal of Social Science* 33(1):23–45.

———. 2009a. "Is There a Meaning in Natural Disasters? Constructions of Culture, Religion, and Science." *Exchange: Journal of Missiological and Ecumenical Research* 38(3):226–43.

———. 2009b. "Religion, Violence, and Diversity: Negotiating the Boundaries of Indonesian Identity." In *Religion, Civil Society, and Conflict in Indonesia,* edited by Mohamad Machasin, Karl Sterkens and Frans Wijsen. Zurich: Lit Verlag.

Adeney-Risakotta, Bernard. 2014a. "Indonesian and Western Social Imaginaries." In *Dealing with Diversity,* edited by Bernard Adeney-Risakotta. Geneva: Globethics.net.

———. 2014b. "Peacemaking in the Indonesian Context." In *(Un)Common Sounds: Songs of Peace and Reconciliation among Muslims and Christians*, edited by Roberta A. King and Sooi Ling Tan. Eugene, OR: Cascade.

———, ed. 2014c. *Dealing with Diversity: Religion, Globalization, Violence, Gender, and Disasters in Indonesia*. Geneva: Globethics.net. Translated into Indonesian as *Mengelolah Perbedaan: Agama, Globalisasi, Kekerasan, Jender, dan Bencana di Indonesia*. Bandung: Mizan, 2015.

———. 2016a "Religion and Disaster, What Is the Question? Moral Wisdom in Ancestors, Religion, and Science." *Asian Journal of Religion and Society* 4(1):29–51.

———. 2016b. "Traditional, Islamic, and National Law in the Experience of Indonesian Women." *Journal of Islam and Christian Muslim Relations*. Volume 27, Issue 3:303–318. http://dx.doi.org/10.1080/09596410.2016.1186422.

———. 2017a. "Indonesian Repertoires for Managing Diversity." In *Religion and Public Piety: Comparing European and Indonesian Experiences*, edited by Dicky Sofjan. Geneva: Globethics.net.

———. 2017b. *Visions of a Good Society in Southeast Asia*. Singapore: Centre for Study of Christianity in Asia (CSCA), Trinity Theological College Press.

Adeney-Risakotta, Farsijana. 2005. *Politics, Ritual, and Identity in Indonesia: A Moluccan History of Religions and Social Conflict*. Nijmegen, Netherlands: Radboud University Njimegen. A digital copy is available from http://webdoc.ubn.ru.nl/mono/r/risakotta_f/poliriani.pdf.

———, ed. 2007. *Perempuan dan Bencana: Pengalman Yogyakarta*. Yogyakarta: Selandang Ungu Press.

Ahmed, Leila. 1986. "Women and the Advent of Islam." *Signs: Journal of Women in Culture and Society* 11(4):665–91.

Ahnaf, Iqbal. 2006. *The Image of the Other as Enemy: Radical Discourse in Indonesia*. Chiang Mai: Silkworm Books.

Anderson, Benedict R. 1965. *Mythology and the Tolerance of the Javanese*. Ithaca, NY: Cornell University Press.

———. 1972. "The Idea of Power in Javanese Culture." In *Culture and Politics in Indonesia*, edited by Claire Holt. Ithaca, NY: Cornell University Press.

———. 1984. "Gagasan tentang Kekuasaan dalam Kebudayaan Jawa." In *Aneka Pemikiran Tentang Kuasa dan Wibawa*, edited by Miriam Budiardjo. Jakarta: Penerbit Sinar Harapan.

———. [1983] 1991. *Imagined Communities: Reflections on the Origins and Spread of Nationalism*. New York: Verso.

———. 1990. *Language and Power: Exploring Political Cultures in Indonesia.* Ithaca, NY: Cornell University Press.

An-Na'im, Abdullahi Ahmed. 1990. *Toward an Islamic Reformation: Civil Liberties, Human Rights, and International Law.* Syracuse, NY: Syracuse University Press.

———. 2008. *Islam and the Secular State.* Cambridge, MA: Harvard University Press.

Antlöv, Hans, and Sven Cederroth. 1994. *Leadership on Java: Gentle Hints, Authoritarian Rule.* Copenhagen: Nordic Institute of Asian Studies.

Aoyama, Toru. 2007. "Indianization Revisited: A Comparative Review and Its Contemporary Significance." Unpublished paper presented at ICRS, Yogyakarta.

Aragon, Lorraine V. 2000. *Fields of the Lord: Animism, Christian Minorities, and State Development in Indonesia.* Honolulu: University of Hawai'i Press.

Arendt, Hannah. 1963. *On Revolution.* New York: Viking.

———. 1970. *On Violence.* London: Allen Lane.

Aritonang, Jan Sihar, and Karl Steenbrink, eds. 2008. *A History of Christianity in Indonesia.* Leiden: Brill.

Asad, Talal. 1993. *Genealogies of Religion: Discipline and Reasons of Power in Christianity and Islam.* Baltimore: Johns Hopkins University Press.

Asyhari, Budi, and Subkhi Ridho. 2010. *Perempuan, Islam, Indonesia: Mengurai Jebakan Revivalisme Keagamaan.* Yogyakarta: Lembaga Studi Islam dan Politik.

Atkinson, Jane, and Shelly Errington, eds. 1990. *Power and Difference: Gender in Island Southeast Asia.* Stanford, CA: Stanford University Press.

Bagir, Zainal Abidin. 2005. *Science and Religion in the Post-colonial World: Interfaith Perspectives.* Adelaide, Australia: ATF Press.

Banchoff, Thomas, and Robert Wuthnow, eds. 2011. *Religion and the Global Politics of Human Rights.* New York: Oxford University Press.

Barber, Benjamin. 1995. *Jihad vs. McWorld: Terrorism's Challenge to Democracy.* New York: Times Books.

Baum, Gregory. 1975. *Religion and Alienation.* Mahwah, NJ: Paulist Press.

Beatty, Andrew. 1999. *Varieties of Javanese Religion. An Anthropological Account.* Cambridge: Cambridge University Press.

———. 2009. *A Shadow Falls: In the Heart of Java.* London: Faber and Faber.

Bellah, Robert N. [1970] 1991. *Beyond Belief: Essays on Religion in a Post-traditional World.* Berkeley: University of California Press.

———. 2011. *Religion in Human Evolution: From the Paleolithic to the Axial Age.* Cambridge, MA: Harvard University Press.

Bellah, Robert, and Hans Joas, eds. 2012. *The Axial Age and Its Consequences.* Cambridge, MA: Belknap Press of Harvard University Press.

Bellah, Robert N., Richard Madsen, William M. Sullivan, Ann Swidler, and Steven M. Tipton. 1985. Habits of the Heart: Individualism and Commitment in American Life. Berkeley: University of California Press.

Benedict, Ruth. [1946] 1989. *The Chrysanthemum and the Sword: Patterns of Japanese Culture.* Boston: Houghton Mifflin.

Berger, Peter L. 1963. *Invitation to Sociology: A Humanist Perspective.* New York: Anchor.

———. 1967. *The Sacred Canopy.* New York: Doubleday.

———. 1969. *A Rumor of Angels.* New York: Doubleday.

———. 1983. "On the Obsolescence of the Concept of Honor." In *Revisions: Changing Perspectives in Moral Philosophy,* edited by Stanley Hauerwas and Alasdair MacIntyre. Notre Dame, IN: University of Notre Dame Press.

———, ed. 1999. *The Desecularization of the World.* Grand Rapids, MI: Eerdmans.

———. 2014. *The Many Altars of Modernity: Toward a Paradigm for Religion in a Pluralist Age.* Berlin: De Gruyter Mouton.

Berger, Peter L., and Thomas Luckmann. 1989. *The Social Construction of Reality.* New York: Anchor.

Bertrand, Jacques. 2004. *Nationalism and Ethnic Conflict in Indonesia.* New York: Cambridge University Press.

Blackburn, Susan, Bianca J. Smith, and Siti Syamsiyatun, eds. 2008. *Indonesian Islam in a New Era: How Women Negotiate Their Muslim Identities.* Clayton, Australia: Monash University Press.

Bourchier, David, and John Legge, eds. 1994. *Democracy in Indonesia, 1950s and 1990s.* Clayton, Australia: Monash University Press.

Bourdieu, Pierre. 1977. *Outline of a Theory of Practice.* Cambridge: Cambridge University Press.

———. 1980. *The Logic of Practice.* Stanford, CA: Stanford University Press.

———. 1984. *Distinction: A Social Critique of the Judgement of Taste.* London: Routledge.

———. 2001. *Masculine Domination.* Translated by Richard Nice. Stanford, CA: Stanford University Press.

Bowen, John Richard. 1993. *Muslims through Discourse: Religion and Ritual in Gayo Society.* Princeton, NJ: Princeton University Press.

———. 2001. *Shari'a, State, and Social Norms in France and Indonesia.* Leiden: International Institute for Study of Islam in the Modern World.

———. 2003. *Islam, Law, and Equality in Indonesia: An Anthropology of Public Reasoning.* Cambridge: Cambridge University Press.

Bruinessen, Martin van, ed. 2013. *Contemporary Developments in Indonesian Islam: Explaining the "Conservative Turn."* Singapore: Institute of Southeast Asian Studies.

Budiardjo, Miriam, ed. 1984. *Aneka Pemikiran Tentang Kuasa dan Wibawa.* Jakarta: Penerbit Sinar Harapan.

Burke, Peter. 2009. *Cultural Hybridity.* Cambridge: Polity.

Butler, Judith, Jürgen Habermas, Charles Taylor, Cornel West, and Craig Calhoun. 2011. *The Power of Religion in the Public Sphere.* New York: Columbia University Press.

Cady, Linell E., and Sheldon W. Simon, eds. 2007. *Religion and Conflict in South and Southeast Asia.* New York: Routledge.

Campbell-Nelson, John. 2006. "Bumi Tidak Tenang." In *Teologi Bencana*, edited by Zakaria J. Ngelow. Makassar: Yayasan Oase INTIM (Indonesia Timur).

Candraningrum, Dewi, ed. 2014. *Ekofeminisme II: Narasi Iman, Mitos, Air, dan Tanah.* Yogyakarta: Jalasutra.

Carey, Peter. 2008. *The Power of Prophecy: Prince Dipanagara and the End of an Old Order in Java, 1785–1855.* 2nd ed., rev. Leiden: KITLV Press.

Casanova, José. 1994. *Public Religions in the Modern World.* Chicago: University of Chicago Press.

Casanova, José. 2012. "Religion, the Axial Age, and Secular Modernity in Bellah's Theory of Religious Evolution." In *The Axial Age and Its Consequences*, edited by Robert Bellah and Hans Joas. Cambridge, MA: Belknap Press of Harvard University Press.

Center for Women's Studies. 2006. *Islam, Women, and the New World Order.* Yogyakarta: Universitas Islam Negeri Sunan Kalijaga.

Chambert-Loir, Henri. 2009. *Sadur: Sejarah Terjemahan di Indonesia dan Malaysia.* Jakarta: Gramedia.

Chambert-Loir, Henri, and Anthony Reid, eds. 2002. *The Potent Dead: Ancestors, Saints, and Heroes in Contemporary Indonesia.* Asian Studies Association of Australia, Southeast Asia Publications, no. 6. Crows Nest, NSW: Allen and Unwin.

Colombijn, F., and J. Lindblad, eds. 2002. *Roots of Violence in Indonesia: Contemporary Violence in Historical Perspective.* Leiden: KITLV Press.

Cook, Alistair D. B., ed. 2007. *Culture, Identity, and Religion in Southeast Asia.* Newcastle: Cambridge Scholars.

Cooley, Frank L. 1966. "Altar and Throne in Central Moluccan Societies." PhD diss., Yale University. Available at https://cip.cornell.edu/DPubS?verb=Display&version=1.0&service=UI&handle=seap.indo/1107135779&page=record.

Cribb, Robert, ed. 1990. *The Indonesian Killings of 1965–1966.* Monash Papers on Southeast Asia, no. 21. Clayton, Australia: Monash University Press.

Crumley, Carole. 1995. "Heterarchy and the Analysis of Complex Societies." In *Archeological Papers of the American Anthropological Association* 6(1):1–5.

Darmawan, Hikmat. 2014. "*99 Cahaya di Langit Eropa 1 & 2:* Imajinasi Islam dalam Nalar Kekalahan." *Film Indonesia,* March 26, accessed January 8, 2015. http://filmindonesia.or.id/article/99-cahaya-di-langit-eropa-1-2-imajinasi-islam-dalam-nalar-kekalahan#.VLM-ZSuUdnA 2014.

Darusmanwati, Aep Saepulloh. 2014. *Mengintip Alam Gaib.* Jakarta, Zaman.

Day, Dorothy. 1952. *Autobiography: A Long Loneliness.* San Francisco: Harper and Row.

D'Costa, Gavin, ed. 1990. *Christian Uniqueness Reconsidered: The Myth of a Pluralistic Theology of Religions.* Maryknoll, NY: Orbis.

de Certeau, Michel. 1984. *The Practice of Everyday Life.* Berkeley: University of California Press.

Deutscher, E. 1973. *What We Say/What We Do: Sentiments and Acts.* Glenview, IL: Scott Foresman.

Donald, Merlin. 1993. *Origins of the Modern Mind: Three Stages in the Evolution of Culture and Cognition.* Cambridge, MA: Harvard University Press.

Donald, Merlin. 2012. "An Evolutionary Approach to Culture: Implications for the Study of the Axial Age" in Robert Bellah and Hans Joas, eds. *The Axial Age and Its Consequences.* Cambridge, MA: Belknap Press of Harvard University Press.

Doorn-Harder, Pieternella van. 2006. *Women Shaping Islam: Reading the Qur'an in Indonesia.* Urbana: University of Illinois Press.

Duara, Prasenjit. 2015. *The Crisis of Global Modernity: Asian Traditions and a Sustainable Future.* Cambridge: Cambridge University Press.

Durkheim, Émile. [1893] 1933. *The Division of Labor in Society.* Translated by George Simpson. New York: Macmillan.

———. [1912] 1915. *The Elementary Forms of the Religious Life.* Translated by Joseph Ward Swain. New York: Macmillan.

Effendy, Bahtiar. 1998. *Islam dan Negara: Transformasi Pemikiran dan Praktik Politik Islam di Indonesia.* Jakarta: Paramadina.

El Fadl, Khaled Abou. 2001. *Speaking in God's Name.* Oxford: Oneworld.

Elson, R. E. 2008. *The Idea of Indonesia: A History.* Cambridge: Cambridge University Press.

Fealy, Greg, and Virginia Hooker. 2006. *Voices of Islam in Southeast Asia: A Contemporary Sourcebook.* Singapore: Institute of Southeast Asian Studies.

Feener, R. Michael. 2007. *Muslim Legal Thought in Modern Indonesia.* Cambridge: Cambridge University Press.

Feener, R. Michael, and Mark E. Cammack, eds. 2007. *Islamic Law in Contemporary Indonesia: Ideas and Institutions.* Cambridge, MA: Harvard University Press.

Florida, Nancy K. 1995. *Writing the Past, Inscribing the Future: History as Prophecy in Colonial Java.* Durham, NC: Duke University Press.

Friend, Theodore. *Indonesian Destinies.* 2003. Cambridge, MA: Belknap Press of Harvard University Press.

Foucault, Michel. 1978. *The History of Sexuality.* Translated by Robert Hurley. London: Penguin.

———. 1980. *Power/Knowledge: Selected Interviews and Other Writings, 1972–1977.* New York: Pantheon.

———. 1997. *Discipline and Punish.* New York: Vintage.

Gadamer, Hans-Georg. 1975. *Truth and Method.* New York: Seabury.

———. 1979. "The Problem of Historical Consciousness" in Rabinow, Paul, and William M. Sullivan, eds. *Interpretive Social Science: A Reader.* Berkeley: University of California Press.

Gade, Anna M. 2004. *Perfection Makes Practice: Learning, Emotion, and the Recited Quran in Indonesia.* Honolulu: University of Hawai'i Press.

Geertz, Clifford. 1960. *The Religion of Java.* Glencoe, IL: Free Press of Glencoe. Republished in 1976 by Chicago: University of Chicago Press.

———. 1973. *The Interpretation of Culture.* New York: Basic Books.

———. 1983. *Peddlars and Princes.* Chicago: University of Chicago Press,.

Geertz, Hildred. [1961] 1989. *The Javanese Family: A Study of Kinship and Socialization.* Long Grove, IL: Waveland Press.

Gilligan, Carol. 1982. *In a Different Voice*. Cambridge, MA: Harvard University Press.

Girard, René. [1972] 2005. *Violence and the Sacred*. New York: Continuum.

———. 2014. *The One by Whom Scandal Comes*. (Studies in Violence, Mimesis, and Culture). East Lansing: Michigan State University Press.

Giri, Ananta Kumar. 2009. *The Modern Prince and the Modern Sage: Transforming Power and Freedom*. New Delhi: Sage Publications India.

Goldstein, Warren S., ed. 2006. *Marx, Critical Theory, and Religion*, Leiden: Brill.

Gottowik, Volker, ed. 2014. *Dynamics of Religion in Southeast Asia: Magic and Modernity*. Amsterdam: Amsterdam University Press.

Gramsci, Antonio. 1971. *Selections from the Prison Notebooks*. New York: International Publishers.

Gross, Rita M. 2014. "No Girls Allowed? Are the World's Religions Inevitably Sexist?" In *Dealing with Diversity: Religion, Globalization, Violence, Gender, and Disasters in Indonesia*. Edited by Bernard Adeney-Risakotta. Geneva: Globethics.net.

Guibernau, Montserrat, and John Rex, eds. 1997. *The Ethnicity Reader: Nationalism, Multiculturalism, and Migration*. Cambridge: Polity.

Gurevitch, Z. D. 1988. "The Other Side of Dialogue: On Making the Other Strange and the Experience of Otherness." *American Journal of Sociology* 93(5):1179–1199.

Gustavo Gutierrez. 1973. *A Theology of Liberation*. Maryknoll, NY: Orbis. The first (Spanish) edition was published in Lima, Peru, in 1971.

Habermas, Jürgen. 1989. *The Structural Transformation of the Public Sphere*. Cambridge, MA: MIT Press.

———. 2006. "Religion in the Public Sphere." *European Journal of Philosophy* 14(1):1–25.

Hamayotsu, Kikue. 2011. "The End of Political Islam? A Comparative Analysis of Religious Parties in the Muslim Democracy of Indonesia." *Journal of Current Southeast Asian Affairs* 30(3):133–59.

Hasbullah, Moeflich. 2014. "A Century of NU-Muhammadiyah in Indonesia: The Failure of Islamic Modernism?" *Islamika Indonesiana*. 1(1):19–37.

Hassan, Riaz. 2002. *Faithlines: Muslim Conceptions of Islam and Society*. Oxford: Oxford University Press.

Hauerwas, Stanley. 1977. *Truthfulness and Tragedy*. Notre Dame, IN: University of Notre Dame Press.

———. 1991. *A Community of Character*. Notre Dame, IN: University of Notre Dame Press.

Hauerwas, Stanley, and L. Gregory Jones, eds. 1997. *Why Narrative? Readings in Narrative Theology*. Eugene, OR: Wipf and Stock Publishers.

Hauerwas, Stanley, and Alasdair MacIntyre, eds. 1983. *Revisions: Changing Perspectives in Moral Philosophy*. Notre Dame, IN: University of Notre Dame Press.

Headley, Stephen C. 2000. *From Cosmogony to Exorcism in a Javanese Genesis*. Oxford: Oxford University Press.

———. 2004. *Durga's Mosque: Cosmology, Community, and Conversion in Central Javanese Islam*. Singapore: Institute of Southeast Asian Studies.

Hefner, Robert W. 1990. *The Political Economy of Mountain Java: An Interpretive History*. Berkeley: University of California Press.

———, ed. 1993. *Conversion to Christianity: Historical and Anthropological Perspectives on a Great Transformation*. Berkeley: University of California Press.

———, ed. 1998. *Market Cultures: Society and Morality in the New Asian Capitalisms*. Boulder, CO: Westview Press.

———. 2000. *Civil Islam: Muslims and Democratization in Indonesia*. Princeton, NJ: Princeton University Press.

———. 2001. "Public Islam and the Problem of Democratization." 2001. In *Religion and Globalization at the Turn of the Millennium*, special issue of *Sociology of Religion* 62(4):491–514.

———, ed. 2011. *Shari'a Politics*. Bloomington: Indiana University Press.

Heider, Karl G. 1991. *Landscapes of Emotion: Mapping Three Cultures of Emotion in Indonesia*. New York: Cambridge University Press.

Heilbroner, Robert L. 1980. *The Worldly Philosophers*. New York: Simon and Schuster.

Hellwig, Tineke. 1994. *In the Shadow of Change: Citra Perempuan dalam Sastra Indonesia*. Berkeley: University of California Press.

Hobbes, Thomas. [1651] 1952. *Leviathan*. Edited by Nelle Fuller. Chicago: Encyclopaedia Britannica.

Hodgson, Marshall. 1974. *Venture of Islam; Conscience and History in a World Civilization*. 3 Vols. Chicago: University of Chicago Press.

———. 1993. *Rethinking World History: Essays on Europe, Islam, and World History*. Cambridge: Cambridge University Press.

Hofstede, Geert. 1980. *Culture's Consequences: International Differences in Work-Related Values*. Beverly Hills, CA: Sage.

Holsti, Ole R. 2008. *To See Ourselves as Others See Us*. Ann Arbor: University of Michigan Press.

Holt, Claire, ed. 1972. *Culture and Politics in Indonesia*. Ithaca, NY: Cornell University Press.

Hooker, M. B. 2003. *Indonesian Islam: Social Change through Contemporary Fatawa*. Honolulu: University of Hawai'i Press.

Hui, Yew-Foong. 2012. *Encountering Islam: The Politics of Religious Identity in Southeast Asia*. Singapore: Institute of Southeast Asian Studies.

Ikhsanudin, K. M., Mohammad Najib, and Sri Hidayati, eds. 2002. *Fiqh Perempuan: Panduan Pengajaran di Peesantren*. Yogyakarta: Yayasan Kesejahteran Fatayat.

Irianto, Sulistyowati, ed. 2008. *Perempuan dan Hukum: Menuju Hukum yang Berperspektif Kesetaraan dan Keadilan*. 2nd ed. Jakarta: Yayasan Obor Indonesia.

Jackson, Karl D., and Lucian W. Pye, eds. 1978. *Political Power and Communications in Indonesia*. Berkeley: University of California Press.

Jameson, Fredric and Masao Miyoshi, eds. 1998. *The Cultures of Globalization*. Durham, NC: Duke University Press.

Jenkins, Phillip. 2002. *The Next Christendom: The Coming of Global Christianity*. Oxford: Oxford University Press.

Jones, Sidney. 2017. "Indonesia's Illiberal Turn." *Foreign Affairs*, May 26, accessed March 23, 2018. https://www.foreignaffairs.com/articles/indonesia/2017-05-26/indonesias-illiberal-turn.

Jouvenel, Bertrand de. 1952. *Power: The Natural History of Its Growth*. Translated by J. F. Huntington. London: Batchworth Press.

Kahin, Audrey. 2012. *Islam, Nationalism, and Democracy*. Singapore: National University of Singapore Press.

Kahin, George McTurnan. 1952. *Nationalism and Revolution in Indonesia*. Ithaca, NY: Cornell University Press.

Kartini, Raden Adjeng. [1920] 1986. *Letters of a Javanese Princess*. Translated by Agnes Louise Symmers. New York: Knopf.

Keeler, Ward. 1987. *Javanese Shadow Plays, Javanese Lives*. Princeton, NJ: Princeton University Press.

Klinken, Gerry van. 2014. "Religion, Politics and Class Divisions in Indonesia." in *Dealing with Diversity: Religion, Globalization, Violence, Gender, and*

Disasters in Indonesia, edited by Bernard Adeney-Risakotta. Geneva: Globethics.

Kodir, Faqihuddin Abdul. 2007. *Hadith and Gender Justice: Understanding the Prophetic Traditions*. Cirebon, Indonesia: Fahima Institute.

Koentjaraningrat. 1984. "Kepemimpinan dan Kekuasaan: Tradisional, Masa Kini, Resmi dan Tak Resmi." In *Aneka Pemikiran Tentang Kuasa dan Wibawa*, edited by Miriam Budiardjo. Jakarta: Penerbit Sinar Harapan.

Kovacs, Amanda. 2014. "Saudi Arabia Exporting Salafi Education and Radicalizing Indonesia's Muslims." *GIGA Focus* [German Institute of Global and Area Studies], no. 7, October.

Kuhn, Thomas S. 2012. *The Structure of Scientific Revolutions*. 4th ed. Chicago: University of Chicago Press. First published in 1962.

Kumar, Ann. 2009. *Globalizing the Prehistory of Japan: Language, Genes, and Civilization*. Abingdon: Routledge.

Kunkler, Mirjam, and Alfred Stepan, eds. 2013. *Democracy and Islam in Indonesia*. New York: Columbia University Press.

Kwok, Pui-lan. 2005. *Postcolonial Imagination and Feminist Theology*. Westminster: John Knox Press.

Kymlicka, Will. 1995. *Multicultural Citizenship: A Liberal Theory of Minority Rights*. New York: Oxford University Press.

Lach, Donald F. 1965. *Asia in the Making of Europe*. Chicago: University of Chicago Press.

La Loubère, Simon de. [1693] 1969. *A New Historical Relation of the Kingdom of Siam*. Kuala Lumpur: Oxford University Press.

Liddle, R. William. 1996. *Leadership and Culture in Indonesian Politics*. Sydney, Australia: Allen and Unwin.

Lindbeck, George A. 1984. *The Nature of Doctrine: Religion and Theology in a Postliberal Age*. Louisville, KY: Westminster John Knox Press.

Lindsey, Tim and Pausacker, Helen, eds. 2016. *Religion, Law and Intolerance in Indonesia*. New York: Routledge.

Lombard, Denys. 1996a. *Nusa Jawa: Silang Budaya*. Bagian 1: *Batas-Batas Pembaratan*. Jakarta: Gramedia Pustaka Utama. Original title: *Le Carrefour Javanais: Essai d'histoire globale*. Part 1: *Le limited de l'occidentalisation*. Paris: Ecole des Hautes Etudes en Sciences Sociales, 1990.

———. 1996b. *Nusa Jawa: Silang Budaya*. Bagian 2: *Jaringan Asia*. Jakarta: Gramedia Pustaka Utama. Original title: *Le Carrefour Javanais: Essai d'histoire globale*. Part 2: *Les Reseaux Asiatiques*. Paris: Ecole des Hautes Etudes en Sciences Sociales, 1990.

———. 1996c. *Nusa Jawa: Silang Budaya*. Bagian 3: *Warisan Kerajaan-Kerajaan Konsentris*. Jakarta: Gramedia Pustaka Utama. Original title: *Le Carrefour Javanais: Essai d'histoire globale*. Part 3: *Le Heritage des Royaumes Concentriques*. Paris: Ecole des Hautes Etudes en Sciences Sociales, 1990.

Lubis, Todung Mulya. 1993. *In Search of Human Rights*. Jakarta: Gramedia Pustaka Utama.

Luhrmann, Tanya Marie. 2012. *When God Talks Back: Understanding the American Evangelical Experience with God*. New York: Knopf.

Lukito, Ratno. 1997. "Islamic Law and Adat Encounter: The Experience of Indonesia." MA thesis, McGill University.

———. 2013. *Legal Pluralism in Indonesia: Bridging the Unbridgeable*. New York: Routledge.

Ma'arif, Ahmad Syafi'i. 2015. *Islam dalam Bingkai Keindonesiaan dan Kemanusiaan: Sebuah Refleksi Sejarah*. 2nd ed. Bandung: Mizan.

MacIntyre, Alastair. 1984. *After Virtue*. Notre Dame, IN: University of Notre Dame Press.

———. 1988. *Whose Justice, Which Rationality*. Notre Dame, IN: University of Notre Dame Press.

Madjid, Nurcholis. 1978. "The Issue of Modernization among Muslims in Indonesia: A Participant's Point of View." In *What Is Modern in Indonesian Culture?*, edited by Gloria Davies. Athens: Ohio University Press.

Magnis-Suseno, Franz. 1984. *Etika Jawa*. Jakarta: Gramedia.

Mangunwijaya, Y. B. "The Indonesia Raya Dream and its Impact on the Concept of Democracy" in Bourchier, David, and John Legge, eds. 1994. *Democracy in Indonesia, 1950s and 1990s*. Clayton, Australia: Monash University Press.

Mbembe, Achille. 1992. "The Banality of Power and the Aesthetics of Vulgarity in the Postcolony." *Public Culture* 4(2):1–30.

Mckinnon, Andrew M. 2006. "Opium as Dialectics of Religion: Metaphor, Expression, and Protest." In *Marx, Critical Theory, and Religion*, edited by, Warren S. Goldstein. Leiden: Brill.

Mendieta, Eduardo, and Jonathan Vanantwerpen. 2011. *The Power of Religion in the Public Sphere*. New York: Columbia University Press.

Miller, Vincent J. 2014 "What Does Globalization Do to Religion" in *Dealing with Diversity: Religion, Globalization, Violence, Gender, and Disasters in Indonesia*, edited by Bernard Adeney-Risakotta. Geneva: Globethics.net.

Mills, C. Wright. [1956] 2000. *The Power Elite*. New York: Oxford University Press.

Minhaji, H. Akh. 2008. *Islamic Law and Local Tradition: A Socio-historical Approach*. Yogyakarta: Kurnia Kalam Semesta.

Moore, Mark W., and Adam Brumm. 2007. "Stone Artifacts and Hominins in Island Southeast Asia: New Insights from Flores, Eastern Indonesia." *Journal of Human Evolution* 52(1):85–102.

Morton, Timothy. 2010. *The Ecological Thought*. Cambridge, MA: Harvard University Press.

Mukhotib, ed. 2002. *Menolak Mut'ah dan Sirri: Memberdayakan Perempuan*. Yogyakarta: Yayasan Kesejahteraan Fatayat dan The Ford Foundation.

Mulia, Siti Musdah. 2007. "Toward a Just Marriage Law: Empowering Indonesian Women through a Counter Legal Draft to the Indonesian Compilation of Islamic Law." In *Islamic Law in Contemporary Indonesia: Ideas and Institutions*, edited by R. Michael Feener and Mark E. Cammack. Cambridge, MA: Harvard University Press.

———. 2008. "Menuju Hukum Perkawinan Yang Adil: Memberdayakan Perempuan Indonesia?" In *Perempuan dan Hukum: Menuju Hukum yang Berperspektif Kesetaraan dan Keadilan*, edited by Sulistyowati Irianto. 2nd ed. Jakarta: Yayasan Obor Indonesia.

Nabhan, Gary Paul. 2014. *Cumin, Camels, and Caravans: A Spice Odyssey*. History of Spice Trade, 45. Berkeley: University of California Press.

Naipaul, V.S. 1998. *Beyond Belief: Islamic Excursions among the Converted Peoples*. New York: Vintage.

Nathan, K.S., and M. Hashim Kamali, eds. 2004. *Islam in Southeast Asia: Political, Social, and Strategic Challenges for the 21st Century*. Singapore: Institute of Southeast Asian Studies.

Ngelow, Zakaria J., ed. 2006. *Teologi Bencana*. Makassar: Yayasan Oase INTIM (Indonesia Timur).

Niebuhr, Reinhold. 1932. *Moral Man and Immoral Society*. New York: Charles Scribner's Sons.

Nietzsche, Friedrich 1978. *Thus Spoke Zarathustra*. Translated by Walter Kaufman. New York: Penguin.

Nussbaum, Martha C. 2007. *The Clash Within: Democracy, Religious Violence, and India's Future*. Ranikhett: Permanent Black.

Olson, Bruce. [1973] 2006. *Bruchko*. Lake Mary, FL: Charisma House.

Ong, Aihwa, and Michael G. Peletz, eds. 1995. *Bewitching Women, Pious Men: Gender and Body Politics in Southeast Asia*. Berkeley: University of California Press.

Oreskes, Naomi, ed. 2003. *Plate Tectonics: An Insider's History of the Modern Theory of the Earth*. Boulder, CO: Westview.

Owen, John M., IV. 2014. *Confronting Political Islam: Six Lessons from the West's Past*. Princeton, NJ: Princeton University Press.

Palmer, David A., Glenn Shive, and Philip A. Wickeri, eds. 2011. *Chinese Religious Life*. Oxford: Oxford University Press.

Placher, William C. 1989. *Unapologetic Theology*. Westminster: John Knox, 1989.

Polanyi, Michael. 1958. *Personal Knowledge*. Chicago: University of Chicago Press.

Rabinow, Paul, and William M. Sullivan, eds. 1979. *Interpretive Social Science: A Reader*. Berkeley: University of California Press.

Rahman, Fazlur. 1982. *Islam and Modernity: Transformation of an Intellectual Tradition*. London: University of Chicago Press.

Rakhmat, Jalaluddin. 1991. *Islam Aktual: Refleksi Sosial Seorang Cendikiawan Muslim*. Bandung: Mizan Press.

Rawls, John. 1971. *A Theory of Justice*. Cambridge, MA: Harvard University Press.

Reid, Anthony. 1974. *The Indonesian National Revolution, 1945–1950*. Melbourne: Longman.

———. 1988. *Southeast Asia in the Age of Commerce, 1450–1680*. Vol. 1: *The Lands below the Winds*. New Haven, CT: Yale University Press.

———. 1993. *Southeast Asia in the Age of Commerce, 1450–1680*. Vol. 2: *Expansion and Crisis*. New Haven, CT: Yale University Press.

———. 2000. *Charting the Shape of Early Modern Southeast Asia*. Chaing Mai, Thailand: Silkworm.

———. 2011. *To Nation by Revolution: Indonesia in the 20th Century*. Singapore: National University of Singapore Press.

———. 2014a. "Urban Respectability and the Maleness of (Southeast) Asian Modernity." *Asian Review of World Histories* 2(2):147–167.

———. 2014b. "Patriarchy and Puritanism in Southeast Asian Modernity." DORISEA Working Papers, no. 8. Dynamics of Religion in Southeast Asia, accessed March 23, 2018. http://www.dorisea.de/de/node/1616.

———. 2014c. "Religious Pluralism as an Asian Tradition." In *Dealing with Diversity*, edited by Bernard Adeney-Risakotta. Geneva: Globethics.net.

———. 2015a. *A History of Southeast Asia: Critical Crossroads.* Hoboken, NJ: Wiley Blackwell.

———. 2015b. "Religious Pluralism or Conformity in Southeast Asia's Cultural Legacy?" *Studia Islamika: Indonesian Journal for Islamic Studies.* 22(3): 23–38.

Ricci, Ronit. 2011a. *Islam Translated: Literature, Conversion, and the Arabic Cosmopolis of South and Southeast Asia.* Chicago: University of Chicago Press.

———. 2011b. *Remembering Java's Islamization: A View from Sri Lanka.* Asia Research Institute Working Papers, no. 153. Singapore: Asia Research Institute, National University of Singapore.

Ricklefs, M. C. 1998. *The Seen and Unseen Worlds in Java, 1726–1749: History, Literature, and Islam in the Court of Pakubuwana II.* Honolulu: University of Hawai'i Press.

———. 2006. *Mystic Synthesis in Java: A History of Islamization from the Fourteenth to the Early Nineteenth Centuries.* White Plains, NY: EastBridge.

———. 2007. *Polarising Javanese Society: Islamic and Other Visions, 1830–1930.* Singapore: National University of Singapore Press.

———. 2008. *A History of Modern Indonesia since c. 1200.* Stanford, CA: Stanford University Press.

———. 2012. *Islamisation and Its Opponents in Java, c. 1930 to the Present.* Honolulu: University of Hawai'i Press.

Rinaldo, Rachel. 2013. *Mobilizing Piety: Islam and Feminism in Indonesia.* Oxford: Oxford University Press.

Riwut, Nila Bawin. 2011. *Dayak: Position, Function, and Roles of Dayaknese Women.* Yogyakarta: Galang Press.

Rodemeier, Susanne. 2014. "Bui Hangi, Istri Manusia Sang Dewa: Analisa Cerita Lisan Pulau Pura, Nusa Tenggara Timur." In *Ecofeminisme II: Narasi Iman, Mitos, Air dan Tanah*, edited by Dewi Candraningrum. Yogyakarta: Jalasutra.

Runzo, Joseph, and Nancy Martin, eds. 2003. *Human Rights and Responsibilities: The Contribution of the World Religions.* Oxford: Oneworld.

Sacks, Jonathan. 2011. *The Great Partnership: God, Science, and the Search for Meaning.* London: Hodder and Stoughton.

Santoso, Soewito. 1975. *Sutasoma, a Study in Old Javanese Wajrayana*. New Delhi: International Academy of Indian Culture.

Schlehe, Judith. 2016. "Contesting Javanese Traditions." *Indonesia and the Malay World*. DOI:10.1080/13639811.2016.1219494.

Scott, James C. 1985. *Weapons of the Weak: Everyday Forms of Peasant Resistance*. New Haven, CT: Yale University Press.

———. 2009. *The Art of Not Being Governed: An Anarchist History of Upland Southeast Asia*. New Haven, CT: Yale University Press.

———. 2012. *Decoding Subaltern Politics: Ideology, Disguise, and Resistance in Agrarian Politics*. London: Routledge.

Sindhunata. 1998. *Mata Air Bulan*. Yogyakarta: Kanisius.

Singgih, Emanuel Gerrit. 2006. "Allah dan Penderitaan di dalam Refleksi Teologis Rakyat Indonesia." In *Teologi Bencana*, edited by Zakaria J. Ngelow. Makassar: Yayasan Oase INTIM (Indonesia Timur).

Smith, Bianca J. 2008. "Kejawen Islam as gendered praxis in Javanese village religiosity." In *Indonesian Islam in a New Era: How Women Negotiate Their Muslim Identities*. Edited by Susan Blackburn, Bianca J. Smith, and Siti Syamsiyatun. Clayton, Australia: Monash University Press.

Smith-Hefner, N. J. 2007. "Youth Language, *Gaul* Sociability, and the New Indonesian Middle Class." *Journal of Linguistic Anthropology* 17:184–203.

Sofjan, Dicky. 2016a. "Religious Diversity and Politico-Religious Intolerance in Indonesia and Malaysia." *Review of Faith and International Affairs* 14(4): 53–64.

———. 2016b. "Minoritization and Criminalization of Shia Islam in Indonesia." *Journal of South Asian and Middle Eastern Studies* 39(2):29–44.

———, ed. 2016c. *Religion, Public Policy, and Social Transformation in Southeast Asia*. Vol. I: *Managing Religious Diversity*. Geneva: Globethics.

Sofjan, Dicky, with Mega Hidayati. 2014. *Religion and Television in Indonesia: Ethics Surrounding Dakwahtainment*. Geneva: Globethics.

Stackhouse, Max. 1984. *Creeds, Society, and Human Rights: A Study in Three Cultures*. Grand Rapids, MI: Eerdmans.

Steenbrink, Karol, and Jan Sihar Aritonang. 2000. *A History of Christianity in Indonesia*. Leiden: KITLV Press.

Sterkens, K., M. Machasin, and F. Wijsen, eds. 2009. *Religion, Civil Society, and Conflict in Indonesia*. Zurich: Lit Verlag.

Sukarno. 1975. *Indonesia accuses!: Soekarno's defence oration in the political trial of 1930*. Edited, translated, annotated, and introduced by Roger K. Paget. New York: Oxford University Press.

Suryadinata, Leo. 2007. *Understanding the Ethnic Chinese in Southeast Asia*. Singapore: Institute for Southeast Asian Studies.

Taussig, Michael. 1991. *Shamanism, Colonialism, and the Wild Man: A Study in Terror and Healing*. Chicago: University of Chicago Press.

Taylor, Charles, 1979. "Interpretation and the Sciences of Man." In *Interpretive Social Science: A Reader*. Edited by Paul Rabinow and William M. Sullivan. Berkeley: University of California Press.

———. 1989. *Sources of the Self*. Cambridge, MA: Harvard University Press.

———. 1994. *Multiculturalism*. With commentary by K. Anthony Appiah, Jürgen Habermas, Steven C. Rockefeller, Michael Walzer, and Susan Wolf. Edited by Amy Gutmann. Princeton NJ: Princeton University Press.

———. 2003. *Modern Social Imaginaries*. Durham, NC: Duke University Press.

———. 2007. *A Secular Age*. Cambridge, MA: Belknap Press of Harvard University Press.

Thomas, Dylan. [1937] 1952. *The Poems of Dylan Thomas*. New York: Publishing.

Tocqueville, Alexis de. 1945. *Democracy in America*. Edited by P. Bradley. New York: Knopf.

Tönnies, Ferdinand. [1887] 2001. *Community and Civil Society*. Edited by Jose Harris. Cambridge: Cambridge University Press. Translated from Tönnies, *Gemeinschaft und Gesellschaft*.

Toulmin, Stephen. 1990. *Cosmopolis: The Hidden Agenda of Modernity*. New York: Free Press.

Traube, Elizabeth G. 1986. *Cosmology and Social Life*. Chicago: University of Chicago Press.

Tsing, Anna Lowenhaupt. 1993. *In the Realm of the Diamond Queen: Marginality in an Out-of-the-Way Place*. Princeton, NJ: Princeton University Press.

Turner, Bryan S. 1974. *Weber and Islam: A Critical Study*. London: Routledge and Kegan Paul.

Utomo, A.J. 2012. "Women as Secondary Earners: Gendered Preferences on Marriage and Employment of University Students in Modern Indonesia." *Asian Population Studies* 8(1):65–85.

Veer, Peter van der. 2014. *The Modern Spirit of Asia: The Spiritual and the Secular in China and India*. Princeton, NJ: Princeton University Press.

Wade, Geoff, and Li Tana, eds. 2012. *Anthony Reid and the Study of the Southeast Asian Past.* Singapore: Institute of Southeast Asian Studies.

Waley, Arthur, trans. 1938. *The Analects of Confucius.* New York: Vintage.

Walzer, Michael. 1983. *Spheres of Justice: A Defense of Pluralism and Equality.* New York: Basic Books.

———. 1994. *Thick and Thin: Moral Argument at Home and Abroad.* Notre Dame, IN: University of Notre Dame Press.

Warner, Michael, Jonathan Vanntwerpen, and Craig Calhoun, eds. 2010. *Varieties of Secularism in a Secular Age.* Cambridge, MA: Harvard University Press.

Weber, Max. 1946. *From Max Weber.* Edited and translated by H. H. Gerth and C. Wright Mills. New York: Free Press.

———. [1930] 2001. *The Protestant Ethic and the Spirit of Capitalism.* New York: Routledge.

White, Joyce. 1995. "Incorporating Heterarchy into Theory on Socio-political Development: The Case from Southeast Asia." In *Heterarchy and the Analysis of Complex Societies,* edited by Robert Ehrenreich, Carole L. Crumley, and Janet E. Levy. Archeological Papers of the American Anthropological Association, no. 6. Hoboken, NJ: Wiley-Blackwell.

White, Lynn. 1967. "The Historical Roots of our Ecological Crisis." 155(3767): 1203–1207.

Winzeler, R. L. 1982. "Sexual Status in Southeast Asia: Comparative Perspectives on Women, Agriculture, and Political Organization." In *Women of Southeast Asia*, edited by Penny V. Esterik. Occasional Papers, no. 9. DeKalb: Center for Southeast Asian Studies, Northern Illinois University.

Wittgenstein, Ludwig. 1953. *Philosophical Investigations*. London: Blackwell.

Woodman, G. R., and A. Allott, eds. 1985 *People's Law and State Law: The Bellagio Papers*. Dordrecht: Foris.

Woodward, Mark R. 1989. *Islam in Java: Normative Piety and Mysticism in the Sultanate of Yogyakarta*. Tucson: University of Arizona Press.

———, ed. 1996. *Towards a New Paradigm: Recent Developments in Indonesian Islamic Thought*. Tempe: Arizona State University Press.

Zurbuchen, Mary S., ed. 2005. *Beginning to Remember: The Past in the Indonesian Present*. Singapore: National University of Singapore Press.

INDEX

1965–1966, 18, 286–87, 289, 384

Abdullah, Amin, 365
Abdurrahman Wahid, Gus Dur, 61, 85,
    90–1, 117, 194, 234, 357, 359, 367,
    368, 376
adat, 38, 40, 53, 75, 85, 121, 122, 161, 166,
    177, 183, 202, 204, 206–7, 251–66,
    274
Adeney/Adeney-Risakotta, Bernard, 21,
    35, 40, 53, 161, 187, 202, 205, 215,
    236, 257, 267, 274, 365, 368, 375
Adeney-Risakotta, Farsijana, 7, 43, 241,
    254–55, 283, 286, 369–70
Ahmadiyah, 18, 52, 211, 278–79, 368, 373
Ahnaf, M. Iqbal, 141–43, 150, 152, 248, 331,
    362
Ahok; Purnama, Basuki Tjahaja, 168–69,
    180, 187, 197, 279, 282, 284–85,
    288, 365, 368, 374
Anderson, Benedict R., 18, 25, 44, 51, 74,
    91, 95–96, 157–66, 168–69, 189,
    360, 362–63
Anwar, Dewi Fortuna, 259
Aragon, Lorraine, 359
Arendt, Hannah, 179, 182, 188–91, 199,
    217, 220, 366
Asad, Talal, 3, 108
authority, 51, 89, 159–61, 165, 169–70, 177,
    181, 187–89, 212, 255–57, 264, 266,
    274, 281, 309, 363
axial civilizations, 5, 10, 21, 30–33, 38, 47,
    55, 59–61, 69, 72–75, 82, 91, 298,
    353, 357

Bagir, Zainal Abidin, 128, 146–48, 150–52,
    219, 249, 361
Beatty, Andrew, 24–25
Bellah, Robert N., 5, 21, 28, 30–33, 45, 60,
    100, 141, 236, 354, 357
Berger, Peter, 35, 44–45, 74, 105, 170–71,
    184, 359
Benedict, Ruth, 215
Bourdieu, Pierre, 143–44, 182, 195–99,

216–17, 368
Bowen, John R., 202, 263–66, 348, 360,
    371–72
Bruinessen, Martin, 24
Buddhism, 26, 28, 34, 58–59, 72, 108, 110,
    209, 234, 353–54
buffered self, 46–47, 127, 147, 325–26

Campbell-Nelson, John, 242, 246
Carey, Peter, 69, 220
Casanova, José, 30, 32
circulatory history, 26, 54, 60, 62, 290
clash of civilizations, 10, 41, 73, 186, 294–
    97, 358
cognition, forms of, 5, 8, 11, 30–33, 60–61,
    69, 88, 99, 238, 298
Colombijn and Lindblad, 18, 287
Compilation of Islamic Law CIL, 266–67,
    274
conflict, 13, 19, 22, 27, 34, 41–42, 52, 54, 73,
    133, 137, 160, 167, 179–82, 184–85,
    211–12, 221, 225, 263, 266–67, 275,
    277–99, 308, 339–42, 374
Confucianism, 18, 28, 34, 55, 62, 108–9,
    167, 209, 219, 358

Darul Islam Indonesia, DII, 288–89, 374
de Certeau, Michel, 40, 102, 219, 375
democracy, 19–21, 25, 68, 70, 92, 167, 179–
    82, 188, 198–99, 213–14, 288, 297,
    340, 342–44, 352
Dewi Sri, 261
dignity, 170–72, 197, 213, 281, 297, 363
disenchanted, disenchantment, 3, 12, 35,
    46, 80, 82, 103–10, 113–14, 126–28,
    145–46, 151–53, 165, 249, 319–35
Donald, Merlin, 30–33, 54, 60
Doorn-Harder, Pieternella van, 270
dreams, 12, 46, 85, 107, 114, 116–20, 127,
    133–35, 140, 142, 144, 147, 305,
    320–21, 324–28, 333
Duara, Prasenjit, 26, 290
Durkheim, Emile, 30, 182–84, 199, 217,
    354–55, 360

403

Embah Selamat, 93–100, 359
essentialism, 6, 10, 19, 27, 39, 54, 64, 235,
    241, 267, 298, 370
Ethical Policy, 69, 111–12
evolution, 5, 28, 30–3, 60–1, 73, 108–10,
    159–60, 162, 165, 355, 363

Fadl, Kahled Fadou El, 53, 365
Feener, Michael, 371
fiqh, 53, 201–2, 264–66, 274, 372
Florida, Nancy K., 25, 28, 92
force, 1, 59, 85, 89–92, 105–6, 108–9, 111,
    124, 145, 151, 161, 170, 186–90, 194,
    199, 206, 216–17, 231, 246, 253,
    255, 265, 280–81, 283, 286, 289–
    90, 295, 329, 348, 357, 363, 368
Foucault, Michel, 98, 102, 143, 182, 190,
    193–95, 199, 216–17, 367

Gadamer, Hans Georg, 4, 45, 103, 354
Gafatar, 278–79, 373
Gandhi, Mahatma, 188, 290, 353, 359, 375
Geertz, Clifford, 25–28, 39, 60, 98, 100–
    101, 256, 354
Gillian, Carol, 241
Girard, Rene, 131, 261, 284
Gross, Rita, 258

Haas, Ernst B., 363
Habermas, Jurgen, 182, 191–93, 199, 366
habitus, 73, 144, 195–97, 216–17, 225, 259,
    278, 368
hadiths, 262
Hassan, Riaz, 268–70
Hauerwas, Stanley, 220, 236
Hefner, Robert W., 24, 359
heterarchy, 253–54, 271, 275
Hinduism, 26, 28, 58–59, 72, 108, 110,
    209, 234, 291, 333, 353–54, 358, 375
Hodgson, Marshall, 351
Holsti, Ole R., 21
honor, 2, 4, 54, 73, 84, 86–87, 89–90, 134,
    138, 170, 176–77, 181, 188, 198, 213–
    14, 231–32, 243, 248, 251, 265, 293,
    304, 306–7, 340–41, 343–44, 347–
    48
human rights, 19, 21–22, 35, 44, 47–52, 57,
    67, 70, 85, 90, 92, 106, 113, 174–75,

    178–81, 187, 191–93, 211–15, 262,
    264–80, 290–91, 296–97, 306,
    308, 339–44, 352, 355, 358, 367,
    371–72

ideal types, 2–7, 10, 26–28, 33, 41, 47, 72–
    73, 104, 106–7, 131, 147, 159–66,
    171, 215, 263, 345, 355
India, 1, 5, 10–11, 19, 21, 23, 26, 28, 30–31,
    37–41, 47, 55, 58–68, 70, 75–77, 83,
    101, 135, 183, 256, 290–91, 298,
    353–54, 357–58, 361, 375,
indigenous religions, 52, 55, 58, 61, 106,
    114, 177, 209–11, 219, 231, 278, 369,
    371
interreligious marriage, 291–93
intolerance, 11, 22, 140, 143, 145, 149, 275,
    277–99, 348
Islamicate, 10–11, 17, 19, 66–67, 291, 296,
    351–52, 369, 372–73
Islam Nusantara, 21, 24

Jakarta Charter, 288–89
Jaspers, Karl, 30,
Jenkins, Phillip, 17
Jokowi, 24, 168–70, 180, 187, 262–63, 278,
    286, 363
Jones, Sidney, 374

Kaharingan, 101, 121, 177, 230, 292, 338,
    360, 364, 375–76
Kahin, Audrey, 289
Kartini, Raden Adjeng, 253, 255
Keeler, Ward, 50, 169
Klinken, Gerry van, 351
Koentjaraningrat, 160–61, 189, 363
Koran, 19, 23–24, 53, 63, 77, 87, 94–95, 110,
    112–13, 133, 136–40, 148–49, 198,
    201, 204, 205, 208–9, 216, 220–21,
    259, 270, 279, 284–85, 292–93,
    306, 314, 317, 337, 351, 353, 358,
    360–61, 365, 374
Kuhn, Thomas S., 61, 245
Kumar, Ann, 57–58

Law, 12–13, 22, 23, 28, 32, 34, 40, 46, 48,
    50–53, 57, 67–70, 75, 83–86, 96,

Law (*continued*)
105, 110, 113, 136, 161, 171, 174, 179,
187, 191–92, 201–13, 224, 234, 244,
248, 250–52, 253–75, 278, 281, 283,
293–97, 304, 306–8, 337–40, 348,
352–56, 366, 368–73, 375
Lev, Daniel, 57
Lindbeck, George, 97
Lombard, Denys, 28, 59
Lukito, Ratno, 263–64, 371
Luhrmann, Tanya Marie, 47, 127, 354

Ma'arif, Ahmad Syafi'i, 119, 125, 132–34,
148–53, 184, 219, 248, 360–61, 365
Machasin, M., 124, 129, 138–41, 149–53,
248–49, 360
MacIntyre, Alastair, 44, 236
Madjid, Nurcholis, 34–35, 201, 354, 365
magic, 3, 12, 35, 46, 60, 62, 80, 81, 93, 95–
96, 99–102, 105–12, 124–25, 136,
140, 144–45, 149, 158, 162–65, 177,
189, 261, 307, 331, 359
Magnis-Suseno, Frans, 50, 89, 161, 169,
256, 368, 376
Magritte, René, 17, 29
Mahabhrata, 31, 59, 65, 161
Majelis Ulama Indonesia, MUI, 279, 356,
373
Mangunwidjaya, 90–92, 358
Marx, Karl, 182, 185–87, 199, 290, 355, 360,
365
matrilineal, 166, 258–59
matrifocal, 256, 258
Merapi, 87, 90–91, 170, 229–30, 241–43,
246, 249, 261, 371
Middle East, 1–2, 5, 10–11, 17–30, 38–39,
58–60, 63, 66–67, 75, 106, 133–34,
141, 143, 184, 256, 269, 281–82,
290, 297–98, 352–53, 358
Minhaji, Akh, 263–64, 371
modernism, Islamic modernism, 12, 28–
29, 35, 66, 80, 82, 101, 104–29, 175,
234, 250, 319–35, 348, 360
Morton, Timothy, 81, 98
Muhammadiyah, 12, 44, 50, 53, 106, 111–
13, 128, 131–38, 146–53, 194, 205,
279, 331, 356, 360–61, 367
Mulia, Siti Musdah, 267

Nahdlatul Ulama, NU, 24, 44, 50, 85, 112–
13, 131, 136, 138–43, 146, 149–53,
193–94, 279, 285, 353, 356, 359,
360–61, 364
Na'im, Abdullahi An, 365
Naipospos, Bonar Tigor, 381
NASAKOM, 27, 289
natural disasters, 13, 69, 86, 97, 116, 126,
133, 136, 142, 225, 229–52, 296,
298, 308, 321, 325, 333, 369–73
nature, 7, 11, 13, 46, 51, 55, 62, 75, 81, 83–
96, 136, 142, 142, 148, 158, 170, 188,
229–52, 274, 297, 307–8, 347–49,
357, 365–67, 369–70, 377
Ngelow, Zakaria J., 241, 370
Niebuhr, Reinhold, 182
ninety-nine names, 285, 374
Nugroho, Garin, 65, 357
Nussbaum, Martha, 41, 64, 358

Olson, Bruce, 98–99
orientalism, 3–5, 351

Pancasila, 50, 52–53, 67, 109, 182, 185, 191,
193, 198, 204, 288–89, 358, 366
Partai Komunis Indonesia, PKI, 262, 289,
375
Patriarchy, 13, 253–54, 256, 270–71, 274–75
Placher, William C., 100, 234
pluralism, legal pluralism, 10, 53, 263, 371
Pujiastuti, Susi, 262–63

Rahman, Fazlur, 132, 365
Ramadan, 26, 67, 82, 94, 216, 218, 292, 358
Ramadan, Tariq, 365
Ramayana, 31, 59, 65, 161, 221, 230
Ratu Kidul, Queen of the South, 87, 170,
261, 359
Reid, Anthony, 18, 58–59, 62, 84, 256, 289,
357
repertoires, 13, 44, 277
revolution, 29, 46, 51, 70, 132, 183, 188,
289, 353, 375
Ricci, Ronit, 64
Ricklefs, M. C., 1, 19, 24–28, 58, 70, 84, 92,
353, 356–57, 360
Rodemeier, Susanne, 260, 271
Ronggowarsito, 92

Sapir-Whorf hypothesis, 97
Said, Edward, 3, 5
scapegoat, 97, 245, 284–85, 288
Schlehe, Judith, 137–38, 362
Scott, James, 40, 58–59, 102, 280
second naïveté, 5–6, 45, 100, 103–4, 141, 354
secular, secularism, secular age, 2–10, 23, 32–35, 45–53, 73, 75, 82, 93, 99, 105, 107–8, 113, 127, 140, 150–51, 173, 205–6, 224, 322, 334, 359,
Semar, 91, 363
shaman, 93–102, 120–22, 136, 142, 144, 160–61, 242–43, 305, 320, 328, 331, 360
Sharia, 22, 53, 67, 75, 181, 187, 201–2, 204–6, 224, 259, 264, 268, 275, 288–89, 348, 372
Shia, 18, 52, 211, 278
Sindhunata, 241–42
Singgih, E. Gerrit, 242
Smith-Hefner, Nancy, 356
spirit possession, 12, 82, 100–101, 107, 114–15, 120–23, 127–28, 133, 135–36, 139–40, 142, 147, 151, 153, 161, 189, 250, 305, 321, 325, 328–33, 360–61
spirits, 11–12, 35, 46–47, 63, 75, 80–86, 89, 93, 98–103, 107, 110, 114–16, 121–23, 127, 133, 139–53, 230–31, 247, 250, 304, 308, 319–34, 361
Sunnah, 23–24, 110–13, 133, 202, 220–21, 351, 360
Syamsiyatun, Siti, 134–38, 148–52, 165, 248, 321, 332, 361
Soeharto, xiii, 18, 21–22, 25, 51, 53, 85, 91, 97, 110, 125, 159, 167–69, 179, 182, 187, 190–95, 198–99, 263, 266–67, 270, 283–90, 297, 342, 353, 355–56, 360–61, 366, 371
Subianto, Prabowo, 169, 363, 366
suicide bombers, 244, 285, 294
Sukarno, 27, 51, 159, 185, 288–89, 365, 374
Suryadinata, 284

Taussig, Michael, 101–2

Taylor, Charles, 2–3, 11, 21, 36, 42–47, 82–83, 127, 354–55, 358, 368
Taoism, 28, 62, 91, 108
terrorism, 1, 20–21, 73, 101, 182, 244, 281–82, 285, 290, 294, 296–98, 375
Tonnies, Ferdinand, 84, 355, 360
traditionalist Islam, 12, 28–29, 106, 112, 131, 193, 360
Trump, Donald, 22, 168, 180, 278, 281, 290–91, 296–97, 352, 365
truth, 3, 12, 18, 32, 67, 80, 83, 98–104, 108–9, 182, 193–95, 243, 251, 284
Tsing, Anna L., 101–2, 262

Udasmoro, Wening, 143–46, 150–52, 195, 248–49, 369

violence, 12–13, 18–19, 83, 101, 113, 141, 145, 149, 170, 179–80, 186–92, 195, 198–99, 217, 253–55, 278, 280–88, 291, 293–94, 296, 298, 352, 357, 363, 371, 373
Veer, Peter van der, 107–9

Waltz, Kenneth, 161, 363
Walzer, Michael, 297
Weber, Max, 3, 30, 35, 46, 60, 95, 105–8, 159–60, 182, 186–88, 199, 355, 360, 362–63, 365–66
White, Lynn, 234
women, 13, 19, 38–39, 43, 67, 76, 76, 101, 121, 134, 149, 153, 196, 201, 225, 237, 240–41, 252–75, 282, 285, 294, 308, 352, 360, 370–71, 373–74
Woodward, Mark, 26, 28

Yijing, 62, 64
Yudhoyono, Susilo Bambang, SBY, 125, 180, 361

Zheng He, 62

∞

design and layout
typography and illustrations
by **H.G. Salome**
Bristol, Vermont USA

www.metaglyfix.com